ILLUSTRATED HISTORY,

COMPRISING IN A CONDENSED FORM A

HISTORY OF THE UNITED STATES,

—A—

GEOGRAPHY OF THE WESTERN CONTINENT,

AND THE CHIEF OBJECTS OF INTEREST ON

THE EASTERN CONTINENT,

INCLUDING A HISTORICAL AND DESCRIPTIVE SKETCH OF

THE HOLY LAND,

BY

W. S. CLARK.

ILLUSTRATED BY STEREOSCOPIC VIEWS

PUBLISHED BY

E. & H. T. ANTHONY, NEW-YORK.

PUBLISHED BY

J. H. CLARK & CO.,

ROCKFORD, ILLINOIS.

ROCKFORD REGISTER STEAM PRINTING HOUSE.

1870.

PREFACE.

This work has been prepared for the purpose of bringing within the reach of all, the important matter of History and Geography in a condensed form, and illustrated in such a manner as to make clear and lasting impressions on the mind of the Scholar, and serve as an incentive to study. This study has been sadly neglected, not because of its unimportance, but from the long, dry, and tedious manner in which it has been presented. The wood cuts which usually accompany Histories, generally give a very imperfect idea of the scene intended to be represented.

Accompanying this work are Stereoscopic Views taken from the object itself, showing nature and art as they actually exist, and as they would appear if seen with the naked eye.

INSTRUCTIONS.

This History, Stereoscope, and Views, will be furnished in Sets. The Views that are sent to a Township all differ, and by changing, from time to time, each district can have the benefit of the whole number. In the back part of the Book will be found a list of headings, giving the page and division of the catalogue under which will be found the title and number corresponding with that on the View. When a view is furnished that is not embodied in the catalogue, figures will be set on the face side of the View, denoting the page in the History, except when a sufficient description is printed on the back of the view.

The History can be used with great success with but a single copy in the School, by giving each scholar in the class so much time for the study. When more are required they can be obtained of Agents, or by ordering.

All orders in the Northwest must be sent to

JAS. H. CLARK & CO.,

Rockford, Illinois.

CONTENTS.

PART I.

PART II.

PART III.

HISTORY

OF THE

UNITED STATES.

CHAPTER I.

DISCOVERY OF AMERICA.

The United States consists of thirty-six States and ten Territories. This country is bounded by the great lakes and the British possessions on the north, the Atlantic ocean on the east, the gulf of Mexico and Mexico on the south, and the Pacific ocean on the west.

The American continent, or New World, as it is sometimes called, was discovered by Christopher Columbus, in the year 1492. Columbus was a native of Genoa—born about 1435. His father was a wool-comber, but gave his son advantages of education, particularly in geography, mathematics, and astronomy, for which he early displayed a decided taste. When he was fourteen years of age he went to sea. A few years later, while in the service of a kinsman who commanded a small Genoese squadron, and taking part in an engagement with some Venetian vessels off the coast of Portugal, his ship caught fire, and he leaped into the waves and barely saved his life by swimming ashore. He was attracted to Lisbon by the fame that Portugal had won by her maritime enterprise, where he married the daughter of an eminent navigator, the access to whose charts and journals awakened within him an ardent desire for discovery.

From this time to 1477 we find him engaged in various voyages to the Canaries, the Azores, Madeira, and the coast of Guinea and Iceland.

The geographical researches of Columbus convinced him that the earth was round, and that there must necessarily be land in the western hemisphere to counterbalance the eastern continent. The maps to be obtained in his day gave but little information respecting the extent of Asia. He imagined that it extended much further east than it really did, or that the coast was lined with large islands extending within a few hundred leagues of Europe. Pieces of wood, strangely carved, had been picked up by sailors in the unknown ocean. Upon one island were found the bodies of two men totally different in appearance from the natives of Europe and Africa. These circumstances confirmed him in his belief, and he sought means of testing its truth. In order to carry out his project effectually he must have men and ships. His first proposals were made to the senate of his native city, but were rejected. His next application was to John II. of Portugal; who, after drawing out his plan, treacherously sent a vessel on the proposed course under another commander, but happily gained nothing by his baseness. Columbus then sent his brother Bartholomew to Henry VII. of England, but he was captured by pirates, and it was years before he reached London. Being unsuccessful in Portugal, in 1484 Columbus went to Spain, where for a time he supported himself and son by making charts and maps. "At last he succeeded in procuring an interview with Ferdinand, king of Aragon. This cautious monarch, after listening to his projects, submitted them to the learned men of the university of Salamanca, by whom they were once more condemned." After several years Columbus finally obtained an interview with Isabella, the wife of Ferdinand, and queen of Castile and Leon. To enable him to appear at court she sent him about seventy dollars, with which he purchased a mule and suitable clothing. The queen was moved by his arguments, but was unwilling to furnish the required aid. More disheartened than ever Columbus was on the point of abandoning Spain, when at last, by the advice of wise counsellors, Isabella determined to embark in the enterprise, even if she had to pledge her jewels in order to procure the necessary funds. Columbus was commissioned as High Admiral and Viceroy of all the countries he might discover, and went to Palos to fit out the expedition.

There was great difficulty in finding sailors for such a voyage, but with the aid of the queen three small vessels, none of them being over one hundred tons burden, and ninety men were obtained. The Santa Maria, which bore the flag of Columbus, was the only one that had a deck. The Pinta and Nina were commanded by two brothers by the name of Pinyon. They provided themselves with provisions enough to last one year. The whole expense of the outfit was only £4,000.

This little fleet sailed from Palos August 3, 1492. A full sense of the dangers they might encounter seized on the sailors when land faded from their sight, and their fears were gradually increased, till, on the expiration of twenty days without seeing any signs of land, they began to talk of throwing Columbus overboard and returning home. "The variation of the compass had not yet been discovered, and their alarm was greatly heightened when they observed that the magnetic needle no longer pointed directly north. It was a trying hour for Columbus, but his great mind was equal to the crisis. Explaining the variations of the compass in a manner satisfactory to his followers, though not to himself, he used every means to induce them to prosecute the voyage, now picturing to their minds the riches they would obtain, and now threatening them with the anger of their sovereign. At last both officers and men insisted on returning, and Columbus was obliged to promise that unless land appeared within three days he would comply with their demand. The shallowness of the water, the numerous birds of the air, the grass and weeds floating by, a branch that was picked up with berries still fresh upon it, all made him sure that he could give this promise with safety." On the evening of October 11th, the sails were furled, and a close watch kept. About ten o'clock a moving light was discovered by Columbus and several others, and at two in the morning a shout from the Pinta proclaimed the discovery of land, and at daybreak was displayed to the overjoyed adventurers a scene of strange beauty. The land was covered with the forests and gay foliage and blossoms of a tropical clime. The natives thronged from the woods and gazed with wonder and astonishment at the ships, which, with their white sails, they regarded as huge birds hovering over the sea. "Columbus was the first to touch the newly discovered shore. Richly attired and with drawn sword, he landed. Kneeling on the sand he kissed the earth and returned thanks to God. When he had taken formal possession of the country in the name of the king and queen of Spain, his followers rendered him homage as viceroy, and the inhabitants, regarding the Spaniards as a superior race, prostrated themselves at his feet." The land first reached was one of the Bahama islands, to which Columbus gave the name of San Salvador, by which name it is still known.

Having learned from the natives that gold was to be obtained further to the south, they soon sailed in that direction and discovered Cuba and Hayti. One of his vessels having been wrecked he left thirty-five of his men in Hayti, and on the 1st of January, 1493, embarked for Spain. A violent storm on the return voyage threatened his frail vessels, and Columbus, fearing his discoveries would be lost to the world, wrote an account of them on parchment, which he secured in a cask and threw into the sea, hoping that the winds and waves might cast it ashore. But he was mercifully spared to make known personally his discoveries. The shattered vessels finally entered the port of Palos in safety, amid the acclamations of the people and the thunder of cannon. Columbus presented himself before the king and queen and laid before them the history of his discoveries, exhibited specimen products of the new world with the natives whom he had brought with him, and in return was loaded with the highest honors.

On the 25th of September, 1493, Columbus started upon his second voyage to the new world. This time he had a fleet of seventeen vessels and one thousand five hundred men. On his arrival at Hayti he found that his colony had been cut off. By their injustice and cruelty to the natives they had provoked them to summary vengeance. After providing for the erection of a fort on this island, Columbus proceeded to explore the surrounding islands. Soon after completing this work he was delighted by the arrival of his brother Bartholomew, whom he had not seen for thirteen years, and who, on returning from his unsuccessful mission to England, was sent by Isabella with supplies to the new world.

The followers of Columbus, being disappointed in obtaining gold, began to murmur and complain of his management of affairs, the result of which was, an emissary of his enemies was sent out to examine into it. Columbus returned to Spain and plead his own cause before the throne. He established his innocence and was received into favor.

In 1498 he made his third voyage, directing his course nearer the equator than he had previously done. During this voyage he discovered the island of Trinidad and the coast of South America, near the mouth of the Orinoco river. In the current from the mouth of this great river his fleet was for a time in great danger. This led him to believe that so mighty a stream must belong to a continent. On his return to his colony on the island of Hayti he found Bovadilla, whom, at the instigation of his enemies, the Spanish sovereign had vested with power to examine into his conduct, and if needful to supersede him in command.

Columbus was sent back to Spain in chains. The captain of the vessel, grieved to see so great a discoverer treated in this manner, offered to remove his chains. But Columbus, indignant at the ingratitude of his country, would not allow them to be removed, and ordered that they should be buried with him. Every charge made against him he repelled, but his sovereign never had the justice to restore him to his station, and when it became necessary to remove Bovadilla on account of his mismanagement, Ovando was appointed his successor.

Though feeling deeply this ingratitude, and also the infirmities of age, in 1502 Columbus set out on a fourth voyage. He still entertained the belief that the land he had discovered formed a part of Asia, which delusion he did not live to have dispelled. The object of this last voyage was to discover a new passage to India by sailing further west. He explored the coast along the gulf of Darien. But at last, after a succession of disasters in the attempt to reach Hayti, he was wrecked off the coast of Jamaica, where, being nearly reduced to starvation and in danger of attacks from the Indians, he saved himself and his followers by an ingenious stratagem. From his knowledge of astronomy he knew that an eclipse of the moon was to take place, and calling the natives around him told them that the Great Spirit was displeased with them on account of their treatment to the white man, and that He would, that night, hide his face from them. When the moon became dark they were convinced of the truth of what he had said, and brought him supplies, and besought him to pray to the Great Spirit to receive them into favor again. After undergoing extraordinary hardships, Columbus finally reached Hayti, and returned to Spain in the summer of 1504. Queen Isabella had died a short time before, and the remaining two years of the great discoverer's life was shrouded in gloom. He died at Valladolid in the 71st year of his age. His chains were put in his coffin as he requested, and his remains now rest in the cathedral of Havana.

Encouraged by the success of Columbus, other Spanish navigators had found their way to the new world. Among these was Ojeda, in whose company was a well educated Florentine gentleman who published an interesting description of the lands he had visited. His name was Americo Vespucci. His was the first written account of the western continent, and as it left Columbus out of view, the continent, instead of being called after its real discoverer, was named from this Florentine, America.

The early inhabitants of this country were the North American Indians, but they, as a nation, have long since passed away, although a remnant still linger in some of the States and in the Indian territory, and beyond the Rocky mountains.

The three oldest towns in the United States are St. Augustine, in Florida, founded by the Spaniards in 1565; Jamestown, in Virginia, founded by the English in 1607; and Plymouth, in Massachusetts, in 1620, also by the English.

CHAPTER II.

NEW ENGLAND.

MASSACHUSETTS AND RHODE ISLAND.

The history of New England begins with the landing of the Pilgrim Fathers, who were Englishmen, belonging to a sect of Christians called Puritans. During the reign of the Roman Catholic Queen, Mary of England, their ancestors had been driven to the continent of Europe, where they had learned a more simple mode of worship than that practiced by the English church. On the accession of Queen Elizabeth, having returned to their country, they refused to become members of the established church, or to submit to its usages. They were therefore nicknamed Puritans, and were persecuted for their non-conformity, as it was called.

These persecutions they endured for about fifty years, when a small company of them, in the year 1608, fled to Holland. Here they remained until 1620, when they resolved to go to America. They went to England in a small vessel called the Speedwell, where they remained about two weeks, and set sail for America. But the Speedwell proving unseaworthy, they were obliged to return, and this vessel and those of the company whose courage failed them were dismissed, and the rest crowded into the Mayflower.

On the 6th of September, 1620, this frail bark, bearing its precious burden, lost sight of English ground. The number of Pilgrims was a hundred and one. While on shipboard they drew up a body of laws which they resolved to obey, and chose John Carver for their governor. This first American constitution was drawn up and signed on the lid of a chest of Norway pine belonging to Elder Brewster. This chest is still preserved in the Athenæum at Hartford.

It was the intention of the Pilgrims to settle near the mouth of the Hudson river, but owing to the ignorance of the captain they were landed on the barren coast of Massachusetts. Considerable time was spent exploring the coast for a suitable landing place, and Plymouth Rock being decided upon, the sea-wearied Pilgrims, on the 21st of December, after a three months' voyage, stepped ashore. "Tradition says it was the foot of Mary Chilton, a young maiden of the band, that first pressed Forefathers Rock, as it is still named and honored by their descendants."

"The heavy night hung dark,
The hills and waters o'er,
When a band of exiles moored their bark
On the wild New England shore.

Ay, call it holy ground,
The soil where first they trod!
They have left unstained what there they found,
Freedom to worship God."

Severe trials awaited them in their new home. Disease and famine did their fearful work. Among the victims were Governor Carver, his wife and child. In the spring, only forty-six of the one hundred and one passengers were living. But during this time they were mercifully preserved from the murderous tomahawk of the Indian, a pestilence, the year before, supposed to have been the small pox, having carried off the most savage of the tribes. The first Indian they met was Samoset, who greeted them with the cheering salutation: "Welcome, Englishmen! Welcome, Englishmen." He was from what is now called Maine, and had learned to speak English from the captain of a fishing vessel on the coast. He informed them that Massasoit, the great chieftain of that region, was approaching with his warriors. Samoset was engaged as interpreter, and by means of a few kindly presents, the sachem's good will was secured, and a treaty made which was faithfully kept for more than fifty years. Through Massasoit's influence, ninety less powerful chiefs were brought into treaty, and Canonicus, the only hostile one, was awed when the Governor returned the arms and rattlesnake skin which the savage had sent him in token of defiance, stuffing the latter with powder and ball.

Between the years 1620 and 1630, various settlements were made by individuals and parties around Massachusetts Bay, at

Charlestown, and Cambridge and Salem. Colonists were enabled to emigrate to this country by means of merchants, residing in London and the west of England, forming themselves into companies and obtaining from the King grants to settle particular plantations in America, with certain rights and privileges of commerce and government. These grants were called charters. These companies furnished ships and sent out colonists who were to cultivate the land, and procure fish and furs, the profits on which articles it was expected would repay the company in England for the expense of sending them out.

Several gentlemen of family and fortune, belonging to the Massachusetts Bay Company, agreed themselves to go to New England, provided they could carry their charter along with them, and their government not managed by a council of the company in England, as was usually the case. This privilege was granted, and Mr. Winthrop and many other distinguished men embarked for New England on the 8th of April, 1630. After a somewhat boisterous voyage, this little fleet of five vessels was anchored at Charlestown. Here they were kindly received by the former colonists, and began to build, intending to make it their permanent home, but they found but one spring of water, and that so brackish that disease carried off many of their numbers. The new colony was threatened with destruction, and, being invited by Mr. William Blackstone to join him on the south side of Charles river, where he had built his lowly hut, they gladly removed thither.

They named their new settlement Boston, in honor of a much beloved pastor of Boston, England, who afterwards joined the new colony, where he was highly honored. "One of the first acts of the colony was to draw up a confession of faith, and enter into a church covenant. This was done with the utmost solemnity, after a day of fasting and prayer. Mr. Blackstone, who was an Episcopalian, was invited to join this church, but he replied very quaintly, 'I came from England because I did not like the Lord Bishops; but I cannot join you because I would not be under the Lord Brethren.'"

The little village of Boston grew rapidly. The inhabitants were noted for their industry, sobriety and honesty. The Governor forbade cards and gaming tables, and discouraged the drinking of toasts. A man was whipped for stealing a loaf of bread, and another for shooting fowls on Sunday. Mechanics and masons worked diligently at their trades. Vessels were built to traffic with other settlements on the coast; one of which, called the Blessing of the Bay, was launched July 4th, 1631. Education was by no means neglected. Harvard College was founded in eight years after the founding of the colony. It was named in honor of John Harvard, who, dying, left to this institution eight hundred pounds. In the year this College was founded, a printing press was set up in it by a man named Glover, but there was little progression made in this art the first forty years of New England history.

The next year after this colony was established, Mr. John Eliot, the first Missionary to the Indians, joined them. He visited the Indians in their wigwams and taught them to read and pray; also translated the Bible into their language. A copy of this book is still preserved, but only the title, "Up Biblum God," meaning the book of God, can now be read. The language has perished with the race.

Between the years 1630 and 1636, persecution in England was revived, driving many wise and able men to the colonies. In the year 1635, three thousand emigrants arrived at Boston, among whom was Sir Henry Vane, an intimate friend of the poet Milton. He was soon elected Governor. Though the Puritans had left England to secure religious liberty, they were unwilling to grant it to others, and required every one to attend their worship and conform to their opinions. Roger Williams, a young preacher settled at Salem, was the first to teach that every one had a right to worship God as he saw fit, and that bigotry in New England, as well as in old England, was contrary to reason and the Bible. His listeners became warmly attached to him, but his enlarged views, so far beyond the age in which he lived, alarmed the Boston Puritans and made him enemies. They were shocked at his saying that civil magistrates were bound to protect the lives and property of peaceful citizens of any creed; and that it was their duty to restrain crime but not to control opinion. The number of his enemies increased, his wife was for a time influenced by his opposers, and his home made unhappy. He was at last censured and pronounced unsound in judgment; and on his election as pastor by the people of Salem, a tract of land was withheld from them by the Boston council by way of punishment. A spirited remonstrance from Williams and his congregation followed; in consequence of which, the town of Salem was disfranchised by the next general court. His supporters, frightened at these measures, finally submitted, and Williams was left to advocate his cause alone. At last the sentence of banishment was pronounced. He had hoped to remain until spring, but the prospect of losing him awakened the affections of his people, and the general court, fearing his influence, commanded him to embark for England, and officers were sent to convey him to the vessel; but he had fled from Salem with the determination to find in some other part of the new world, the freedom which was denied him there. For fourteen weeks he was a wanderer in the wilderness, amid the snows of a severe winter, "sorely tost in a bitter season, not knowing what bread or bed did mean." He was kindly received by the Indians, whose language he had learned, and to whom he ever proved a patient missionary. Massasoit and the chief of the Narragansetts received him as their guest. Of them he purchased a tract of land on the bay bearing their name. Here, with but five companions, he commenced a settlement which he named Providence, in grateful acknowledgment of the hand which had guided his wanderings. Thus originated the first settlement in Rhode Island.

In 1639, Newport was founded near an old stone tower. This curious structure, twenty-four feet high, was evidently of great antiquity. The Indians were unable to give any information respecting its origin. The same principles prevailed and were carried out in both the Providence and Rhode Island colonies, though they were at first independent of each other. In 1644 they received a charter and were united under the name of the Rhode Island and Providence Plantations.

CONNECTICUT.

The Connecticut, so called from its Indian name, which means long river, was discovered by the Dutch in 1614. They established a trading place near where Hartford now stands. Until the year 1630, they enjoyed undisputed possession of the country, when reports of the fruitfulness and beauty of this region reaching England, it was granted to the Earl of Warwick, who transferred it to Lord Say-and-Seale and Lord Brook.

Previous to this, settlements had been made from both Massachusetts colonies. The Dutch had tried to prevent the first comers from sailing up the river, but without success. The founders of the busy little State of Connecticut were the excellent of the earth. Between the years 1633 and 1636 four flourishing villages had sprung up on the banks of its beautiful river, viz: Windsor, Hartford, Saybrook and Wethersfield, and in 1638, New Haven, now one of the loveliest cities in all New England, was founded by a Puritan pastor.

The country between the Connecticut river and the Narragansett Bay, was thickly peopled with Indian tribes, the most powerful of which were the Pequods, Mohegans and Narragansetts. The Pequods, fearing the power of the English, endeavored to form a league with the Narragansetts. Roger Williams learned that proposals of this kind were being made, and resolved to plead for his persecutors and defeat the plans of the Pequods. Setting out in a fearful storm, he made his way to the nearest Narragansett village, where he found the Pequod embassadors and nearly lost his life by interfering; but he pleaded his cause nobly, and after some hesitation the Narragansetts refused to become the Pequod's allies.

In May of the year 1637, the authorities of Connecticut declared war against the Pequods. With a band of ninety men, seventy from Connecticut and twenty from the Bay Colony, the colonists entered upon their first warfare. The Pequod confederacy consisted of twenty-six tribes, numbering over two thousand men. Their principal villages were on what is now called the

Thames River, and to attack them the colonist soldiers now directed their march. On the 26th of May, just before sunrise, they cautiously approached the huts of the sleeping savages. The Indians had set no sentry, and the barking of a dog gave the first alarm. In confusion, amid cries of "Owanux!" "Owanux!" (the English! the English!) they rallied with bow and arrow for the fight, and defended themselves with great bravery. The result of the battle was still doubtful, when a blazing brand was thrown among the mats with which one of the wigwams was covered, and thus were the fortunes of the day decided. The English and their red allies, the Mohegans, formed a circle around the burning huts, and slew their enemies without mercy, as they were driven into sight by the fire. Only two of the English were lost, while the fort and the wigwams of the Indians were burned, and six hundred Pequods, men, women, and children, were slain. The next morning a body of three hundred Pequods arrived from another village; and though they fought with desperation on seeing the destruction of their homes and relatives, they too were defeated. Two hundred of the survivors surrendered in despair to the English. They were either sold into slavery or incorporated among the friendly tribes; and the name of Pequod became extinct.

After the first victory the Narragansett tribe had joined the English, but the latter made a poor return to their chief, Miantonomah, for his services. A war having broken out between the Narragansetts and Mohegans, Miantonomah was captured. "Let him be delivered to his old enemy, Uncas," said the ungrateful men of Connecticut. The savage Mohegan took him to a solitary place and in the presence of two settlers tomahawked him, and, cutting a piece of quivering flesh from his victim's shoulder, ate it, declaring it the most delicious morsel he had ever tasted.

Connecticut, now free from danger, grew and prospered. It was her happy lot to be blessed with God-fearing governors. The rights of voting and holding office were confined to church members, and the Bible was adopted as the rule of public action.

MAINE AND NEW HAMPSHIRE.

The territory which now constitutes the States of Maine and New Hampshire was divided between Sir Ferdinand Gorges, John Mason and others. In 1623 the settlement of New Hampshire was commenced at Dover and Portsmouth by the gentlemen to whom the country had been granted. John Mason became sole proprietor of a large part of the country, and the claims of his heirs furnished a fruitful source of contention. The settlements were annexed to Massachusetts in 1614, and so continued till 1679, when a separate government was instituted for New Hampshire. In after years, when Massachusetts had lost her charter, and was under royal rule, the two provinces were occasionally united under one governor. In 1741 they were finally separated, and from that time until the war of independence, the two colonies had separate royal governors.

THE UNION OF THE COLONIES.

The New England colonies began about this time to feel the necessity of union. They were threatened by the Indians on one side, and the Dutch and French on the other, which, with the attempts in England to take away their charters, led them to unite. This first confederation of New England colonies took place in 1643. It lasted fifty years, and when broken up by the loss of their charters, the colonists still cherished a desire for union. The colonies forming this union were Plymouth, Massachusetts Bay, New Haven, and Connecticut, under the name of "The United Colonies of New England." At this time the population numbered about twenty thousand, scattered through fifty villages. Each colony retained the control of its own territory; but all matters of common interest and questions of war and peace were decided by a council consisting of two commissioners from each. In times of war each colony was to furnish men and money in proportion to its population. This confederacy may be considered as the germ of the American union.

Rhode Island refusing to be included in the Plymouth colony was not admitted to the confederation.

DOMESTIC LIFE, CHARACTER, AND LAWS OF THE PURITANS.

Their condition, of course, was materially the same as that of the English people at that time. The use of chimneys was becoming common, though opposed by some who thought smoke improved their health and hardened the timbers of their houses. Pewter dishes and spoons were taking the place of wooden ones. Boards and unhewn logs were mostly used in building. Rye, barley and oats were the principal food, and the taste of meat was hardly known in thousands of families. The condition of the people in Massachusetts was considerably better than this. After the first few years of scarcity they lived more comfortably and independently than the same class in the old world.

The Puritans of New England imbibed a strong aversion to the manners and customs of those who had persecuted them. They opposed the use of veils, wigs, silken hoods and scarfs, and discountenanced all frivolous fashions in dress, and forbade the observance of Christmas. Comparing themselves to the Israelites of old, they tried to conform to the laws and habits of the chosen people who fled from bondage in Egypt to an unknown wilderness. Like them, their Sabbath began at the going down of the sun on Saturday evening, and was observed with the utmost strictness. Prayers and sermons were esteemed according to their length, and the children and servants were regularly catechised.

Their laws condemned all wars that were not defensive, and penalties were attached to gambling, intemperance, and other immoralities. Interest on loaned money was forbidden, and blasphemy and idolatry were punished with death.

Persecuted Christians, of their own faith, were supported for a time at the public expense; but priests, Jesuits and Quakers shared the hatred of the Puritans and were forbidden to set foot within their limits.

The Quakers were first known as a religious body in England in 1644. They were followers of George Fox. They believed that God communicated directly with the spirits of men, and considered all human interference in religious matters as wrong, and boldly proclaimed that "God was come to teach his people himself." They practiced the utmost simplicity in dress and language. They would neither bear arms nor take an oath. They denounced ceremonies, pleasures and show, and abhorred titles; and generally addressed others by the appellation of Friends. Anxious to propagate their religion, they had turned their eyes to America, but here they met with persecution as well as in England. The Puritans seemed to have forgotten their own sufferings, and displayed the same persecuting spirit from which they had themselves fled. If one of the Quakers was found in their colonies he was to lose an ear, and if he returned the other ear was forfeited, and for a third offence his tongue was to be pierced with a red-hot iron. But they gloried in their persecutions. Fines, whippings and tortures could not keep them away. Finally the sentence of death was pronounced on all that should appear the second time in the colonies. Three men and one woman were victims of this cruel law. This law was finally repealed, and the Quakers being whipped out of the colony the excitement gradually died away.

The Puritans were only carrying out the intolerant principles that were being practiced in every Christian country. To Roger Williams and Lord Baltimore belongs the honor of first rising above the bigotry of the age.

KING PHILIP'S WAR.

The Puritans, during the long struggle between Charles I. and his parliament, had sided against the king, and were therefore treated with great liberality and favor when Cromwell assumed the government.

In 1658 Cromwell died, and Charles II. was restored to the throne of England. The first vessel that left for the colonies after this event brought over three of the regicides, Goffe, Whalley, and Dixwell. They found refuge in the house of Mr. Russel, minister of Hadley, where they lived in profound concealment.

The Massachusetts colonists were obliged to acknowledge the authority of the new sovereign of England. A public address was presented to his majesty, in which they appealed to him for a continuation of their liberties, and pardon for having sided against his father. The king confirmed their charter and pardoned past offenses, but required the Puritans to extend the right of voting to those who were not church members, to take the oath of allegiance, and to tolerate the church of England.

Scarcely were these troubles ended when the colonists were involved in a long and bloody war known as King Philip's war. Philip was the younger of the two sons of Massasoit. He had become hostile to the English on account of the death of his brother, which he ascribed to them. Alexander had died of a fever brought on by mortification at being arrested and imprisoned by the English. Philip was the most powerful sachem of the New England tribes, and determined to avenge the death of his brother. The first hostile deed was the murder of nine men at Swanzy, of the Plymouth colony. All the horrors of the Pequod were renewed, and on a much larger scale. The mother retired to rest to be awakened at midnight by the dreadful war-whoop, to see her children cut down by the merciless tomahawk. The family on their way to church were exposed to the attacks of a cruel and cunning enemy. Goffe, the regicide, had been a military commander. Looking from the window of his hiding place, on a sabbath day, after the people were collected for public worship, he saw a body of ambushed Indians stealing upon them. He suddenly made his appearance before the gathering worshippers, his white hair and beard and loose garments streaming to the winds. "He gave the alarm and word of command, and the men already armed, at once formed and bore down upon the foe. After they had conquered they looked around for their preserver, but he had vanished, and they fully believed an angel was sent for their deliverance."

When this war ended twenty-five villages were in ruins and one white family in every twenty had been burned out. But the fate of the Indians during this struggle was more terrible than that of the whites. They often perished in their burning wigwams. Many were made prisoners and sold into slavery, some

2

wandered away and joined other tribes, and when King Philip was shot he was almost the last of his tribe.

In 1677 the charter struggle was again commenced. The king declared that Massachusetts had no jurisdiction over the provinces of Maine and New Hampshire. Maine was purchased by a Boston merchant for about six thousand dollars, and thus became a part of Massachusetts.

New Hampshire was made a royal province, and a governor and council were appointed. The colonists were obliged to use the liturgy of the English church and observe its fasts and festivals. King Charles II. also demanded that Massachusetts should submit to laws passed in the English parliament, oppressing the commerce of the infant colonies. Willing to yield everything but their charter, they, by an act passed in their own general court, bound themselves to obey the English laws of trade. They would willingly and cheerfully give up Maine and everything except the right of "government within themselves," which their charter granted. This struggle was at its heigh when Charles II. died, and the Roman Catholic James II. ascended the throne. He declared there should be no free governments in his dominions, and determined to take away from the New England colonies their charters. Sir Edmond Andros was chosen to carry this plan into effect, and was appointed governor of the New England province.

On the 30th of December, 1686, Sir Edmond Andros landed at Boston. He demanded the charters, and those of Massachusetts and Rhode Island were surrendered. He then proceeded across the country to Connecticut with an armed force, determined to take away their liberty; but the Connecticut people were not wanting in shrewdness; the charter was not immediately presented but the subject discussed until evening, when the lights were suddenly put out, and during the darkness the charter was carried off by William Wadsworth, and hid in the hollow of an old oak tree. Being unable to obtain the charter, Andros inquired for the records of the colony wrote under them the Latin word "finis," which means the end. Sir Edmond began his career with the most flattering professions of his regard to the safety and happiness of the people, but "Nero concealed his tyrannical disposition more years than Sir Edmond did months." But the day of his power was soon over. In April, 1689, news reached the colonies that James II. had been driven from the throne, and that Mary and William had been placed upon it. All Boston was aroused; companies marched through the streets with drums and colors, and Governor Andros was thrown into prison. Joy was universal throughout the colonies; the general court assembled; the charter oak yielded its precious treasure, and "finis" was erased from the records.

In 1688 the union of the Connecticut and Massachusetts colonies was broken up. Rhode Island and Connecticut were permitted to keep their charters, but Massachusetts by a new charter was made a royal province with a governor appointed by the king. New Hampshire was separate from Massachusetts and had also a royal governor.

The principal event in New England between the years 1689 and 1700 was a war carried on with the French and Indians. When King William ascended the throne he was at war with Louis XIV. of France. This was soon extended to the French and English colonies in America. In conducting this war the French called to their assistance the services of the Indians. Nova Scotia was given up to the French, and peace was made between the countries in 1697.

The first war of the eighteenth century was Queen Anne's war. The cruelties practiced in King William's war were repeated in this. The town of Deerfield, in Massachusetts, was attacked in February, 1704, by a party of two hundred French and one hundred and forty-two Indians. They concealed themselves in a pine forest until midnight; then, with their fearful warwhoop they fell upon the defenseless village. A dreadful scene ensued; the village was burned, forty-seven were killed and one hundred and twelve carried into captivity. A treaty of peace was made in 1713, called, from the place in Holland where it was signed, the peace of Utrecht. For thirty years succeeding the close of Queen Anne's war the colonists enjoyed comparative repose.

In 1774 France again declared hostility to England, and the colonies prepared to commence the contest known in America as King George's war. The principal event of this war in America was the capture of the fortress of Louisburg, on the island of Cape Breton. This fortress had been constructed by the French at an expense of five and a half millions of dollars.

In 1748 a treaty of peace was concluded at Aix-la-Chapelle, in Germany, when it was agreed that all prisoners should be released and all acquisitions of property or territory were to be restored. But soon disputes about local boundaries began, and it was not long before these two nations were involved in another bloody struggle for dominion in the new world.

CHAPTER III.

THE MIDDLE STATES.

At the time of the early settlement of America nearly all the nations of Europe were at war with each other on account of different religious opinions. To escape persecution the English Quaker, the French Huguenot, and many from the shores of the Baltic and the banks of the Danube and Rhine sought refuge on the banks of the Hudson and Delaware.

Henry Hudson, while exploring the eastern coast of America, seeking for a north-west passage to India, sailed up the river which now bears his name. His little ship, called the Half Moon, was the first European sail ever borne upon its waters.

For fifteen years no regular attempt at settlement was made. The island of Manhattan, consisting of twenty-two thousand acres, was purchased in 1624 by the Dutch from the Indians, for about twenty-four dollars. This island, called New Amsterdam, contained a few Dutch cottages with thatched roofs and wooden chimneys. It is now the wealthy and populous city of New York.

The country claimed by the Dutch was called New Netherlands. To encourage emigration to New Netherlands, the Dutch West India company offered every man who, in four years, would plant a colony of fifty souls, a tract of land sixteen miles in length, and as wide as they required, with the privilege of governing all who settled upon it. Van Swiller was appointed governor in 1633, and from the beginning had difficulties with the English colonies on the Connecticut river. In 1638 he was succeeded in office by Sir William Kieft, who was a bold and unprincipled man, and soon involved his colony in serious troubles. The Indians, excited by the rum which they had purchased from the Hollanders, committed various trespasses which Kieft punished severely. An Indian warrior had been made drunk and robbed, and, on returning to a sense of his injuries, murdered two of the Dutch. About this time a band of Indians, driven by the Mohawks, sought shelter with the

Hackensacks, on the Hudson, and solicited the protection of the Dutch. But Kieft could not be satisfied without a flow of blood. He sent a party of his countrymen across the river in the night, who fell upon the unsuspecting fugitives, and in the general massacre, women and children, old and sick, shared the same cruel fate. The fiery hatred and vengeance of all the surrounding tribes was aroused, and a desperate and bloody war was the result. It was for a time feared that every Hollander would be swept from the country. Roger Williams using his influence in behalf of peace, hostilities were for a time suspended. But the war was afterward renewed, and for two years the colony suffered dreadfully. John Underhill was made captain of their forces. He successfully beat back and defeated the Indians. The river Indians were adopted into the Mohawk tribe, and a treaty of peace was made with the Dutch.

Kieft was succeeded by Peter Stuyvesant, an eminent soldier, and possessed of every requisite for an efficient governor. He was kind and just in his treatment to the Indians; settled boundary disputes, granted the colony a more liberal system of trade, and promoted its interests. But while he was removing all causes for trouble with his neighbors, there was a power at work within his own colony which caused him much anxiety and uneasiness. The people had for a number of years shown an ardent desire for greater freedom. Stuyvesant was an aristocrat and opposed to democracy. He soon found himself at variance with his people. At last, without the approbation of their governor, a general assembly of two deputies from each village was convened for the purpose of asserting the rights of the people. Taxation was resisted, and a willingness expressed to bear English rule, if they might enjoy English liberty. The change of government was not long delayed. The whole territory of New Netherlands had been granted by Charles II. of England, to his brother James, Duke of York, and the name of New Amsterdam was changed to New York, in honor of the Duke, and the name of Albany was given to the settlement on the Hudson, called by the Dutch Fort Orange.

The people of New York soon perceived that a change of government did not bring with it the blessings they had hoped. In the hope of having a representative government they were disappointed, and the taxes to support the government were increased.

War was declared between England and Holland in 1672. Holland being successful, New York again passed into the hands of the Dutch. This state of things, however, lasted but about fifteen months, when New York was restored to the English, in whose possession it remained until the time of the revolution. All the Atlantic coast, now from Maine to Georgia, belonged to the English.

NEW JERSEY.

In 1623 the territory between the Hudson and the Delaware was granted to Lords Berkeley and Carteret by the Duke of York. Carteret's share consisted of the territory included in the state of New Jersey. Elizabethtown, then consisting of four houses, became the capital of the province.

At the end of ten years Berkeley sold his province to the Friends, a large number of whom settled there the next year. They purchased lands from the Indians, who thus expressed their kind welcome and desire for peace: "You are brothers, and we will live like brothers with you. We will have a broad path for you and us to walk in. If an Englishman fall asleep in this path, the Indian shall pass him by and say: He is an Englishman; he is asleep; let him alone. The path shall be plain; there shall not be in it a stump to hurt the feet."

East Jersey also fell into the possession of the Friends, being purchased by William Penn and eleven of his brethren. They obtained a charter and appointed Robert Barclay governor for life. When the Duke of York ascended to the throne, he considered his contracts as duke not binding upon his honor as king. Through the instrumentality of Andros he endeavored to annul the American charters. He succeeded in subverting the governments of several, among which were the Jerseys. New Jersey from this period presents but few items of interest up to the time the independence of the colonies was declared, in 1776.

PENNSYLVANIA.

Pennsylvania is the only instance of an American colony founded without bloodshed. It was intended to be an asylum for the persecuted English Friends.

William Penn was the only son of an English admiral, who had won distinction by his conquest of Jamaica, and brilliant achievements during the war with Holland. He was born in 1644. While a student at Oxford, and at the age of sixteen, he became interested in the doctrines of the Quakers, for which he was expelled from the university. This displeased his father, who beat him and turned him out of doors, but afterwards forgave him, and sent him to travel on the continent, in the hope that by intercourse with the world his opinions would be changed. At the age of twenty-two he was sent by his father to Ireland on business, and while there became so impressed by the preaching of Thomas Loe, the Quaker minister, that he joined their society, and became so firm a convert that all his father's reproaches, and even a second expulsion from home could not change his faith. His firmness and gentleness afterward won for him the admiration and forgiveness of his father.

During the next three years he was three times imprisoned for his religion and pleading the cause of his brethren. At one time a jury was starved two days and nights to compel them to convict him. They insisted on returning a verdict of acquittal, for which they were fined.

On his release from imprisonment, he, with several others of his persuasion, embarked for Holland, distributed tracts and preached to the people. On his return to England he found the condition of the Friends as suffering as ever, and determined to found a free and happy home for them in the new world. In 1681 he obtained a tract of land on the western bank of the Delaware river, in payment of a claim against the government for sixteen thousand pounds, left him by his father. The king gave to this territory the name of Pennsylvania, "the woody land of Penn."

Within the domain granted to Penn were some Swede and Dutch settlements. These he had no desire to remove. He sent them a copy of his grant, and a message informing them that he had no intention of usurping their rights, but intended they should be governed by their own laws.

The year before Penn was able to join his colony, he sent out a number of emigrants with instructions for building a city. He did not wish it to be a crowded city with the pure air and light of heaven shut out, but to each house there was to be a large garden attached, so that it might be a "faire greene country towne."

In November of the year 1682, Penn, with a hundred settlers, sailed for the new world in the ship Welcome. During the long voyage of nine weeks thirty of his companions died of small pox. He was warmly welcomed on his arrival by the Friends who had preceded him. He sailed up the Delaware, on the banks of which he determined to found his city. The ground was purchased from the Swedes. The city thus commenced was called Philadelphia, or city of Brotherly Love.

Soon after this Penn made his famous treaty with the Indians. They met under a large elm tree in what is now called Kensington. This tree was preserved until 1810 when it was blown down during a severe storm. A monument, which has since been erected, marks the place where it stood. Here, beside the Delaware, Penn met the chieftains. The old warriors took their seats on the ground in the form of a half moon, while the younger ones arranged themselves behind in a similar form. Their new governor, who had inspired their confidence by means of a few presents, occupied the central space before them. "We meet," said he, "on the broad pathway of good faith and good will. I will not call you children, for parents sometimes chide their children too severely; nor brothers only, for brothers differ. The friendship between me and you I will not compare to a chain, for that the rains might rust or the falling tree might break. We are the same as if one man's body were divided into two parts. We are one flesh and one blood."

The Indians trusted him and presented him with a belt of wampum as an emblem of friendship. "We will live," said they, "with William Penn and his children so long as the sun and moon shall endure." This treaty of peace between the English Quaker and the red man of the forest was never violated. While other white settlements suffered severely from Indian wars, "not a drop of Quaker blood was ever shed by an Indian."

The government of Pennsylvania was republican. An assembly, composed of six members from each county, was organized. All sects were tolerated. Every freeman could vote and hold office, who believed in God and abstained from work on the Sabbath. This peaceful colony grew and prospered. In 1683 Philadelphia consisted of four cottages, but in two years the houses numbered six hundred. It grew more in three years than New York did in fifty.

DELAWARE.

In 1631 the Dutch planted a feeble settlement near the present site of Lewiston, but difficulties with the natives had excited savage vengeance, and they exterminated the Dutch colony.

Gustavus Adolphus, the monarch of Sweden, determined to plant a colony in America, which should be an asylum for persecuted Christians. He died before his plans were carried out. When his daughter, Christiana, succeeded to the throne, the minister, Oxenstiern, accomplished the noble purpose which her father had formed. A church and fort were built on the site of Wilmington. The place was called Christiana, in honor of their young queen. Their territory was named New Sweden. The jealousy of the Dutch was aroused, and they resolved to expel or subdue the Swedes. For a few years Delaware was in the possession of the Dutch, although the inhabitants were Swedes.

CHAPTER IV.

THE SOUTHERN STATES.

MARYLAND.

In England, during the reign of King James, the Puritans were subjected to very severe penalties on account of their religious belief. But, although the king persecuted the Puritans for non-conformity with the rites and views of the English church, he, on the other hand, oppressed the Roman Catholics still more severely; and the Puritans also, as they became more numerous and increased in influence, raised a fierce outcry against the Romanists, persecuting them as far as they were able, even while they were themselves suffering persecution at the hands of King James and the supporters of the English church. The Roman Catholics, being thus oppressed on both sides, turned, in their distress, to America, which was, even at that early day, an asylum for the oppressed.

George Calvert, one of the most influential of the Roman Catholics, was a leading member of the London company, and he also held the office of Secretary of State at the time of the embarkation of the Pilgrims for America. For his services to his country and sovereign, he was, in 1621, created an Irish peer, with the title of Lord Baltimore.

In 1628, Lord Baltimore went to Virginia with the view of establishing a Roman Catholic colony there, but he found the Virginians hostile to the cause, opposing it as violently as the king himself. He then went beyond the Potomac, where he found a beautiful country which was as yet unoccupied. He went back to England and applied for a charter to establish a colony there. The charter was granted by Charles I. (who had ascended the throne in 1625,) after the death of Lord Baltimore, to his son Cecil, who had inherited his title and property. The province was called *Maryland*, in honor of the Catholic queen, Henrietta Maria.

The first company of emigrants, with Leonard Calvert, brother of Cecil, as their governor, arrived in March, 1634. They sailed up the Chesapeake and purchased a village of the Indians, which they named St. Mary. By their honesty in paying for their land, they secured the friendship of the Indians, and being well supplied with the necessaries of life, the colony prospered.

Some time previous to the establishment of this colony, William Clayborne had obtained a license from the king to traffic with the Indians, and he, in company with others, had established trading stations at different points along the Chesapeake. Clayborne and his followers denied the authority of Lord Baltimore, and collected on the eastern border of Maryland, resolved to sustain their claims at all hazards. Their obstinacy caused some trouble, but Baltimore sent a force against them, which, after a severe skirmish, succeeded in making the insurgents prisoners. Clayborne's property was confiscated, and he was sent to England to answer to a charge of treason.

The first legislative assembly in Maryland was held at St. Mary in 1635. At this time every freeman was entitled to a voice in the enactment of laws, and it was not until 1639 that a representative government was established. At first each county chose as many representatives as it pleased, while the proprietor appointed others, but afterwards the counties were confined to four each, and the city of Annapolis was allowed two.

Although the Indians were at first amicably disposed towards the Maryland colony, they afterwards became jealous of their increasing power and began to harass them in many ways. The whites at last determined to endure their encroachments no longer, and declared war against them. This war lasted from 1642 to 1645, when peace was again restored. But now disturbances came in another direction. During this same year, William Clayborne, having been acquitted of the charge of treason in England, returned to Maryland determined on revenge. He infused a spirit of rebellion into some of the colonists, and his party became so powerful that the governor was obliged to flee into Virginia, where he remained a year and a half before the rebellion was quelled, and he was permitted to resume his office.

The colony went on from this time with but little disturbance until 1654, when Cromwell became Protector of England. By this time the Protestants were greater in numbers and influence than the Romanists in Maryland, and, instigated by Clayborne they forgot the generosity of Baltimore in allowing them religious freedom, and passed a law withdrawing the protection of the laws of Maryland from the Catholics.

At this the Catholics raised the standard of rebellion. A civil war was begun which lasted, with occasional interruptions, until 1691, when an end was put to the disturbances by King William III. who made Maryland a royal province, thus depriving Lord Baltimore of his rights as proprietor. Maryland continued to be a royal province until 1716, when the rights of Lord Baltimore were again recognized, and the colony was restored to an heir who had embraced the Protestant religion. The original form of representative government was now again established, and Maryland grew and prospered under wise governors until the beginning of the revolutionary war.

VIRGINIA.

In 1584, after an unsuccessful attempt by Sir Humphrey Gilbert, an English nobleman, to explore the coast of America from St. Johns, Newfoundland, southward, his step-brother, Sir Walter Raleigh, obtained a patent from Queen Elizabeth which granted to him all lands which he might discover in America, between the Delaware and Santee rivers. He sent out two men, named Arthur Barlow and Philip Amidas, to explore the American coast. After taking possession of the country in the name of Queen Elizabeth, they, in a few weeks, returned to England with the most animated statements concerning the country. Upon hearing their glowing descriptions, the queen pronounced this one of the most illustrious events of her reign, and in remembrance of her unmarried state, she gave to the newly discovered region the name of *Virginia.*

Some time after this a strife ensued between England and France respecting the possession of the new territory, which did not end until 1604. The English then claimed a tract of country extending from Halifax, Nova Scotia, on the north, to Cape Fear, North Carolina, on the south. A district, extending from the mouth of the Potomac river to Cape Fear, was granted to an association of merchants and noblemen, a majority of whom were residents of London. This association was called the London company.

The first company of emigrants to Virginia under the auspices of the London company, left England in December, 1606, in three vessels, commanded by Captain Christopher Newport. The colonists numbered one hundred and five, but in all that number there were but "twelve laborers and a few mechanics." The remainder of them were dissolute and indolent men, not at all fitted for an undertaking such as that in which they had embarked.

These men left England with no charter permitting them to govern themselves, but they were, on the contrary, to be governed by a council of seven from the company in England. In lesser affairs they were to be ruled by a subordinate council chosen from their number by the council at home. The colonists were not to know until they reached their destination who composed this subordinate council, for their names and instructions were placed in a sealed box which they were commanded not to open until they reached Virginia. Thus, when, on board the vessels, any disputes arose between the colonists, there was no one who could check the disturbance and re-establish concord.

Upon arriving at the American coast, the vessels were driven by a storm into Chesapeake Bay. They gave to the two capes, at the entrance of the bay, the names of Charles and Henry, in honor of the sons of King James. They soon entered the James river, which they named in honor of the king, and about fifty miles up the river they landed on the 23d of May, 1607, and commenced the settlement which they called Jamestown.

According to the instructions contained in the sealed box which the colonists brought to America with them, Edward Maria Wingfield was their first governor. The colonists began to suffer from want in a few weeks, as some of their provisions had been spoiled while they were on their way, and the rest had been consumed. They had not planted any grain upon their arrival, and as the Indian tribes adjoining their settlement showed signs of hostility, they were in a very deplorable condition. In addition to the famine and hostility of the Indians, the extreme dampness of the climate, together with the insufferable warmth, carried away a great many of them, so that at the close of the summer but one half of their number were living.

At this time they discovered that their governor was living bountifully on some private stores, and also making preparations to leave the colony and flee to the West Indies. They immediately deposed him, and chose Ratcliffe as his successor. Ratcliffe, however, proving inefficient, the settlers looked to Captain John Smith, who was, in reality, the ablest man among them, but whom they had before treated unkindly on account of envy.

Smith assumed the reins of government, and soon, by his indomitable energy, restored order in the colony, and compelled the Indians to supply them with food. The autumn also brought plentiful supplies of wild game, so that the colony again began to prosper.

Smith, taking advantage of the prosperous condition of the colony, started out with a few companions on a tour of exploration. He ascended the Chickahominy river fifty miles, then, leaving the boat, he, with two of his companions plunged into the forest. They were soon surrounded by a band of Indians who slew his companions and made him a captive. They exhibited him in several of their settlements, and then took him before Powhatan, the chief of their tribe. Here, a council of warriors condemned him to death. In accordance with this decision, he was led out to execution, his arms were pinioned and his head was laid upon the stone. The clubs of the Indians were raised to strike, when Pocahontas, the loved and only child of Powhatan, threw herself upon the prisoner and entreated her father not to slay him. The chief granted her prayer, and, by this circumstance, the Indians were changed from enemies to friends, as they believed him to be under the protection of some powerful Manitou or guardian angel.

They immediately made a treaty with him, and sent a guard of twelve men to escort him back to Jamestown in safety.

Upon Smith's return he found every thing in disorder in the colony. The colonists were an improvident and lazy set of men, and their number was increased early in 1608. At this time, Captain Newport, who had returned to England shortly after the arrival of the first company of immigrants at Jamestown, arrived with one hundred and twenty men. These men were as idle and dissolute as those who had preceded them. Soon after their arrival some glittering particles were discovered in the earth near Jamestown which were mistaken for gold, and, in spite of Smith's remonstrances, the colonists bestowed all their labor upon it, and indulged in dreams of wealth. Smith soon became disgusted with them, and, with a few men, went on another tour of exploration. They sailed up the Chesapeake bay and Potomac river in an open boat. They also traveled through the forests, and made treaties with several Indian tribes. They traveled three thousand miles in three months, and on their return Smith constructed a very accurate map of the country.

When Smith returned from his second trip he was made president of the council at Jamestown. He did all in his power to turn the attention of the settlers from seeking gold to agriculture. He met with success in a degree, but the colonists were none of them accustomed to such labor, and he found it a hard task to keep them from idleness. He wrote to the Supreme Council in England, entreating them to "send but thirty carpenters, husbandmen, gardeners, fishermen, blacksmiths, masons, and diggers of trees' roots, rather than a thousand" of such as were then there. They were obliged to depend upon the Indians for a greater portion of their food.

In June, 1609, the London company obtained a new charter, giving them more extended advantages. By it, the Supreme Council in England was furnished with the right to fill any vacancies which might occur in its own body, and also to choose a governor for Virginia. This governor was to be vested with absolute power, having at his disposal the property and even the lives of the colonists.

Under the new charter the Supreme Council appointed Lord Delaware governor of Virginia for life. Not being able to go immediately to Virginia, he sent Captain Christopher Newport, Sir George Somers, and Sir Thomas Gates, authorizing them to govern the colony until his arrival. They left England on the 12th of June, 1609, with nine ships and over five hundred emigrants.

When they had come near to the coast, the fleet was scattered by a hurricane, and the vessel which contained the three commissioners was wrecked on the Bermuda islands. The majority of the emigrants, however, reached Jamestown in safety.

The new settlers were as dissolute and improvident as the others, and caused Smith considerable trouble. He, however, ruled the settlement until the close of the year, when, having met with a severe accident, he was obliged to return to England for surgical attendance.

As soon as the colonists were freed from the control of Smith, they returned to their old habits of idleness. Their supply of food being soon consumed, they were in a deplorable condition, and as Smith was the only man whom the Indians respected, they would not supply the settlers any longer. On the contrary, soon after his departure they began to evince signs of hostility, and, reading their own fate in the growth and increasing power of the whites, they formed a plan for exterminating them. This plan, however, was defeated by Pocahontas, who remained friendly to the English, and revealed it to them.

In June, 1610, one year from the time of their departure from England, the commissioners, who had fitted up a vessel on the island where they were wrecked, arrived at Jamestown. But, instead of being met and welcomed by a flourishing colony, as they had expected, they were received by a few starving creatures; for, of the five hundred left by Smith six months before, only sixty were now living. They immediately resolved to leave the town where they had suffered so much, and, had it not been for the interference of Sir Thomas Gates, they would have set fire to the settlement. They left the settlement in four little vessels, and a more wretched or dejected company than those who floated down the James river on the 17th of June, 1610, could not well be imagined. On the following morning, when they had nearly reached the mouth of the river, their sorrow was turned into joy on meeting their new governor, Lord Delaware, who was coming with more immigrants and an abundant supply of provisions. They immediately returned to Jamestown, and that night the air was resonant with songs of praise to the Giver of all good.

Under the wise administration of Lord Delaware, the colony prospered, but he was obliged, on account of ill health, to return to England in March of the following year. Sir Thomas Gates was then appointed governor of Virginia, and he arrived during the month of September following, with six ships, three hundred immigrants, one hundred kine, and an abundant supply of provisions. The settlers greeted him gladly, and under his government the little colony flourished greatly.

Another charter was granted to the London company in 1612. By it the power of the king over the council and colony was abrogated, and the Supreme Council in England was also abolished. The whole company, as a body, made laws and elected officers for the colony. The settlers were contented, although they had no voice in the government. They acquiesced in all the measures taken and decisions made by the company, and there were about a thousand English settlers in Virginia at the beginning of the year 1613.

Ever since the departure of Smith the Indians had been hostile to the colonists in Virginia. During the fore part of the year 1613, Pocahontas, who was dearly loved by her father, was kidnapped by a scouting party from the white settlement and taken to Jamestown. This party stole her, hoping that Powhatan would pay a large ransom for her release, or at least consent to a treaty of peace; but, on the contrary, he was exasperated, and made immediate preparations for war. This threatened evil was, however, averted by Pocahontas and a young Englishman by the name of John Rolfe, between whom a mutual attachment had sprung up. Pocahontas was educated in the language and religion of the English, and in April, 1613, she received the rite of baptism, and was joined in marriage to young Rolfe. Powhatan gave his consent to this union, and from that time until his death he was a friend to the English.

The colony now began to prosper, and in 1619 a great many people came from England and settled in Virginia. In this year also, the people first held a representative assembly. By the intercession of George Yeardley, who was then governor, they were granted a share in the enactment of laws for the colony. On the 28th of June, in this year, they held the first representative assembly at Jamestown. Virginia was divided into eleven boroughs, from each of which two representatives were chosen. These representatives were called burgesses, and the assembly consisted of them together with the governor and his council. After two years they obtained from the London company a written constitution, and at about the same time one hundred and fifty young women came over "to become wives to the planters," so that now the settlers regarded this as their permanent abode, and set to work in earnest.

Powhatan continued to be the friend of the English until his death, when his brother, Opechancanough, became chief of the tribes. Opechancanough was hostile to the whites, and in 1622, soon after he became chief, he set on foot a plot to annihilate the white settlements. On the first of April, the settlements farthest from Jamestown, were attacked, and great numbers of the inhabitants slain. Jamestown and the settlements bordering upon it, being warned by Chanco, a friendly Indian, were saved, and those inhabitants of the towns which were attacked, who were not massacred, fled to Jamestown. The colony which numbered eighty settlements was reduced to eight within a few days.

When the English were collected at Jamestown, they made preparations for war. This war, which commenced immediately, lasted, with occasional interruptions, until 1646, when, Opechancanough having died in captivity, the Indians gave up their lands and left the country.

The London company having become very much increased in numbers and influence, King James I. regarded their growing power as hostile and injurious to his own, and so he sought to dissolve the company. In this he succeeded. He took away their charter and made Virginia a royal province. He appointed George Yeardley governor, and twelve councilors to assist him in the administration of the government. Both this monarch and his son Charles I., who succeeded to the throne upon the death of his father, April 6th, 1625, were very selfish, and ruled the Virginia colony more for their own benefit than for that of the settlers.

After Charles I. was beheaded, and during the time that Oliver Cromwell ruled England as *Protector*, the Virginia planters were allowed to govern themselves, and the colony prospered remarkably, but at the death of Cromwell, in 1658, his son, to whom he had left the government, not having the ability to rule as his father had done, soon resigned his office, and the next year after that, the line of Stuart kings was continued in the person of Charles II, the son of Charles I. At his accession a powerful aristocracy arose in Virginia, formed by the rich planters. This party, who were more numerous than the republicans, attempted to deprive them of any part in the government. In addition to this, King Charles II. made very tyrannical and rigorous laws regarding their commercial transactions. These laws required them to ship all goods to and from England in English vessels; they also forbade them to trade with any European power except England, and their traffic among themselves was either excessively taxed or altogether forbidden.

In the year 1675, the Susquehannah Indians, a tribe of southern Pennsylvania, invaded their northern border, and committed many fearful ravages. Upon the refusal of Governor Berkeley to give the people arms with which to protect themselves, they resolved to arm themselves without his authority, and at the earnest solicitation of his countrymen, Nathaniel Bacon, a young republican, placed himself at their head. He was, at first, declared a traitor by the governor, but, as he was supported by a body of five hundred resolute patriots, Berkeley was compelled to listen to the popular demand, and allow him a commission. The republican assembly immediately confirmed this action of the governor, and gave Bacon command over a thousand men. Bacon advanced against the Indians without delay, but he had no sooner left Jamestown than Governor Berkeley again declared him guilty of treason, and with an army equal to that of Bacon took possession of the settlement. When Bacon heard of this action, he marched against Berkeley and compelled him to evacuate Jamestown. He marched into the town, confiscated the property of Berkeley's followers, and proclaimed himself governor. Soon afterward, however, he heard of the arrival of a large body of troops which had been sent from England to suppress the insurrection, and, as he was not able to hold the town against the united forces, he set it on fire. The whole town, with the exception of the old church tower, was destroyed.

Jamestown was burned on the evening of September 30th, 1676, and Bacon marched to the York river, where he conceived a plan to expel the governor's forces from the colony; but before it was carried into execution, he died from the effects of a disease contracted in the swamps about Jamestown. There being no one of sufficient ability to lead his party after his death, they were soon overpowered, and many of them were executed. Berkeley ruled the colony tyrannically for a year, when he was recalled, and another governor was sent from England.

During the rest of the reign of Charles II. and that of his brother James II., the Virginians were very much oppressed by the tyranny of governors appointed over them, but from the revolution of 1688, which deposed James II., and enthroned William and Mary, to the beginning of the French and Indian war, the whole colony of Virginia thrived remarkably.

THE FRENCH AND INDIAN WAR.

Almost at the commencement of the 18th century, the French began to intrude upon the territory of the English. They already possessed Louisiana and Canada, and continued to form settlements west of Pennsylvania and Virginia. The English endured their encroachments, until, in 1753, the French devised a scheme for constructing a line of forts from Canada to Louisiana, passing through the English colonies of Pennsylvania and Virginia. Upon this the governor of Virginia sent a letter of remonstrance to the commander of the French. George Washington, who was then but twenty-one years of age, was chosen as the messenger. There was much danger connected with the mission, and the route was an exceedingly difficult one, but a better man to undertake it, than Washington, notwithstanding his youth, could not have been chosen.

On the 31st of October, 1753, Washington, accompanied by three or four attendants, started upon his perilous mission. After enduring many hardships and privations, he, at last, reached the headquarters of the French commander. He delivered his message, and after four days received a written reply. He then returned to Virginia, where he arrived after an absence of eleven weeks.

The answer of the French commander had been a refusal to relinquish the claim of the French to the territory where they had settled; so the English made immediate preparations for war. Upon attempting to build a fort at the point where the Ohio, Alleghany, and Monongahela rivers meet, they were driven away by a party of French soldiers, who finished the fort, and gave it the name of Du Quesne.

In May, 1754, Washington surprised an advanced party of the French at the Great Meadows, and gained a complete victory. The French commander was slain, and only fifteen of the fifty under his command escaped. On account of a lack of men, however, the English were obliged to withdraw their forces, so that the French again occupied the Ohio valley.

In February, 1755, General Edward Braddock was sent from England to take command of the provincial troops. He was entirely unaccustomed to Indian warfare, and drilled his army according to European tactics, notwithstanding Washington, who had consented to attend him as aid-de-camp, repeatedly attempted to advise him to act differently. He haughtily refused to act upon the advice of Washington, believing that a lack of bravery on the part of the colonists was the only cause of their defeats.

After a long delay, Braddock commenced his march. When near Fort Du Quesne, on the 9th of July, they were surprised by a quick discharge of bullets and arrows from the adjoining thickets. The English army was thrown into confusion, and, not knowing where to fire, expended their ammunition by firing into the air. General Braddock, after having three horses shot under him, was mortally wounded. Washington, although fired at many times, was not touched, so that the Indians regarded him with a superstitious dread.

At the time of the expedition of Braddock against Fort Du Quesne, two others were sent out. One of them was against Niagara and Kingston, under Governor Shirley, and the other against Crown Point, under General William Johnson, both of which, though not as calamitous as that of Braddock, failed to accomplish the end in view.

This war continued, each side alternately gaining advantages, until 1760, when the French were subdued. Articles of peace, however, were not signed until February 10th, 1763.

THE CAROLINAS.

Numerous attempts were made during the sixteenth century to establish settlements in the region called, by the English, South Virginia; the first of which was by the Huguenots, or French Protestants, who had fled from persecution in their own land. They gave to the country the name of *Carolina*, in honor of the King of France, Charles IX., which name it still retains. This attempt at settlement proved unsuccessful, as did also those made by several expeditions afterwards fitted out by Sir Walter Raleigh, and sent from England. The first permanent settlements in that region were formed by dissatisfied and adventurous colonists from the other American settlements and Barbadoes.

In the year 1663 Charles II., King of England, granted this territory to eight noblemen, and the same country which, in

1562, was named Carolina, in honor of the French king, now, one hundred years afterward, received the same name in honor of the King of England.

The Barbadoes planters came to Carolina in 1665, and established a colony with Sir John Yeamans as governor. In honor of Lord Clarendon, Prime Minister of England, and one of the proprietors, this colony was called the Clarendon County Colony. This colony was established in the northern part of Carolina, and soon became known entirely as *North Carolina.*

In January, 1670, three vessels bearing emigrants, under the command of Joseph West and William Sayle, were sent out from England by the proprietors, for the purpose of establishing another colony. After settling in two or three places, which they afterwards abandoned, they finally founded a settlement on the site of the present city of Charleston, in the year 1682.

As soon as permanent settlements had been founded in the Carolinas, the proprietors conceived the plan of drawing up a grand constitution for this country, which they confidently hoped would far outstrip any government in Europe. They appointed Lord Ashley Cooper, Earl of Shaftesbury, one of the proprietors, and John Locke, one of the most distinguished philosophers of that time, to frame the instrument. It was finished in March, 1669, and was highly commended in Europe, but when taken to Carolina and tested, it was found to be exceedingly unpractical. The people would not receive it, but preferred laws of their own making. After a long endeavor to render the grand scheme practical in its workings, the proprietors gave up the attempt and permitted the people to rule in their own way. Representative government was first established in 1672, in the southern part of Carolina. This was called, in honor of Sir George Carteret, one of the proprietors, the Carteret County Colony, but it soon after received the name of *South Carolina.*

For a period of five or six years, beginning with the year 1680, great numbers of immigrants came and settled in the Carolinas, comprising the persecuted, as well as the adventurous from England, Scotland, and Ireland, the Huguenots from France, and many of the Dutch from New York. The colonists were industrious, and in both North and South Carolina many soon became wealthy. The contest between the proprietors and people lasted for twenty years, but the first legislative assembly was convened in 1688. After that, during the remainder of the seventeenth century, both the Carolinas prospered remarkably. At the beginning of the seventeenth century, on account of a war existing between England and Spain, the Spanish colony at St. Augustine, Florida, disturbed the Carolina settlements. The neighboring tribes of Indians also at times showed signs of hostility, but the colonists held both their Spanish and Indian foes in check, and were not long disturbed by them. In the year 1715, a powerful Indian confederacy was formed against the whites. This confederacy numbered about six thousand men, and, headed by the *Yamassees* and *Tuscaroras*, and instigated by the Spaniards, they made many fearful ravages in the Carolinas. Energetic and wise measures were immediately taken by Governor Craven; the colonies were placed under martial law, the white inhabitants and slaves were armed, and a strong force went out against the Indians, who were soon overpowered, and fled, part of the tribes to the south, and part to the north.

The people of the Carolinas were heavily taxed by the proprietors, who also refused to aid them against their enemies, and in 1719 the people of South Carolina called a convention and sent a petition to the king to make South Carolina a royal province. The petition was granted, the colony was purchased by the king, who appointed a governor, and allowed the people to choose their own representatives. Ten years later North Carolina was also sold to the king.

By this arrangement, the people of neither colony derived much benefit. The royal governors appointed over them were generally weak, selfish, and tyrannical, as they had proved in Virginia, Maryland and other colonies, and from this time until the beginning of the Revolutionary War, North and South Carolina, in common with other American colonies under royal rule, were involved in contentions with their governors concerning their rights and privileges.

GEORGIA.

At the time that the Carolinas became royal provinces, the whole country between the Savannah and Altamaha rivers was uninhabited except by Indian tribes. At this time also, the cruel laws against debtors were in full force in England, and men of all classes who were unable to pay their debts were thrown into prison.

Moved with pity for these unfortunate men, a band of philanthropists, at the head of whom was General James Edward Oglethorpe, conceived the plan of establishing on the free soil of America an asylum for those who were oppressed on account of their poverty, and persecuted for their religious belief. This plan was approved by Parliament, and sanctioned by the king, and all who were in prison for debt were released on condition that they would accompany the expedition. A charter was granted to Oglethorpe and his associates, "in trust for the poor," in the year 1732, to found a colony in the region between the Savannah and Altamaha rivers, which was called *Georgia,* in honor of King George II.

General Oglethorpe, with the first band of emigrants, numbering one hundred and twenty, sailed from England in November, 1732, and touched at Charleston in the following January. From there he went to Port Royal, when, after landing the greater portion of the settlers, he ascended the Savannah river as far as Yamacraw bluff, where he laid the foundation of the city of Savannah.

Treaties of peace were immediately made with the Indians of the country, who appeared friendly, and sold their lands to the new comers at a price satisfactory to both parties. Many immigrants came from different parts of Europe, on account of the religious freedom in Georgia. A colony was founded by a pious sect from Austria, called the Moravians, who had fled from Roman Catholic persecution in their native country. They gave the name of Ebenezer to their settlement, and lived happily in the enjoyment of religious liberty.

Governor Oglethorpe went back to England, and when he returned, in 1736, he brought with him about three hundred new settlers, among whom were one hundred and fifty Scotch Highlanders, who were well versed in military tactics. These Highlanders built a town on the Altamaha river, to which they gave the name of Darien. John Wesley—the founder of the denomination known as the Methodists—and his brother Charles also came with Oglethorpe, as missionaries in Georgia and among the Indians. Their labors were not crowned with very great success, and they returned to England in 1738. The distinguished preacher, George Whitfield, who was then only twenty-three years of age, came to Georgia at that time. He met with greater success than Wesley had done, and his eloquence was so great that vast multitudes were attracted to hear him preach wherever he went. He founded an orphan asylum at Savannah, which was supported by contributions received by him at various places in England and America where he preached. During his lifetime it was of great benefit to the colony, and flourished under his powerful influence. At his death, however, which occurred at Newburyport, Massachusetts in 1770, being deprived of its sole support, it became extinct.

During the year 1739, England being at war with Spain, the Spanish settlers of St. Augustine made several attacks upon the Georgian settlements. Governor Oglethorpe had been expecting this, and had established a firm friendship with the neighboring Indian tribes. In 1740, having been appointed commander-in-chief, he went with an army of over two thousand men, consisting of English soldiers, Scotch Highlanders and friendly Indians, to attack St. Augustine. In this attack, however, he was unsuccessful, on account of sickness among his troops, caused by the oppressive heat of the climate and impurity of the atmosphere, and he was obliged to return to Savannah.

After Oglethorpe's departure, the Spaniards determined again to attack the Georgian settlements. They accordingly fitted out a fleet of thirty-six vessels, and in 1742 landed above the town of St. Simon's with three thousand men. Oglethorpe, by a stratagem, decoyed them into a swamp where his men lay in ambush. The Spaniards were surprised and completely routed. They immediately retreated to their ships, and returned to St. Augustine.

General Oglethorpe left Georgia in 1743, never again to return, and went to England. He had been dearly loved by the colonists, and his departure was greatly lamented. During Oglethorpe's stay in Georgia he had firmly prohibited the introduction of slavery in the colony; but soon after his departure, slaves were brought there and employed on the plantations.

The charter which had been obtained by Oglethorpe and his colleagues was granted to them for twenty-one years. The colony had proved extremely unprofitable to the trustees, and at the end of the term of years named in the charter they willingly gave up the instrument, and Georgia was from that time until the beginning of the war of independence, a royal province.

CHAPTER V.

CAUSES OF THE REVOLUTION.

An act for taxing the American colonies was passed in the English parliament March 22d, 1765. Heavy expenses had been incurred by the English government for the protection of the colonies during the French and Indian war; and these, it was claimed, should be repaid by the colonists. The Americans would have been willing to have contributed their share, if they had been allowed to send representatives to the English parliament; but as they were not, they maintained that England had no right to tax them without their consent.

By the provisions of the Stamp Act, a tax was imposed on all paper used in business transactions. No deed, bond, note, agreement, receipt, lease or contract was valid, without a stamp costing from three pence to six pounds. Every newspaper was also required to be stamped, and for every advertisement they contained a duty of two shillings was imposed.

When the news of the Stamp Act reached America it caused great excitement and indignation among the people.

Patrick Henry was the youngest member of the legislature of Virginia. After waiting in vain for some of the older members to oppose it, he tore a fly leaf from an old law book, and drew up five resolutions, declaring that the sole right and power to levy taxes was vested in the General Assembly, and to vest that power in any other assembly was to destroy British, as well as American freedom. He spoke eloquently in favor of his resolutions; "and in the midst of an impassioned harangue, exclaimed," "Cæsar had his Brutus, Charles I. his Cromwell, and George III."—"Treason! treason!" was shouted from every part of the house—"may profit by their example. If this be treason, make the most of it."

The act was to go into operation on the 1st of November, and the excitement increased as the day approached. In Boston, handbills were posted up, warning those who should use or distribute stamped paper to take care of their lives and property. The day was ushered in by the tolling of bells; flags were hung at half mast, and every sign of a funeral solemnity was displayed. In New York, ten boxes of stamps were destroyed by the people. The business men of both these places resolved to import nothing from England until the act was repealed. Domestic manufactures were commenced in almost every family. Homespun clothes were worn by the wealthiest as well as the middling classes.

In Boston, "a paper was issued, bearing for its device, a snake, on the head of which were the letters N. E. [New England], while the body was divided into several pieces, marked with the initials of the other colonies. The motto, *join or die*, explained its meaning. In New Hampshire, on the morning of the eventful day, the bells tolled, and the people assembled as for a funeral procession. A coffin, bearing the name of *Liberty* was borne to a grave on the shoulders of eight persons, to the sound of minute guns. A funeral oration was pronounced, and the coffin was lowered into the grave. Suddenly signs of life appeared. It was raised to the surface, and now bore the inscription, *Liberty revived.* Enthusiastic shouts from the multitude, and the triumphant sounds of drums and trumpets greeted the resurrection."

The obnoxious Stamp Act was repealed in March, 1766; but the parliament still maintained the *right* to tax the colonies.

Among other harsh measures resorted to by Great Britain was the Mutiny Act, obliging the colonies to find quarters and supplies for soldiers that were sent to keep them in order. These troops were stationed at New York and Boston. The people were exasperated against the troops, and finally blood was shed in the streets of Boston.

A rope-maker got into difficulty with a soldier and struck him. Out of this grew an affray between several soldiers and rope-makers. A few evenings after this, about seven hundred citizens assembled for the purpose of attacking the troops. The soldiers fired upon the citizens, and killed three and dangerously wounded several others. Then several thousand of the exasperated citizens collected, and a terrible scene of blood would have occurred, had not the governor assured the people that justice should be vindicated. Captain Preston and his men were tried for murder. Through the influence of John Adams and Josiah Quincy, Preston and all his men were acquitted, except two, who were found guilty of manslaughter.

Parliament still claimed the right to tax the colonies, and a duty was laid on glass, lead, tea, etc. In 1770, all the taxes, excepting the one on tea, were removed.

In 1773, several ships, laden with tea, entered the American ports, but the people determined not to receive it. In Boston, a party of men, disguised as Indians, marched to the wharf where the ships were anchored, and threw three hundred and forty-two chests of tea into the sea. The same feeling existed in New York, Philadelphia, and Charleston. Ships that entered these ports were obliged to return to England without landing their cargoes.

The conduct of Boston produced a powerful sensation in the British Parliament, and harsh measures were now adopted toward this offending town. Parliament, by enactments, ordered the port of Boston to be closed against all commercial transactions, and the general court, the custom house, and other public offices should be removed to Salem.

This Act was called the Boston Port Bill. All the American colonies sympathized with the Bostonians. The merchants of Salem offered their port to those of Boston. Rice and money were sent them by the people of Georgia; five hundred and twenty-five bushels of wheat were sent from New York; and sympathizers in London presented one hundred and fifty thousand dollars for the poor of Boston.

In 1774 a Congress, composed of delegates from the thirteen colonies, met at Philadelphia. It was composed of the wisest and best men the colonies afforded. Among them were Washington, Patrick Henry and John Adams. Their meeting was opened with prayer by the Rev. Mr. Duche, an Episcopalian clergyman. Mr. Adams says, "he prayed fervently and in language sublime and beautiful, for Congress, for the province of Massachusetts Bay, and especially the town of Boston."

This Congress, which was convened the 5th of September, remained in session until the 26th of October, when they adjourned to meet again the 10th of May, 1775. But before the second Congress assembled the people had armed themselves to protect their rights and establish their freedom.

CHAPTER VI.

THE WAR OF INDEPENDENCE.

1775.

This war, generally known as the Revolutionary War, commenced with the skirmishes of Lexington and Concord, April 19th, 1775. Feeling that war was inevitable, hundreds of brave men armed themselves. Their leaders were Greene, Stark, Putnam, and others who had learned war in the contests with the French and Indians.

On the night of the 10th of May, an expedition from Connecticut, commanded by Colonel Ethan Allen, reached Ticonderoga, a strongly fortified place on Lake Champlain. Just as day was breaking on the morning of the 11th, they marched upon the fortress. The sentinel, too much frightened to give the alarm, retreated, and the Americans captured the fortress without striking a blow. Allen entered the commander's quarters, and awaking him, ordered him to surrender instantly. Seeing resistance was useless, he obeyed, and the fort, with its muskets, guns and ammunition, fell into the hands of the Americans.

Crown Point was also taken a short time after Ticonderoga.

June 17th, 1775, the battle of Bunker's Hill was fought. The Americans fought with great bravery and drove the British back as long as their ammunition held out, when they were obliged to give up their fort. Many were lost on both sides. Among those who were lost on the American side was Mr. Warren, whose death was deeply felt by his countrymen. The colonists were encouraged by the result of this battle, and the enemy was convinced that the Americans were not so feeble as they imagined.

In the midst of these excitements the second Continental Congress convened at Philadelphia, and George Washington was appointed commander-in-chief of the army. He refused all pay, except enough to defray his expenses. The army numbered fourteen thousand, and there were but nine cartridges to each soldier.

December 31st, 1775, General Arnold and General Montgomery attacked the city of Quebec from different quarters. Montgomery was shot; the British surrounded them and the division was forced to surrender. Arnold commanded the troops that effected a retreat, and entrenched himself on the opposite side of the river, a few miles below the town. With the unfortunate attack on Quebec the first year of the war closed.

1776.

A heavy cannonade was opened upon Boston from the American batteries, on the 2d of March. General Howe, who had succeeded General Gage, being alarmed for the safety of the city, resolved to evacuate it, which he did on the 17th of March, and embarked for Halifax.

On the 20th, Washington, at the head of his troops, marched into the city with drums beating and banners waving, greeted on every side with demonstrations of joy by the people. But they were shocked when they beheld the ruined condition of their beautiful town. Old South Church had been converted into a riding school; Faneuil Hall had been used for a theatre; wood had become so scarce that the pews of churches, the counters of stores, and even valuable libraries, had been used for fuel.

As soon as Washington had placed Boston in a state of security, he repaired to New York. Before attempting New York, Parker and Clinton were sent by the British to attack Charleston. General Lee and Colonel Moultrie had erected a fort on Sullivan's Island; the engagement commenced on the 28th of June. The British were repulsed, and sailed for New York. The slaughter of the British was frightful; the number of killed and wounded amounted to two hundred and twenty-five; of the Americans, only two were killed, and twenty-two wounded.

About this time, the people recommended Congress to declare the colonies absolved from allegiance to the crown, and Richard

Henry Lee, Benjamin Franklin, Roger Sherman and Robert Livingston, were appointed a committee to draw up a Declaration of Independence. Thomas Jefferson, the youngest member of the committee, was chosen chairman, and to him was assigned the task of preparing the important document. After being discussed several days, and slightly amended, it was adopted by Congress at two o'clock on the 4th of July, 1776. This act of Congress did much to animate the hearts and support the people during the disastrous military campaign that followed.

In July the British fleet left Halifax, and entering New York harbor, the troops landed on Staten Island, where in a few days, they were joined by Parker and Clinton from the south.

In August, the British and Hessians landed on Long Island and attacked the American division posted at Brooklyn. The Americans were defeated, and during the night effected a retreat to New York, carrying with them every thing but their heavy cannon. Leaving the city in the hands of the British, the Americans continued their march to Harlem, where a skirmish occurred in which they were partially victorious. They then retreated to White Plains, where they encountered the British and were defeated.

Washington now made preparation for the defense of Philadelphia. He had been pursued by the enemy, under Lord Cornwallis, as far as the Delaware, but they were unable to cross it for want of boats, and awaited the freezing of the river. Congress had departed, and there were many loyalists in the town; this led them to think the city could be easily taken. Cornwallis returned to headquarters at New York, and his troops were scattered in small divisions through New Jersey.

Washington determined to attack a body of Hessians stationed at Trenton. Christmas night was chosen for his enterprise. Knowing that they would pass the day in sports and drinking, he resolved to take advantage of their condition. The surprise was complete. Colonel Rahl, while trying to rally his panic-stricken soldiers, fell mortally wounded, and the Hessians surrendered to the Americans.

1777.

The first battle of this year was fought at Princeton.

On new year's day Washington was at Trenton. Cornwallis arrived about sunset and attempted to cross the river, but was repulsed, and awaited the approach of day. The British army being fresh and strong, the Americans feared the result of the next day's encounter, and determined to leave their post during the night and attack the British at Princeton. Their camp fires were left burning to deceive the enemy on the opposite side of the river. At Princeton the British were surprised and defeated. Cornwallis, on awaking at Trenton, found the American camp fires still burning, but not a soldier, tent or cannon was to be seen. He made a hasty march to Princeton, but did not arrive in time to prevent the victory Washington had gained.

On the 11th of September the British crossed the Brandywine, attacked and defeated the Americans, who retreated to Chester, and then to Philadelphia, hoping to save that city; but in this they were disappointed, and on the 26th of September it passed into the hands of the British.

Hearing that the enemy's force at Germantown was somewhat weakened, an attack upon it was planned. They succeeded at first in driving the British from their post, and for a time victory seemed secure; but some of the divisions failed to move to the attack as ordered, and the Americans were obliged to retreat with a considerable loss.

A British army under General Carleton, consisting of seven thousand men, was stationed in Canada. Carleton was succeeded in command by Burgoyne, who took possession of Fort Edward, and, being greatly in want of military stores, dispatched Colonel Baum, with a large force, to seize some that the Americans had deposited at Bennington. The approach of Burgoyne on the western frontier had caused a large force to be collected in New Hampshire, under the command of Major Stark. This detachment reached Bennington just in time to encounter Colonel Baum's force. In the severe battle that was fought the Americans were victorious. Baum, seven hundred prisoners and large quantities of arms and ammunition were captured.

The battle of Stillwater, fought on the 19th of September, in which the Americans were victorious, was one of the severest battles of the war.

The next encounter took place on the 7th of October, in which the British lost more than four hundred men, and the Americans were again victorious. The situation of Burgoyne was now desperate. The British held a council of war, in which it was agreed that a surrender of Burgoyne and his troops should be made to General Gates, and on the 17th of October the ceremony of surrender took place.

1778.

After the surrender of Burgoyne, a treaty was made between the Americans and the French, on February 6th, 1778, by which the latter nation recognized the independence of the former, and decided to help her fight for it.

A French fleet being expected in the Delaware, the British general determined to evacuate Philadelphia and proceed to New York. His movements being discovered by Washington, he sent a division of his army, under General Lee, to pursue them and give them battle. He overtook them at Monmouth Court-house, but, being alarmed at the sudden attack of the British, ordered a retreat. But Washington arrived just as the retreat commenced; he reprimanded Lee, and inspired the soldiers with courage and led them against the foe. During the night Clinton retreated towards New York, and the Americans were masters of the field.

1779.

The British, wearied of their unsuccessful attempts to conquer the New England and Middle States, now turned their attention to the south, where they knew the American forces were weakest. Here they met with better success. Their first conquest was Savannah; then followed Sunbury and Augusta. In fact, at the beginning of 1779 nearly all Georgia was in their possession. The royal governor was restored, and a royal province once more existed in the colonies. These victories encouraged the British, who now demanded the surrender of Charleston. Governor Rutledge and General Lincoln animated the people and soldiers to great exertions for the defense of the city, and the enemy retreated without attacking the place. Active operations in the south were suspended until the autumn of this year.

But in the north the ravages of war were carried on. Portsmouth and Norfolk, in Virginia, Norfolk, Fairfield, New Haven and other villages on Long Island Sound, were burned. The next important victory was the capture of Stony Point. The Americans entered the fort by means of the countersign, which they obtained from a negro who was in the habit of selling fruit in the garrison. After a short resistance, Colonel Johnson and his garrison surrendered prisoners of war. The following report was sent to the commander-in-chief:

"The fort and garrison, with Colonel Johnson, are ours; our officers and men behaved like men who are determined to be free."

The Americans were unable to retain Stony Point, as the British sent large reinforcements up the river. They, however, removed the cannon and military stores and destroyed the fort.

The Americans, aided by Count D'Estaing, attacked the city of Savannah, but they were unsuccessful, and the close of the year found Georgia still under a royal governor.

1780.

In May, of 1780, the city of Charleston passed into the hands of the British. After the surrender of General Lincoln, he was succeeded by General Gates, who advanced through the Carolinas and encountered the British at Camden, where a battle was fought and the Americans again defeated with great loss. The British, elated by their success, now pushed towards the north, hoping to drive the enemy from Carolina. They advanced as far as Charlotte, when, hearing that Major Ferguson had been killed, and his eleven hundred troops made prisoners, Cornwallis returned and took up his quarters at Winnsboro, South Carolina.

Although Charleston and Camden were in possession of the British, the Americans were cheered by the brilliant exploits of Marion, Sumpter and Lee. Marion so many times and in such rapid succession cut off detachments of Cornwallis' army, that Tarleton gave him the name of Swamp Fox.

Benedict Arnold was a bold soldier, but a bad and unprincipled man. He had married a tory lady, and lived in such an extravagant style as to awaken the suspicions of the Pennsylvania Legislature. A court-martial was appointed to try him. He was convicted of procuring public money by fraudulent means, and sentenced to be reprimanded by the commander-in-chief. This duty was performed by Washington with the utmost delicacy, but Arnold felt the disgrace, and, his bad passions being fully aroused, he agreed to place West Point in the hands of the British for fifty thousand dollars and a brigadier's commission in their army. Communications between the two armies were carried on through Adjutant General Major Andre. Andre was arrested and suffered death as a spy. Arnold escaped in safety to the British lines.

Another year now drew to a close, and England had expended vast treasures and much blood in endeavoring to subjugate the colonies, without success.

1781.

The first battle in the campaign of this year was fought at Cowpens. Victory was decided in favor of the Americans, and the British were obliged to retreat, leaving behind them three hundred killed or wounded, and over five hundred of their troops prisoners.

General Greene gave battle to the British on the 15th of March, at Guilford Court-house. After an engagement lasting two hours, the Americans were obliged to retreat, but the enemy had suffered too much to pursue them. Numerous encounters between the two armies took place during the summer. Greene was defeated at Camden, but other Generals had at the close of the season succeeded in driving the British into the south-east corner of the state. In the battle of Eutaw springs in September, the Americans were victorious. The British now abandoned all their posts, and retreated to Charleston. The last battle of the Revolution occurred at Yorktown. The allied armies,—French and American—after compelling the British to abandon their outworks, commenced a siege on the 28th of September. On the 9th of October they opened a heavy cannonade on the British works; red hot balls were hurled among the English shipping, causing several vessels to be burned. Cornwallis, perceiving that all would be lost unless he could escape, attempted to cross York river, but a sudden storm arose and dispersed the boats, and they were compelled to put back, and the project was abandoned. Hope now failed, and Cornwallis, on the 19th of October, surrendered the posts at Yorktown and Gloucester, and almost seven thousand soldiers and his shipping and seamen, to General Washington and De Grasse. The terms of surrender were the same as those the British had required of General Lincoln at Charleston.

Negotiations for peace were commenced in the spring of 1782. Before the close of the year the Southern cities were given up, but New York remained in the hands of the British until fall of the following year. The treaty of peace was signed September 3d, 1783, by commissioners who met at Paris. On the eighth anniversary of the first battle of the Revolution, a cessation of hostilities was proclaimed, and on the 3d of November following, the army was disbanded. During the Revolution many naval battles were also fought. The most important occurred off the coast of England in 1779. During the course of the war the Americans captured eight hundred and three vessels, with merchandise, amounting to about eleven millions of dollars.

The darkest period of American history succeeded the Revolution. A debt of forty millions of dollars had been contracted, and Congress had no means of paying it. The articles of confederation formed a sufficient constitution of government during the war, but were not adapted to the public wants of an independent sovereignty.

In May, of the year 1787, a convention assembled at the state house in Philadelphia. All the states were represented except Rhode Island. George Washington was chosen to preside, and, after long deliberation, the articles of confederation were cast aside, and the national constitution, under which we now live, was formed. After it had been signed by each member of the convention, it was submitted to Congress, September 28th, and that body sent copies of it to the several legislatures, that it might be approved of by the people of each individual state. Eleven of the states ratified it within a year, and it was adopted the 4th of March, 1789.

George Washington, by the unanimous voice of the people, became their first president, and John Adams was chosen vice president.

CHAPTER VII.

THE ADMINISTRATIONS.

WASHINGTON'S ADMINISTRATION—1789–1797.

On the 14th of April, Washington received an official announcement of his election as president of the United States, under the new constitution. The ceremony of inauguration took place at New York on the 13th of April. The oath of office was administered by Chancellor Livingston.

At this time the condition of the country was a very trying one. The Spanish authorities had prohibited the Americans from navigating the Mississippi; our ships in the Mediterranean sea were attacked by pirates of the Barbary states, and many an American citizen was condemned to slavery or an Algerine dungeon; and no treaty of commerce had been made with England, nor had they sent a minister to our country. And in addition to these, the French endeavored to solicit the Americans to aid them in their revolution.

Three executive departments were created. Mr. Jefferson was secretary of state; Mr. Hamilton of the treasury, and General Knox secretary of war. These officers comprised the president's cabinet. The first difficulty to be encountered was the payment of the public debt.

In 1791, on the recommendation of Hamilton, a United States bank and national mint was established at Philadelphia.

Vermont was claimed by New York and New Hampshire until 1791, when it became independent, and was admitted into the Union, the first addition to the thirteen original states.

Great opposition was made to the mode of raising money by taxation. In western Pennsylvania it met with so much resistance that Congress was obliged to send troops to put down the rebellion.

The hostility of the Indians on the frontier was a constant source of trouble. Three armies were, at different times, sent to subdue them. A treaty of peace was made after the war had continued five years, and our western country was left unmolested by Indian hostility for many years.

In 1795, negotiations were entered into with the Barbary powers, which protected our commerce, and by a treaty with Spain, the same year, its claims upon our western territory were abandoned, and the navigation of the Mississippi was thrown open to us. The year 1795 witnessed the treaties with England, Spain, Algiers, and the Indians.

In 1797, Washington's second term of office closed, and he refused to be re-elected.

ADAMS' ADMINISTRATION—1797–1801.

John Adams was the second president, and Thomas Jefferson vice president. Adams adopted the national cabinet council, left by Washington, as his own.

The recent treaty with England very nearly brought on a war between France and America. The government of France refused to receive the American embassadors. Preparations for war were made, and General Washington was summoned to take command of the armies. Hostilities commenced, and a vessel of each nation was captured, but the army was not summoned to the field. Three envoys were appointed to proceed to France and negotiate for peace, but Napoleon Bonaparte had overthrown the government, and had the control of affairs in his own hands. He promptly received the United States embassadors, and entered into a treaty with their nation. On the return of the ministers the United States army was disbanded.

Washington died at his home, in Mount Vernon, on the 14th of December, 1799, in the sixty-eighth year of his age. The national grief was sincere; the spirit of party was hushed, and the nation mourned at the grave of the man who was "first in war, first in peace, and first in the hearts of his countrymen."

During the summer of 1800, the seat of government was removed from Philadelphia. Thomas Jefferson was inaugurated in the capitol at Washington.

JEFFERSON'S ADMINISTRATION—1801–1809.

Mr. Jefferson was inaugurated March 4th, 1801. The oath of office was administered by Chief Justice Marshall.

In 1803, Louisiana having been ceded to France, our government purchased it of Napoleon Bonaparte for fifteen millions of dollars. Out of it two territories were formed, called the territory of New Orleans and the district of Louisiana.

The treaty with Algiers, in 1795, had provided that the United States should pay a sum of money annually for the protection of her commerce in the Mediterranean Sea, but the insolence of the piratical powers became so unendurable that the government determined to cease paying tribute to them. The Bashaw then declared war, and our little navy, under Commodore Preble, was sent to the Mediterranean to humble the pirates. He succeeded in bringing the Emperor of Morocco to terms, and appeared before Tripoli with his squadron. One of his vessels—the Philadelphia—grounded in the harbor of Tripoli; she was captured and her crew made slaves.

In February, of 1804, after the capture of the Philadelphia, Lieutenant Decatur boarded her, killed the guard, set her on fire, and escaped without losing a man.

Through the aid of the brother of the governor of Tripoli, peace was secured the following year. For ten years longer, however, our commerce suffered in the Mediterranean from the pirates. In 1815, the final treaty of peace was made, the Barbary powers compelled to pay for the injury they had done, and to give up all claim to tribute from the United States.

The whole of Jefferson's second term was one of anxiety and trial. In 1805, and the two following years, the American commerce suffered much from British aggressions. The United States had maintained a strict neutrality in the wars that were convulsing Europe, but the belligerents, in their anxiety to do each other damage, adopted measures destructive to American commerce. The British and French governments issued orders forbidding the ships of neutrals to enter the ports of their respective enemies, and the American commerce dwindled to a domestic coast trade.

MADISON'S ADMINISTRATION–1809–1817.

Jefferson was succeeded, March 4th, 1809, by James Madison. The difficulties with Great Britain first engaged his attention. Hopes of more friendly relations between France and England were entertained, but they proved false.

During the year 1811, the Shawnee Indians, through the agency of the British, threatened hostility against the western settlements. General Harrison was sent against them, and defeated them in the battle of Tippecanoe, in the north-west part of Indiana. This act of hostility, on the part of Great Britain, together with aggressions on the commerce of the United States, led Congress, on the 18th of June, 1812, to declare war with Great Britain.

General Dearborn was appointed commander-in-chief of the American forces. The first event of this war was disastrous to the Americans. General Hull was ordered to invade Canada, but was obliged to retreat to Detroit, which place he surrendered to the British without attempting to defend it. In the following year Commodore Perry repaired this loss. On the 10th of September he defeated and captured the British fleet on Lake Erie. This victory gave them command of the lake, and enabled them to recover Detroit. During the battle at Detroit, the fierce Indian chief, Tecumseh, was killed. Early in this year Toronto was captured by the Americans. On the 3d of July, 1814, Fort Erie was captured. On the 4th, the British were defeated at the battle of Chippewa, and on the 25th the Americans were again victorious at Lundy's Lane. These victories drove the British from the Niagara frontier.

The American navy consisted of twenty ships, that of the English one thousand and sixty. In August, 1812, the Constitution captured the British Guerriere, and on the 29th of

December, of the same year, compelled the frigate Java to surrender. Commodore Decatur, commanding the United States, captured the Macedonian.

The ravages of war were felt along the Atlantic coast during the year 1813. Several towns were plundered and burned; large numbers of negroes were seized and sold in the West Indies, and General Ross entered Washington city and burned the capitol and president's house, and very nearly succeeded in making the president and his cabinet prisoners. The battle of New Orleans, in which the Americans were victorious, closed the war.

Commissioners met in Belgium, and a treaty of peace was made, the terms of which were satisfactory to both parties.

MONROE'S ADMINISTRATION—1817–1825.

On the 4th of March, 1817, James Monroe was inaugurated at Congress Hall. During the first year of Monroe's administration a portion of the Mississippi territory was admitted into the union as a state.

About this time a difficulty arose with the Seminole Indians, outlaws from the Creek nation, and negroes who had fled from their masters. Massacres became so frequent that the inhabitants were obliged to flee from their homes for security. General Jackson marched into Florida and soon defeated and dispersed them.

In 1818, the Indians ceded to the government of the United States all their lands west of the Tennessee river, in the states of Kentucky and Tennessee. Alabama was admitted into the union as a state, and the territory of Arkansas separated from Missouri territory. During the year 1819, the Floridas were ceded to the United States by Spain, and became a territory in 1821, and General Jackson was appointed governor. Maine was admitted in March, 1820, and Missouri in August, 1821.

During the remainder of Monroe's administration, little of general importance occurred, aside from the rapid progress of the country. In the autumn of 1824, four candidates for the presidency, representing the different sections of the union, were nominated. The choice being devolved upon the house of representatives, John Quincy Adams was chosen president.

ADAMS' ADMINISTRATION—1825–1829.

John Q. Adams became President March 4th, 1825. He renewed a proposition which Monroe had made, to purchase the land the Indians held east of the Mississippi. Some of the tribes were unwilling to do this; but in February all the territory in Georgia, except a thousand acres, was ceded to the United States.

Internal improvement and domestic manufactures were the principal subjects that engrossed the president's attention. During Adams' administration more than five millions of dollars had been distributed among the surviving revolutionary soldiers, the national debt had been greatly diminished, and five millions of dollars were in the treasury.

JACKSON'S ADMINISTRATION—1829–1837.

During this administration two Indian wars occurred. In 1832, Black Hawk, a powerful chief of the Sac Indians, together with the Fox and Winnebago tribes, waged war on the Illinois frontier. General Atkinson was sent against them, and, after a few skirmishes, Black Hawk was captured and taken to Washington, and the Indians were driven beyond the Mississippi.

Towards the close of 1835 another Indian war, of a more serious nature, arose. The Seminole Indians, led on by their principal chief, Osceola, commenced a distressing warfare on the frontier settlements of Florida. This war lasted seven years. On one occasion Major Dode was surrounded by Indians, and his command, consisting of one hundred men, were cruelly massacred; four escaped alive, but afterwards died of their wounds. A treaty of peace was not concluded until Osceola died in prison, at Fort Moultrie, in 1842.

Jackson was possessed of strong passions, an iron will and an uncorrupt heart. He entered upon the duties of his office, determined to guide the ship of state according to his conception of the constitution. The people were divided into two distinct classes. By one he was thoroughly loved, and by the other intensely hated. His energetic administration gave general satisfaction, and he was re-elected. He vetoed a bill passed by Congress to renew the charter of the United States bank, in 1836. In 1833, he went so far as to direct the secretary of the treasury to withdraw the government funds, and deposit them in certain state banks. The secretary refused to do this, and was dismissed from office. In October, 1833, the act was accomplished. Intense excitement prevailed throughout the country; numerous failures followed; the president was censured by a resolution of the senate, but, being supported by the house of representatives, he persevered, and finally triumphed. The state banks enlarged their operations, and commercial prosperity revived.

Arkansas was admitted into the Union in June, 1836, and Michigan, in January following.

VAN BUREN'S ADMINISTRATION—1837–1841.

Van Buren was inaugurated March 4th, 1837. The great apparent prosperity during the last year of Jackson's administration, was succeeded by a revulsion in monetary affairs. The mercantile failures in New York alone, amounted to more than a hundred millions of dollars. In New Orleans failures to the amount of twenty-seven millions occurred within two days.

In 1837, a portion of the Canadas rose in rebellion against the British, and determined to secure their independence. Individuals and companies from the United States joined these rebels. This displeased Great Britain, and it became necessary for the president to issue a proclamation preventing further aggressive movements. About this time the dispute concerning the boundary between the state of Maine and the British possessions was renewed, and the peaceful relations between Great Britain and the United States were endangered. General Scott was sent to the frontier, and harmony between the two countries was restored.

HARRISON'S AND TYLER'S ADMINISTRATION—1841–1845.

William Henry Harrison, who succeeded Van Buren, was inaugurated March 4th, 1841. His cabinet counselors were wisely chosen. Daniel Webster was appointed secretary of state. The only official act of importance performed by Harrison, was the issuing of a proclamation calling an extra session of congress to legislate upon important matters connected with the revenue and finances of the country. He died the 4th of April, just one month after his inauguration.

On the 6th of April the oath of office was administered to John Tyler. The extra session of congress, called by president Harrison, occupied itself with the financial interests of the country. A general bankrupt law was enacted, which freed those who had failed from their obligations, and enabled them to recommence business. The sub-treasury act was repealed. The chief object sought to be obtained during this session was the establishment of a national bank. Two bills providing for such an institution passed both houses, but were vetoed by the president, who was severely censured by the party who had elected him. His cabinet all resigned, except Mr. Webster, who retained his seat on account of public interests which would have suffered by his withdrawal at this time.

The second year of Mr. Tyler's administration was signalized by the return of the United States exploring expedition. This expedition had been sent, four years before, by the United States navy to explore the southern ocean. It was commanded by Charles Wilkes. He made many important discoveries; among which was the Antarctic continent, along which he coasted for a distance of seventeen hundred miles.

During this administration, difficulties in Rhode Island originated in attempts to abandon the old charter granted by Charles II., under which the government had been administered one hundred and eighty years, and adopt a state constitution of government. The disputes which arose concerning the manner in which their government should be altered, assumed a serious aspect. The state was on the verge of civil war, and national troops were sent to restore quiet and order. A free constitution was framed, and went into operation in May, 1843.

Florida was admitted into the union in 1845, and Iowa in 1846.

Towards the close of Tyler's administration the country was much agitated concerning the admission of the republic of Texas as a state of the union. By the north it was strongly opposed, because it would increase the political strength of slavery, and lead to a war with Mexico.

POLK'S ADMINISTRATION—1845–1849.

James K. Polk entered the presidential mansion, as its occupant, March 4th, 1845. May 29th, 1844, the news of his nomination was transmitted from Baltimore to Washington by the *magnetic telegraph*, "being the first dispatch ever so communicated."

On the 4th of July, 1845, Texas became one of the United States. Its admission into the union, as had been predicted, caused a war between Mexico and the United States. Although the independence of the state of Texas had been acknowledged by the United States, England and France, a portion of its territory was claimed by Mexico. American vessels were plundered in the Gulf of Mexico, and the property of American merchants confiscated to the amount of six millions of dollars. These aggressions continued, and the president ordered General Zachary Taylor, with his troops, to the Rio Grande. The boundary between Texas and Mexico was still unsettled. The territory between the Rio Grande and the Nueces was claimed by both parties.

While war was gathering in the south-west, difficulties arose between the governments of the United States and Great Britain, concerning the boundary between the two countries on the north-west, which was finally settled by a treaty of peace in June, 1846, the boundary being fixed at forty-nine degrees north latitude.

Hostilities commenced on the part of the Mexicans on the 26th of April, 1846, when a reconnoitering party, under Captain Thornton, was killed or captured by the Mexicans.

Taylor's army, consisting of fifteen hundred men, was called "the Army of Occupation." On the 8th of May, as he was advancing to Fort Brown, he encountered six thousand Mexicans, under General Arista. In the severe conflict which ensued, the Mexicans were defeated, with a loss of nearly five hundred in killed and wounded. The Americans lost fifty-three. The next day a shorter, but bloodier battle occurred between the same armies at Resaca de la Palma. The Mexicans were again defeated, with a loss of one thousand, while the Americans lost but one hundred and ten. Congress declared that war had begun, and Taylor was ordered to invade Mexico, advancing from Matamoras towards Monterey. His first division was commanded by General Worth. They encountered and defeated two armies, raised to oppose them, one at Monterey, on the 24th of September, under General Ampudia, and another at Buena Vista, February 23d, under Santa Anna.

Santa Anna approached Buena Vista with twenty thousand men, and ordered General Taylor, with his five thousand troops, to surrender, which he politely refused to do, and made ready for an encounter he felt would be the most trying in which he had yet engaged. The Mexicans commenced the battle at sunrise on the 23d. This bloody conflict lasted until night, when the Mexicans withdrew, leaving their dead and wounded behind them. The Mexicans lost two thousand, and the Americans two hundred and sixty-seven.

On the 29th of March, 1847, General Scott compelled the city of Vera Cruz and the castle of San Juan d' Ulloa to surrender. He defeated the enemy in the great battle of Cerro Gordo, and entering the valley of Mexico, he won the victories of Contreras, Churubusco, Molino del Rey, Chapultepec, and on the 14th of September, entered the capital in triumph, and planted the American flag on the national palace.

In August of 1846, General Kearney, commander of the army of the west, had taken possession of New Mexico, and started for California to aid Colonel Fremont and Commodores Sloat and Stockton, in the conquest of that country.

The Americans being every where victorious, the Mexican congress sued for peace. On the 2d of February, 1848, a treaty of peace was signed at Guadalupe Hidalgo. Including this peace, Mexico ceded to the United States New Mexico and California, for the sum of fifteen millions of dollars.

Wisconsin was admitted into the union in May, 1848.

General Taylor's brilliant victories in Mexico rendered him so popular that he was nominated for president of the United States. He was elected by a large majority, with Millard Fillmore as vice president.

TAYLOR'S AND FILLMORE'S ADMINISTRATION—1849–1853.

The 4th of March occurring on Sunday, the oath of office was administered on the 5th. The first object which claimed the attention of the new president was California. After the discovery of gold, its population increased so rapidly, that in 1849 the people took measures for its admission into the union. A constitution was adopted which prohibited slavery. Intense excitement existed throughout the whole country. Part of the state was south of the dividing line established by the Missouri compromise, and senators from the south declared the prohibition of slavery there would cause a dissolution of the union.

In the midst of this excitement the senate was deprived of one of its most effective orators, by the death of John C. Calhoun.

He died at Washington, on the 31st of March, 1850. On the 9th of July following, the country, a second time, suffered bereavement, in the loss of its chief magistrate. The disease, which terminated his life, was similar to the cholera. He was succeeded by Vice President Fillmore. The former cabinet resigned, and Daniel Webster was appointed secretary of state.

The first important measure adopted by Mr. Fillmore was the Compromise act. After the requirements of the act had been thoroughly discussed in congress, Mr. Fillmore gladly affixed his signature to the bill, and California was admitted into the union as a free state.

During this administration the territory of Washington was formed out of the northern part of Oregon.

PIERCE'S ADMINISTRATION—1853–1857.

Franklin Pierce, the fourteenth president of the United States, was inaugurated March 4th, 1853.

The most exciting question that arose during Pierce's term related to the organization of a vast region in the interior of the continent into two territories, to be called respectively Nebraska and Kansas. The slavery agitation was revived again in all its strength. The bill for organizing these territorial governments passed both houses, and after receiving the signature of the president, became a law. The question of slavery or freedom was left to its occupants to decide, when they should seek admission into the union as states.

BUCHANAN'S ADMINISTRATION—1857–1861.

March 4th, 1857, Franklin Pierce was succeeded by James Buchanan, the democratic candidate. The two great political parties, into which the people were divided, were the whigs and democrats. But after the Missouri compromise was repealed a new party was formed, styled republican. It was composed chiefly of those who had formerly belonged to the whig party. The republicans were opposed to the extension of slavery into free territory; and yet maintained that Congress had no right to interfere with it in the slave states. The country was violently agitated by the slavery question throughout Buchanan's term. The excitement reached its highest pitch in October, 1859, when John Brown, with fifteen white and five colored men, seized the arsenal at Harper's Ferry, with the view of establishing the freedom of the slaves by force of arms. Federal troops were sent to suppress the insurrection. Thirteen of the invaders were killed. Brown and the remainder were captured, tried, convicted of treason, and were executed December 2d, under the laws of Virginia. The southern leaders attempted to implicate the people of the north in this mad enterprise, and the bitterness of feeling existing between them was greatly increased.

During the close of Buchanan's administration, preparations were made for the rebellion which soon followed. Cobb, Thompson, and Floyd, members of his cabinet, took an active part in the secession of the slave states. Floyd, the secretary of war, sent United States arms and munitions of war to the southern states.

LINCOLN'S ADMINISTRATION.

On the 4th of March, 1861, Chief Justice Taney administered the oath of office to Abraham Lincoln, the president elect of the United States. The leaders of the democratic party in the south claimed that Mr. Lincoln was the representative of the so-called "abolitionists," who now expected, through him, to abolish the institution of slavery from the United States. They, therefore, made his election a pretext for attempting to dissolve the union, and establish a southern confederacy with slavery as its corner stone.

At the time agreed upon, the politicians in the several states met in convention, and, without consulting the people, passed the ordinance of secession from the United States. South Carolina took the lead on the 20th of December, 1860, in a convention at Charleston, and her action was imitated by the following states, in order, namely: Mississippi, Florida, Alabama, Georgia, Louisiana, Texas, Virginia, Arkansas, North Carolina and Tennessee. On the 4th of February a convention assembled at Montgomery, Alabama, and established a "southern confederacy," with the title of *Confederate States of America.* Jefferson Davis, of Mississippi, was chosen president, and Alexander H. Stephens, of Georgia, vice president of the "confederacy." The conspirators immediately raised an army to sustain their revolt, and seized all forts, arsenals, ships, arms, and other government property which they could lay hold of.

It had been the intention of the conspirators from the first to take possession of Forts Sumter and Moultrie, in Charleston harbor, especially Sumter, as it was the stronger. (See view No. 3133.) Major Robert Anderson, who was stationed at that point, suspected their design, and removed his garrison from Fort Moultrie to Sumter. At this, the rebels were enraged, and immediately determined to bombard the fort. They cut off all communication between the garrison and its friends, and demanded the surrender of the fort to the authorities of the state. On the refusal of Anderson to surrender, General P. G. T. Beauregard, who had raised a large army, prepared to seize the fort. On the 12th of April, 1861, the fort was assaulted, and its interior fired. Anderson held out as long as he was able, but his supplies having become exhausted, "he evacuated the fort on the 14th, carrying with him the garrison flag."

It was while the preparations for the attack upon Fort Sumter were going on that president Lincoln was inaugurated. He declared his intention to execute the laws of the country and protect the property of its citizens. As soon as tidings of the assault upon Sumter reached Washington, the president issued a call for seventy-five thousand men, to serve for three months in quelling the rebellion, and in less than twenty days nearly two hundred thousand had volunteered, and about forty millions of dollars had been subscribed by the loyal people of the north for the purpose of carrying on the war. Then a contest was begun, which, "in numbers engaged, territorial extent of operations, and destructive engines used," is unparalleled in the history of the world.

CHAPTER VIII.

THE CIVIL WAR.

1861.

The condition of the national army at the commencement of the war was extremely unfavorable. It consisted of only sixteen thousand men, the greater part of whom were on the western border, holding the Indians in check, and at least one-half of the entire land force of the United States was surrendered by General Twiggs to the "authorities of Texas," one of the revolted states. The naval force consisted of but ninety vessels, bearing twenty-four hundred guns and but seven thousand men. These, however, at the beginning of the war were all in foreign waters, with the exception of one steamship bearing twenty-five guns, and a small relief ship of two guns. John B. Floyd, the former secretary of war, had caused most of the arms to be taken from the forts in the northern states to those in the slave states. From this, it will be seen, that almost every instrument which might have been employed for the protection of the government, had been put away from its control by the conspirators.

From the beginning, the conspirators had determined to gain possession of the capital, and it was now in great danger of being seized. As a movement preparatory to the seizure of Washington, the navy yard at Gosport, and the arsenal and armory at Harper's Ferry were attacked by the insurgents. Not being able to hold them, the commander of the national forces set fire to them, and evacuated Harper's Ferry on the 18th, and Gosport on the 21st of April. On the 19th of the same month, the sixth Massachusetts regiment passed through Baltimore on its way to Washington, and was attacked by a mob of ten thousand men. Two of its number were killed, and one mortally wounded. This was the first blood shed in the great conflict. A monument to the memory of the two who fell as the first victims of the rebellion, was erected in Lowell, Massachusetts. (See view No. 6617.)

On account of the entensive preparations which the conspirators had made, and the increasing strength of the conspiracy, the president issued a call for over sixty-four thousand additional troops for the army and eighteen thousand for the navy "to serve during the war."

Baltimore was seized by a detachment from the United States forces under General Benjamin F. Butler, and troops after that passed through the city without molestation. The city of Washington was occupied by a large body of national troops under General Winfield Scott, and no more trouble was anticipated from the rebels in that quarter. Up to the time that congress assembled, July 4th, there had been, besides the three months troops, two hundred and thirty thousand men enlisted, and on the 10th congress appropriated five hundred millions of dollars for defraying the expenses of the war, and authorized the president to call for five hundred thousand more men. On the 20th of the same month, the seat of the confederate government was removed from Montgomery to Richmond, Virginia.

On the 24th of May occurred the first entrance by loyal troops into a rebellious state. Alexandria and Arlington Heights, in Virginia, were seized by United States forces. The first commander who entered Alexandria was Colonel E. E. Ellsworth, at the head of his gallant New York Fire Zouaves. He was shot on the same day by the proprietor of the "Marshall House," in that city. (See views No. 2294 and No. 2295.)

The seat of war was soon extended as far west as Missouri, but that state was rescued from the hands of the conspirators by the energetic Captain Nathaniel Lyon, aided by his troops and the loyal citizens. The first battle after the declaration of war by the United States government, was fought on the 3d of June at Philippi, Barbour county, Virginia. A body of national forces, commanded by Colonel B. F. Kelley, assaulted and defeated a detachment of seventeen hundred confederate soldiers. General Butler, who was in command at Fortress Monroe, learned that batteries had been planted on the creek at Big Bethel by Colonel Magruder, a confederate officer, and he, on the night of the 10th, sent Brigadier General Pierce, with two columns from Fortress Monroe and Newport News, to seize them. The two detachments, when they met, fired upon each other, each supposing the other to be a hostile force. In this disaster, the first officer of the regular army who fell a victim to the rebellion, was killed. This was Lieutenant John T. Greble, an artillery officer.

The next day Colonel Lewis Wallace, with his Indiana Zouaves, scattered a force of five hundred rebel troops at Romney, Hampshire county, Virginia, and drove the confederate force, which was stationed at Harper's Ferry, to Winchester. At about this time a considerable force, commanded by General George B. McClellan, entered West Virginia from the Ohio. A detachment from this army, under Colonel W. S. Rosecrans, defeated a body of three thousand confederate troops at Rich Mountain, on the 11th of July.

At the time these military operations were being carried on, the loyal people of Western Virginia were excited over the ordinance of secession which had lately been passed at Richmond. They refused their consent to that action, and representatives from thirty-nine counties assembled in convention at Wheeling, on the 11th of June. On the 17th they declared their independence of the government of the state of Virginia, and on the 20th the commonwealth of West Virginia was established, with Frank H. Pierpont as Governor.

In July, a movement was set on foot for the capture of Richmond, the confederate capital, and on the 18th of this month, General Irwin McDowell, with about fifty thousand men, comprising the army around Washington, advanced from Fairfax Court-house, Virginia, for the purpose of attacking the confederates at Manassas Junction. It had been the design, if successful at Manassas, to advance against Richmond, and take possession of that city. The same day on which they left Fairfax Court-house, they came upon a body of confederate troops at Blackburn's Ford, near Centreville, where a sharp skirmish occurred.

No advantage was gained by either side, and at Bull Run, on the 21st, the contest was renewed. (See views No. 2328 and 2329.) At this time a very severe battle was fought. The rebel forces were under the command of Beauregard and other able generals. At first the federal forces were triumphant; but just as the confederates were about to retreat, General Joseph E. Johnston arrived with reinforcements. The confederates were then rallied, and the federal forces were completely routed, and fled toward Washington. The national loss at this battle was over three thousand men. On the 22d, General McClellan was invested with the command of the forces in the vicinity of Washington, called "The Army of the Potomac;" and on the 31st, General Scott having resigned his position on account of his failing health, General McClellan received the appointment of general-in-chief of the armies of the union.

During the time that these military movements were in progress in Virginia, the war was progressing in the west. A severe contest occurred near Carthage, in Missouri, on the 5th of July. The union forces were led by Colonel Franz Sigel, and the rebels by the governor of Missouri, C. F. Jackson. Although the forces under Jackson far outnumbered those of Sigel, the latter conducted his retreat so ably that not one union soldier fell into the hands of the enemy; and, as the confederate loss was almost four times that of the national, it was, substantially, a union victory. On the 2d of August, an indecisive fight took place at Day Spring, between the nationals, under General Lyon, and the confederates, under General Ben McCulloch, which was renewed on the 10th at Wilson's Creek, near Springfield. McCulloch's force in this battle was about twenty-two thousand strong, while that of Lyon, with the exception of a small column under Sigel, consisted of only five thousand. General Lyon was killed at nine o'clock in the morning. The victory, which was very indecisive, was claimed by the rebels, although their loss was more than double that of the federals.

During the summer of 1861 a large navy had been created, and in the latter part of August an expedition was fitted out at Fortress Monroe against Forts Hatteras and Clark, at the entrance of Pamlico Sound. This expedition, the military force of which was under General Butler, and the naval under Commodore Stringham, proved remarkably successful. A great many prisoners were taken, besides several vessels, heavy cannon, and one thousand stand of small arms.

When the conspirators received tidings of the action of the people of West Virginia, they resolved to compel them to submit to secession. Accordingly, three bodies of troops were sent against them, commanded respectively by Colonel Robert E. Lee, ex-Governor Henry A. Wise, and John B. Floyd, the former secretary of war. The latter was met at Carnifex Ferry, in West Virginia, by a federal force under General Rosecrans, and, in a severe engagement of three days' duration, the rebels were defeated. At about this time, also, the union troops at Lexington, in Missouri, under Colonel James A. Mulligan, were attacked by a confederate force under General Sterling Price. The rebels gained possession of the town and held it until the 16th of October, when it was recaptured by a body of federal cavalry led by Major Frank J. White.

On the 31st of October, a body of national troops, under General Charles P. Stone, was defeated at Ball's Bluff, in Virginia, by a vastly superior confederate force under General Evans, and on the 7th of November, one week later, another victory was gained by the rebels at Belmont, Missouri. Their forces, under the command of General Cheatham, were attacked by General Ulysses S. Grant, at the head of a body of union troops, and they were at first compelled to abandon their position, but, having received re-enforcements from Columbus, Kentucky, they rallied and drove the federal troops to their boats. On the same day, however, Forts Beauregard and Walker, guarding the Port Royal entrance, on the coast of South Carolina, were captured by a union naval force under Rear-Admiral Samuel F. Dupont. "This was a very important victory, for it led to the permanent occupation, by government troops, of the Sea Islands along the South Carolina coasts, between Charleston and Savannah, so famous for the production of fine cotton."

This was the last important movement during this year, but the hostile feeling which existed at the time of the bombardment of Fort Sumter was now as strong as ever, and both armies made extensive preparations for a vigorous campaign the coming season.

1862.

Hostilities were commenced this year by another joint military and naval expedition from Fortress Monroe, under the command of General Ambrose E. Burnside and Commodore L. M. Goldsborough. The expedition set out from Hampton Roads on the 11th of January, and proceeded southward as far as Hatteras Inlet, whence it turned and went back to Roanoke Island, in Albemarle Sound, which it took, after a sharp contest, on the 8th of February, together with over three thousand stand of arms, and a large number of prisoners.

While this expedition was in progress, on the 19th of January a severe battle was fought at Mill Spring, in the eastern part of Kentucky, between union forces, commanded by General George H. Thomas and General Schoepf, and confederates under Generals George B. Crittenden and F. R. Zollicoffer. In this battle the federal troops gained a decisive victory. The rebel General Zollicoffer was shot by Colonel S. S. Fry, of the 4th Kentucky regiment.

Soon after this battle several other important victories were successively won by the national forces. The first of these was the capture of Fort Henry, on the Tennessee river, on the 6th of February, by land troops, under General Grant, and a naval force commanded by Commodore Andrew H. Foote. Grant, then, with about fifteen thousand of his troops advanced to Fort Donelson, on the Cumberland river, which was held by a large garrison under the command of Generals John B. Floyd, Simon B. Buckner, and Gideon J. Pillow. Being here joined by other troops, which increased his force to about forty thousand strong, Grant laid siege to the fort. After sustaining the siege for three days, General Buckner, on the 16th of February, surrendered the fort, together with over thirteen thousand men and valuable spoils. Generals Floyd and Pillow deserted Buckner when they saw that the fort must be surrendered; but the latter, more honorable than they, remained, and suffered himself to be made a prisoner with his soldiers.

On the 5th of March, a battle was commenced at Pea Ridge, in western Arkansas, between federal troops under Generals Samuel R. Curtis, Franz Sigel, and Jeff. C. Davis, and confederates under Generals Earl Van Dorn, Sterling Price, and Ben McCulloch, in which, after a three days' contest, the union forces were victorious. The noted Texan, General Ben McCulloch, was killed in this battle. On the day this battle closed, "a new kind of vessel, called a 'ram,' and named *Virginia* (late *Merrimac*), produced great havoc and consternation in Hampton Roads." This vessel was plated with iron, and had been constructed by the confederates at Norfolk. On the same night, however, a "floating battery," lately invented by Captain J. Ericsson, a native of Sweden, made its appearance in Hampton Roads. Like the *Merrimac*, it was constructed chiefly of iron. It was named the *Monitor*, and was commanded by Lieutenant John H. Worden. The next day it went out against the *Merrimac*, and, after a severe engagement, the "Rebel Apollyon" was so badly disabled that it retreated to Norfolk, leaving the little *Monitor* in command of Hampton Roads.

At the beginning of this year, there were four armies in the field, viz: The *Army of the Potomac*, the army at Fortress Monroe, the army of Western Virginia, and the army in Kentucky. An order had been issued by President Lincoln on the 27th of January, for all the armies to move upon the enemy on the 22d of February. We have seen that this order had been obeyed by the armies at Fortress Monroe, and in Kentucky. The *Army of the Potomac*, also, under General McClellan, advanced to Manassas, and the confederate force stationed there, being less than one-fourth the number of the federal force, retreated to Richmond; and, as was afterward known, the national army might have advanced and taken possession of Richmond without being very strongly resisted; but General McClellan had formed a plan of advance different from that originally fixed upon, and on this account the army was delayed until the 3d of April. On that day, General McClellan, at the head of the *Army of the Potomac*, left Fortress Monroe on an expedition against Richmond. One month later, May 4th, Yorktown, which was occupied by a rebel force under General Magruder, and which McClellan was preparing to besiege, was evacuated by the garrison stationed there, who fled toward Richmond. The federal troops immediately entered the town, and on the 5th a force was sent in pursuit of the fugitives. They were overtaken on the same day at Williamsburg, and in a severe engagement which ensued, the union troops were victorious. On the 9th, General John E. Wool, who was then in command at Fortress Monroe, advanced with a body of troops against Norfolk. The rebels at that place made no attempt to defend it, but fled to Richmond, after having utterly destroyed the famous ram *Merrimac*, leaving behind them about two hundred cannon. On the 25th, a force of about four thousand men, under General Nathaniel P. Banks, was defeated at Winchester, in the Shenandoah valley, by a confederate force of fifteen thousand, but made good their retreat. A great part of the Potomac army crossed the Chickahominy river on the 22d, and on the 29th captured Hanover Court-house from the rebels. A severe engagement took place at Fair Oaks on the 31st of May and 1st of June, between the rebels under General Joseph E. Johnston, and a portion of the army of the Potomac, under General Silas Casey. The rebel force was more than double that of the nationals, but no advantage was gained by either side, while each sustained a fearful loss. The army of the Potomac changed its position in about three weeks from this time, which led to a succession of battles during the last week of June, the most important of which were the battles of Mechanicsville, June 25th; Gaines' Mill, June 27; Peach Orchard Station, and Savage's Station, June 29; Glendale, or White Oak Swamp, June 30, and Malvern Hill, July 1.

While these movements were in progress in Virginia, the other branches of the army were not idle. On the 14th of March, the expedition from Fortress Monroe, known as "Burnside's expedition," captured Newbern, in North Carolina, and Grant was following up his victories at Forts Henry and Donelson, by advancing further into the confederate territory, so that at the beginning of April, he had ascended the Tennessee river almost to the southern boundary of the state. On the 6th of the month, his army was attacked before daylight by a strong rebel force under General A. Sydney Johnston. This engagement took place at Shiloh, near Pittsburgh Landing. The union troops were scattered, and General Benjamin M. Prentiss, together with twenty-five hundred men, was taken prisoner. During the night, however, strong re-enforcements arrived under General Don Carlos Buell, and, on the morning of the 7th, General Grant renewed the contest, and, after a very severely fought battle, gained a complete victory. On the same day, Island No. 10, a strongly fortified island in the Mississippi river, together with the surrounding batteries on the shore, was surrendered to Commodore Foote, after a twenty-three days' bombardment.

Four days after this, the national army gained control over the entrance to Savannah river, by the surrender of Fort Pulaski, at its mouth, to General David Hunter, and on the same day Huntsville, in Alabama, was captured by a federal force under General Ormsby M. Mitchel. On the 18th, General C. C. Augur captured Fredericksburg, in Virginia, and on the 28th, New Orleans, the most important and populous city of the confederacy, next to Baltimore, was taken by a naval force under Commodores David G. Farragut and David D. Porter, and a military force under General Butler.

Eight days after the capture of New Orleans, a naval force, commanded by Colonel Charles Ellet, after a hard fought battle, overpowered the confederates at Memphis, Tennessee, and the city was surrendered to the nationals. Colonel Ellet was mortally wounded, but Commodore Davis immediately assumed command, and took possession of the city.

The troops commanded by General John C. Fremont, Nathaniel P. Banks, and Irwin McDowell, were united into one force, called the *Army of Virginia*, on the 25th of June, and General John Pope was invested with the command. This army was comparatively idle during the greater part of the month of July, but in the latter part of this month the rebels advanced from Richmond with the intention of making an attempt to seize Washington. General Pope, with great difficulty, held them in check until the 22d of August, when McClellan came to his assistance. General McClellan was placed in command of all the forces around Washington on the 1st of September.

On the 14th, a severe engagement occurred at South Mountain, in Maryland, in which each army was commanded by its General-in-Chief, George B. McClellan, on the national side, and Robert E. Lee on the side of the confederates. The union forces won the day, but the heroic General Jesse L. Reno was among the slain. On the following day, Harper's Ferry, in Virginia, together with over eleven thousand men, two hundred wagons, seventy cannon, and thirteen thousand small arms, was surrendered to the confederates, under General Thomas J. ("Stonewall") Jackson. (See views of Harper's Ferry.)

Two days after the surrender of Harper's Ferry, Generals McClellan and Lee, each with a force of about one hundred thousand men, met at Antietam Creek, in Maryland, and, in a severe engagement, lasting from daylight till dark, the union forces were victorious. The rebels lost about twenty thousand men. The union General J. K. F. Mansfield was killed, and Generals I. P. Rodman and Israel B. Richardson were mortally wounded. General Lee retreated toward Richmond, but McClellan made no attempt to pursue him, and the army of the Potomac remained in Maryland until the 27th of October, when General Burnside, with a portion of it, entered Virginia. The rest of the army followed on the 31st, led by McClellan, who was, on the 5th of November, superseded by General Burnside.

In August, Middle Kentucky was ravaged by bands of guerrillas, who were fighting for the confederate cause. The most famous leader of these depredators was John Morgan, who, at the head of a large band, committed many ravages. At about the same time, the state of Kentucky was invaded by rebel troops led by General E. Kirby Smith, who, on the 29th of August, defeated a federal force of infantry and cavalry, commanded by Generals Manson and Cruft, near Richmond, in Kentucky, and then advanced toward Cincinnati. General Wallace, who was in command of northern Kentucky, was so well prepared to receive the rebels when they approached, that they beat a hasty retreat. A confederate force, under General Braxton Bragg, also invaded Kentucky with the intention of seizing the city of Louisville. That place, however, was well defended by General Buell, and the attempt to capture it was given up. On the 8th of October, Bragg was met and defeated near Perryville, in Kentucky, by a federal force under the command of Generals A. D. McCook, Lovell H. Rousseau, and Philip H. Sheridan, and he soon after left the state.

Nothing of importance was done by the army of the Tennessee, after the battle of Shiloh, except the expulsion of the rebels from Corinth on the 26th of May, by a body of troops under General Henry W. Halleck, until October. On the 3d and 4th of this month, the confederate Generals Van Dorn and Price carried on an engagement with the force at Corinth. They compelled the federal force to flee into the town the first day, but, on the second day, after a severely contested battle, they were badly worsted, and fled, leaving behind them fourteen flags, and several stands of arms.

After Burnside had been placed in command of the army of the Potomac, he advanced toward Fredericksburg, on the Rappahannock. He halted opposite the city on the 17th of November, where the army lay encamped for almost a month. On the 13th of December, a portion of the army, led by Generals Joseph Hooker, Edwin V. Sumner, and William B. Franklin, attacked the rebel force at Fredericksburg, but they were defeated with the loss of about eight thousand men. The army remained inactive from that time until near the end of April, 1863.

During the year 1862, Pensacola, in Florida, had been captured by national forces, and several victories had been won by the national arms in Texas and on the lower Mississippi. The last important engagements of the year were an unsuccessful attempt, by union troops, under General William T. Sherman, to gain possession of Vicksburg, in Mississippi, on the 27th of December, and a severely fought battle at Murfreesboro, in Tennessee, between federal troops under General William S. Rosecrans, and confederates, commanded by General Bragg. This battle, which continued from the 29th of December, 1862, until the 4th of January, 1863, was won by the union troops, but with the loss of almost twelve thousand men.

While these contests on land and water were going on, the government at Washington "was devising and executing measures for the suppression of the great insurrection. Congress made ample provisions for money and men ; the latter by draft, if not otherwise obtained. Believing that a heavy blow at slavery had become a military necessity, it authorized the president to proclaim the emancipation of the slaves. He did not do so immediately ; but, by proclamation, September 22d, 1862, he assured the confederates that, unless they should lay down their arms within a hundred days, he should issue an edict which would proclaim the freedom of all bondmen in territory wherein rebellion existed."

1863.

As the confederates did not heed the warning of President Lincoln, September 22d, 1862, he, on the 1st of January, 1863, issued the famous Emancipation Proclamation, which proclaimed liberty to all slaves in those states which were in rebellion against the government.

The last session of the thirty-seventh congress closed on the 4th of March. "It had placed the entire resources of the country in the hands of the president, and adopted measures for the increase and efficiency of the army." All the national forces were ordered to their posts, and, in the early part of May, the president ordered a draft of three hundred thousand men. This measure met with considerable opposition; and, in New York city, on the day when the draft was commenced, a fearful riot broke out among the laboring classes and rebel sympathizers, which was not quelled until the end of three days. "The draft was enforced in twelve states," and "the government, sustained by every right-minded citizen, went steadily on in its duty." After the emancipation proclamation had been issued, thousands of slaves came within the lines of the union army, and, at the close of the year, sixty thousand colored troops were in the service of the government.

On the 25th of January, General Burnside was relieved of the command of the army of the Potomac, and General Hooker appointed in his place. Near the close of April, General Hooker crossed the Rappahannock, and, on the 2d, 3d and 4th of May, he encountered a large rebel force, under General Lee, at Chancellorsville. This was a severe contest, in which neither party gained any advantage. Both sides sustained a heavy loss, and among the rebel slain was the famous "Stonewall" Jackson.

On the 28th of June, Hooker was superseded by General George G. Meade. General Lee had advanced from Virginia, through Maryland, into Pennsylvania, during the month of June, and his presence in the latter state produced great terror among the inhabitants. At length, on the 1st of July, he was met at Gettysburg, in Adams county, by General Meade. (See views Nos. 2384, '5, '6 and '7, and 2394, '5 and '6.) The first engagement, on the morning of the 1st, was commanded, on the federal side, by General John F. Reynolds, and on the side of the confederates, by General D. H. Hill. General Reynolds was slain (see view No. 2392). The battle raged, with interruptions, until the evening of the 3d, when the national forces gained a complete victory. They captured three cannon, forty-one banners, over twenty-eight thousand small arms, and nearly fourteen thousand prisoners.

The confederates, followed by the army of the Potomac, retreated into Virginia beyond the Rappahannock. Both armies lay quiet until the 5th of October, when Lee again moved northward, and destroyed the railroad between the Rapidan river and Manassas Junction. Several skirmishes took place between that time and the early part of November, when Meade drove the rebel force back across the Rappahannock, and there encamped. Nothing more of importance was done by these armies until the next year.

During the year 1863, the union troops in North Carolina, under General J. G. Foster, after a series of engagements, gained possession of all of eastern North Carolina north of the Neuse river. The Department of the Gulf, also, under General Banks, with headquarters at New Orleans, was active during this year. In a vigorous raid between New Orleans and Alexandria, on the Red river, Banks captured twenty-two cannon and two thousand prisoners, besides considerable public property and several steamboats. In company with Admiral Farragut, he captured Port Hudson, on the Mississippi, on the 8th of July. General Banks reports his captures during this campaign to be over ten thousand men "seventy-three guns, six thousand small arms, beside three gunboats, eight other steamboats, and cotton, cattle, &c., to an immense value." He also sent out a successful expedition to Texas.

Admiral Dupont, on the 7th of April, attempted the capture of Fort Sumter, but was unsuccessful, because he was not aided by any land forces. General Quincy A. Gillmore was sent to his assistance, and, "on the 23d of August, after a terrible bombardment for seven days, Fort Sumter was reduced, it was reported, to a 'shapeless and harmless mass of ruins.'" (See views of Fort Sumter.)

After Sherman's unsuccessful attack on Vicksburg, in December, 1862, he went with General John A. McClernand, who, with the assistance of Admiral Porter, in January, 1863, took possession of Arkansas Post, on the Arkansas river, together with "five thousand prisoners, seventeen guns, three thousand small arms, besides large quantities of munitions and commissary stores."

General Grant, who was now at the head of the Army of the Mississippi, began to lay plans for the capture of Vicksburg, a post considered impregnable by the confederates. After several unsuccessful attempts to pass around the city, he, on the 14th of April, crossed the Mississippi and gained two battles near

Port Gibson, south of Vicksburg, whence he advanced to the rear of the city. He laid siege to the city on the 19th of May. At first he had some trouble in retaining his position, for General Joseph E. Johnston was in his rear with a large force. He persevered, however, in the assault upon Vicksburg, and, on the 4th of July, General John C. Pemberton, the officer in command, surrendered the city to General Grant, and a force was sent, under General Sherman, to hold Johnston in check.

General Grant gives, as the result of this campaign, "the defeat of the enemy in five battles outside of Vicksburg; the occupation of Jackson, the capital of the state of Mississippi, and the capture of Vicksburg and its garrisons and munitions of war; a loss to the enemy of thirty-seven thousand prisoners, among whom were fifteen general officers; at least ten thousand killed and wounded, and among the killed Generals Tracy, Tilghman and Green, and hundreds, perhaps thousands of stragglers, who can never be collected and reorganized. Arms and munitions of war for an army of sixty thousand men have fallen into our hands; besides a large amount of other public property, consisting of railroads, locomotives, cars, steamboats, cotton, &c.; and much was destroyed to prevent our capturing it." This was the most brilliant and memorable campaign of the war, and "the heaviest single blow ever given to the muscular resources of the rebellion."

This victory, coming, as it did, on the day after that of Meade, at Gettysburg, caused great rejoicing throughout the country.

After his victory at Murfreesboro, Tennessee (January 4), General Rosecrans remained quiet until the 25th of June. At that time, however, he again advanced against Bragg, compelling him to retire as far as Chattanooga, on the Tennessee river, in the southern part of the state. Rosecrans moved on, took possession of Chattanooga, and, on the 19th of September, encountered the forces under Bragg, and re-enforcements from Lee, under General James Longstreet, in the Chickamauga valley. Rosecrans was compelled to retire to Chattanooga, where he remained until Grant arrived with additional forces. That commander, on the 19th of October, left General J. B. McPherson in command at Vicksburg, and went himself to take command of the army of the Cumberland, at Chattanooga. He restored communication with that place, and, being re-enforced by Sherman in November, he, on the 23d, commenced the memorable battle of Lookout Mountain and Chattanooga. (See views of Lookout Mountain). A force under General Hooker gained possession of Lookout Mountain, and, on the 25th, the battle terminated in favor of the national army. Bragg fled into Georgia, and Longstreet went to Knoxville, in East Tennessee. Here, on the 29th, he attacked a union force under General Burnside, but, Sherman arriving with re-enforcements from Grant's army, Longstreet fled back to the army under General Lee, in Virginia.

During this year, the states of Missouri and Arkansas passed into the hands of the national force in that department, and, on the 26th of July, General John Morgan, the noted guerrilla, surrendered a large force under his command, to General Shackleford, in Morgan county, Ohio. The navy had also been at work. The rebel ram *Atlanta* was captured by the *Weehawken*, of Dupont's fleet, under Captain John Rodgers, off the coast of Georgia, on the 17th of June. Farragut and Porter had also won several victories on the Mississippi river and its tributaries. At the close of this year, therefore, the people of the loyal north had great cause for rejoicing, and the prospects for the speedy success of the armies of the republic were greater than ever before.

1864.

On the 1st of February, of this year, President Lincoln again ordered a draft for three hundred thousand men; and, on the 15th of March, he issued a call for two hundred thousand more volunteers for the army and navy. Preparations were made at the beginning of the year for another attempt to gain possession of Richmond.

On the 16th of January, fifteen miles of the track of the Virginia and Tennessee railroad, west of Lynchburg, were destroyed by a band of Union cavalry from the army of the Potomac, under General W. W. Averill.

On the 3d of February, General Sherman left Vicksburg on an invasion eastward. He was gone twenty-four days, and his expedition was exceedingly successful. An invading force, under General Truman Seymour, left Port Royal, in South Carolina, on the 5th, and succeeded in making its way to Olustee, where, on the 20th, it was defeated by a large confederate force, and was compelled to fall back to Jacksonville. On the 13th of March, General A. J. Smith, from the army at Vicksburg, together with the fleet of Admiral Porter, captured Fort De Russey, on the Red river. Then, in conjunction with General Banks, they gained two victories—one at Cane river, on the 26th of March, and one at Pleasant Hill on the 9th of April.

At this time, General Steele, in command at Arkansas, in endeavoring to join the Red river expedition, was attacked, and lost two hundred wagons and two thousand men. On the 24th of March, the rebel cavalry leader, General N. B. Forrest, captured Union City, in Tennessee, and on the 25th he plundered Paducah, in Kentucky. On the 12th of April he took possession of Fort Pillow, in western Tennessee, on the Mississippi river, where he instituted a general massacre upon colored troops stationed there.

The armies of the east and west made preparations for a great campaign at the beginning of the year. The army of the Potomac, under General Meade, and the three armies of the west, united under General Sherman, were all eager to meet the foe. On account of his valuable services to the government, General Grant, on the 9th of March, received a commission as Lieutenant-General, and was appointed General-in-Chief of the national forces. He took command of the army of the Potomac, with his headquarters in the field, and, on the 3d of May, sent an order to General Sherman to advance against the rebels in Georgia, while he, with the Potomac army, should move upon Richmond. He crossed the Rapidan and encountered the army of Lee in the "Wilderness," near Chancellorsville, on the 5th of

May. The number of men engaged in this battle is estimated at two hundred and fifty thousand men. After a severe contest of three days, the confederate army retreated toward Richmond. Grant followed Lee so closely that, in the early part of June, the latter was close upon the outskirts of that city. A force from Fortress Monroe, under General Butler, fortified itself on the Appomattox river, and kept back Beauregard, who was coming up from the Carolinas to the assistance of Lee. Grant soon gained a position near Petersburg, and Lee went south of the Appomattox for the purpose of defending Petersburg. Grant commenced a siege immediately, and destroyed the railway connections between Lee's position and Richmond at the close of July, so that the safety of both the army and city were imperiled. He gained several victories over Lee's army during the months of July and August. On the 18th of August, he seized the Weldon railway, the principal line of communication between Lee and the southern part of the confederacy. Several attempts were made by the rebels to recapture it, but in vain. Grant, after having demolished it for a distance of twelve miles, intrenched himself near by, and kept the army of Lee in continual terror. (See views of Atlanta, Georgia.)

After receiving Grant's order to march, Sherman, with his vast army, left Chattanooga, and moved toward Atlanta, in Georgia. He fought three heavy battles near there with the confederate force, under General John B. Hood (who had superseded Johnson), and utterly defeated them each time. In the second battle, July 22d, General McPherson was killed. Sherman sent out detachments of cavalry to cut off the railway communications with the city, and closely besieged it until the 2d of September, when Hood abandoned the place, and Sherman entered in triumph.

While these operations were in progress in the United States, a powerful rebel privateer, called the *Alabama*, under the command of Captain Raphael Semmes, was producing great havoc among American merchantmen in foreign waters. She carefully avoided all vessels sent against her by the government, until finally, on the 15th of June, the French government ordered her to leave their waters, and, in doing so, she encountered a national vessel named the *Kearsarge*, commanded by Captain John Winslow. The *Alabama* was sunk, but her commander escaped in an English vessel.

In the early part of July, an invading force, under General Jubal A. Early, left Lee's army for the purpose of seizing supplies. General Lewis Wallace, with a force numbering about one-third that of Early, met the latter at the Monocacy river. He kept the confederates from Baltimore and Washington, but was compelled by superior numbers to fall back, and Early carried off a large amount of booty. On the 30th of the same month, another force ascended through Maryland, into Pennsylvania, as far as the village of Chambersburg, which they set on fire. (See views Nos. 2018, 2019, and 2020.) They immediately returned, after gathering supplies in the Shenandoah valley, closely pursued by a force from Grant's army, under General Sheridan.

On the 5th of August, a fleet under Admiral Farragut, and a co-operating land force under General Gordon Granger, entered Mobile. On the 8th, Fort Gaines, and on the 23d, Fort Morgan were surrendered to Farragut. Both these forts were strong posts at the entrance of Mobile Bay, and were well garrisoned.

In view of this and other victories, the president, on the 3d of September, issued a proclamation recommending the next Sunday, September 11th, as a day of thanksgiving and prayer.

In the beginning of November, General Sherman sent General George H. Thomas, with a considerable force, to Tennessee, against Hood, and, on the 14th, he himself left Atlanta on a march to the sea. He captured Milledgeville, the capital of the state of Georgia, on the 29th, and continued his advance toward Savannah, taking possession of that city on the 21st of December. General Hood coming up toward Nashville, he was met at Franklin by a portion of Thomas' army, under General Schofield, on the 30th of November. Schofield was driven back to Nashville, but, on the 15th of December, General Thomas advanced against Hood, and compelled him to flee into Alabama, after suffering great losses.

On the 8th of November, Abraham Lincoln was re-elected president of the United States, and Andrew Johnson, of Tennessee, vice president, by the republican party. The democratic candidate was General George B. McClellan.

1865.

After the capture of Savannah by General Sherman, he was joined by the army in South Carolina, under General Foster. He moved northward to Columbia, the capital of South Carolina, which he captured on the 17th of February. Thence he advanced to Goldsboro, in North Carolina, where, on the 22d of March, he was joined by General Schofield, from Newbern, and General Terry, who had captured Wilmington, on the Cape Fear river, on the 15th of January, assisted by a naval force under Admiral Porter. This united force held Johnston in check at Raleigh, the capital of the state.

General Sheridan held command of the Shenandoah valley, and, in the early part of March, he attacked General Early at Charlottesville, and gained a great victory. He then destroyed the railway communication between Richmond and Lynchburg, and, at about the middle of March, he, with General Edward O. C. Ord, and the army of the James, joined General Grant before Richmond. (See views of Richmond, Virginia.)

Lee now endeavored to escape from Richmond, and go to join Johnston, in North Carolina, but, in this he was foiled by Grant, who would not allow him to leave Richmond. After several severely fought battles, in which Lee suffered a loss of over twenty thousand men, he was, at length, obliged to sign terms of capitulation. On the 9th of April, the main army of the confederates was surrendered by their general-in-chief to General Grant, and they were paroled as prisoners of war. This was "the death blow to the rebellion." The "president," Jefferson Davis, and the other ring-leaders of the conspiracy fled, and, on the 26th, General Johnston surrendered to General Sherman "on the terms accorded to Lee." The inferior forces were speedily dispersed, and the war was substantially ended in May.

CHAPTER IX.

THE CLOSE OF THE WAR.

JOHNSON'S ADMINISTRATION.

President Lincoln went down to the front on the 24th of March, 1865, and, at the time of the fall of Richmond, he was at Grant's headquarters in City Point, Virginia. The next day, April 4th, he went to Richmond, and held a levee in the deserted mansion of the late confederate "president."

On the 14th of April, four years after the evacuation of Fort Sumter, General Anderson, together with a great many officers, soldiers and civilians, celebrated this anniversary by raising over the ruins the old flag which Anderson carried away with him at the time of the evacuation. (See views Nos. 3137 to 3146, inclusive.)

At this time the whole land was filled with rejoicing concerning the surrender of Lee, and the probable speedy surrender of Johnston, but, on the morning of the 15th of April, the joy was turned into sorrow by the announcement that, on the previous evening, the president had been stricken down by the hand of an assassin. President Lincoln and General Grant had been invited to visit Ford's theatre on that evening, and it had been publicly announced that they would be present. General Grant, on that day, was suddenly called out of the city, but the president, not willing to disappoint the public, went, with his wife and two others. During the progress of the play, John Wilkes Booth, an actor of some note, came into the box from behind, shot the president, and, jumping on the stage, escaped through the back door of the theatre. At the same time, Secretary Seward, who was lying ill at his residence, was severely wounded by a man who had entered the house ostensibly for the purpose of delivering a message from Mr. Seward's attending physician. A plot had been concocted to murder the president, vice president, General Grant, the cabinet officers, and other distinguished persons, and the leaders of the "confederacy" were suspected of forming it, in the hope that "in the midst of the confusion that might ensue, their wicked cause might gain an advantage." The plan, however, was unsuccessful. The president was the only one killed. Secretary Seward recovered, and the men appointed to assassinate the other intended victims, failed to carry out their part of the plot.

Andrew Johnson was inaugurated president at ten o'clock on the 15th of April, and "the government went steadily on in its course." The remains of the martyred president were taken, by the way of the most important cities of the United States, to his former residence, Springfield, Illinois. Large crowds of people accompanied the funeral procession in every city through which it passed. In Philadelphia the body was seen by one hundred and twenty thousand citizens, and in New York, both to and from the City Hall, where the body was exhibited, the mournful cortege was attended by an immense concourse. (See views of the "funeral of President Lincoln, New York city.")

On the 26th of April, the day of the surrender of Johnston, Booth and one of his accomplices, David C. Harrold, were found in a barn near Port Royal, Virginia. Upon their refusal to surrender themselves, the barn was set on fire. At this, Harrold came out and gave himself up, but Booth, still refusing, was shot by a sergeant named Corbett.

On the 10th of May, the fugitive president of the "Confederate States" was captured by a portion of the fourth Michigan cavalry, under Colonel B. D. Pritchard. They surprised his party in their camp near Irwinsville, Georgia, and, while Davis was attempting to escape in the disguise of a woman, he was made a prisoner. He was taken to Washington to await his trial on a charge of treason.

On the 7th of July, Harrold, and some others convicted of complicity in the assassination conspiracy, were hung, and other accomplices punished by banishment or imprisonment.

On the 29th of May, 1866, the nation was again thrown into mourning by the intelligence that the veteran General Scott had died at West Point, New York, at the advanced age of eighty years.

On the 22d of February, 1866, President Johnson made a speech to a crowd that had assembled in front of his house, in which he placed himself in opposition to the party who had elected him, and, from that time until the close of his administration, attempted to enforce a policy odious to the great mass of the loyal people of the north, and in direct opposition to the legislation of congress. From the date of his speech until the adjournment of the thirty-ninth congress, March, 1867, out of fifteen bills which had passed both houses of congress, ten were vetoed by the president, six of which were passed over his head; one was a pocket veto, and four became laws without his signature.

On the 6th of May, 1867, Jefferson Davis was admitted to bail in the sum of one hundred thousand dollars. His bail bond was signed by Horace Greeley, Augustus Schell, J. Minor Botts, and several leading Richmond secessionists.

After two unsuccessful attempts, by members of the fortieth congress, to impeach the president for "high crimes and misdemeanors," one in June and the other in December, 1867, articles of impeachment were finally drawn up in March, 1868. The trial closed on the 6th of May. The members of the senate constituted the jury. A vote of two-thirds of the members was required to convict the president, and he was acquitted by a vote of nineteen to thirty-five; so he continued the occupant of the presidential chair until the close of his term.

On the 3d of November, General Ulysses S. Grant was elected president of the United States, and Schuyler Colfax, of Indiana, the speaker of the house of representatives, vice president. On the 4th of March, 1869, Chief Justice Salmon P. Chase administered the oath of office to President Grant.

Now, with this battle-scarred chieftain at the helm of the ship of state, let us hope that the great work of reconstruction, which has been so successfully commenced, may be speedily completed; that the whole nation, from the lakes to the gulf, and from ocean to ocean, may be united in advancing the best interests of the government; and that our common country, by the blessing of Almighty God, may henceforth, as heretofore, be an asylum for the oppressed and persecuted of all lands, and continue, in all future time, to hold her proud position at the head of the nations of the earth.

CHAPTER X.

THE NORTH AMERICAN INDIANS.

The term Indian, as applied to the various nations and tribes that inhabited the western continent at the time of its discovery by the Spaniards, originated in the mistaken idea that the newly-found continent formed a part of Asia. By some ethnologists the American Indians are classed as a distinct variety of the human race, and are as peculiar to the American continent as its fauna and flora. Their history, previous to the settlements made among them by the Europeans, is involved in obscurity. But the supposition that they are not the descendants of Adam and Eve is erroneous, as it is contrary to the Bible.

Other ethnologists refer their origin to the great Mongolian family, who have found their way from Asia across Behring's Strait. This Strait is only thirty-six miles wide, and during severe winter seasons it is frozen over, forming an easy mode of communication between the two continents; or the passage across may have been made in boats which have been driven over by storms.

According to some historians, the Indians owe their origin to the "lost tribes of Israel," who, we are told, "took counsel to go forth into a farther country, where never mankind dwelt." These tribes, it is thought by some, crossed over into America, and are the progenitors of the Indian race. This theory is, however, unsupported by acknowledged facts.

The era of their existence as a distinct nation probably dates back to a short time subsequent to the dispersion at Babel, which gave to each branch of the human family its language and individuality. At this time mankind penetrated beyond the Plains of Shinar, and gradually spread over Northern Asia, where, by adventure or accident, they reached the new continent.

After the confusion of tongues, a large body of shepherds, driving their flocks before them, moved to Egypt, made a conquest of the country, founded an empire under the name of the Shepherd Kings, built large cities, and constructed the massive pyramids on which their history is recorded in hieroglyphics. Their tyranny became unendurable, and the Egyptians drove them from their land. These defeated shepherds, it is thought by some, crossed into America in the manner before described, and it is probable they are the progenitors of the Indians who inhabited Mexico. The mounds and ancient works, the ruins of which still remain ; also the manner of interring their dead, corresponding with the Egyptians, confirm this opinion.

The character and language of the various tribes that peopled our country, differed so materially from Mexican Indians, that it is highly probable that they were descendants from a later body of Asiatic adventurers than the latter.

The first settlers were somewhat advanced in civilization and the mechanical arts. Remains of some of their structures are still to be seen in various parts of our country. They were probably driven from their settlements further to the south by less civilized tribes, until the whole continent was peopled.

The traditions of the Indians do but little to lift the veil of mystery that shrouds their origin. They entertain the idea that they are an insulated race, distinct from other people, and had their origin in the ground. Hence their name, Aborigines. According to one tradition, they climbed from the interior to the surface of the globe, by means of the roots of a large vine. By another account, their ancestors, after living under ground for ages, discovered the light of day through an aperture of a cavern, and by almost superhuman efforts, emerged from their subterranean prison. By another tradition, their fathers crossed a tract of water to reach their present habitation.

The Indian tribes are classified in reference to their dialects, into eight distinct families, of which the Algonquins is the largest. This name was given them by the French. They occupied a great portion of the United States east of the Mississippi and north of North Carolina and Tennessee. It was composed of several powerful tribes, and the number of its warriors exceeded those of all the other tribes together.

The Huron Iroquois tribes occupied the territory of Canada south of the Ottawa river, and portions of the states of New York, Ohio, and Pennsylvania. To this family belonged the Five Nations. They were joined by the Tuscaroras, making a confederacy known as the Six Nations. The English obtained their friendship and assistance during the French war. Chiefs from each of these nations met the colonial representatives at a congress assembled at Albany, where a plan of an American union was presented by Benjamin Franklin. Hendric, the Mohawk warrior, urged its acceptance. "We thank you," he said, "for brightening the covenant chain. We will take this belt to Onondaga, where our council fire always burns, and keep it so securely that neither the thunderbolt nor the lightning shall break it. Strengthen yourselves, and bring as many as you can into this covenant chain."

The Dakotahs, or Sioux, were a large family west of the Mississippi; hence but little was known about them by the early settlers.

The Catawbas were a powerful family, inhabiting the interior of South Carolina, but were vanquished and nearly exterminated by the Iroquois. They assisted the people of South Carolina in their wars with the Cherokees and other hostile tribes; also aided them during the revolution. When the civil war broke out in 1861, the survivors of this nation, numbering less than one hundred souls, occupied a small village on the Catawba river.

The Catawbas were joined on the west by the Cherokees, who occupied the territory of the Blue Ridge and Alleghanies, one of the most delightful places in the United States. They had long and bloody wars with the Five Nations. They aided the British during the revolution, and for a number of years thereafter the frontier of the Carolinas suffered from their ravages. A treaty was made with them in 1791, and no more trouble ensued. In 1812, they assisted the United States in subjugating the Creeks, under their fierce chief, Tecumseh. They rapidly advanced in civilization, and schools and a printing press were established, but they were obliged to seek a new home in the wilderness. They now constitute the largest, most civilized, and prosperous of the Indian tribes, notwithstanding the injuries they suffered during the late civil war. They now number about fifteen thousand souls.

The Uchees, a remnant of a once powerful tribe, were the sixth of the Indian families. But little of their history is known. They never occupied any other region than the northern part of Georgia. They boasted that they were the descendants of the most ancient inhabitants of the region in which they were found. Their language differed from the other families in being more harsh and guttural.

The Natchez occupied territory on the east bank of the Mississippi, in the vicinity of the city which bears their name. Their early history is not known, but from a tradition which they retained of having seen "warriors of fire" where they formerly lived, which no doubt refers to Cortes' soldiers, we may infer that they were connected with the Mexican Indians. The Natchez were jealous of the French, whom they considered as intruders, and determined to drive them from their country. They were unsuccessful, and were nearly exterminated by their enemy. Those who survived joined the Creek confederacy, and their original language has become extinct.

The Mobilian family was composed of a group of tribes. Their territory extended over the region between the Atlantic and the Mississippi, bounded on the north by the Ohio river, and on the south by the Gulf of Mexico. The most powerful and important tribe of this family was the Creeks. Though strong and warlike, considerable attention was given to agriculture, and, when not engaged in war, they assisted the women in cultivating the soil. They were a source of great annoyance to the white settlers on the Georgia frontier, and during the revolution they assisted the British. The Seminoles, a part of the Creek confederacy, caused much trouble in Florida. They were finally subjugated in 1842, after which the greater portion of the tribe moved beyond the Mississippi. The Choctaws and Chickasaws are also members of the Mobilian family. The Choctaws, when first discovered by the Europeans, were engaged in agricultural pursuits, were possessed of quiet habits, and never engaged in war, except for their defense. The brave Chickasaws were the early friends of the English. They aided the English during the revolution, but since that time have been friendly with the United States.

Light is often shed upon the history of a people by a study of their language. A great variety of dialects were used by the Indians, bearing a general resemblance to each other, but sufficient difference was discovered to group them into eight families. Their language possesses a wild grandeur, and much less irregularity than cultivated tongues. The simple child of nature, unacquainted with art, science, commerce, and mechanical industry, had need of but few words; yet, as an intelligent being, governed by passions and affections, he required some mode of expressing his thoughts and feelings, and we find him in all parts of the continent possessing a language suited to his condition. None of the Indian languages were written, but an ingenious Cherokee seeing the books used by missionaries, and learning that the characters which they contained represented the sounds used by them in speaking, without any knowledge of other languages, succeeded in making an alphabet for his own language, consisting of eighty-five characters, representing syllables, of which there are but eighty-five in their language. The Cherokee words are short, and it requires but little study to enable one to read and write it with ease.

The Indians, though unable to write, like the Egyptians and other ancient nations, conveyed their thoughts by pictures or hieroglyphics, by which means they communicated with each other. The Mexicans, at the time of Cortes' invasion, informed their king of the arrival of the Spaniards and their ships, by pieces of white linen, on which were painted objects resembling vessels and men in Spanish garb.

Hieroglyphics have been found on rocks and trees in different parts of our country. These, with their oral traditions, are all they possess of their past history. Figures abound in the Indian language, often rendering it sublime. "Many Indian chiefs were as distinguished for their eloquence as for their courage. Their delivery was animated, dignified and forcible; their gesticulation graceful and natural. Some of their speeches have scarcely been surpassed by the greatest efforts of civilized orators."

The relics of the Aborigines may be considered under two classes. Those of recent origin, such as rude weapons and ornaments, and those of ancient origin, among which are ruins of fortifications, fire places, weapons, utensils and ornaments of copper, brass and silver, walls of cities, sculptured columns, and catacombs containing mummies. In the Illinois salt works were found the remains of a well and drain, also ashes and fragments of pottery, and in other salt-springs have been found vessels suitable for evaporating water. From discoveries made in the copper mines of Lake Superior, it is probable they have been worked before. In Ohio, a silver cup was discovered in a mound which had been partially undermined by a stream. Isinglass mirrors have been discovered many feet below the surface.

The number of mounds erected in North America is variously estimated at from five to ten thousand. These are most numerous in Mexico and Central America. They also abound in ruins and remains of cities, temples, pyramids, and sculptured columns which equal in grandeur and magnificence those of the old world. (See views of Central America.)

The Mexicans and Peruvians were the only two of the many nations that peopled this continent at the time it was first explored by the Spaniards, who had attained to any high degree of civilization.

The Indians are characterized by a red or copper color, a square head with a low, broad forehead, full face and prominent cheek bones, their eyes dark and expressive, their hair black, coarse, and straight; their forms erect and well proportioned, and their powers of endurance remarkable.

The men were employed in war, hunting and fishing. When engaged in the chase or war, the ground, without shelter, formed their bed; they had no protection except the fires they kindled to prevent attacks from wild beasts. The women bore all the burdens during journeys. They built the huts or wigwams in which they lived, planted and gathered their crops, and dressed skins for clothing. Manual labor was considered beneath a warrior; hence all menial labor was performed by the women.

Their wigwams were made of poles, covered with skins, mats, or bark of trees. They were constructed with little labor, and abandoned when a change of residence was desired. They were generally found grouped together in villages. (See Indian views.)

For a great portion of the year they subsisted on game, fish, and roots. When these resources failed they resorted to maize or Indian corn. Their money consisted of little tubes, made of common clam shells; they were fastened upon belts and called *wampum*.

A regular union between husband and wife was universal among all the tribes. The men had a right to as many wives as they could support. The marriage tie generally lasted till death, but by some, wives were taken and dismissed at pleasure. The Indian warrior compelled his wife, or squaw, to do all the drudgery, and often treated her with cruelty. For his children he entertained a stronger affection.

Education among the Indians consisted chiefly in such training as would enable them to endure hardships, hunger and fatigue; they also practiced athletic exercises. The Indian boy, at the age of eight years, was required to do without food and drink for half a day. When he was twelve his face was blackened, and he was required to fast a whole day at a time. At eighteen his face was blackened for the last time; he was taken into the woods and remained there without food as long as life could be so supported. He was then taken home, praised for his endurance, and henceforth considered himself a man.

Indian wars were usually carried on by small parties; they could not act in large bodies with much success, from a want of discipline. Their object was to surprise the enemy, and kill as many as possible. Their honors were counted by the number of scalps they obtained. They depended for food on the game they might secure in the forest. Their weapons were bows and arrows, tomahawks of stone, and scalping-knives of bone, until the arrival of the Europeans, when they were made of iron.

A captive was taken to the village of his conquerors, where he was obliged to "run the gauntlet" between two lines of the savages, who beat him as he passed. He then was adopted into the tribe or burned at the stake.

Each tribe, among the Indians, had its chief or sachem, who generally excelled the rest of his tribe in cunning, bravery or eloquence. They had no laws, and during peace the chiefs exercised no authority. If a wrong was perpetrated, its punishment was left to the party who suffered it, and not to the tribe.

Different modes of burial prevailed in different tribes. Some bodies were buried in a sitting posture, some were laid on the ground, and a little house, covered with bark, erected over them. By some tribes bodies were deposited in rude coffins and placed on a high scaffold. By others they were placed on the boughs of trees, where they remained until, from decomposition, the bones fell to the ground. The dead were buried with their bows and arrows, tomahawks, saddles, food and tobacco. Sometimes a favorite horse and dog were killed and interred with their master; in fact, every thing they value in life is buried with them, so as to be ready for use on entering the spirit land. (See views of Indian graves.)

The Indians of the present day preserve these customs. The funeral service consists of a prayer to the Great Spirit, of which the following is an example: "We are sorry to part with our brother, who was a daring brave and a good Indian, and whose lodge contained many scalps of his enemies. But we have yielded to Thy will, and we commit him to Thy care. We have outfitted him as Thou seest, for his journey; and now we desire Thee to lead him to the fair land beyond the setting sun, where game is always plentiful, and bad Indians and white men never come."

The Indians believed in a God or "Great Spirit" whom they worshiped, and to whom they prayed for courage and success in war. It was a general belief among the different tribes that the Deity possesses a human form. With their general idea of the Deity and the creation various traditions were blended. According to the tradition of the Chippewas, a man was created and placed on the earth during the summer season. He subsisted on berries until winter, when he supported life by hunting. Finding it difficult to walk through deep snow, he attempted to make a snow-shoe. He succeeded, without difficulty, in making the frame, but being unable to weave in the web, he abandoned it. Every evening, on returning from hunting, he perceived that the work was progressing. This he attributed to a bird which he captured by strategem, and it immediately changed into a beautiful woman.

The Indians believe in the existence of good and evil spirits; the former of whom endow certain persons with superior power. These were called medicine men. If in case of disease a cure was effected by one of them, he was thought to have gained a victory over the evil spirit, and if unsuccessful it was through no fault of the medicine man, and the blame was attached to the evil spirit.

They imagined that the soul when freed from the body passed over a dark river, into which the wicked were precipitated, where they remained forever struggling among the waves, or were borne to a place of torment. The good crossed in safety, and hastened to the happy hunting grounds which abounded in the choicest game.

A want of foresight is peculiar to the Indian race. This deficiency in their character has been the cause of much distress. They provide but little food at a time, and consequently when no game is to be obtained they suffer greatly from want of food. Among other prominent traits of character are caution and fortitude. When among friends or enemies every word and action is looked upon with suspicion, and, when undergoing the most excruciating tortures at the hand of an enemy, their sufferings are betrayed by neither sigh nor groan.

The Indians inhabiting the Indian territory at the present time number about one hundred and fifty thousand. The United States purchased the lands they occupied, and gives them others within the new territory which the government has assigned them, transports them, furnishes agricultural implements, plows and fences a portion of their fields, erects school-houses and supports teachers in them the year through. (See views of government school.)

A form of government in each tribe has been established similar to the state governments.

The Choctaws inhabit the southern part of the territory, and are engaged in the cultivation of corn, flax, hemp, tobacco, and cotton. Their government is divided into four departments; legislative, executive, judicial and military.

The Chickasaws have amassed considerable wealth from the sale of their lands east of the Mississippi, to the United States. They have a fund of ten thousand dollars annually applied to education.

The Cherokees take the lead in civilization. Their form of government is similar to the Choctaws. They work the lead mines, manufacture salt, and are also engaged in agriculture.

The Creeks, among which are about sixteen hundred Seminoles, are less advanced in civilization, and their form of government less perfect than the other tribes.

The emigrating tribes are the Senecas, Shawnees, Pottawatomies, Iowas, Weas, Piankashaws, Peorias, Kaskaskias, Ottawas, Delawares, Kickapoos, Wyandots, Sacs and Foxes, all of which are more or less civilized, and receive annuities from the government.

The native tribes residing in the Indian territory are the Pawnees, Sioux, Quapaws, Kansas, Otoes, Omahoes and Ponsars, all of which are in a degraded condition. They receive annuities from the United States. (See views of Sioux and Pawnees.)

The Camanches are a warlike tribe, living south of the Great Platte. They follow the buffalo north in summer, and in winter return with them to the plains of Texas.

North of the Great Platte are fifteen or twenty small tribes.

In the vicinity of the Rocky Mountains are Shoshonees or Snakes, Arapahoes, Crows and Blackfeet, the last two of which are very warlike tribes. The Blackfeet stole a blanket, infected with small pox, from the American Fur company, which caused the disease to spread all through their tribe, and they were reduced in number about two-thirds.

Such is the brief history of the Aboriginal nations that inhabited our country, and annihilation seems to be their destiny. "The great garden of the western world needed tillers, and white men came. They have thoroughly changed the condition of the land and the people. The light of civilization has revealed, and industry developed, vast treasures in the soil, while, before its radiance, the Aboriginals are rapidly melting like snow in the sunbeams. A few generations will pass, and no representatives of the North American Indians will remain upon the earth."

CHAPTER XI.

DECLARATION OF INDEPENDENCE.

A DECLARATION BY THE REPRESENTATIVES OF THE UNITED STATES OF AMERICA, IN CONGRESS ASSEMBLED.

When, in the course of human events, it becomes necessary for one people to dissolve the political bands which have connected them with another, and to assume, among the powers of the earth, the separate and equal station to which the laws of nature and of nature's God entitle them, a decent respect to the opinions of mankind requires that they should declare the causes which impel them to the separation.

We hold these truths to be self-evident—that all men are created equal; that they are endowed by their Creator with certain inalienable rights; that among these are life, liberty and the pursuit of happiness. That, to secure these rights, governments are instituted among men, deriving their just powers from the consent of the governed; that, whenever any form of government becomes destructive of these ends, it is the right of the people to alter or abolish it, and to institute a new government, laying its foundations on such principles, and organizing its powers in such form, as to them shall seem most likely to effect their safety and happiness. Prudence, indeed, will dictate that governments long established should not be changed for light and transient causes; and, accordingly, all experience hath shown that mankind are more disposed to suffer, while evils are sufferable, than to right themselves by abolishing the forms to which they are accustomed. But when a long train of abuses and usurpations, pursuing invariably the same object, evinces a design to reduce them under absolute despotism, it is their right, it is their duty, to throw off such government, and to provide new guards for their future security. Such has been the patient sufferance of these colonies, and such is now the necessity which constrains them to alter their former systems of government. The history of the present king of Great Britain, is a history of repeated injuries and usurpations, all having in direct object the establishment of an absolute tyranny over these states. To prove this, let facts be submitted to a candid world.

He has refused his assent to laws the most wholesome and necessary for the public good.

He has forbidden his governors to pass laws of immediate and pressing importance, unless suspended in their operations till his assent should be obtained; and, when so suspended, he has utterly neglected to attend to them.

He has refused to pass other laws for the accommodation of large districts of people, unless those people would relinquish the right of representation in the legislature—a right inestimable to them, and formidable to tyrants only.

He has called together legislative bodies at places unusual, uncomfortable, and distant from the repository of their public records, for the sole purpose of fatiguing them into compliance with his measures.

He has dissolved representative houses repeatedly, for opposing, with manly firmness, his invasions on the rights of the people.

He has refused, for a long time after such dissolutions, to cause others to be elected, whereby the legislative powers, incapable of annihilation, have returned to the people at large for their exercise; the state remaining, in the meantime, exposed to all the dangers of invasions from without, and convulsions within.

He has endeavored to prevent the population of these states; for that purpose obstructing the laws for the naturalization of foreigners; refusing to pass others to encourage their migration hither, and raising the conditions of new appropriations of lands.

He has obstructed the administration of justice, by refusing his assent to laws for establishing judiciary powers.

He has made judges dependent on his will alone for the tenure of their offices, and the amount and payment of their salaries.

He has erected a multitude of new offices, and sent hither swarms of officers to harass our people and eat out their substance.

He has kept among us in times of peace, standing armies, without the consent of our legislatures.

He has affected to render the military independent of, and superior to, the civil power.

He has combined with others to subject us to a jurisdiction foreign to our constitutions, and unacknowledged by our laws; giving his assent to their acts of pretended legislation;

For quartering large bodies of armed troops among us;

For protecting them, by a mock trial, from punishment for any murders which they should commit on the inhabitants of these states;

For cutting off our trade with all parts of the world;

For imposing taxes on us without our consent;

For depriving us, in many cases, of the benefits of trial by jury;

For transporting us beyond seas, to be tried for pretended offenses;

For abolishing the free system of English laws in a neighboring province, establishing therein an arbitrary government, and enlarging its boundaries, so as to render it at once an example and fit instrument for introducing the same absolute rule into these colonies;

For taking away our charters, abolishing our most valuable laws, and altering, fundamentally, the forms of our governments;

For suspending our own legislatures, and declaring themselves invested with power to legislate for us in all cases whatsoever.

He has abdicated government here, by declaring us out of his protection, and waging war against us.

He has plundered our seas, ravaged our coasts, burned our towns, and destroyed the lives of our people.

He is at this time transporting large armies of foreign mercenaries, to complete the works of death, desolation, and tyranny, already begun with circumstances of cruelty and perfidy scarcely paralleled in the most barbarous ages, and totally unworthy the head of a civilized nation.

He has constrained our fellow-citizens, taken captive on the high seas, to bear arms against their country, to become the executioners of their friends and brethren, or to fall themselves by their hands.

He has excited domestic insurrection among us, and has endeavored to bring on the inhabitants of our frontiers, the merciless Indian savages, whose known rule of warfare is an undistinguished destruction of all ages, sexes, and conditions.

In every stage of these oppressions we have petitioned for redress in the most humble terms; our repeated petitions have been answered only by repeated injury. A prince whose character is thus marked by every act which may define a tyrant, is unfit to be the ruler of a free people.

Nor have we been wanting in our attentions to our British brethren. We have warned them, from time to time, of attempts by their legislature to extend an unwarrantable jurisdiction over us. We have reminded them of the circumstances of our emigration and settlement here. We have appealed to their native justice and magnanimity, and we have conjured them by the ties of our common kindred, to disavow these usurpations, which would inevitably interrupt our connections and correspondence. They, too, have been deaf to the voice of justice and of consanguinity. We must, therefore, acquiesce in the necessity which compels our separation, and hold them as we hold the rest of mankind—enemies in war—in peace, friends.

We, therefore, the representatives of the United States of America, in general congress assembled, appealing to the Supreme Judge of the world for the rectitude of our intentions, do, in the name and by the authority of the good people of these colonies, solemnly publish and declare that these united colonies are, and of right ought to be, free and independent states; that they are absolved from all allegiance to the British crown, and that all political connection between them and the state of Great Britain is, and ought to be, totally dissolved; and that, as free and independent states, they have full power to levy war, conclude peace, contract alliances, establish commerce, and do all other acts and things which independent states may of right do. And for the support of this Declaration, with a firm reliance on the protection of Divine Providence, we mutually pledge to each other our lives, our fortunes, and our sacred honor.

CHAPTER XII.

CONSTITUTION OF THE UNITED STATES.

We, the People of the United States, in order to form a more perfect Union, establish justice, insure domestic tranquillity, provide for the common defence, promote the general welfare, and secure the blessings of liberty to ourselves and our posterity, do ordain and establish this Constitution for the United States of America.

ARTICLE I.

SECTION 1. All the legislative powers herein granted shall be vested in a congress of the United States, which shall consist of a senate and house of representatives.

SEC. 2. The house of representatives shall be composed of members chosen every second year by the people of the several states, and the electors in each state shall have the qualifications requisite for electors of the most numerous branch of the state legislature.

No person shall be a representative who shall not have attained to the age of twenty-five years, and been seven years a citizen of the United States, and who shall not, when elected, be an inhabitant of that state in which he shall be chosen.

Representatives and direct taxes shall be apportioned among the several states which may be included within this union, according to their respective numbers, which shall be determined by adding to the whole number of free persons, including those bound to service for a term of years, and excluding Indians not taxed, three-fifths of all other persons. The actual enumeration shall be made within three years after the first meeting of the congress of the United States, and within every subsequent term of ten years, in such manner as they shall by law direct. The number of representatives shall not exceed one for every thirty thousand, but each state shall have at least one representative; and until such enumeration shall be made, the state of New Hampshire shall be entitled to choose three, Massachusetts eight, Rhode Island and Providence plantations one, Connecticut five, New York six, New Jersey four, Pennsylvania eight, Delaware one, Maryland six, Virginia ten, North Carolina five, South Carolina five, and Georgia three.

When vacancies happen in the representation from any state, the executive authority thereof shall issue writs of election to fill such vacancies.

The house of representatives shall choose their speaker and other officers; and shall have the sole power of impeachment.

SEC. 3. The senate of the United States shall be composed of two senators from each state, chosen by the legislature thereof, for six years; and each senator shall have one vote.

Immediately after they shall be assembled in consequence of the first election, they shall be divided as equally as may be into three classes. The seats of the senators of the first class shall be vacated at the expiration of the second year, of the second class at the expiration of the fourth year, and of the third class at the expiration of the sixth year, so that one-third may be chosen every second year; and if vacancies happen by resignation, or otherwise, during the recess of the legislature of any state, the executive thereof may make temporary appointments until the next meeting of the legislature, which shall then fill such vacancies.

No person shall be a senator who shall not have attained to the age of thirty years, and been nine years a citizen of the United States, and who shall not, when elected, be an inhabitant of that state for which he shall be chosen.

The vice president of the United States shall be president of the Senate, but shall have no vote, unless they be equally divided.

The senate shall choose their other officers, and also a president *pro tempore*, in the absence of the vice president, or when he shall exercise the office of president of the United States.

8

The senate shall have the sole power to try all impeachments. When sitting for that purpose, they shall be on oath or affirmation. When the president of the United States is tried, the chief justice shall preside; and no person shall be convicted without the concurrence of two-thirds of the members present.

Judgment in cases of impeachment shall not extend further than to removal from office, and disqualification to hold and enjoy any office of honor, trust or profit under the United States; but the party convicted shall nevertheless be liable and subject to indictment, trial, judgment and punishment, according to law.

Sec. 4. The times, places and manner of holding elections for senators and representatives, shall be prescribed in each state by the legislature thereof; but the congress may at any time by law make or alter such regulations, except as the places of choosing senators.

The congress shall assemble at least once in every year, and such meeting shall be on the first Monday in December, unless they shall by law appoint a different day.

Sec. 5. Each house shall be the judge of the elections, returns, and qualifications of its own members, and a majority of each shall constitute a quorum to do business; but a smaller number may adjourn from day to day, and may be authorized to compel the attendance of absent members, in such manner and under such penalties as each house may provide.

Each house may determine the rules of its proceedings, punish its members for disorderly behavior, and, with the concurrence of two-thirds, expel a member.

Each house shall keep a journal of its proceedings, and from time to time publish the same, excepting such parts as may in their judgment require secrecy; and the yeas and nays of the members of either house on any question shall, at the desire of one-fifth of those present, be entered on the journal.

Neither house, during the session of congress, shall, without the consent of the other, adjourn for more than three days, nor to any other place than that in which the two houses shall be sitting.

SEC. 6. The senators and representatives shall receive a compensation for their services, to be ascertained by law and paid out of the treasury of the United States. They shall in all cases, except treason, felony, and breach of the peace, be priviliged from arrest during their attendance at the sessions of their respective houses, and in going to and returning from the same; and for any speech or debate in either house, they shall not be questioned in any other place.

No senator or representative shall, during the time for which he was elected, be appointed to any civil office under the authority of the United States, which shall have been created, or the emoluments whereof shall have been increased during such time; and no person holding any office under the United States shall be a member of either house during his continuance in office.

SEC. 7. All bills for raising revenue shall originate in the house of representatives; but the senate may propose or concur with amendments as on other bills.

Every bill which shall have passed the house of representatives and the senate, shall, before it becomes a law, be presented to the president of the United States. If he approve, he shall sign it; but if not, he shall return it, with his objections, to that house in which it shall have originated, who shall enter the objections at large on their journal, and proceed to reconsider it. If, after such reconsideration, two-thirds of that house shall agree to pass the bill, it shall be sent, together with the objections, to the other house, by which it shall likewise be reconsidered, and if approved by two-thirds of that house, it shall become a law. But in all such cases the votes of both houses shall be determined by yeas and nays, and the names of the persons voting for and against the bill shall be entered on the journal of each house respectively. If any bill shall not be returned by the president within ten days (Sundays excepted) after it shall have been presented to him, the same shall be a law, in like manner as if he had signed it, unless the congress, by their adjournment, prevent its return, in which case it shall not be a law.

Every order, resolution, or vote to which the concurrence of the senate and house of representatives may be necessary (except on a question of adjournment) shall be presented to the president of the United States; and before the same shall take effect, shall be approved by him; or, being disapproved by him, shall be repassed by two-thirds of the senate and house of representatives, according to the rules and limitations prescribed in the case of a bill.

SEC. 8. The congress shall have power—

To lay and collect taxes, duties, imposts and excises, to pay the debts and provide for the common defense and general welfare of the United States; but all duties, imposts and excises shall be uniform throughout the United States;

To borrow money on the credit of the United States;

To regulate commerce with foreign nations, and among the several states, and with the Indian tribes;

To establish an uniform rule of naturalization, and uniform laws on the subject of bankruptcies throughout the United States;

To coin money, regulate the value thereof and of foreign coin, and fix the standard of weights and measures;

To provide for the punishment of counterfeiting the securities and current coin of the United States;

To establish post offices and post roads;

To promote the progress of science and useful arts, by securing for limited times to authors and inventors the exclusive right to their respective writings and discoveries;

To constitute tribunals inferior to the supreme court;

To define and punish piracies and felonies committed on the high seas, and offenses against the law of nations;

To declare war, grant letters of marque and reprisal, and make rules concerning captures on land and water;

To raise and support armies; but no appropriation of money to that use shall be for a longer term than two years;

To provide and maintain a navy;

To make rules for the government and regulation of the land and naval forces;

To provide for calling forth the militia to execute the laws of the union, suppress insurrections and repel invasions;

To provide for organizing, arming, and disciplining the militia, and for governing such part of them as may be employed in the service of the United States, reserving to the states respectively the appointment of the officers, and the authority of training the militia according to the discipline prescribed by congress;

To exercise exclusive legislation, in all cases whatsoever, over such district (not exceeding ten miles square) as may, by cession of particular states, and the acceptance of congress, become the seat of the government of the United States, and to exercise like authority over all places purchased by the consent of the legislature of the state in which the same shall be, for the erection of forts, magazines, arsenals, dock yards, and other needful buildings; and

To make all laws which shall be necessary and proper for carrying into execution the foregoing powers, and all other powers vested by this constitution in the government of the United States, or in any department or officer thereof.

SEC. 9. The migration or importation of such persons as any of the states now existing shall think proper to admit, shall not be prohibited by the congress prior to the year one thousand eight hundred and eight, but a tax or duty may be imposed on such importation, not exceeding ten dollars for each person.

The privilege of the writ of habeas corpus shall not be suspended, unless when, in cases of rebellion or invasion, the public safety may require it.

No bill of attainder or ex post facto law shall be passed.

No capitation, or other direct tax, shall be laid, unless in proportion to the census or enumeration hereinbefore directed to be taken.

No tax or duty shall be laid on articles exported from any state.

No preference shall be given by any regulation of commerce or revenue to the ports of one state over those of another; nor shall vessels bound to or from one state, be obliged to enter, clear, or pay duties in another.

No money shall be drawn from the treasury but in consequence of appropriations made by law; and a regular statement and account of the receipts and expenditures of all public money shall be published from time to time.

No title of nobility shall be granted by the United States; And no person holding any office of profit or trust under them shall, without the consent of the congress, accept of any present, emolument, office, or title, of any kind whatever, from any king, prince, or foreign state.

SEC. 10. No state shall enter into any treaty, alliance, or confederation; grant letters of marque or reprisal; coin money; emit bills of credit; make anything but gold and silver coin a tender in payment of debts; pass any bill of attainder, ex post facto law, or law impairing the obligation of contracts, or grant any title of nobility.

No state shall, without the consent of the congress, lay any imposts or duties on imports or exports, except what may be absolutely necessary for executing its inspection laws; and the net produce of all duties and imposts, laid by any state on imports or exports, shall be for the use of the treasury of the United States; and all such laws shall be subject to the revision and control of the congress.

No state shall, without the consent of congress, lay any duty of tonnage, keep troops, or ships of war in time of peace, enter into any agreement or compact with another state, or with a foreign power, or engage in war, unless actually invaded, or in such imminent danger as will not admit of delay.

ARTICLE II.

SECTION 1. The executive power shall be vested in a president of the United States of America. He shall hold his office during the term of four years, and, together with the vice-president, chosen for the same term, be elected as follows:

Each state shall appoint, in such manner as the legislature thereof may direct, a number of electors, equal to the whole number of senators and representatives to which the state may be entitled in the congress; but no senator or representative, or person holding an office of trust or profit under the United States, shall he appointed an elector.

[The electors shall meet in their respective states, and vote by ballot for two persons, of whom one, at least, shall not be an inhabitant of the same state with themselves. And they shall make a list of all the persons voted for, and of the number of votes for each; which list they shall sign and certify, and transmit sealed to the seat of the government of the United States, directed to the president of the senate. The president of the senate shall, in the presence of the senate and house of representatives, open all the certificates, and the votes shall then be counted. The person having the greatest number of votes shall be the president, if such number be a majority of the whole number of electors appointed; and if there be more than one who have such majority and have an equal number of votes, then the house of representatives shall immediately choose by ballot one of them for president; and if no person have a majority, then from the five highest on the list the said house shall in like manner choose the president. But in choosing the president, the votes shall be taken by states, the representation from each state having one vote; a quorum for this purpose shall consist of a member or members from two-thirds of the states, and a majority of all the states shall be necessary to a choice. In every case, after the choice of the president, the person having the greatest number of votes of the electors shall be the vice-president. But if there should remain two or more who have equal votes, the senate shall choose from them by ballot the vice-president].*

The congress may determine the time of choosing the electors, and the day on which they shall give their votes; which day shall be the same throughout the United States.

No person except a natural born citizen, or a citizen of the United States, at the time of the adoption of this Constitution, shall be eligible to the office of president; neither shall any

* This clause is annulled. See amendments, article XII.

person be eligible to that office who shall not have attained to the age of thirty-five years, and been fourteen years a resident within the United States.

In case of the removal of the president from office, or of his death, resignation, or inability to discharge the powers and duties of the said office, the same shall devolve on the vice-president, and the congress may by law provide for the case of removal, death, resignation, or inability, both of the president and vice-president, declaring what officer shall then act as president, and such officer shall act accordingly, until the disability be removed, or a president shall be elected.

The president shall, at stated times, receive for his services a compensation, which shall neither be increased nor diminished during the period for which he shall have been elected, and he shall not receive within that period any other emolument from the United States, or any of them.

Before he enters on the execution of his office, he shall take the following oath or affirmation:—"I do solemnly swear (or affirm) that I will faithfully execute the office of president of the United States, and will, to the best of my ability, preserve, protect and defend the constitution of the United States."

SEC. 2. The president shall be commander-in-chief of the army and navy of the United States, and of the militia of the several states, when called into the actual service of the United States; he may require the opinion, in writing, of the principal officer in each of the executive departments, upon any subject relating to the duties of their respective offices, and he shall have power to grant reprieves and pardons for offenses against the United States, except in cases of impeachment.

He shall have power, by and with the advice and consent of the senate, to make treaties, provided two-thirds of the senators present concur; and he shall nominate, and, by and with the advice and consent of the senate, shall appoint ambassadors, other public ministers and consuls, judges of the supreme court, and all other officers of the United States, whose appointments are not herein otherwise provided for, and which shall be established by law; but the congress may by law vest the appointment of such inferior officers as they think proper, in the president alone, in the courts of law, or in the heads of departments.

The president shall have power to fill up all vacancies that may happen during the recess of the senate, by granting commissions, which shall expire at the end of their next session.

SEC. 3. He shall from time to time give to the congress information of the state of the Union, and recommend to their consideration such measures as he shall judge necessary and expedient; he may, on extraordinary occasions, convene both houses, or either of them, and, in case of disagreement between them, with respect to the time of adjournment, he may adjourn them to such time as he shall think proper; he shall receive ambassadors and other public ministers; he shall take care that the laws be faithfully executed, and shall commission all the officers of the United States.

SEC. 4. The president, vice-president and all civil officers of the United States, shall be removed from office on impeachment for, and conviction of, treason, bribery, or other high crimes and misdemeanors.

ARTICLE III.

SECTION 1. The judicial power of the United States shall be vested in one supreme court, and in such inferior courts as the congress may from time to time ordain and establish. The judges, both of the supreme and inferior courts, shall hold their offices during good behavior, and shall, at stated times, receive for their services, a compensation, which shall not be diminished during their continuance in office.

SEC. 2. The judicial power shall extend to all cases, in law and equity, arising under this Constitution, the laws of the United States, and treaties made, or which shall be made, under their authority;—to all cases affecting ambassadors, other public ministers, and consuls;—to all cases of admiralty and maritime jurisdiction;—to controversies to which the United States shall be a party;—to controversies between two or more states;—between a state and citizens of another state;—between citizens of different states;—between citizens of the same state claiming lands under grants of different states, and between a state, or the citizens thereof, and foreign states, citizens or subjects.

In all cases affecting ambassadors, other public ministers and consuls, and those in which a state shall be party, the supreme court shall have original jurisdiction. In all the other cases before mentioned, the supreme court shall have appellate jurisdiction, both as to law and fact, with such exceptions and under such regulations as the congress shall make.

The trial of all crimes, except in cases of impeachment, shall be by jury; and such trial shall be held in the state where the said crimes shall have been committed; but when not committed within any state, the trial shall be at such place or places as the congress may by law have directed.

SEC. 3. Treason against the United States shall consist only in levying war against them, or in adhering to their enemies, giving them aid and comfort.

No person shall be convicted of treason unless on the testimony of two witnesses to the same overt act, or on confession in open court.

The congress shall have power to declare the punishment of treason, but no attainder of treason shall work corruption of blood, or forfeiture except during the life of the person attainted.

ARTICLE IV.

SECTION 1. Full faith and credit shall be given in each state to the public acts, records, and judicial proceedings of every other state. And the congress may by general laws prescribe the manner in which such acts, records and proceedings shall be proved, and the effect thereof.

SEC. 2. The citizens of each state shall be entitled to all privileges and immunities of citizens of the several states.

A person charged in any state with treason, felony, or other crime, who shall flee from justice, and be found in another state, shall, on demand of the executive authority of the state from which he fled, be delivered up, to be removed to the state having jurisdiction of the crime.

No person held to service or labor in one state, under the laws thereof, escaping into another, shall, in consequence of any law or regulation therein, be discharged from such service or labor, but shall be delivered up on claim of the party to whom such service or labor may be due.

Sec. 3. New states may be admitted by the congress into this union; but no new state shall be formed or erected within the jurisdiction of any other state; nor any state be formed by the junction of two or more states, or parts of states, without the consent of the legislatures of the states concerned, as well as of the congress.

The congress shall have power to dispose of and make all needful rules and regulations respecting the territory or other property belonging to the United States; and nothing in this constitution shall be so construed as to prejudice any claims of the United States, or of any particular state.

Sec. 4. The United States shall guarantee to every state in this union a republican form of government, and shall protect each of them against invasion; and, on application of the legislature, or of the executive (when the legislature can not be convened,) against domestic violence.

ARTICLE V.

The congress, whenever two-thirds of both houses shall deem it necessary, shall propose amendments to this constitution, or, on the application of the legislatures of two-thirds of the several states, shall call a convention for proposing amendments, which, in either case, shall be valid to all intents and purposes, as part of this constitution, when ratified by the legislatures of three-fourths of the several states, or by conventions in three-fourths thereof, as the one or the other mode of ratification may be proposed by the congress; *Provided*, that no amendment which may be made prior to the year one thousand eight hundred and eight, shall in any manner affect the first and fourth clauses in the ninth section of the first article; and that no state, without its consent, shall be deprived of its equal suffrage in the senate.

ARTICLE VI.

All debts contracted and engagements entered into before the adoption of this constitution, shall be as valid against the United States, under this constitution, as under the confederation.

This constitution and the laws of the United States, which shall be made in pursuance thereof; and all treaties made, or which shall be made, under the authority of the United States, shall be the supreme law of the land; and the judges in every state shall be bound thereby, any thing in the constitution or laws of any state to the contrary notwithstanding.

The senators and representatives before mentioned, and the members of the several state legislatures, and all executive and judicial officers, both of the United States and of the several states, shall be bound by oath or affirmation to support this constitution; but no religious test shall ever be required as a qualification to any office or public trust under the United States.

ARTICLE VII.

The ratification of the conventions of nine states shall be sufficient for the establishment of this constitution between the states so ratifying the same.

Done in convention, by the unanimous consent of the states present, the seventeenth day of September, in the year of our Lord one thousand seven hundred and eighty-seven, and of the independence of the United States of America the twelfth. In witness whereof, we have hereunto subscribed our names.

GEORGE WASHINGTON,
President and Deputy from Virginia.

New Hampshire.

JOHN LANGDON, NICHOLAS GILMAN.

Massachusetts.

NATHANIEL GORHAM, RUFUS KING.

Connecticut.

WILLIAM SAMUEL JOHNSON, ROGER SHERMAN.

New York.

ALEXANDER HAMILTON.

New Jersey.

WILLIAM LIVINGSTON, DAVID BREARLEY,
WILLIAM PATTERSON, JONATHAN DAYTON.

Pennsylvania.

BENJAMIN FRANKLIN,
ROBERT MORRIS,
THOMAS FITZSIMONS,
JAMES WILSON,
THOMAS MIFFLIN,
GEORGE CLYMER,
JARED INGERSOLL,
GOUVERNEUR MORRIS.

Delaware.

GEORGE READ,
JOHN DICKINSON,
JACOB BROOM.
GUNNING BEDFORD, JR.,
RICHARD BASSETT,

Maryland.

JAMES M'HENRY,
DANIEL CARROLL.
DANIEL OF ST. THOMAS JENIFER,

Virginia.

JOHN BLAIR,
JAMES MADISON, JR.

North Carolina.

WILLIAM BLOUNT,
HUGH WILLIAMSON.
RICHARD DOBBS SPAIGHT,

South Carolina.

JOHN RUTLEDGE,
CHARLES PINCKNEY,
CHARLES COTESWORTH PINCKNEY,
PIERCE BUTLER.

Georgia.

WILLIAM FEW,
ABRAHAM BALDWIN.

Attest: WILLIAM JACKSON, *Secretary.*

AMENDMENTS

To the Constitution of the United States, ratified according to the Provisions of the Fifth Article of the foregoing Constitution.

ARTICLE I.

Congress shall make no law respecting an establishment of religion, or prohibiting the free exercise thereof; or abridging the freedom of speech, or of the press; or the right of the people peaceably to assemble, and to petition the government for redress of grievances.

ARTICLE II.

A well-regulated militia, being necessary to the security of a free state, the right of the people to keep and bear arms, shall not be infringed.

ARTICLE III.

No soldier shall, in time of peace be quartered in any house, without the consent of the owner, nor in time of war, but in a manner to be prescribed by law.

ARTICLE IV.

The right of the people to be secure in their persons, houses, papers, and effects, against unreasonable searches and seizures, shall not be violated, and no warrants shall issue, but upon probable cause, supported by oath or affirmation, and particularly describing the place to be searched, and the persons or things to be seized.

ARTICLE V.

No person shall be held to answer for a capital, or otherwise infamous crime, unless on a presentment or indictment of a grand jury, except in cases arising in the land or naval forces, or in the militia, when in actual service in time of war and public danger; nor shall any person be subject for the same offense to be twice put in jeopardy of life or limb; nor shall be compelled in any criminal case to be a witness against himself, nor to be deprived of life, liberty, or property, without due process of law; nor shall private property be taken for public use, without just compensation.

ARTICLE VI.

In all criminal prosecutions, the accused shall enjoy the right to a speedy and public trial, by an impartial jury of the state and district wherein the crime shall have been committed, which district shall have been previously ascertained by law, and to be informed of the nature and cause of the accusation; to be confronted with the witnesses against him; to have compulsory process for obtaining witnesses in his favor, and to have the assistance of counsel for his defense.

ARTICLE VII.

In suits at common law, where the value in controversy shall exceed twenty dollars, the right of trial by jury shall be preserved, and no fact tried by a jury shall be otherwise re-examined in any court of the United States, than according to the rules of common law.

ARTICLE VIII.

Excessive bail shall not be required, nor excessive fines imposed, nor cruel and unusual punishments inflicted.

ARTICLE IX.

The enumeration in the constitution, of certain rights, shall not be construed to deny or disparage others retained by the people.

ARTICLE X.

The powers not delegated to the United States by the constitution, nor prohibited by it to the states, are reserved to the states respectively, or to the people.

ARTICLE XI.

The judicial power of the United States shall not be construed to extend to any suit in law or equity, commenced or prosecuted against one of the United States by citizens of another state, or by citizens or subjects of any foreign state.

ARTICLE XII.

The electors shall meet in their respective states, and vote by ballot for president and vice-president, one of whom, at least, shall not be an inhabitant of the same state with themselves; they shall name in their ballots the person voted for as president, and in distinct ballots the person voted for as vice-president, and they shall make distinct lists of all persons voted for as president, and of all persons voted for as vice-president, and of the number of votes for each, which lists they shall sign and certify, and transmit sealed to the seat of the government of the United States, directed to the president of the senate; the president of the senate shall, in the presence of the senate and house of representatives, open all the certificates, and the votes shall then be counted;—the person having the greatest number of votes for president, shall be the president, if such number be a majority of the whole number of electors appointed; and if no person have such majority, then from the persons having the highest numbers not exceeding three on the list of those voted for as president, the house of representatives shall choose immediately, by ballot, the president. But in choosing the president, the votes shall be taken by states, the representation from each state having one vote; a quorum for this purpose shall consist of a member or members from two-thirds of the states, and a majority of all the states shall be necessary to a choice. And if the house of representatives shall not choose a president whenever the right of choice shall devolve upon them, before the fourth day of March next following, then the vice-president shall act as president, as in the case of the death or other constitutional disability of the president. The person having the greatest number of votes as vice-president, shall be the vice-president, if such number be a majority of the whole number of electors appointed, and if no person have a majority, then from the two highest numbers on the list, the senate shall choose the vice-president; a quorum for the purpose shall consist of two-thirds of the whole number of senators, and a majority of the whole number shall be necessary to a choice. But no person constitutionally ineligible to the office of president shall be eligible to that of vice-president of the United States.

ARTICLE XIII.

SECTION 1. Neither slavery nor involuntary servitude, except as a punishment for crime whereof the party shall have been duly convicted, shall exist within the United States, or any place subject to their jurisdiction.

SEC. 2. Congress shall have power to enforce the article by appropriate legislation.

ARTICLE XIV.

SECTION 1. All persons born or naturalized in the United States and subject to the jurisdiction thereof, are citizens of the United States and of the state wherein they reside. No state shall make or enforce any law which shall abridge the privileges or immunities of citizens of the United States; nor shall any state deprive any person of life, liberty, or property, without due process of law, nor deny to any person within its jurisdiction the equal protection of the laws.

SEC. 2. Representatives shall be apportioned among the several states according to their respective numbers, counting the whole number of persons in each state, excluding Indians not taxed. But when the right to vote at any election for the choice of electors for president and vice president of the United States, representatives in congress, the executive and judicial officers of a state, or the members of the legislature thereof, is denied to any of the male inhabitants of such state, being twenty-one years of age and citizens of the United States, or in any way abridged, except for participation in rebellion or other crime, the basis of representation therein shall be reduced in proportion which the number of such male citizens shall bear to the whole number of male citizens twenty-one years of age in such state.

SEC. 3. No person shall be a senator or representative in congress, or elector of president and vice president, or hold any office, civil or military, under the United States or under any state, who, having previously taken an oath, as a member of congress, or as an officer of the United States, or as a member of any state legislature, or as an executive or judicial officer of any state, to support the constitution of the United States, shall have engaged in insurrection or rebellion against the same, or given aid and comfort to the enemies thereof. But congress may, by a vote of two-thirds of each house, remove such disability.

SEC. 4. The validity of the public debt of the United States authorized by law, including debts incurred for payment of pensions and bounties for services in suppressing insurrection and rebellion, shall not be questioned. But neither the United States nor any state shall assume or pay any debt or obligation incurred in aid of insurrection or rebellion against the United States, or any claim for the loss or emancipation of any slave; but all such debts, obligations or claims shall be held illegal and void.

SEC. 5. The congress shall have power to enforce, by appropriate legislation, the provisions of this article.

ARTICLE XV.

SECTION. 1. The right of the citizens of the United States to vote shall not be denied or abridged by the United States or by any state on account of race, color, or previous condition of servitude.

SEC. 2. The Congress shall have power to enforce this article by appropriate legislation.

Twenty-one states have now (November 1st, 1869,) given their sanction to the fifteenth amendment. Seven more are required to make it a part of the constitution of the United States.

CHAPTER XIII.

THE EMANCIPATION PROCLAMATIONS

OF SEPTEMBER, 1862, AND JANUARY, 1863.

"On the 22nd of September, 1862, Mr. Lincoln issued one of the two most important proclamations ever penned by a president of the United States: that which announced to the negroes held as slaves in the rebellious states that on and after the first day of the new year, they should be forever released from bondage. This great document, which was read with joy by the loyal residents of the north, and which was a source of such infinite happiness to the unfortunate class of beings who were to be more particularly affected by its provisions, was as follows:

"I, Abraham Lincoln, president of the United States of America, and commander-in-chief of the army and navy thereof, do hereby proclaim and declare, that hereafter, as heretofore, the war will be prosecuted for the object of practically restoring the constitutional relation between the United States and the people thereof in those states in which that relation is, or may be, suspended or disturbed; that it is my purpose upon the next meeting of congress to again recommend the adoption of a practical measure tending pecuniary aid to the free acceptance or rejection of all the slave states, so-called, the people whereof may not then be in rebellion against the United States, and which states may then have voluntarily adopted, or thereafter may voluntarily adopt, the immediate or gradual abolishment of slavery within their respective limits, and that the effort to colonize persons of African descent, with their consent, upon the continent or elsewhere, with the previously obtained consent of the government existing there, will be continued; that on the first day of January, in the year of our Lord one thousand eight hundred and sixty-three, all persons held as slaves within any state, or any designated part of a state, the people whereof shall then be in rebellion against the United States, shall be then, thenceforward and forever, free, and the executive government of the United States, including the military and naval authority thereof, will recognize and maintain the freedom of such persons, and will do no act or acts to repress such persons, or any of them, in any efforts they may make for their actual freedom; that the executive will, on the first day of January aforesaid, by proclamation, designate the states and parts of states, if any, in which the people thereof respectively shall then be in rebellion against the United States; and the fact that any state, or the people thereof, shall on that day be in good faith represented in the congress of the United States by members chosen thereto, at elections wherein a majority of the qualified voters of such state shall have participated, shall, in the absence of strong countervailing testimony, be deemed conclusive evidence that such state and the people thereof have not been in rebellion against the United States.

"That attention is hereby called to an act of congress entitled 'An act to make an additional article of war,' approved March 13, 1862, and which act is in the words and figures following:

"'*Be it enacted by the Senate and House of Representatives of the United States of America, in Congress assembled*, That hereafter the following shall be promulgated as an additional article of war for the government of the army of the United States, and shall be observed and obeyed as such.

"'ARTICLE —. All officers or persons of the military or naval service of the United States, are prohibited from employing any of the forces under their respective commands for the purpose of returning fugitives from service or labor, who may have escaped from any persons to whom such service or labor is claimed to be due, and any officer who shall be found guilty by a court martial of violating this article, shall be dismissed from the service.

"'SEC. 2. And be it further enacted, That this act shall take effect from and after its passage.'

"Also to the ninth and tenth sections of an act entitled, 'An act to suppress insurrection, to punish treason and rebellion, to seize and confiscate property of rebels, and for other purposes,' approved July 17, 1862, and which sections are in the words and figures following:

"'SEC. 9. And be it further enacted, That all slaves of persons who shall hereafter be engaged in rebellion against the government of the United States, or who shall in any way give aid or comfort thereto, escaping from such persons and taking refuge within the lines of the army; and all slaves captured from such persons or deserted by them, and coming under the control of the government of the United States, and all slaves of such persons found on (or being within) any place occupied by rebel forces and afterwards occupied by the forces of the United States, shall be deemed captives of war, and shall be forever free of their servitude and not again held as slaves.

"'SEC. 10. And be it further enacted, That no slave escaping into any state, territory, or the district of Columbia, from any of the states, shall be delivered up, or in any way impeded or hindered of his liberty, except for crime, or some offense against the laws, unless the person claiming said fugitive shall first make oath that the person to whom the labor or service of such fugitive is alleged to be due, is his lawful owner, and has not been in arms against the United States in the present rebellion, nor in any way given aid and comfort thereto; and no person engaged in the military or naval service of the United States shall, under any pretence whatever, assume to decide on the validity of the claim of any person to the service or labor of any other person, or surrender up any such person to the claimant, on pain of being dismissed from the service.'

"And I do hereby enjoin upon, and order all persons engaged in the military and naval service of the United States to observe, obey and enforce within their respective spheres of service the act and sections above recited.

"And the executive will in due time recommend that all citizens of the United States who shall have remained loyal thereto throughout the rebellion, shall (upon the restoration of the constitutional relation between the United States and their respective States and people, if the relation shall have been suspended or disturbed) be compensated for all losses by acts of the United States, including the loss of slaves.

"In witness whereof, I have hereunto set my hand and caused the seal of the United States to be affixed.

"Done at the city of Washington, this twenty-second day of September, in the year of our Lord one thousand eight hundred and sixty-two, and of the independence of the United States the eighty-seventh.

"By the President: "ABRAHAM LINCOLN.

"WM. H. SEWARD, *Secretary of State.*"

"Such a bold movement was necessarily distasteful to the traitors, and while the southern journals pronounced it to be a bid for the slaves to rise in insurrection, a bid which none but a barbarian would devise, it was denounced in the Richmond congress, and a resolution was there offered, exhorting the people to slay every union soldier and raider found within their borders, and offering a reward to every negro, who would, after the first of January, 1863, kill a unionist.

"The other important proclamation was issued on the first of January, 1863, and was worded as follows:

"*Whereas*, on the twenty-second day of September, in the year of our Lord one thousand eight hundred and sixty-two, a proclamation was issued by the president of the United States, containing among other things the following, to wit:

"That on the first day of January, in the year of our Lord one thousand eight hundred and sixty-three, all persons held as slaves within any state, or designated part of a state, the people whereof shall then be in rebellion against the United States, shall be then, thenceforth and forever free, and the executive government of the United States, including the military and naval authorities thereof, will recognize and maintain the freedom of such persons, and will do no act or acts to repress such persons, or any of them, in any efforts they may make for their actual freedom.

"That the executive will, on the first day of January aforesaid, by proclamation, designate the states and parts of states, if any, in which the people therein respectively shall then be in rebellion against the United States, and the fact that any state, or the people thereof, shall on that day be in good faith represented in the congress of the United States by members chosen thereto, at elections wherein a majority of the qualified voters of such states shall have participated, shall, in the absence of strong countervailing testimony, be deemed conclusive evidence that such state and the people thereof are not then in rebellion against the United States.

"Now, therefore, I, Abraham Lincoln, president of the United States, by virtue of the power in me vested as commander-in-chief of the army and navy of the United States in time of actual armed rebellion against the authority and government of the United States, and as a fit and necessary war measure for suppressing said rebellion, do, on this first day of January, in the year of our Lord one thousand eight hundred and sixty-three, and in accordance with my purpose so to do, publicly proclaimed for the full period of one hundred days from the day of the first above-mentioned order, and designate, as the states and parts of states wherein the people thereof respectively are this day in rebellion against the United States, the following to-wit: Arkansas, Texas, Louisiana, except the parishes of St. Bernard, Plaquemines, Jefferson, St. John, St. Charles, St. James, Ascension, Assumption, Terre Bonne, La fourche, St. Mary, St. Martin and Orleans, including the city of New Orleans. Mississippi, Alabama, Florida, Georgia, South Carolina, North Carolina, and Virginia, except the forty-eight counties designated as West Virginia, and also the counties of Berkeley, Accomac, Northampton, Elizabeth City, York, Princess Ann, and Norfolk, including the cities of Norfolk and Portsmouth, and which excepted parts are, for the present, left precisely as if this proclamation were not issued.

"And by virtue of the power and for the purpose aforesaid, I do order and declare that all persons held as slaves within said designated states, and parts of states are, and henceforward shall be free; and that the executive government of the United States, including the military and naval authorities thereof, will recognize and maintain the freedom of said persons.

"And I hereby enjoin upon the people so declared to be free, to abstain from all violence, unless in necessary self-defense, and I recommend to them, that in all cases, when allowed, they labor faithfully for reasonable wages.

"And I further declare and make known that such persons of suitable condition will be received into the armed service of the United States to garrison forts, positions, stations, and other places, and to man vessels of all sorts in said service.

"And upon this, sincerely believed to be an act of justice, warranted by the constitution, upon military necessity, I invoke the considerate judgment of mankind and the gracious favor of Almighty God.

"In witness whereof, I have hereunto set my hand and caused the seal of the United States to be affixed.

[L. S.] "Done at the city of Washington, this first day of January, in the year of our Lord one thousand eight hundred and sixty-three, and of the Independence of the United States of America the eighty-seventh.

"By the President: "ABRAHAM LINCOLN.

"WILLIAM H. SEWARD, *Secretary of State.*"

PART II.

GEOGRAPHICAL HISTORY

OF THE

UNITED STATES.

CHAPTER I.

NEW ENGLAND STATES.

MAINE.

Maine, the most eastern of the United States, and by far the largest of the New England States, lies between latitude 42° 57′ and 47° 32′ N., and longitude 66° 52′ and 71° 6′ W. It is bounded on the north by Canada East; on the south by the Atlantic Ocean; on the east by New Brunswick and Passamaquoddy Bay; and on the west by New Hampshire and Canada East. Its greatest length from north to south is 303 miles; from east to west, 212 miles; area, 31,766 square miles, or 20,330,240 acres. In 1860, only about one-eighth of this vast territory, or about 2,704,133 acres, was under cultivation.

Maine, as a general thing, is hilly and mountainous, and has its culminating point at Mount Katahdin, at an altitude of 5,385 feet. A broken range of mountains, supposed to be a continuation of the White Mountains of New Hampshire, extends across the state in a north-easterly direction, and terminates with Mars Hill, in Aroostook county, about one mile from the eastern boundary of the state. This mountain chain forms the water-shed between the basin of the St. Johns river and the Atlantic ocean. Extensive quarries of granite, of the finest quality, are found upon the coast; and in the interior are metamorphic rocks and minerals. The coast line is very irregular, being indented with numerous bays, which receive some of the largest rivers of New England. Passamaquoddy, the largest bay, is at the south-eastern extremity of the state. It is fifteen miles long, and ten miles wide, and is entered by three passages. The other principal indentations are Englishman's, Frenchman's, Penobscot and Casco bays. The principal rivers are Penobscot, Kennebec, Androscoggin and Saco. The Penobscot is the largest, and is formed by the junction of the Seboois river with the

West Branch. The extreme length of the river is above 300 miles, and it has a course, after its junction with the Seboois, of 135 miles. The western branch rises in the extreme western part of the state, at the foot of the Green mountains, and in its course drains the Chesuncook and Bamedumpok lakes. At Bangor, 58 miles from the mouth of the river, vessels of the largest size are received. The source of the Kennebec river is Moosehead lake, which is about 1,000 feet above the level of the sea. It has a length of 160 miles, and receives the waters of the Dead and Sebasticook rivers. The Androscoggin river originates in Coos county, New Hampshire, in Umbagog lake, and, after a very irregular course of about 150 miles, enters the Kennebec, about 20 miles above the mouth of the latter river. The Saco river rises among the White mountains, in the southern part of Coos county, New Hampshire, and, after flowing in a south-easterly direction, through Maine, enters the Atlantic in York county. The St. John river separates Maine from Canada East, and the St. Croix partially separates the same state from New Brunswick.

No other state in the union contains so great a number of beautiful lakes, as Maine. Of these, Moosehead, in a wild and picturesque region, lying between the counties of Somerset and Piscataquis, is the largest. It is 35 miles long and 10 miles broad. There is a steamboat upon the lake, used to convey lumber to the Kennebec river. The water is deep, and abounds with fish, among which trout are conspicuous. Chesumcook lake, 26 miles long and four miles broad, is merely an expansion of the Penobscot river. Schoodic lakes are two beautiful sheets of water in Washington county, drained by an affluent of the St. Croix river.

On the south-eastern coast of the state are a number of islands, of which the principal are Fox islands, and Grand Menan and Mount Desert Islands. The latter, in Frenchman's bay, is 15 miles long and 11 miles broad. The inhabitants, numbering more than 200, are chiefly engaged in shipping and fisheries.

Maine has extensive forests of pine, spruce, hemlock, and maple, and it is estimated that one-third of the ships of America are built in this state. The white and red oak abound in the vicinity of the coast; and in the districts at the headwaters of the Kennebec and Penobscot, are found the pine and spruce. Butternut and white walnut are scarce, but maple, birch and ash grow in abundance. The mineral productions of Maine are not very extensive. Considerable iron is found upon the Aroostook river, and small quantities of copper and lead are found in the vicinity of Dexter and Lubec. Large quantities of slate are found between the Kennebec and St. Johns rivers.

The climate of Maine is extremely regular, the temperature ranging from 30° below zero to 100° above. The soil in the mountainous regions, and in districts bordering upon the south-eastern coast, is poor, and wholly unadapted to cultivation. The most fertile portions of the country comprise the basin of the St. John's river, and the territory lying between the Kennebec and Penobscot rivers. The staple products are corn, rye, barley, buckwheat, beans, potatoes, oats and hay. Wheat is produced, though in limited quantities. Hops and flax are also cultivated, and large quantities of maple sugar are manufactured.

No other state in the union has as great a number of good harbors, or affords such natural advantages for commerce, as Maine. The length of the coast, in a direct line, is 278 miles. Considering the irregularity of the coast, and following the same in all its windings, the former length is increased three times. The most of the rivers flowing into the Atlantic are safe for the largest vessels, from ten to fifty miles from the ocean. Lumber, which is produced by means of these rivers, is the chief export. The lumber produced in 1860 was valued at $6,598,565. In 1863 the exports amounted to $7,016,342; imports $3,911,468. The increase of exports of the latter year over 1862 was over $1,500,000.

AUGUSTA

Is the capital, and Portland and Bangor the largest cities of the state. Augusta is the seat of justice of Kennebec county, and is sixty miles north-east of Portland, on both sides of the Kennebec, about forty-five miles from the mouth of that river. The business portion of the city lies under an elevation, which rises a short distance from the river. On the summit of this elevation are a number of hotels, and a large portion of the city residences. The state house, in the southern portion of the city, is an imposing building, of light granite construction, in front of which is a spacious park, containing ornamental trees and flowers, and intersected with gravel walks. Augusta contains twelve churches, ten hotels, six banks, several public schools, and a female academy. A dam, five hundred and ninety feet long, has been constructed across the river, in the northern limits of the city, which greatly improves the navigation above, and affords immense hydraulic power to the manufactories and foundries below. A passenger and railroad bridge span the river, about one-fourth of a mile apart, the former being five hundred and the latter nine hundred feet long. The Portland and Kennebec railroad passes through Augusta, and terminates at Waterville. Population in 1860, 7,609.

PORTLAND,

The capital of Cumberland county, is on the eastern side of Casco bay, one hundred and five miles north-east of Boston, two hundred and ninety-two miles south-east of Montreal, and three hundred and seventeen miles in the same direction from Quebec. It is the largest city of Maine, and is the southern terminus of the Atlantic and St. Lawrence railroad. Its site is a hilly peninsula, about three miles long, and averaging three-fourths of a mile in breadth. The harbor, nearly surrounded by land, is one of the finest in the world, being of sufficient depth to receive the largest vessels, and guarded at its principal entrance by several strong fortresses. Portland is finely laid off, and contains a large number of handsome buildings, generally constructed of brick. Congress street, extending from Munjoy's to Bramhill's, the former on the eastern, and the latter on the western side of the peninsula, is the principal thoroughfare of the city.

The most prominent public building of the city is the city hall, erected in 1859. The building, of dark sandstone construction, is surmounted by a lofty dome. The other principal buildings are the custom house, mechanics' hall, a natural history building, mercantile association and Maine charitable mechanics' association buildings, and a large number of churches. Portland is rich in commerce and manufactures. Her exports for the year 1864 amounted to $3,824,591; imports $3,018,063. The city is extensively engaged in ship building, and contains manufactories of locomotives, railway carriages, &c. Portland has an abundant supply of pure water, and is lighted with gas. Population in 1860, 26,342.

BANGOR,

The capital of Penobscot county, is sixty-six miles north-east of Augusta, and one hundred and twenty-six miles in the same direction from Portland. It is on the right bank of the Penobscot, and on both sides of the Kenduskeig, which enters the former river about sixty miles from the ocean. A bridge, one thousand three hundred and twenty feet long, extends to Brewer, on the opposite bank of the river, and a short distance below is the Portland harbor, five hundred yards long, and deep enough, at high water, to receive the largest ships. The city has a pleasant location, commanding a fine view of the river and surrounding country. Bangor has a large number of hotels, colleges, and churches. A first class hotel, called the Bangor house, is probably inferior to none in the state. The city contains four large foundries, four steam furniture manufactories, a large number of steam sawing and planing mills, fifteen banks, twelve churches, and a theological seminary. Bangor has railway communications with Old Town, and cities on the Penobscot and Kennebec railroad. Population in 1860, 16,407.

Main has six hundred miles of railroad, sixty-nine banks, and four thousand five hundred public schools. The latter are supported by money arising from the sale of public lands, and a tax of one-half of one per cent. on the capital of banks. The state also contains three colleges, twelve hundred churches, and forty-nine periodical publications. The government consists of a governor, senate, and house of representatives. Excepting criminals and paupers, persons have the right of suffrage after residing in the country three months. Maine sends six members to congress, and is entitled to eight electoral votes for president.

NEW HAMPSHIRE.

New Hampshire, one of the original thirteen United States, and next to Maine, the largest of the New England states, lies between latitude 42° 41′ and 45° 11′ N., and longitude 70° 40′ and 72° 28′ W. It is bounded on the north by Canada East, on the south by Massachusetts, on the east by Maine and the Atlantic ocean, and on the west by Vermont and Canada East. Its greatest length from north to south is one hundred and seventy-six miles; width, forty-five miles; area, nine thousand two hundred and eighty square miles, or five million nine hundred and thirty-nine thousand two hundred acres. New Hampshire is often called the "Granite State," on account of the abundance of that mineral. From the magnificent scenery of the White mountains, it is also styled the "Switzerland of America."

With the exception of a small district in the south-eastern portion of the state, the country is hilly and mountainous. The White mountains extend nearly across the state from north to south. They commence near the head waters of the Aroostook river, in Maine, and reach their culminating in Coos county, New Hampshire. The base of the mountains is a broad platteau, from sixteen to eighteen hundred feet high. The White mountains are more admired by travelers, and attract a larger number of tourists than any other natural objects in the United States, excepting Niagara. The lofty mountains, wild valleys, beautiful lakes, grand cascades and torrents, alike contribute beauty and grandeur to this delightful region. Twenty bold peaks, with deep, narrow gorges, rise abruptly to the hight of five thousand feet. Mount Washington, the highest summit, and culminating point of New England, is eighty-five miles north of Concord, in Coos county, and has an altitude of six thousand two hundred and eighty-five feet. The sides, which are remarkably steep, are covered for about three-fourths of the distance from the base to the summit, with a thick growth of trees. The upper part has a conical form, and is frequently enveloped in mist and fog. Mount Adams, next in hight to Mount Washington, is in the same county, and has an altitude of five thousand seven hundred and fifty-nine feet. Mount Jefferson, directly north of Mount Washington, between the latter peak and Mount Adams, has an altitude of five thousand six hundred and fifty-seven feet. Mount Lafayette is a peak of the Franconia range, in Grafton county, seventy-five miles north-west of Concord. Hight, five thousand five hundred feet. Immediately across the valley is Profile or Cannon mountain, which is covered with dense forests, till you arrive in the vicinity of the summit. This peak, though exceeded in hight by the surrounding mountains, is none the less interesting. At the foot of this mountain, near the Franconia notch, is the Profile house, a favorite resort of tourists.

Other elevations of importance are Mount Madison, five thousand four hundred and fifteen feet high, Mount Monroe, five thousand three hundred and forty-nine feet high, and Mount Franklin four thousand eight hundred and fifty feet high. (See views of White mountains.) The principal elevations, independent of the main chain, are the Kearsarge mountains, in Merrimac county, two thousand four hundred and sixty-eight feet high, and the Blue hills, in the south-eastern portion of the state, one thousand one hundred and fifty-one feet high. The upper portions of the former consist of bare granite rock.

The most important rivers of New Hampshire are the Connecticut and Merrimac. The Connecticut has its source in a small sheet of water, a few miles north of Connecticut lake. The Merrimac river, formed by the confluence of the Pemigewasset and Winnipiseogee rivers, flows first in a southerly, and, after entering Massachusetts, in a north-easterly direction, and reaches the Atlantic near Newburyport. Winnipiseogee, the principal lake in the state, is drained by the river of the same name. This large and beautiful sheet of water, lying between Carroll and

Belknap counties, is twenty-five miles long and ten miles wide. Its multitude of islands, and irregular form, in connection with the romantic beauty of the surrounding scenery, render it one of the most pleasing places in the state. Its waters are very deep and pure, and it is thought by some to rival Loch Lomond in beauty.

The forest trees of New Hampshire are various. On the mountain slopes are vast forests of pine, which sometimes grow over two hundred feet high. The other principal trees are the oak, maple, spruce, beech and hemlock. The climate of New Hampshire resembles that of Maine, the summers being short, and the winters long and severe.

Though there are some fertile districts, the state, as a general thing, is not adapted to agricultural pursuits. In 1860 there were two hundred and thirty-eight thousand nine hundred and sixty-six bushels of wheat, and one million four hundred and fourteen thousand six hundred and twenty-eight bushels of corn produced.

Concord is the capital. Manchester and Portsmouth are the principal towns.

CONCORD,

The capital of New Hampshire, and seat of justice of Merrimac county, is on the western bank of the Merrimac river, fifty-nine miles north-west of Boston. The ground on which the city is built is slightly elevated, and comprises a district two miles long, and three-fourths of a mile broad. Main street, the principal thoroughfare, extends through the entire length of the city from north to south, and contains the business houses, hotels, churches, etc. State street contains a Methodist general biblical institute, and a huge state prison of granite construction. The state house is a hewn granite edifice, one hundred and twenty-six feet long, forty-nine feet wide, and two stories high, standing in the center of a common, finely ornamented with maple and elm trees. The falls in the Merrimac at Concord afford valuable water power to the foundries, mills, etc. The city contains nine churches, four newspaper offices, eight banks, and a state lunatic asylum. Population in 1860, 10,896.

MANCHESTER,

A town of Hillsborough county, and chief city of New Hampshire, is on the eastern bank of the Merrimac river, eighteen miles south-east of Concord, and fifty-nine miles north-west of Boston. The city is finely laid off on an elevated plain ninety-five feet above the river. The principal street is a mile and a half long, and one hundred feet broad, and divides the city into two nearly equal parts. The western portion of the city is chiefly built of wood, and contains a number of handsome villas and residences. The eastern portion, or the part bordering on the river, is built almost wholly of brick, and contains the business establishments, hotels, etc. The most important buildings are the town house, the different churches and public schools, and the athenæum. The latter, established in 1844, has a free reading room, and a library of thirty-five hundred volumes. "The system of public instruction comprises a high school, two grammar schools, an intermediate, six middle, and twelve primary schools, besides others not classed." The city is furnished with gas by a company established in 1851, having a capital, at the present time, amounting to about one hundred thousand dollars.

Near Manchester the Merrimac has a descent of fifty feet, called Amoskeag Falls, which, in connection with a dam a short distance below, affords sufficient hydraulic power to run several hundred thousand spindles.

The most important corporations of Manchester are the Amoskeag manufacturing company, and the Stark mills, the former employing twenty-five hundred persons, both male and female, and producing daily sixty-five thousand yards of tickings, drillings, sheetings, and pantaloon stuffs, and the latter twelve hundred persons, and manufacturing daily thirty thousand yards of sheetings, seventeen thousand yards of drilling, and upwards of five thousand seamless bags.

The city contains twelve churches, ten newspaper publications, five insurance companies, and four banks with a capital exceeding five hundred thousand dollars. Population, 20,107.

PORTSMOUTH,

A city and semi-capital of Rockingham county, is on the southern bank of the Piscataqua river, three miles from its mouth, and fifty-five miles north-east of Boston. The site of the city is a slightly elevated peninsula, formed by the Piscataqua river. It is connected by bridges with Grand island and Kittery, directly opposite in Maine. Prominent among the public buildings are the state arsenal and athenæum, the finest structures in the city. The latter has a library of ten thousand choice volumes. On an island facing the city is a United States navy yard, containing "three immense ship houses, and a floating balance dock, constructed at a cost of about eight hundred thousand dollars."

Portsmouth is the only port of entry in the state. The harbor, having an average depth of about fifty-five feet, lies between the city and the sea, and is large enough to accommodate upwards of two thousand vessels. The city contains nine churches, four newspaper publications, five banks, a large number of manufactories, and an excellent system of public schools. Population in 1860, 9,335.

New Hampshire has forty-four cotton, sixty-one woollen, and twenty-nine iron factories; a large number of paper mills, fifty-one banks, seven hundred churches, thirty-eight newspaper publications, and numerous and well conducted free schools. Population of the state in 1860, 326,073, of which 325,579 were white, and 494 colored.

In New Hampshire the governor, senate, and house of representatives are elected annually. The senate is composed of twelve and the house of representatives of two hundred and eighty-six members. The governor receives a salary of one thousand dollars per annum.

VERMONT.

Vermont, one of the United States, and the first state admitted after the adoption of the federal constitution, lies between latitude 42° 44′ and 45° N., and longitude 71° 33′ and 73° 25′

W. It is one hundred and fifty miles long, and from forty to eighty-five miles wide, including an area of ten thousand two hundred and twelve square miles, or six millions five hundred and thirty-five thousand six hundred and eighty acres. It is bounded on the north by Canada East, on the south by Massachusetts, on the east by the Connecticut river, which separates Vermont from New Hampshire, and on the west by Lake Champlain and New York.

The surface of the country is hilly and mountainous. The Green mountains traverse the entire length of the state from north to south. In the southern part of the state they form a single chain, but at Northfield, twelve miles south of Montpelier, a range branches off in a north-easterly direction, and forms the boundary line between Canada East and the states of Maine and New Hampshire. The highest peak is Mount Mansfield, twenty-two miles north of Montpelier, having an altitude of four thousand three hundred and fifty-nine feet. The other peaks range from a hight of two thousand to five thousand feet, and are all covered with vegetation, and cultivated to their summits.

The principal rivers of Vermont are the Missisque, Lamoille, Winooski, Otter, and Passumpsic. The Missisque and Lamoille rise among the mountains in Orleans county, and, after a course of seventy-five and seventy miles, enter Lake Champlain, the former in Missisque, and the latter in Chittenden county. The Winooski river rises in Washington county, and flows into Lake Champlain, five miles west of Burlington. At Winooski village, near Burlington, the river has a fall of twenty feet. Lake Champlain separates Vermont from New York, for over one hundred miles. Its entire length is one hundred and thirty-five miles, and it has a width varying from one to twelve miles. Its outline is very irregular, and its surface is diversified by numerous beautiful islands. Its depth varies from fifty to three hundred feet. Its waters are discharged into the St. Lawrence through the Richelieu river. Vessels of the largest size navigate the lake with perfect safety. It is connected with the Hudson river by the Champlain canal, thus establishing uninterrupted water communication with the principal cities of New York. The lake abounds with trout, salmon, pike, and other fish.

The Vermont side of the lake is extremely fertile, but on the opposite shore the country is wild, rocky, and desolate.

Vermont shares Lake Memphremagog with Canada East. This lake is about thirty miles long, and has a width varying from one to five miles. About eight miles of its length is in Orleans county, Vermont; the remainder is in Canada. Its waters are discharged through Magog outlet, into the St. Francis river, and from thence into St. Peter's lake, an expansion of the St. Lawrence river.

Vermont, though subject to severe weather, is one of the healthiest states in the union. The temperature ranges from seventeen degrees below to ninety-two degrees above zero. The country suffers from frost as early as the first of September, though the weather does not become severe till December.

The best quality of iron ore is found along the western base of the Green mountains, and considerable quantities of lead, zinc and copper are found in different parts of the state. At Rutland are rich quarries of statuary marble. Small quantities of gold have also been discovered. A lump weighing ten and a half ounces was discovered in Newfane, in 1826. At the towns of Bridgewater, Stowe, and Plymouth this precious ore is found.

The soil of Vermont is a rich marl, and produces Indian corn, oats, wheat, rye, potatoes, and hops in great abundance. The mountainous district is covered with a heavy grass, affording excellent pasturage for cattle. Among the forest trees are found the hemlock, fir, spruce, oak, beech, sugar-maple, pine, hickory, elm, butternut, birch, cedar, and basswood. Vermont has a valuable lumber trade, and is extensively engaged in the manufacture of maple sugar. In 1860, there were two millions eight hundred and twenty-three thousand one hundred and fifty-seven acres of land under cultivation.

In manufactures, Vermont holds only a secondary rank among the United States. The number of manufacturing establishments in the state in 1850, engaged in mining and the mechanical arts, numbered fourteen hundred and eighty-nine.

The commerce of Vermont is carried on by means of Lake Champlain. Her imports for the year 1862, amounted to two millions five hundred and sixty-seven thousand eight hundred and ninety-two dollars; exports, seven hundred and thirty-six thousand six hundred and sixty-three dollars.

The state contains five hundred and fifty-six miles of railroad, fifty woollen mills, ten cotton mills, five hundred and ninety-six churches, one hundred and eighteen academies and high schools, two thousand nine hundred and thirty-seven district free schools, and thirty-six weekly and six daily newspapers.

Montpelier is the capital, and Burlington is the largest city.

MONTPELIER,

The capital, is the seat of justice of Washington county, on the right bank of the Onion river, two hundred miles north-west of Boston, on the Boston and St. Lawrence railroad.

The most important building is the state house, a rich granite edifice one hundred and fifty feet long, one hundred feet wide, and surmounted by a dome, the top of which is one hundred feet above the ground. Montpelier contains six churches, five newspaper offices, three banks, an academy, and several other schools. Population in 1860, 2,411.

BURLINGTON,

The metropolis of Vermont, and seat of justice of Chittenden county, is on Burlington bay, forty miles north-east of Montpelier. At the mouth of the bay, on Juniper island, is a light house, erected by the United States government, and a breakwater to protect shipping. Burlington has excellent water communication by means of Lake Champlain, and is on railroad lines leading to important cities of New England and Canada. The Vermont university is located in the eastern suburbs of the the town, on an elevation, two hundred and eighty-one feet above the level of the sea. This institution, consisting of four buildings, was founded in 1791. The city has four newspapers offices, four banks, several churches, and seven thousand three hundred and seventy-five tons of shipping. In 1860 the inhabitants numbered 7,713.

ST. JOHNSBURY,

An important town and capital of Caledonia county, Vermont, is thirty-six miles north-east of Montpelier, and fifty miles east of Burlington. It is on the western bank of the Passumpsic river, which affords abundant water power for the mills and manufactories in the town. It contains forty stores, and a manufactory for Fairbanks' scales. It has also four foundries with machine shops, two banks, and a number of churches. Population 3,500. (See views of St. Johnsbury.)

St. Johnsbury Centre is two miles north of St. Johnsbury, on the Passumpsic river, and Passumpsic river railroad. It contains four churches, two carriage manufactories, and three mills. Population 750. (See views of St. Johnsbury Centre.)

Waterford is a township of Caledonia county, about forty-five miles north of Montpelier, intersected by the Connecticut river and the Passumpsic river railroad. The surface is very uneven, and is traversed by ridges of hills and cliffs. (See views of Waterford.)

The population of Vermont has a steady, though not rapid increase. In 1790 the inhabitants numbered only eighty-five thousand four hundred and sixteen. In 1860 the state had a population of three hundred and fifteen thousand and ninety-eight, of which three hundred and fourteen thousand three hundred and eighty-nine were white, and seven hundred and nine colored. The government of the state is administered by a governor, lieutenant governor, senate and house of representatives. The senate consists of thirty and the house of representatives of two hundred and thirty members. Vermont sends three members to the national house of representatives, and is entitled to five electoral votes for president.

MASSACHUSETTS.

Massachusetts, one of the thirteen original United States, lies between latitude 41° 15′ and 42° 53′ N., and longitude 69° 56′ and 73° 32′ W. It is bounded on the north by Vermont and New Hampshire; on the south by Connecticut, Rhode Island,

Buzzard's Bay and Vineyard Sound; on the east by Cape Cod Bay, Massachusetts Bay, and the Atlantic Ocean; and on the west by New York. Its length from east to west is one hundred and sixty miles; from north to south, forty-seven to one hundred and ten miles; area, seven thousand eight hundred square miles, or four millions nine hundred and ninety-two thousand acres.

In the western part of the state are the Green mountains, and, scattered over the country, are solitary peaks, sometimes attaining a great hight. Mounts Tom and Holyoke, on opposite sides of the Connecticut river, in Hampden county, are isolated peaks, having respective hights of twelve hundred and fourteen and nine hundred and thirty feet. Mount Wachusett, in Worcester county, two thousand and eighteen feet high, commands a brilliant prospect. Saddle mountain, the culminating point of the state, is in Berkshire county, and has an altitude of three thousand eight hundred feet. The north-eastern portion of the state is hilly, and the south-eastern low and sandy.

The western part of the state is remarkable for the variety and beauty of its scenery. Berkshire county, in particular, deserves the attention of all lovers of the picturesque. It has an area of one thousand square miles, and lies east of the Green mountains, occupying the entire length of the state from north to south. The surface is very uneven, and in some parts mountainous. Saddle mountain, in the northern, and Bald Peak, in the southern part of the county, are the principal elevations. Monument mountain, in the township of Stockbridge, has a bold and rocky summit, and a perpendicular ascent of over two hundred feet, from the valley below. (See views of Monument mountain.) A deep ravine, of great wildness, in the same township, called the Ice Glen, contains ice during the whole year. (See views of the Ice Glen.) Among the other remarkable natural objects of Berkshire county, may be mentioned the Falls of the Housatonic, near Dalton; a rock in Marlborough, weighing nearly fifty tons, and so accurately balanced that it will move, when slightly pressed; Hanging mountain, rising perpendicularly three hundred feet above the Farmington river; and the Natural Bridge, on Hudson's brook, in North Adams. (See views of Natural Bridge.) At this point, a fissure, fifty feet deep and five hundred feet long, has been worn through solid rock, forming a bridge forty-seven feet above the water.

The principal rivers of the state, are the Connecticut, Merrimac and Housatonic. The Merrimac has a course of forty miles, in the state, and on its banks are the cities of Lowell, Lawrence, Andover and Newburyport. The falls and rapids of both this river and the Connecticut, render navigation difficult, but afford immense water-power for the manufacturing cities through which they pass.

The soil and climate of Massachusetts are unfavorable for agriculture. The south-eastern portion of the state is low and sandy, and salt marshes abound near the coast. The western half is the most productive, and in the Connecticut and Housatonic valleys there are extremely fertile districts. The staple productions are, Indian corn, oats, potatoes, rye, buckwheat, barley, fruits, hay, and maple sugar. In 1860, Massachusetts produced one hundred and nineteen thousand seven hundred and eighty-three bushels of wheat, two millions one hundred and fifty-seven thousand and sixty-three bushels of corn, three millions two hundred and thirty-three thousand one hundred and ninety-eight pounds of tobacco, and three hundred and seventy-seven thousand two hundred and sixty-seven pounds of wool.

In proportion to her size, Massachusetts holds the first rank in the union as a manufacturing state. According to the manufacturing statistics of 1860, there were eight thousand one hundred and seventy-six establishments in the state, employing a capital of one hundred and thirty-three millions of dollars. The value of her manufactures for the same year amounted to two hundred and sixty-six millions of dollars. There are also in the state one hundred and fifty woollen mills, three hundred cotton mills, thirteen carpet mills, and many iron foundries and nail factories. The manufacture of boots and shoes alone amounts to fifty millions of dollars a year.

In commercial importance, Massachusetts is second only to New York. Her principal exports are her manufactures, rocks and ice. She is largely engaged in fisheries, which give employment to over thirty thousand persons. Boston exports an average of one hundred thousand tons of ice yearly. Granite and iron are the most important mineral products. Mines of lead were worked as early as 1765, at Northampton. Coal is found in limited quantities in the vicinity of Mansfield.

Boston is the capital, and largest city of the state. Other important cities are Lowell, Cambridge, Roxbury, Charlestown and Worcester.

BOSTON,

The capital, is one of the oldest towns in the union, and, next to New York, is the most important commercial city in the United States. It is the capital of Suffolk county, and is situated at the western extremity of Massachusetts bay, four hundred and sixty-four miles northeast of Washington, and about one-half of that distance from New York. The city is divided into three parts, viz: Boston Proper, or Old Boston, East Boston and South Boston. A very hilly and uneven peninsula, of five hundred acres, forms the site of Boston Proper, which is connected with Roxbury by a narrow isthmus, about a mile and a quarter long. This isthmus was formerly, during rainy weather, flooded with water, but it has recently been improved, and is now traversed by several good roads. Boston is also connected with the surrounding cities by a number of bridges, of which the Charles river bridge, connecting the city with Charlestown; Old Cambridge bridge, two thousand seven hundred and fifty-eight feet long, crossing the Charles river to Cambridge road; South Boston bridge, one thousand five hundred and fifty feet long, leading to South Boston; and Canal bridge, connecting Boston with Letchmere Point, now Cambridge, are the most important. South Boston is on the southern side of the harbor, between Boston Proper and Fort Independence. East Boston, the terminus of the Grand Junction Railroad, occupies about six hundred and sixty acres of the western portion of Noddle's Island.

Originally, the streets of Boston were narrow and crooked; but much has recently been done to improve them. The most important streets are Tremont and Washington. Some of the fashionable promenades are bordered with beautiful elms, some of which are over a century old. The Boston Common, an inclosure of fifty acres, in the western part of Old Boston, near the Charles river, is one of the finest public parks in America. It was formerly called "Tower's Field," and was used as a town cow-pasture. In the center of the common is a pond, from which spouts a large fountain, from fifty to sixty feet high. The grounds are surrounded by an elegant and costly iron fence, three hundred and sixty rods in length. Between the common and the river is a botanic garden, covering twenty-five acres of ground.

The state-house was built in 1798, and holds a conspicuous place among the public buildings of the city. The building is one hundred and seventy feet long, sixty-five feet wide, and is surmounted by a dome thirty feet high, and one hundred and twenty feet above the ground. On the entrance floor is a statue of Washington, by Chaucer. Faneuil Hall, the "Cradle of Liberty," as it is called, is an object of much interest, as being the place where the orators, in the days of Hancock and Adams, roused the people to resistance against British oppression.

The Quincy Market, erected at a cost of one hundred and fifty thousand dollars, is five hundred feet long, fifty feet wide, two stories high, and surmounted by a lofty dome. The City Hall, erected in 1864 and 1865, is one of the handsomest buildings in the United States. It is constructed of granite, which was brought from Concord, New Hampshire, and cost the city nearly six hundred thousand dollars. The Merchant's Exchange, on State street, is two hundred and fifty feet long, seventy-five feet broad, and cost one hundred and seventy-five thousand dollars. "The front is composed of Quincy granite, with four pilasters, each a single stone forty-five feet high, and weighing about fifty-five tons." In the Music Hall, on Winter street, is the "Great Organ," the richest and most powerful instrument of the kind ever constructed. It was built at Ludwigslust, Germany, and cost sixty thousand dollars. It is sixty feet high, forty-eight feet wide, twenty-four feet deep, has eighty-nine stops, and about six thousand pipes.

Prominent among the Boston hotels, is the Tremont house, a first-class hotel on Tremont street. The Winthrop house is also a fine hotel, on Tremont street. The other principal hotels are the Revere house, on Bowdoin square; the American house, on Hanover street; and the Parker house.

Boston contains, also, a large number of libraries, the most noted of which are the Boston Athenæum, containing sixty thousand volumes; the Massachusetts Historical Society, having twelve thousand volumes; the American Academy of Arts and Sciences, having fifteen thousand volumes; the Mercantile Library Association, thirteen thousand five hundred volumes; and the State Library, having ten thousand volumes. The Public Library building, erected in 1858, at a cost of three hundred and sixty-three thousand six hundred and thirty-three dollars, is directly opposite the Common, on Boylston street, and contains ninety-five thousand volumes.

Boston supports an immense foreign and domestic commerce. Of the three thousand and eleven vessels that entered the port of Boston during the year ending June 30, 1863, eight hundred and thirty-six were American, and two thousand one hundred and seventy-five foreign. Boston receives an abundant supply of fresh water from Lake Cochituate, twenty miles west of the city. The water is received in an immense reservoir in Brookline, by means of a brick water-pipe, from whence it is conveyed to different reservoirs throughout the city. Boston contains one hundred churches, and the same number of periodical publications. Population, in 1860, one hundred and seventy-seven thousand eight hundred and forty. (See views of Boston.)

LOWELL,

A city of Massachusetts, and, next to Boston, the largest in the state, is at the junction of the Concord with the Merrimac river, thirty miles north-west of Boston, and eight miles south from the dividing line between New Hampshire and the state in which it is situated. Five railroads, establishing an uninterrupted line of communication with cities on the sea coast, and in the interior, have their terminus at Lowell. The city is regularly laid off, and contains three handsome public parks, or commons as they are more commonly called. The streets are very direct, and intersect each other at right angles.

The principal public buildings are the court house and county jail, the former erected in 1851, at a cost of one hundred thousand dollars, the latter in 1855–56, at a cost of one hundred and fifty thousand dollars. Other noted edifices are Mechanics' building, Huntington hall, and Wentworth's, Carlton, and Appleton blocks. The chief libraries of the city are the Merchants' association and city library, the former containing nine thousand and the latter twelve hundred volumes.

At Lowell the Merrimac river has a perpendicular pitch of thirty-three feet, called the Pawtucket falls, which affords immense water power to this great manufacturing town. Thirteen manufacturing companies in Lowell, in 1864, had in their possession fifty-four mills, and employed a capital of thirteen millions eight hundred and fifty thousand dollars. Lowell has thirty-two churches, forty-five primary, eight grammar, and one high school, several private schools, seven banks, two insurance companies, five newspaper offices, extensive manufactories of of cotton and woollen goods, carpets, prints, etc., consuming twenty-five millions pounds of cotton per annum; eleven machine shops, six carriage manufactories, four lumber dealing firms, four sash, door, and blind factories, and three paper mills.

"The sixth Massachusetts regiment, principally from Lowell, was the first to enter the field in response to the call of President Lincoln, April 15th, 1861, for seventy-five thousand volunteers. The regiment left Lowell on the 16th; on the 19th was attacked by a mob in Baltimore, and two of its members—Ladd and Whitney—both of Lowell, were killed. A monument to these first martyrs of the great American rebellion, has been erected in a public square in the heart of the city." The population of Lowell has been greatly increased by foreign emigration. Population in 1860, 36,827.

CAMBRIDGE,

An important city and semi-capital of Middlesex county, is on the northern bank of the Charles river, three miles north-east of Boston, with which city it is connected by water communication, and by the old Cambridge and canal bridges. Cambridge is finely laid off, the streets being broad, and shaded with lofty and majestic elms, some of which are nearly one hundred years old.

Cambridge is one of the oldest towns in the union, and is the seat of Harvard university. (See views of university.) This institution, founded in 1648, is the most interesting object connected with the town. It was named in honor of Rev. John Harvard, who bequeathed to it a legacy of seven hundred and eighty-one pounds. Its present fund exceeds one million dollars. A law and theological school, and a medical college, are connected with the university, and there is also a department for those wishing to enter upon a scientific course, independent of other branches. Of the twenty-one buildings belonging to the university, twenty are in Cambridge, and one in Grove street, Boston. Cambridge contains twenty churches, six banks, several hotels, the county buildings, post office, and a large number of manufactories. Population, 26,060.

ROXBURY,

Is an important town of Massachusetts, in Norfolk county, three miles south-west of Boston, on the Boston and Providence railroad. It is connected with Boston by several stage roads crossing the "Boston Neck." The site of the city presents every variety of surface, from the lofty hill, down to districts nearly level with the sea. From the summit of many of these hills, a good view can be obtained of the city of Boston, and much of the surrounding scenery. Roxbury might justly be regarded as a suburb of Boston, being closely connected in wealth and interest with that city. Many of the Boston business men have beautiful residences in Roxbury. Roxbury has manufactories of fire and steam engines, steam boilers, carpetings, fringe, tassels, leather, etc. Population, 25,137.

CHARLESTOWN,

A city of Middlesex county, .is on the northern side of the Charles river, directly opposite Boston. The peninsula on which the city is built, formed by the confluence of the Mystic with the Charles river, is, like most of the country in the vicinity, rugged and hilly. Charlestown is connected with Boston and Cambridge by the Prison Point bridge, which strikes the centre of canal bridge, which connects the two former cities. The city is finely built, having wide and shady streets, and many elegant edifices. Main, Bunker Hill, and Medford, running north and south, are the principal streets. The city contains four banks, a huge state prison, with accommodations for five hundred convicts, and a United States navy yard, occupying eighty acres, at the foot of Bunker Hill. The dry dock, built at a cost of six hundred and seventy thousand dollars, is at the upper end of the yard. It is three hundred and forty-one feet long, eighty feet wide, thirty feet deep, and constructed of granite.

"The chief object of interest, however, to persons visiting Charlestown, is the Bunker Hill monument, erected in commemoration of the first great battle fought between the British and Americans. It stands on Breed's Hill, usually called Bunker Hill, near the spot where the brave Warren fell. Its foundations, which are fifty feet above the level of the sea, are enclosed twelve feet under ground. The corner stone was laid by Marquis de Lafayette, June 17th, 1825. The fifteenth anniversary of the battle, June 17th, 1843, the completion of the monument was celebrated, in the presence of the president of the United States, many of the members of his cabinet, and a vast concourse of citizens. It consists of a plain granite shaft, two hundred and twenty feet high, thirty-one feet square at the base, and fifteen feet at the top. Within is a winding stairway, by which it is ascended to a chamber immediately under the apex, eleven feet in diameter, containing four windows, which afford a magnificent panoramic view of the surrounding country. In this chamber are two of the four cannon which constituted the whole train of field artillery possessed by the Americans at the commencement of the war, in April, 1775. These two pieces are named respectively Hancock and Adams." (See views of Bunker Hill.)

Mystic lake, five miles from the city, supplies Charlestown with a stream of pure, fresh water. Population in 1860, 25,063.

WORCESTER

Is the seat of justice of Worcester county, forty-five miles south-west of Boston. It is on the northern bank of the Blackstone river, partially environed with beautiful hills, and is intersected by six important railways. Main street is the chief business thoroughfare, and contains the court house, churches, and all the important public buildings of the city. The American antiquarian society building is eighty feet long, fifty feet wide, contains thirty-five thousand volumes, and "plaster casts of Michael Angelo's celebrated statues of Christ and Moses."

Worcester contains eighteen churches, seven banks, five newspaper offices, six insurance companies, an excellent system of schools, and a large number of rolling and woollen mills, foundries, etc. Population in 1860, 24,960.

In 1860 the population of Massachusetts was one million two hundred and thirty-one thousand and sixty-six, of whom one million two hundred and twenty-one thousand four hundred and sixty-four were white, and nine thousand six hundred and two were colored. The state contains one hundred and seventy-six banks, sixteen hundred miles of railroad divided between fifty-one companies, sixteen hundred and thirty-six churches, twenty-two daily papers, two hundred and eighty-two periodical publications, four thousand four hundred and forty-four public schools, seven hundred and fifty academies, four normal schools, five colleges, and three lunatic asylums.

The governor of Massachusetts receives a salary of two thousand five hundred dollars per annum. The senate is composed of forty and the house of representatives of three hundred and fifty-six members. Massachusetts is represented by eleven members in the national house of representatives, and is entitled to thirteen electoral votes for president.

CONNECTICUT.

Connecticut, one of the thirteen original United States, lies between latitude 41° and 42° 3′ N., and longitude 71° 55′ and 73° 50′ W. It is bounded on the north by Massachusetts, on the south by Long Island sound, on the east by Rhode Island, and on the west by New York. It greatest length from north to south is sixty-eight miles, from east to west about ninety-three miles, including an area of four thousand six hundred and seventy-four square miles, or two millions nine hundred and ninety-one thousand three hundred and sixty acres.

The surface of Connecticut is greatly diversified by mountains and hills. The Green mountains, which extend nearly across the state, reach no great hight, and would more properly be denominated hills. Many subordinate ridges are found between the Connecticut and Housatonic, and east of the former river are elevations supposed to be a part of the White mountain chain. On either side of the Connecticut, near its mouth, are walls of trap rock, through which the river, at some early period, has worn for itself a channel.

The principal rivers of Connecticut are the Housatonic, Connecticut, and Thames. The Housatonic rises in Berkshire county, Massachusetts, and, after a southerly course of one hundred and fifty miles, enters Long Island sound, fifteen miles below Derby. The river has a fall of one thousand feet from its source to its mouth, which, though derogatory to navigation, affords valuable water power to the numerous manufacturing towns upon its banks. The most beautiful descent of the river, occurs between Falls village and Canaan, thirty-seven miles north-east of New Haven. (See views of the Housatonic.) The Connecticut river is safe for large vessels as far north as Middletown, and the Housatonic as far as Derby. The Thames traverses the eastern portion of the state, and is navigable as far as Norwich, fourteen miles from its mouth.

In regard to climate, Connecticut ranks among the foremost of the United States. Her winters, like all of the New England states, are generally severe, but her springs are earlier, and summers, owing to her proximity to the sea, less subject to intense heat. The soil, especially in the valleys of the Connecticut, Housatonic, and Thames, is exceedingly fertile. The beautiful valley of the Connecticut, called by the Indians "the pleasant country," contains some of the oldest towns of the United States. The western half of the state is devoted to agriculture, the eastern chiefly to grazing and pasturage. The staple productions are butter, cheese, wool, maize, oats, barley, wheat, flax, hemp, and tobacco. Principal minerals, marble, freestone, and iron.

The commerce and manufactures of Connecticut, though not very large, are important. The value of the exports of the year ending June 30th, 1861, amounted to four hundred and twenty-one thousand three hundred and twenty dollars; imports, seven hundred and fifty-three thousand three hundred and nine dollars. According to the manufacturing statistics of the same year, the capital invested amounted to forty-five millions seven hundred and seventy thousand dollars; amount of the annual product, eighty-three millions.

The capitals of the state are Hartford and New Haven. Other important cities are Middletown, New London, and Norwich.

NEW HAVEN,

A city and capital of a county of the same name, and semi-capital of the state of Connecticut, is at the head of New Haven bay, a branch of Long Island sound, seventy-six miles north-east of New York, and one hundred miles south-west of Boston. The city is on a level and undulating plain, sloping gently back from the sea. The scenery which surrounds New Haven is in the highest degree picturesque and beautiful. On every side, except where it is bordered by the sea, the city is surrounded by lofty hills, two of which, one upon either side of the town, have a perpendicular ascent of nearly four hundred feet, and are called from their position, east and west rocks. Chapel street, the fashionable promenade of the city, extends in a north-westerly direction from Mill river, through the entire length of the city.

In New Haven a neatness and regularity is observable, which is rarely found in other cities. The city covers from six to seven square miles, and is regularly laid off, the streets running in parallel directions, and crossing each other at right angles. Beautiful elms, lining the streets, and ornamenting public squares and parks, are scattered throughout the city. From the great abundance of these trees, New Haven is appropriately styled the "City of Elms." In Temple street they are so numerous and large that the rays of the sun seldom penetrate through the mass of foliage to the walk beneath. A succession of beautiful residences on Hill House avenue are almost entirely hid from view by the profusion of foliage and flowers. A public square of sixteen acres, called the "Green," is one of the finest parks in the United States. Wooster and York are the other principal squares, the former containing five acres, and lying in the eastern part of the city.

New Haven is the seat of Yale college, which is, undoubtedly, the greatest institution of its kind in the union. It was founded in 1700, by ten farmers, who each donated a number of books for its support; and named in honor of Elihu Yale, who at his death, left to the institution a large sum of money. A whole block, immediately east of the public green, is occupied by the college and its buildings. On the eastern side of the square are five brick buildings, each four stories high, and containing study rooms and sleeping apartments. In the same row are the chapel, observatory, and lyceum. Farther back is the Trumbull gallery, containing a choice collection of historical paintings. Near the western end of the square is the library building, a handsome gothic structure one hundred and fifty feet long.

"Among the principal public edifices may be mentioned the state house, standing in the western section of the green. It is a large stuccoed building, modeled after the Parthenon, and contains, besides the legislative halls, apartments for the supreme, superior, and county courts."

"The new railroad depot, recently erected on Chapel street, near State street, is a fine brick structure, with towers." The other principal buildings are St. Paul's chapel and Trinity church, both handsome stone buildings.

The harbor of New Haven is very shallow, rendering a near approach to land both difficult and dangerous. To meet this difficulty, a wharf has been built in the bay, which extends nearly three thousand five hundred feet from the shore. The city has four newspaper offices, five banks, with an aggregate capital of two millions of dollars, and a savings institution, having eight hundred and thirty-five thousand one hundred and twelve dollars on deposit. Population in 1860, 39,268. (See views of New Haven.)

HARTFORD,

Semi-capital, and, next to New Haven, the largest city of Connecticut, is in Hartford county, on the western bank of the Connecticut river, about one hundred and twenty-four miles south-west of Boston, and thirty-six miles north-east of New Haven. The city covers about two thousand acres of very uneven ground, which is intersected by upwards of seven hundred streets and alleys. Main street, two miles long, and containing the most important business buildings, extends through the entire length of the city from north to south, dividing it in two nearly equal parts. State street, extending from Main street to the river, contains a large number of wholesale establishments.

Brick and freestone are the chief building materials. The court house, erected in 1792, is one of the finest buildings in the city. This structure, of the Doric order, is one hundred and fourteen feet long, seventy-six feet wide, fifty-four feet high, and is surmounted by a lofty dome. Trinity college, in a richly ornamented inclosure, one mile south of the state house, is one of the finest educational establishments in the state. Wadsworth athenæum, devoted to science, literature, and the arts, and having a library of five thousand volumes, is a turreted gothic building of granite construction. "A gallery of paintings, and other rooms devoted to the fine arts occupy the central portion of the building." The American asylum for deaf and dumb, founded in 1820, is a four story building, one hundred and thirty feet long, and fifty feet wide, attended by about two hundred and thirty pupils. Hartford contains twelve banks, twenty-four churches, seven newspaper offices, and seventeen fire and life insurance companies. Population, 29,152.

MIDDLETOWN,

An important city of Connecticut, and semi-capital of Middlesex county, is twenty-four miles north-east of New Haven, at the head of ship navigation on the Connecticut, and on the Air Line railway extending from New York to Boston. It is pleasantly situated on the slope of a hill, on the western bank of the river. Main street, the principal thoroughfare, comprises the business portion of the town. The principal buildings are the custom house, court house, and the Wesleyan university, the latter occupying an eminence, and commanding an extensive view of the valley of the Connecticut.

Middletown has a fine harbor, and enjoys important water communications with cities on the river. The city contains four banks, two savings institutions, and manufactories of hardware, guns, leather, etc. Population in 1860, 5,182.

NEW LONDON,

An important city of Connecticut, and semi-capital of New London county, is on the western bank of the Thames river, about three miles from Long Island sound. The ground on which the city is built was formerly covered with huge granite rocks, in consequence of which the city was laid off with little regard to regularity. Much has been done of late, however, to overcome the original inequalities of the surface. In the western suburbs of the city is a lofty hill, from the summit of which a varied and extensive view can be obtained.

Prominent among the public buildings are the custom house, an elegant granite structure, and court house.

New London is extensively engaged in commerce and fisheries, and is also rich in manufactures. The harbor is three miles long, and thirty feet deep, and is encircled on nearly every side by lofty hills, and defended by two strong fortresses, only one of which, however, is garrisoned. The receipts from the whale fishery for the year 1852, were one million three hundred and forty-nine thousand eight hundred and seventy-two dollars.

New London has ten churches, four newspaper offices, sixteen public schools, five banks, with a capital of six hundred thousand dollars, and a savings institution with seven hundred and six thousand one hundred and forty-four dollars on deposit. Population in 1860, 10,115.

NORWICH,

Beautifully situated at the head of the Thames river, is the semi-capital of New London county, and, next to New Haven and Hartford, is the largest city in Connecticut.

The Yantic and Shetucket rivers, which here unite to form the Thames, have each falls and rapids which afford immense hydraulic power to the foundries, mills, etc., of this manufacturing city. The southern portion of the city occupies the slope of a large hill, but to the north it stretches over an elevated and extensive plain. Norwich contains the county buildings, an excellent high school, and a large number of elegant and costly private residences. About three hundred and fifty men are employed by the Norwich arms company in the manufacture of government fire-arms.

Norwich forms communications with cities on the seaboard, and in the interior by means of the Norwich and Worcester and the New London northern railroads. The city contains seventeen churches, three newspaper offices, four insurance companies, forty public schools, seven banks, three savings banks, and about one hundred manufactories of cotton and woollen goods, paper, machinery, etc. Population in 1860, 14,048.

NORWALK,

Is a city of Fairfield county, on both sides of the Norwalk river, on the route of the New York and New Haven railroad, forty-five miles north-east of New York, and thirty-one miles south-west of New Haven.

Norwalk is noted for the manufacture of felt cloth, of which two companies make over five hundred thousand yards per annum. The city contains nine churches, five banks, three union school houses, one of which ranks among the finest educational establishments in the state, and two newspaper offices. The Danbury and Norwalk and New York and New Haven railroads form a junction at Norwalk, by means of which an unbroken line of railway communication is established with all important cities in the state. Vessels drawing six feet of water ascend the river from Long Island sound as far as Norwalk. Population in 1860, 7,582. (See views of Norwalk.)

In 1790 the population of Connecticut was two hundred and thirty-eight thousand one hundred and forty-one; in 1860, four hundred and sixty thousand one hundred and forty-seven. This small increase is, doubtless, owing to the fact that a large portion of the population are yearly emigrating to other states.

Connecticut has seven hundred and sixty miles of railroad in use. The state contains eight hundred and two churches, five colleges, eighteen hundred and ten public schools, and one hundred and ninety-five academies. The governor and lieutenant governor are elected by universal suffrage, the former receiving eleven hundred dollars and the latter three hundred dollars per annum. The senate is composed of twenty-one and the house of representatives of two hundred and fifteen members. Connecticut is represented by four members in the national house of representatives, and is entitled to six electoral votes for president.

RHODE ISLAND.

Rhode Island, the smallest of the United States, and the last of the thirteen original states, lies between latitude 41° 18′ and 42° N., and longitude 71° 8′ and 71° 52′ W. It is bounded on the north and north-east by Massachusetts, on the south and south-east by the Atlantic ocean and the Narragansett bay, on the east by Massachusetts, and on the west by Connecticut. It is forty-seven miles long, and thirty-seven miles broad, and includes an area of thirteen hundred and six square miles, or eight hundred and thirty-five thousand eight hundred and forty acres.

Though the general character of the country is hilly and rugged, there are level districts bordering upon the Atlantic ocean and Narragansett bay. The most important elevations are the Woonsocket hills in the northern, Mount Hope in the western, and Hopkin's hill in the central part of the state.

The principal rivers are the Blackstone and Patuxet, the former rising in Massachusetts, and crossing the north-eastern portion of Rhode Island, and both entering the Narragansett bay. The other rivers of the state, though small, are rapid, and afford valuable water powers. The Narragansett bay is a beautiful sheet of water, thirty miles long and twelve broad, and containing numerous picturesque islands. Block island, ten miles from the coast, is eight miles long, and from two to five miles broad.

The climate of Rhode Island resembles that of Connecticut. The soil of the state is not very fertile, more attention being given to grazing than to tilling. Some of the adjoining islands, however, are extremely productive. The chief productions are wheat, Indian corn, rye, oats, potatoes, buckwheat, beans, wool, butter, honey, wine, and flax.

Rhode Island is extensively engaged in manufactures. According to the manufacturing statistics of the year ending June 30, 1861, the capital invested amounted to twenty-three millions of dollars; value of the annual product, forty-seven millions five hundred thousand dollars. The commerce of Rhode Island is chiefly confined to the neighboring states. Her exports for the year 1861 amounted to two hundred and fifty-five thousand two hundred and ninety-seven dollars; imports, five hundred and forty-three thousand six hundred and fifty-two dollars.

Providence and Newport are the capitals and largest cities in the state. Other important towns are Southfield and Warwick.

PROVIDENCE,

The largest city and semi-capital of Rhode Island, and seat of justice of Providence county, is situated on both sides of an arm of the Narragansett bay, called Providence river, one hundred and seventy-five miles north-east of New York, and forty-three miles south-west of Boston. The ground on which the city is built is very uneven, and rises on the eastern side, in a single instance, to a hight of two hundred and four feet. The greatest elevation on the western side is seventy-eight feet. In consequence of the irregularity of the surface, the city was laid off with little regard to beauty or neatness. Much has recently been done, however, to overcome the original defects, though the city is not, as yet, a pattern of beauty or elegance. Several bridges connect East and West Providence, one of which is over one hundred and forty feet wide.

Prominent among the public buildings is the Arcada, on the western side of the river, fronting on Broad street. This structure, two hundred and twenty-five feet long, eighty feet wide, and three stories high, is built of granite, and in richness and elegance surpasses every building in the city. "What Cheer" is the name applied to a beautiful freestone edifice in Market square. The other principal buildings are the custom house, erected at a cost of two hundred and fifty thousand dollars, state house, a fine brick structure, and the market house on Market square, containing city government offices. The principal churches are Grace and First Congregational, gothic edifices of granite construction.

Providence contains the Butler hospital for the insane, which is located on the right bank of the Seekonk river. It was established in 1844, and called the Rhode Island hospital, but in 1851 it received its present name from Cyrus Butler, Esq., who contributed forty thousand dollars to aid in the support of the institution. The Dexter asylum for the poor, one hundred and seventy feet long, and three stories high, is on the eastern bank of the river, in an enclosure of forty acres. The wall that encloses the building is ten feet high, and was constructed at a cost of twenty thousand dollars.

On an eminence on the same side of the river is the Brown university, established first at Warren, and removed to Providence in 1770. The Athenæum, a costly stone structure, founded in 1836, contains a free reading room, and a carefully selected library of twenty-seven thousand six hundred and ninety-five volumes. Near the centre of the city is a circular park or promenade, eighty feet wide, enclosing a delightful sheet of water about one mile in circumference, which constitutes the head waters of Narragansett bay.

Providence formerly carried on a large foreign trade, but her commerce at the present time is chiefly domestic. The city contains fifty-two churches, ten newspaper offices, twenty-seven school buildings, forty-five banks, four steam fire engines, two manufactories of wood screws, two musket manufactories, and one hundred stationary steam engines, worked by three hundred and ten steam boilers. Population of the city in 1865, 55,000.

NEWPORT,

Semi-capital of Rhode Island, and seat of justice of Newport county, is on the western end of a large island of the same name as the state to which it belongs, in the Narragansett bay, twenty-eight miles south-east of Providence.

Newport has one of the finest harbors in the union, and, up to the time of the revolutionary war, was second to none of the New England cities in commercial wealth. During that war her population was reduced more than one-half, and she has since never been able to regain her former standing. The site of the city is a beautiful rounded elevation, overlooking the harbor and bay, and commanding a varied and extensive prospect.

The most important public buildings are the state house, an imposing brick edifice, surmounted by a cupola, market house, and custom house. Among the churches may be mentioned the Synagogue and Friends' meeting house. The Redwood library, established in 1788, contains fifteen thousand volumes, and an apartment devoted to the fine arts.

Newport is a fashionable watering place, and during the summer months is much frequented by tourists, and made the home of wealthy gentlemen, who have established beautiful country seats in the vicinity. For those in quest of sea air and change of scenery, Newport presents unrivaled attractions. A large number of elegant and fashionable hotels have been erected for the accommodation of visitors. Of these the Bellevue house and Ocean house are the most important. The city contains fifteen churches, two newspaper publications, an academy, an excellent system of public schools, ten banks, and manufactories of carriages, clocks, calicoes, muslins, etc. Population in 1860, 10,508.

In 1860, Rhode Island had one hundred and seventy-four thousand six hundred and twenty inhabitants, of which one hundred and seventy thousand six hundred and sixty-eight were white, and three thousand nine hundred and fifty-two colored. Rhode Island has fifty miles of railroad, three hundred and ten churches, one college, four hundred and twenty-six public schools, fifty-eight academies, three hundred and two libraries, and twenty-six newspaper publications.

The governor receives for his services one thousand dollars, and the lieutenant governor three hundred dollars per annum. The senate consists of thirty-one and the house of representatives of seventy-two members. In November, 1862, the state contained twenty-one savings banks, in which was deposited nine millions five hundred and sixty thousand four hundred and forty-one dollars.

CHAPTER II.

THE MIDDLE STATES.

NEW YORK.

New York, the largest of the Middle States, and the most important and populous of the United States, is bounded on the north by Canada; on the south by Pennsylvania and New Jersey; on the east by Vermont, Massachusetts and Connecticut; on the south-east by Long Island Sound; and on the west by Canada, Pennsylvania and Lake Erie. Lakes Erie and Ontario, and the St. Lawrence and Niagara rivers, separate the state from Canada; Lake Champlain, from Vermont; and the Delaware river, from Pennsylvania. It lies between latitude 40° 30′ and 45° N., and longitude 72° and 79° 55′ W. Greatest length of the state from north to south, three hundred and eight miles; from east to west, including Long Island, three hundred and thirty-five miles; area, forty-seven thousand square miles, or thirty million and eight hundred thousand acres.

The eastern portion of the state is rugged and mountainous. The Highlands, formed by the Schooley mountains, the eastern ridge of the Alleghanies, are from five hundred to one thousand five hundred feet high. These elevations are continued across the south-eastern portion of the state, by the Taconic mountains, which take the name of Green mountains, in Massachusetts and Connecticut. The Adirondacks, the most important group, are in the north-eastern part of the state, and border upon Lake Champlain. Mount Marcy has an altitude of five thousand four hundred and sixty-seven feet, and is the culminating point of the state. Mount Anthony, in the wild region of Lake Champlain, is five thousand feet high. The Catskill mountains extend from Catskill, on the Hudson, to Utica, on a branch of the Mohawk. These mountains abound with wild glens and beautiful water-falls, and are one of the greatest resorts for tourists in the state. They attain their greatest elevation at Roundtop, at an altitude of three thousand eight hundred and four feet. The Catskill Mountain House is found at an elevation of two thousand two hundred and seventy-six feet, and commands an extensive prospect. In the Kauterskill Gorge, three miles south of the hotel, is the Kauterskill Fall, which is precipitated one hundred and eighty feet, into a chasm of great wildness. The Bastion Fall has a descent of eighty-five feet. The scenery among the Catskills is grand and imposing. An unbroken view of from fifty to seventy miles is obtained from the piazza of the Mountain House. Directly at their base is the beautiful valley of the Hudson, and away in the distance, in the state of Massachusetts, the Green mountains are perceptible. (See views of Catskill mountains.) In the western and southern parts of the state, though there are no mountain ranges, the country, as a general thing, is rugged and hilly.

The principal rivers of the state are the Hudson, and its principal branch, the Mohawk, the Genesee, and the sources of the Delaware and Susquehanna. The Hudson river has its source in the mountainous district, in the northern part of the state, and enters New York bay in latitude 40° 42′ N., and longitude 74° 1′ 30″ W. The headstreams of this river are found at an altitude of four thousand feet, and are the outlets of numerous mountain lakes. At Glens Falls, the river has a perpendicular descent of fifty feet. It is affected by the tide as far as the mouth of the Mohawk, one hundred and fifty miles from New York. Its width, at this point, varies from three hundred to seven hundred yards; and between Harverstraw and its mouth it is often five miles broad. Its entire length, from its source to its mouth, is three hundred miles. Justice can hardly be done to the beauty and grandeur of the scenery of this river. The Hudson highlands, originating in the Schooley mountains, commence about twenty miles from New York, and extend in an unbroken mass along the bank of the river for fifty-five miles. They frequently rise fifteen hundred feet above the Hudson, in perpendicular ascent, but the average hight is not so great. On the south, the highlands are known as palisades, which consist of a vast wall of trap-rock, rising to the hight of from three hundred to five hundred feet. Many of the hights are crowned with the ruins of fortifications, which were erected during the revolutionary war, to prevent British ships from ascending the river. At Newburg, on the left bank of the river, sixty-one miles from New York, was the headquarters of Washington during a critical period of the war. Mount Taurus, an elevation among the Highlands, on the left bank of the river, is forty miles north of New York. Breakneck Hill is an eminence in Putnam county, on the eastern bank of the Hudson, at the northern entrance of the Highlands. It is one thousand one hundred and eighty-seven feet high, and terminates in the promontory of St. Anthony's Nose. Polypus Island, a short distance north, is an elevated body of land, of oval formation, near the middle of the river. Its principal tributaries are the Walkill, entering near Kingston, and the Mohawk flowing into it near Troy. In 1820, there were only twenty-two sailing vessels on the river. The total number plying on its waters at the present time, is supposed to exceed eight hundred. The Hudson river steamboats are among the finest and fastest in the world, being frequently over four hundred feet long, and furnished with great luxury. The first successful experiment in steamboat navigation, was made on the Hudson by Robert Fulton, in 1807. The Hudson river was discovered by Henry Hudson, an English navigator, in the service of the Dutch East India company. It was at first called North river, to distinguish it from the Delaware, which was then called South river, but it has subsequently received the name of its discoverer. (See views of the Hudson.)

The Mohawk river rises between Lewis and Oneida counties; receives the West Canada creek, its principal affluent, fourteen miles east of Utica, and enters the Hudson after a course of one hundred and sixty-five miles. On West Canada creek, fifteen miles north-east of Rome, are Trenton falls, which descend three hundred and twelve feet in six cascades. These falls occur in a narrow and deep ravine, about two miles long, with perpendicular walls of limestone on either side, frequently rising to the hight of one hundred and ninety feet. They are less remarkable for the volume of water, than for the wildness and variety of the surrounding scenery. The highest fall has a descent of one hundred feet. (See views of Trenton falls.)

At Little falls, the Mohawk has a descent of forty-five feet in three-quarters of a mile, forming the celebrated Mill-dam falls, which affords valuable water power to the village. At Cohoes, about two miles from its confluence with the Hudson, the river has a perpendicular descent of seventy feet. From Rome to its mouth, the river is followed by the Hudson and Erie canal. Rome, Utica, and Little Falls, are the chief towns on its banks. (See views on the Mohawk river.)

The Genesee river has its source in the northern part of the state of Pennsylvania, and, after a northerly course of one hundred and sixty miles, reaches lake Ontario a short distance north of Rochester. Near the source of the river are three falls, sixty, ninety, and one hundred and ten feet high; and near its mouth there are falls one hundred feet high. At Rochester the river has a perpendicular pitch of ninety-seven feet, giving immense water power to the factories and mills of that city. (See views of Genesee falls.)

The chief branches of the Susquehanna in New York, are the Chemung and Chenango; of the Delaware, Oquago and Popachton. The Ramapo river rises near Newburg in Orange county, and flows in a south and south-east direction, through Bergen and Passaic counties, New Jersey, and discharges its waters into the Atlantic ocean, through the Pompton and Passaic rivers. This river is more remarkable for the beauty and variety of its scenery, than for any manufacturing or commercial worth. It passes through one of the wildest and most picturesque valleys in the state. Near its source a range of hills branches off from the highlands, and follows the river for a considerable distance. Along the Erie railway, which intersects the valley, are a number of beautiful villages, the principal of which, Ramapo and Greenwood, have rolling mills and furnaces.

NIAGARA RIVER AND FALLS.

The Niagara and St. Lawrence rivers form a portion of the boundary between New York and Canada. In the former occur the world renowned falls and rapids. The river takes its rise in the eastern extremity of Lake Erie, and, after flowing about thirty-four miles, empties into Lake Ontario. It is from half a mile to three miles broad. It is deep, its sides level and its course smooth until it reaches the rapids which extend three miles immediately above the falls, the last half mile of which surges and foams with terrific fury.

The cataract of Niagara is not the highest in the world, but it is remarkable for forcing over the precipice a greater amount of water than any other. The highest waterfall in the world is the Yosemite, being over two thousand feet in hight. The falls of Niagara have a descent of only about one hundred and seventy feet, "but the immense body of water that rushes in an almost undivided mass down this distance produces upon the beholder the most intense wonder, and furnishes one of the most sublime objects to be found in the world. Such is the mighty scale on which this cataract is constructed that the beholder does not, at first sight, comprehend its full grandeur, but by degrees it seems to increase in size; its awful front appears to rise higher, its prodigious volume to expand, and its whole aspect to assume a more fearful and sublime physiognomy."

The falls are twenty-three miles from Lake Erie. The river is here divided by an island containing about seventy-five acres, called Goat island, the extremity of which is perpendicular and in a line with the precipice over which the water is precipitated. In consequence of a bend in the river the greater volume of water is sent down on the Canada side. On this side is therefore the greater cataract, which, from its form, has been named Horse Shoe fall, but it no longer bears that name appropriately, as the precipice has been, by the dropping and wearing away of the rock, changed from a circular to a triangular form. On the Canada side of of Goat island stands Terrapin tower, from the top of which is afforded a commanding view of the falls and river below. The falls next the United States, and to the left of Goat island, are called the American falls.

The process of wearing away goes on gradually. Six hundred and seventy thousand tons of water are precipitated over the falls into the gulf every minute. The upper layer of rock is hard, but the strata beneath are soft and easily worn away by the continued action of the water, and then the weight of water causes large pieces of the crust to break off from time to time. The rate of retrocession has been estimated to average from one foot to one yard per year. The present rate is probably not equal to what it was when the falls were near Lake Ontario, nor what it will be as they approach Lake Erie, the rock in these places being softer. Geologists think there is abundant proof that the river between the falls and Queenstown flows in a different channel than it did formerly. Three miles below the falls the contiguity of the bank is broken by a ravine filled with sand and gravel. This being filled up when the continent was submerged, the river was obliged to seek a new route, and has worn away this gorge seven miles long and one hundred and fifty feet deep. Some geologists have thought the erosion was made by other agencies than the river, but the work which is constantly going on there from year to year proves that it has only required time to complete this excavation. It has been supposed, that should the falls ever recede to Lake Erie, a terrible inundation of the region eastward would be the result. But De La Beache has proved satisfactorily, that the only effect would be a gradual draining of Lake Erie, with a slight increase of Niagara river.

The hight of the Horse Shoe fall is not so great as that of the American, yet it surpasses the latter in beauty. The concussion of air caused by this immense cataract is so great that the windows of a hotel, about three hundred yards distant from the falls, are constantly in a tremulous motion. In cold weather the spray freezes on the surrounding buildings, covering them with sheets of ice. On the trees it is accumulated in such masses as to bend them to the ground, and from the margin of the rocks are suspended huge clusters of icicles, sometimes one hundred feet in length, and massive ice mounds are also found which add much to the grandeur of the scene.

The street between the Cataract and International hotels leads to the iron bridge over the rapids to Goat island. The bridge is three hundred and sixty feet long, having four arches of ninety feet span. It is twenty-seven feet wide, has a double carriage way and two foot paths. To the left of Goat island is the Centre fall, which, in contrast with American fall, when seen at a distance, seems like a mere ribbon of water, while its real breadth is two hundred and forty feet. Knowing the actual, and observing the apparent width of this fall, serves to give the spectator a more correct idea of the great size of the whole cataract. This fall, situated at the right of the American, may be seen in the views of the American fall from the Canada side.

The Suspension bridge is two miles below the falls, and at the head of the rapids. Between the bridge and the falls the water is perfectly calm and smooth. Below the bridge are two rapids, caused by the narrowing of the bed of the river and the rocks at the bottom. These rapids run at the rate of twenty-five miles per hour, with breakers rising from ten to twenty feet. The Suspension bridge is constructed of wire, and is considered by some as great a curiosity as the falls themselves. It is eight hundred feet long, twenty-four wide and about two hundred and fifty above the river, and is supported by four cable wires nine and a fourth inches in diameter. These cable wires are composed of small wire twisted together. The force of the current under the bridge is so great that a piece of lead, weighing two hundred pounds, dropped from the bridge, was carried down stream the length of the rope without sinking. At the extremity of the first rapids is the whirlpool, caused by an abrupt turn in the river. The rapids below the whirlpool are about one half mile in extent.

Table Rock, on the Canada side, formerly afforded a good view of the fall. It derived its name from its projecting over the river in the form of a table. The rock has now fallen. A number of people were standing upon it just a few minutes before it fell into the abyss below. Near this point is a staircase which must be descended in order to pass under Horse Shoe fall to Termination rock. One writer, who visited this rock, vowed never again to encounter the blinding, hissing spray, the deafening roar of the falling waters, and the dread possibilities of a second visit to that indescribable, awe-inspiring, terribly magnificent, infernal region.

Lewiston, a flourishing village at the head of navigation on the Niagara, is about half way between the falls and Lake Ontario, and about five miles from the Suspension bridge. About one mile above Lewiston, on the American side, the bluffs diverge off from the river and terminate in what is called Lewiston mountain, the top of which affords a grand and imposing view overlooking the village of Lewiston and the valley and river below to its junction with Lake Ontario. (See views of Niagara.)

New York abounds with beautiful lakes, among which may be mentioned Cayuga, Oneida, Seneca, Chautauqua, Lake George, and Long Lake. The former three are drained by the Oswego river, which empties into lake Ontario. Cayuga lake is forty miles long, and from one to four miles broad. The water is very deep, and is seldom frozen. A steamboat plies from the northern end of the lake, to Ithaca, at the southern. Oneida lake, eighteen miles long, and from three to six miles wide, passes into the Oswego, through Oneida river. Its waters abound with fish, among which trout, salmon, salmon trout, pike and bass, are conspicuous. Seneca lake is a beautiful sheet of water, forty miles long, and from three to five miles wide, lying between Tompkins and Seneca counties on the east, and Steuben and Yates on the west. Chautauqua lake is a beautiful expanse of water in Chautauqua county, eighteen miles long, and from one to three miles broad, and drained by a branch of the Alleghany river. Its name is derived from an Indian phrase, signifying a "foggy place."

Lake George, also called Horicon, is a beautiful expanse of water, between Warren and Washington counties, remarkable for the transparency of its waters, and the grandeur of the surrounding scenery. It is thirty-four miles long, and from one to three and a half miles wide. It is four hundred feet deep in some places, and contains over three hundred picturesque islands. Few places in the United States can boast of more beautiful natural scenery than that which surrounds Lake George. The Narrows, or narrowest portion of the lake, commence thirteen miles from the south-western shore, and are continued from six to eight miles. One mile farther north is an island of about twenty acres, called, from its position, Twelve Mile island. At the entrance of the Narrows, on the western bank of the lake, commence the Black mountains, which reach their greatest hight at an altitude of twenty-two hundred feet. Rogers' Slide, an immense rock, two hundred feet high, received its name from the daring exploit of Major Rogers, who, during the French and Indian war, being closely pursued by the Indians, slid down the steep declivity, and reached the ice below without injury. In the vicinity of the lake is the monument erected to the memory of Colonel Ephraim Williams, who fell in the French war, on the 8th of September, 1755. On the battle ground, near the monument, is a collection of water called Bloody Pond. (See views of Lake George.)

Fort Ticonderoga, near the mouth of the lake, is one hundred feet above the water level. It is surrounded by water upon three sides, and upon a greater portion of the fourth by a deep morass. The ruins of this fort are yet quite picturesque. (See views of Fort Ticonderoga.)

Several important islands are found off the coast of New York, the principal of which are Long, Staten, and Manhattan islands. Long Island, separated from New York by a strait half a mile wide, is one hundred and fifteen miles long and fifteen miles broad. The soil is exceedingly rich, and extensively cultivated. The Long Island railroad extends through the centre of the island from Brooklyn to Greenport. Staten Island, in New York bay, is fifteen miles long and from three to eight miles broad, and constitutes the county of Richmond. Richmond hill is a term applied to a beautiful elevation in the northern portion of the island, which has an elevation of over three hundred feet. Manhattan Island is fifteen miles long and from one to three miles wide, and is the site of New York city.

New York presents a great variety of climate. The severity of the winters and the intense heat of the summers is greatly modified in the western and south-eastern portions of the state by the vicinity to the lakes and the sea coast. In the north the winters are long and severe, and the summers, though short, are excessively hot. New York, as a general thing, is very fertile. Among the mountains and hills there are sterile districts, but on the plains in the western portion of the state, and in the river valleys, the soil is exceedingly rich, and in every way adapted to agriculture. The chief products are oats, Irish potatoes, grass seeds, fruits, hay, hops, maple sugar, butter, cheese, honey, Indian corn, wheat, barley, beans, flax, buckwheat, sweet potatoes, and tobacco. According to the agricultural statistics of 1860, the amount of wheat produced in that year was eight millions six hundred and eighty-one thousand and one hundred bushels; amount of corn, twenty millions sixty-one thousand and forty-eight bushels; amount of wool, nine millions four hundred and fifty-four thousand four hundred and seventy-three pounds. The principal forest trees are oak, pine, tamarack, spruce, hemlock, larch, walnut, fir, chestnut, beech, butternut, elm, ash, and sugar maple.

The manufactures of New York are very important. According to the census of 1860, the state contained twenty-two thousand six hundred and twenty-four manufacturing establishments, with a capital of one hundred and seventy-five millions four hundred and forty-nine thousand two hundred and six dollars, and an annual income of three hundred and seventy-nine millions six hundred and twenty-three thousand five hundred and sixty dollars. In commercial wealth New York takes the lead among all the United States. According to the commercial statistics of the year ending June 30, 1861, her exports amounted to one hundred and fifty-eight millions six hundred and six thousand five hundred and eighteen dollars; imports, two hundred and thirty-seven millions four hundred and two thousand seven hundred and twenty-six dollars.

Albany is the capital of the state, and New York is the chief city. The other principal cities are Brooklyn, Buffalo, Rochester, Troy, Syracuse, Utica, Oswego, Kingston, Newburg, and Elmira.

ALBANY,

The capital of the state, and seat of justice of Albany county, is finely situated on the western bank of the Hudson, one hundred and forty-five miles north of New York, and one hundred and sixty-four miles north-west of Boston. The site of the city, from being low and level on the shore, becomes rugged and uneven as you advance from the river. State street, running from the capitol to the river, is the most important promenade in the city. Broadway, intersecting the former thoroughfare at right angles, contains the greater portion of the business buildings.

The most important public buildings are the capitol, city hall, and state hall. The former is an imposing stone edifice with marble columns, one hundred and fifteen feet long, ninety feet wide, and fifty feet high, surmounted by a lofty dome, supporting a wooden statue of the goddess *Themis*, "with a sword in her right hand and a balance in her left." The city hall, surmounted by an elegant dome, and state hall, are beautiful marble buildings, on the eastern side of the capitol grounds. Connected with the capitol is the state library, a substantial brick edifice, containing upwards of seventy-five thousand volumes. The other important libraries are the Young Men's association, containing ten thousand, and the Albany institute having six thousand volumes.

The educational establishments of Albany are a credit to the city. The most important of these are the university, founded in 1852, and the Albany academy, situated on the eastern side of the capitol grounds, and attended by over four hundred pupils. The state normal school, founded in 1844, has a library of one thousand volumes.

Albany is one of the greatest lumber markets in the world. In 1863, the value of the lumber received in the city amounted to seven millions of dollars.

Albany is the centre of a large number of railroads, by means of which an uninterrupted line of communication is established with all important cities in the state. The city contains fifty-seven churches, seventeen newspaper offices, an excellent system of public schools, belonging to which are libraries containing in all eight thousand volumes, and fifteen banks. Population in 1860, 62,367.

NEW YORK,

The great metropolis of the United States, and, in connection with the surrounding cities, which might properly be regarded as suburbs, the third city in importance in the civilized world, is situated on Manhattan island, in latitude 40° 42′ 43″ N., and longitude 74° 3″ W. Its site is formed by the confluence of the East with the Hudson river, and is separated from the mainland by the Harlem river and Spuyten Duyvel creek. The city also comprises several adjacent islands, containing fortifications and public institutions. The most densely populated portion of the city occupies about four miles of the southern part of the island.

In the New York harbor are twelve forts, mounting fifteen hundred guns. The Narrows, at the entrance of the bay, are one mile wide, and are defended by Fort Lafayette, in the water, two hundred yards from the shore, and Fort Hamilton, on Long Island.

The city of New York is very compactly built, and is regularly laid off into one hundred and forty-one thousand four hundred and eighty-six lots. Broadway, the principal street, is four miles long and five rods wide. It commences at the Battery, in the south-western portion of the island, and extends, in a north-easterly direction, to Grace church, where it bends to the north-west, and passes through the newer portions of the city. Of the many streets which cross Broadway at right angles, Chatham street is the most important.

Fifth avenue, the most fashionable promenade of the city, is lined with massive hotels, stores, and public buildings, many of which are built of marble, and contains, also, elegant private residences and imposing churches. Rialto and Lombard streets contain insurance and brokers' offices and banking houses, and is the great financial district of the United States. Wall street, running east from Broadway, is lined with a compact mass of buildings, of marble, granite and sand-stone construction, and contains the merchants' exchange and the old custom house.

One of the most prominent features of New York, is Central Park, in the northern portion of the city. It is laid out in the finest style of landscape gardening, and has cost the city over fifteen millions of dollars. The park is from one to two miles long, and nearly three-fourths of a mile wide. It formerly covered an area of about seven hundred and fifty acres, but a small portion of this space is now occupied by the city. For a traveler visiting New York, a more pleasing and attractive spot could not be found, than this park. Its uneven surface, over which are scattered masses of rock; its broad and handsome carriage roads, and winding gravel walks; its labyrinth of ornamental trees, and profusion of flowers, all add to the beauty of the place, and unite to render it one of the most pleasing and delightful retreats in existence. Superior architectural and engineering faculty have been employed in the construction of various buildings, bridges, etc. Scattered over the grounds are artificial sheets of water, containing beautiful fountains, and crossed by rustic bridges. During the winter, the park is a favorite resort for a multitude of skaters, of both sexes. A substantial stone wall, six feet high, has recently been built around the park. (See views of Central Park.)

The City Hall Park is a triangular enclosure of eleven acres, beautifully adorned with shade trees, and containing the city hall and other public buildings. Castle Garden, near the Battery, was formerly used as a place of public exhibitions, concerts and fairs.

Prominent among the public buildings, is the city hall, two hundred and sixteen feet long, one hundred and five feet wide, and sixty-five feet high. The sides and south front are of marble, and the north front is of red sand-stone. Annual art exhibitions are given by the National Academy of Design, a handsome edifice on the corner of Fourth avenue and Twenty-third street. The United States Treasury, formerly the custom-house, is on the corner of Wall and Nassau streets, and occupies the site of the old federal hall, from the street gallery of which Washington delivered his first inaugural address, and received the oath of office, which was administered by Chancellor Livingston. The building is two hundred feet long, ninety feet wide, and eighty feet high. At each end is a portico, supported by eight immense pillars. Edwin Booth's theatre is a handsome marble building, recently erected on Twenty-third street, between Fifth and Sixth avenues. The Bible house is a six story brick building, two hundred and thirty-two feet long, and seventy-seven feet wide, on the corner of Eighth street and Fourth avenue. The city hospital is an immense building, of grey-stone construction, on Broadway, one hundred and twenty-four feet long, fifty feet wide, and three stories high, with accommodations for two hundred patients.

New York contains numerous academies and schools, of both public and private character. The New York University, founded in 1831, is a beautiful white marble edifice, built in gothic style, on Washington square. It is a four story building, one hundred and eighty feet long, and one hundred feet wide. Connected with the institution are apartments, devoted to law and medicine. The General Theological Seminary, established in 1817, comprises two stone buildings, each one hundred and ten by fifty feet, situated on West Twentieth street. The Free Academy is a handsome gothic brick structure, founded in 1848, and located on the corner of East Twenty-third street and Lexington avenue. The entire cost of the building exceeded one hundred and fifty-two thousand dollars. Columbia College, known as King's College before the revolution, and the oldest school in the city, was founded in 1754. Rutger's Female Institute is a fine structure, on the corner of Fifth avenue and

Forty-second street, established in 1838. The New York Academy of Music, or Opera House, on the corner of Fourteenth street and Irving place, contains seats for four thousand seven hundred persons. The Cooper Institute, directly opposite the Bible house, is a present to the city from Mr. Peter Cooper, who appropriated nearly three hundred thousand dollars for its establishment. It is one hundred and ninety-three feet long, one hundred and forty-three feet wide, five stories high, and has a free reading room, picture gallery, art schools, etc.

The largest library in the city is the Astor, founded by John Jacob Astor, who, at his death, bequeathed four hundred thousand dollars for that purpose. The Mercantile library, founded in 1820, and recently removed to the Astor place, contains sixty thousand volumes, and a large reading room. One of the largest and most imposing buildings in New York is Stewart's store, an elegant white marble building, occupying a whole block, and being 152 feet on Broadway. Distributed throughout the building are nearly two thousand panes of glass, fifteen of which, in the lower story, fronting on Broadway, are eleven by seven feet. In the evening, the various departments of the store are lighted up by four hundred gas-burners.

New York contains a large number of elegant and fashionable hotels. The most important of these are the Fifth avenue, Hoffman house, Astor house, St. James, and La Farge house. The former two are opposite Madison square, six stories high, and constructed of pure white marble. The Astor house is a substantial building on Broadway, two hundred and one feet long, one hundred and eighty-five feet wide, and six stories high. It is built of Quincy granite, and contains three hundred and twenty-six chambers.

In 1865, New York had three hundred and eleven churches, of which Trinity, Grace, Calvary, Holy Communion, and St. Paul's were the most conspicuous. Trinity church, built of red sandstone, is on the corner of Broadway and Wall street. It is gothic style, one hundred and eighty-nine feet long, eighty-four feet wide, and has the highest spire in the United States. The tower contains a rich chime of bells, and, including the spire, is two hundred and sixty-four feet high. Near where Broadway bends to the north-west, stands Grace church, a handsome white marble edifice, with a tower and spire, surmounted by a cross. St. Paul's church is a handsome structure, immediately to the right of the Astor house, on Broadway, having a lofty spire rising from the rear end of the building.

Union square, on the corner of Broadway and Fourteenth street, is an oval inclosure, containing a life-like and imposing equestrian statue of Washington. The Worth monument, erected in honor of General Worth, an able officer of the Mexican war, who died in Texas, in May, 1849, is in Madison square, a truncated triangular space, directly opposite the Hoffman house.

The streets of New York are traversed by twenty-four lines of omnibuses and horse railways, five of which carried in one year over thirty-two millions of passengers.

A river of pure soft water is received in the city by the Croton aqueduct. This water is conveyed from the Croton river, forty miles distant, through sixteen tunnels, and received in reservoirs of sufficient magnitude to hold conjointly, one billion and two hundred millions of gallons. New York employs sixteen hundred police, with salaries varying from eight hundred to five thousand dollars annually. A volunteer fire department of four thousand two hundred and twenty-seven members, mans fifty steam and hand engines, fifty-six hose carts, and seventeen hooks and ladder trucks.

New York is extensively engaged in both foreign and domestic commerce. Her matchless harbor is formed by the upper bay, which, with its two arms, nearly surrounds the city. New York is connected with Canada and the great lakes, by the Hudson river and the Erie Canal; with the New England states, by Long Island Sound; has easy access to the Atlantic ocean, by which it carries on a trade with nearly every maritime nation on the earth. Elegant steamboats of great magnitude and speed, form connections with the most important cities in the world. The harbor is literally crowded with masts, bearing aloft flags of every maritime nation on the globe. New York has twenty-five ship-yards and manufactories of steam engines, machinery, clothing, carriages and pianoforte factories, and contains twelve large book-publishing establishments. In 1790, the population of New York was 23,831; in 1860, 813,669. (See views of New York.)

BROOKLYN.

Brooklyn, a city at the western end of Long Island, and the capitol of King's county, is, next to New York and Philadelphia, the largest city in the United States. It is separated from New York by the East river, and is connected with that city by numerous steam ferries, which cross every few minutes during the day, and every half-hour during the night.

Brooklyn is regularly laid off, the streets being about sixty feet wide, and crossing each other at right angles. Fulton, the most important exception of the general directness of the streets, is the principal thoroughfare of the city. The rapid growth of Brooklyn is owing partially to the healthiness of the climate, but chiefly to its proximity to the great metropolis. The most beautiful private residences are erected by wealthy gentlemen, and business men of New York.

The principal public buildings are the city hall, court-house, and academy of music. The city hall, occupying a triangular space on Fulton street, is a three story white marble edifice, one hundred and sixty-two feet long, by one hundred and two feet wide, and surmounted by a dome seventy-five feet high. The court-house, built in Corinthian style, also on Fulton street, was erected at a cost of five hundred and forty thousand dollars.

Brooklyn contains one hundred and twenty-one churches, the finest of which are the Holy Trinity, Church of the Puritans, Grace church, Church of the Restoration, and Plymouth church. The Church of the Holy Trinity is a gothic brown stone structure which cost nearly one hundred and fifty thousand dollars. The Church of the Puritans, Grace church, and Church of the Restoration, are also built in gothic style, the former of gray-stone, and the latter of brown-stone.

In the south-eastern portion of the city, on the southern side of Wallabout bay, is the national navy-yard, covering forty acres of ground, and enclosed by a high stone wall. Within the yard are two ship-houses, where are built torpedo boats, war sloops, and other vessels useful in naval warfare. The navy-yard also contains workshops, officers' quarters, and a vast amount of military stores. (See views of Brooklyn navy-yard.)

Brooklyn has several flourishing banks, various literary institutions, and numerous seminaries of education—an ample share, in short, of all that characterizes a wealthy, populous, and intelligent community. Population in 1865, 350,000. (See views of Brooklyn.)

GREENWOOD CEMETERY.

One of the most attractive features of Brooklyn, is Greenwood Cemetery, three miles south-east of Fulton ferry, on Gowanus hights. In beauty of location and adornments of art, Greenwood has no rival. A more beautiful spot for the great necropolis of New York, could not have been easily selected. From its verdant and breezy hills, a glowing and extensive prospect of the surrounding country is gained. A good view is obtained of Long Island, Staten Island, the matchless harbor of New York, beyond which rise the lofty edifices, domes and church spires of the metropolis. The grounds, beautifully laid off, are traversed by broad and handsome carriage-ways and multitudes of avenues, shady lanes, and winding gravel walks, leading to artificial lakes and ponds. The avenues are variously denominated, Alder, Aspen, Baltic, Bayside, Birch, Central, Cypress, Dale, Edgewood, Elm, etc. The length of the various avenues, taken conjointly, and excluding the numerous foot-paths, is sixteen miles. Among the hills, valleys, ridges, and waters, occur the following characteristic and beautiful names: Alpine Hill, Arbor Water, Battle Hill, Bayside Dell, Cedar Dell, Cherry Hill, Crescent Water, Evergreen Ridge, Maple Ridge, Fountain Hill, Ocean Bluff, Grassy Hill, Edge Hill, etc.

Greenwood Cemetery has been a chartered institution for about thirty-one years. John Hanna, who died in September, 1840, was the first person interred in its limits. In 1844,

DeWitt Clinton, once governor of New York, and whose autograph is carved in the soil of that state, from the Hudson river to Lake Erie, was buried in Greenwood. The first bronze casting America ever produced, stands upon his tomb in Bayside Dell. (See view.) The figure is an imposing representation of the statesman, and is the work of the same skillful hand that produced the equestrian statue of Washington in Union Square. Other noted men, who repose in Greenwood, are James K. Paulding, author of *Dutchman's Fireside*, and other works of prose and poetry, which will keep his name forever fresh in the memory of the people; Dr. Samuel L. Mitchell, a distinguished United States senator; Dr. Valentine Mott, the celebrated surgeon; and James Kent, the celebrated chancellor and writer of the well-known commentaries on American law. An Alabamian named Dixon H. Lewis, after a ramble in Greenwood, expressed his desire to be buried there. He was styled the "stout member" at congress, and actually required two seats in the halls of that house for his accommodation. Generals O. M. Mitchell and George C. Strong, of the union, and General Garnet, of the rebel army, are among the noted soldiers that repose in Greenwood. In the poets' corner, are the remains of "Poor McDonald Clarke," a poetical writer of eccentric fancies, who flourished about forty years ago. The neat obelisk, which marks his grave, is surrounded by a circular iron railing. A fine likeness of Clarke is sculptured on the face of the monument, and below is the epitaph, written by himself: "Sacred to the memory of Poor McDonald Clarke." The monument adjoining Clarke's, was erected to the memory of Dohum-mee, a young Indian princess of the Sac tribe, who died while in New York, whither she had come with a delegation of Sacs and Iowas. A plain white monument marks her grave, on which the modest legend, "Mrs. Eliza Gilbert, died January 17, 1861," would fail to stimulate curiosity, or awaken interest.

Among the costly monuments of Greenwood, the one erected to the memory of Charlotte Canda, is really the most important. (See view.) Her death occurred on the evening of her seventeenth birthday, and was occasioned by a fall from her carriage, as she was returning from a party. The fortune which the bereaved father had intended as her dowry, was expended on her tomb. Under the spire-flanked arch, is a picture of the young girl, as she was dressed on the evening of the accident. An oblong space in front of the statue, is surmounted by a balustrade, which forms an ornate porch to the monument. A monumental slab, in the middle of this space, has at its head an urn, with books and instruments of music and drawing. Upon the esplanade fronting the statue, are two guardian angels gazing upon her.

Another handsome monument is the one recently erected by James Brown, in memory of several members of his family who perished on board the ill-fated vessel, the Arctic. It is constructed of Italian marble and Aberdeen granite, is forty-six feet high, and has four columns, surmounted with gables, upon which are crockets, wrought in imitation of white lilies and twining ivy. Upon the different sides of the monument are inscribed appropriate texts of scripture, and upon the groining of the arches are four angels looking down on the sinking steamer, which is most admirably represented in marble. Groups of coral, seaweed, and shells, are carved on the moulding of the pedestal, and the entire monument, standing at the top of "the Tower," near Landscape avenue, is delicately designed and executed.

The Pilot's monument, which stands on Battle hill, is a lofty and slender shaft, erected to the memory of a gallant seaman. The Firemen's monument, on Summit avenue, is a pyramidal marble column, surmounted by a well executed figure of a fireman. The Sea Captain's monument, and monument of Henry Ruggles, and the tombs of Niblo, W. W. Grosbeck, and many others, also attract general attention.

A chapel, for the purpose of conducting the funeral services of foreigners and strangers, has been established in the cemetery. After turning a certain corner of the city, the procession is observable, when the tolling of the chapel bell announces its approach.

BUFFALO,

The third city in importance of New York, and seat of justice of Erie county, is at the eastern end of Lake Erie, at the point where it merges into the Niagara river, covering about the same space on the river as on the lake. It is three hundred miles west of Albany, four hundred miles north-west of New York, and five hundred and thirty-eight miles north-east of Chicago, and is the terminus of the New York and Erie and New York Central railroads, and the Hudson and Erie canal. The site of the city, bordering on the lake and river, is low and level, but before reaching the western suburbs the ground rises to a hight of sixty feet. Niagara street, the most important thoroughfare, is four miles long, and extends nearly across the city from north to south. In the western section of the city the streets are bordered with magnificent shade trees, frequently of great magnitude, and contain many elegant and costly private residences. Among the finest buildings may be mentioned the city hall, four large markets, two court houses, and the city penitentiary.

The literary and educational institutions of Buffalo are important. The Germans' Young Men's association, contains a free reading room, and a library of over two thousand volumes. In the Young Men's association buildings, costing about one hundred and forty thousand dollars, is a well selected library of twelve thousand volumes. The Buffalo female academy, on Delaware street, is one of the finest institutions of the kind in the state.

Buffalo is extensively engaged in commerce. The total trade for the year 1863, amounted to two hundred and fifty-six millions two hundred and fourteen thousand six hundred and fourteen dollars. The city has seventy churches, eighteen newspaper publications, a school for colored children, twenty-five district schools, one high school, nine banks, seventy-five insurance offices, twenty iron manufactories, extensively engaged in the manufacture of steam boilers and engines, nails, car-axles, anchors, etc., and a rolling mill, in which are nine heating and sixteen puddling furnaces.

The entire length of the streets in Buffalo is two hundred and ninety-six miles, fifty-three miles of which were paved at a cost of one million five hundred and forty-one thousand six hundred and ninety-three dollars. Population in 1860, 81,131.

ROCHESTER,

One of the most important cities of New York, and seat of justice of Monroe county, is on the Genesee river, about seven miles from the point where that stream pours its waters into Lake Ontario. It is on the route of the New York Central railroad and Erie canal, the latter of which crosses the Genesee, at this place, by a freestone aqueduct of nine arches, each fifty feet span, and constructed at a cost of six hundred thousand dollars. The city is two hundred and thirty miles west by north of Albany, and sixty-eight miles north-east of Buffalo. It occupies a plain of about five thousand five hundred acres, which is intersected by well paved streets from sixty to eighty feet wide. Marble, stone, and brick are the chief building materials.

The most important public buildings are the Arcade, city hall, and court house, the two latter of which were constructed at a cost of about seventy-five thousand dollars each. Among the libraries may be mentioned the Rochester athenæum, having twelve thousand, and the free library ten thousand volumes. The Rochester university is a brown stone edifice, completed in 1859. The building cost two hundred thousand dollars, and is attended by upwards of one hundred and seventy-five students. The chief hotels are Bracket, Waverly, National, and Congress Hall.

The Genesee river, at Rochester, has a descent, in between two and three miles, of two hundred and twenty-six feet, thus establishing that immense hydraulic power to which the city owes its manufacturing prosperity. Rochester has manufactories of flour, paper, cotton, woollen, machinery, locomotives, etc. The city has forty-five churches, fifteen newspaper offices, three collegiate institutes, a free academy, two commercial colleges, eighteen public schools, several ladies' seminaries, two orphan asylums, an industrial school, an insane asylum, and a city hospital.

It contains, also, twenty-two mills, which produce, on an average, seven thousand three hundred and twenty barrels of flour per day. The Rochester gas company has twenty-nine miles of gas pipe distributed over the city in various directions, which keeps in lighting order upwards of one thousand public lamps. Population in 1865, 60,000. (See views at Rochester.)

TROY,

A city of New York, and seat of justice of Rensselaer county, is at the head of steamboat navigation on the Hudson, on both sides of the river, one hundred and fifty-one miles above New York. The site of the city is a fertile and undulating plain, about three and one half miles long and one and one half miles wide. Mounts Olympus and Ida, the former in the northern and the latter in the southern suburbs of East Troy, are the only important elevations in the city. River street, the most important thoroughfare, is lined with massive warehouses and fine hotels, and follows the course of the river through nearly the entire length of the city.

Prominent among the public buildings is the court house, a fine marble building of the Doric order. Among the schools may be mentioned the Troy female seminary, academy, and the Renssalaer institute, the former attended by from two hundred and seventy to three hundred pupils, and all containing valuable libraries. The most important churches are St. John's, of brown sandstone, St. Paul's, of blue limestone, and the Presbyterian of brick, stuccoed in imitation of granite. Among the hotels, the Troy house, Mansion house, Washington hall, Charles house, and Union hall, are the most important.

The commerce of Troy is important. Large steamboats ascend the river as far as this city, where they receive cargoes brought hither by the Hudson and Erie and the Champlain canals. Troy is connected with Philadelphia by a line of propellers and barges, and with Boston by a line of sailing packets. The city contains thirty churches, eight newspaper publications, fifteen banks, a large number of flour and paper mills, and cotton, woollen, and leather factories, and malleable iron works. Population in 1860, 39,235.

SYRACUSE,

A thriving city of New York, and seat of justice of Onondaga county, eighty miles west of Albany, and thirty-five miles south-east of Oswego, is at the extreme southern end of a small lake bearing the same name as the county in which it is situated. It is the terminus of the Syracuse and Oswego, and Syracuse and Binghampton railroads, and is on the route of the New York Central railroad. The ground on which the city is built is generally level, and is intersected by broad, and, with but few exceptions, regular streets. The chief building materials are brick and stone.

The most important buildings are the hotels and churches. Among the former may be mentioned the Syracuse house, Voorhees house, and Globe hotel. There are twenty-three churches, nineteen of which are Protestant, and four Roman Catholic. The city contains two public halls of sufficient capacity to accommodate upwards of six thousand persons. It has also twelve large public schools, twelve newspaper offices, and ten banks.

Syracuse has the greatest salt works in the United States. The springs from which the salt is produced are owned by the state. Those engaged in its manufacture receive a lease from the state government, by which they are bound to pay a duty of one cent on every bushel produced, and to use the water for no other than saline purposes. The tax, formerly twelve and a half cents per bushel, was afterward reduced to six, and finally to the present rate. Syracuse has a number of flour mills and manufactories of machinery, steam engines, and leather. Population in 1865, 33,000.

UTICA,

A finely built and prosperous city of Oneida county, on the New York Central railroad, and on both sides of the Mohawk river and the Erie canal, ninety-five miles west of Albany, and three hundred and eighty-three miles north by east of Washington. It is connected with the St. Lawrence river by the Black river railroad, and with Binghampton by the Chenango canal. The ground on which the city is built is the site of old Fort Schuyler, and is level with a single exception on the northern side of the river.

Genesee street, the principal thoroughfare, contains the city hall, a handsome Milwaukee brick building, other public buildings, and a large number of mercantile houses. The principal hotels are the National house, Central house, and Bragg's hotel. The city contains twenty-six churches, two fine academies, and two public libraries. Utica is the seat of the state lunatic asylum, occupying a number of stone buildings in the western part of the city. Of the five hundred and fourteen patients in this institution in 1863, two hundred and sixty-two were males, and two hundred and fifty-two females. The city, also, contains eight newspaper publications, besides a number of periodicals, and is extensively engaged in the manufacture of railway carriages, and organs. Population in 1860, 22,529.

OSWEGO,

An important city of New York, and semi-capital of Oswego county, is on the south-eastern shore of Lake Ontario, and is the most important city of the United States on that body. The city is on both sides of the Oswego river, which here enters the lake. It is thirty-five miles north-east of Syracuse, and one hundred and seventy miles west by north of Albany, and is the northern terminus of the Syracuse and Oswego railroad. The city is divided into two nearly equal parts by the river, which is crossed by several substantial bridges.

Oswego is beautifully laid off, in a rich and fertile district, and is intersected by streets frequently one hundred feet wide, and crossing each other at right angles. The principal buildings are the city hall, custom house, and court house. The city contains ten churches, two public libraries, five newspaper publications, a fine system of free schools, and five banks.

The commerce of Oswego is rapidly increasing. The harbor, formed by the mouth of the river, is one of the finest in the state. A pier one thousand two hundred and fifty-nine feet long has been built on the western bank of the river, and one two hundred feet long on the eastern, and other improvements made at the expense of the United States government. Population of the city in 1860, 16,816.

KINGSTON

Is a city and seat of justice of Ulster county, situated on the western bank of the Hudson river, at the terminus of the Delaware and Hudson canal, fifty-five miles south of Albany, and ninety miles north of New York. The city is connected with Albany and New York by steamboats, and with the Hudson river railroad by a steam ferry. It contains eight churches, four banks, four newspaper offices, an excellent academy, and has a large commerce in coal, stone, ice, lime, and cement. Population in 1860, 7,000.

NEWBURG,

A finely built city and semi-capital of Orange county, is beautifully situated among the highlands, on the western bank of the Hudson river, eighty-four miles south of Albany, and sixty-one miles north of New York. The ground on which the city is built has a continual rise as it recedes from the river, and in the outskirts of the city is three hundred feet high. Fishkill, directly opposite Newburg, is connected with the latter city by a steam ferry. By means of a branch railroad to Chester, railway communication is established between Newburg and all important cities on the Erie railway. Newburg has a large number of elegant villas, and beautiful parks and gardens. It contains a number of foundries, tanneries, plaster mills, and manufactories of cotton, wool, machinery, etc. Large quantities of grain, flour, and products of the dairy are exported.

Newburg contains a court house, twenty-three churches, four newspaper offices, six banks, and numerous schools and academies. Railway carriages and steam engines are extensively manufactured. It has forty-one thousand tons of shipping, and carries on a large lumber trade. Population in 1860, 15,196.

YONKERS

Is a beautiful town on the eastern bank of the Hudson river, seventeen miles north of New York. The Hudson river railroad passes through the town, which has also a number of steamboats, establishing water communication with New York. It has ten churches, several banks, four newspaper offices, and a number of manufactories, mills, and foundries. It also contains male and female schools, and academies.

Yonkers is a favorite summer resort for wealthy citizens of New York and Brooklyn, who have established in and around the town a number of splendid residences. Population in 1860, 11,848. (See views of Yonkers.)

WEST POINT.

West Point, the seat of the United States Military Academy, is on the western bank of the Hudson river, in Cornwall township, Orange county, fifty-two miles north of New York. The site of the academy is an elevated and nearly circular plain, from one hundred and seventy to one hundred and ninety feet high, and about one mile in circuit. This national military seat was established in 1802, by forty cadet artillerists and ten engineers, and is supported by the government. The tuition is free —each pupil connected with the institution, however, being obliged to serve the government eight years. The president is allowed to send ten cadets to the academy, and each member of congress, one; the latter from the districts which they represent. No person under sixteen or above twenty-one years of age, is allowed to enter. In 1808, six years after the academy was founded, the school numbered one hundred and fifty-six; in 1812, two hundred and fifty, the latter being the largest number allowed in the academy at one time. The course of study embraces four years: (1) Mathematics, engineering, fencing, and bayonet exercises; (2) French, mathematics, fencing, tactics of infantry, cavalry and artillery; (3) natural philosophy, chemistry, drawing and riding; (4) military and civil engineering, mineralogy, geology, chemistry, law, literature, practical military engineering, tactics.

West Point is picturesquely situated among the Highlands, on the summits of which are ruins of forts, where occurred many important battles between the Americans and British, during the revolutionary war. On one of these elevations, six hundred feet high, is old Fort Putnam, "surrounded on three sides by deep ravines and steep descents." Fortresses in the vicinity of West Point were captured by the British in 1777, but abandoned after the surrender of Burgoyne. Stronger forts were then constructed by the Americans, which the traitor, Arnold, bargained to betray—a plot foiled by the arrest of Major Andre. (See views at West Point.)

ELMIRA

Is a city of Chemung county, on the northern side of the Chemung river, on the route of the Erie railroad, two hundred and seventy-seven miles west by north of New York. It is connected by railroad with Philadelphia, Baltimore and Harrisburg, on the south, and is the southern terminus of the Rochester and Elmira railroad, which connects the Erie with the northern tier of the Central railroad. It is on the route of the Erie railroad, which crosses the Chemung at this place, and is connected with Seneca lake by the Chemung canal. The city contains a court-house, a fine ladies' college, fifteen churches, four newspaper publications, five hotels, six banks, a piano manufactory, and a number of boot manufactories. Population, in 1865, 14,000. (See views at Elmira.)

LITTLE FALLS,

A thriving town of Herkimer county, is picturesquely situated in a narrow and romantic valley, on both sides of the Mohawk river, seventy-five miles north-west of Albany, and two hundred and fifty miles in the same direction from New York. The falls of the Mohawk at this place afford abundant water-power to the foundries and mills on its banks. "The Erie canal here passes, by a deep cut in the solid rock, through a picturesque defile, two miles in extent." (See views of Erie canal.) The elevations on either side of the canal frequently reach a great hight, and greatly resemble the Palisades of the Hudson. A mass of rugged rock, in the outskirts of the town, is called Profile Rock. (See view of Profile Rock.) The town has eight churches, two banks, and four newspaper offices. Population, 5,989.

SARATOGA SPRINGS

Is a fashionable watering place and summer resort in Saratoga county, in the eastern part of New York, thirty-eight miles north of Albany, and one hundred and sixty-seven miles in the same direction from New York. "Saratoga owes its celebrity to its mineral springs, the surrounding scenery possessing few, if any, extraordinary attractions." A single street, lined with massive hotels, stores and elegant private residences, constitutes the chief portion of the town. There are about twenty-three springs, variously impregnated with iron, iodine, soda, magnesia, etc., and all highly charged with carbonic acid. Empire and Iodine springs have been but recently discovered. Congress, the most important of the springs at the present time, was discovered as early as 1792. The waters of High Rock spring, discharged through a conical limestone rock, about five feet high, are "strongly charged with carbonic acid gas." These waters are prescribed in cases of chronic dyspepsia, diseases of the liver, etc. Saratoga Springs is annually visited by from thirty thousand to forty thousand pleasure-seekers and invalids, who receive accommodations at a number of large and fashionable hotels. Congress Hall, in the centre of a finely ornamented enclosure, has a commodious piazza, across the entire front of the building. Union Hall, though equaling the others in splendor and elegance, is in a more retired spot. There are also in the town several concert halls and opera houses, much frequented by the fashionable circle. Population of the town in 1860, 7,496. (See views of Saratoga Springs.)

OWEGO.

Owego is a finely built and prosperous town of Tioga county, New York, at the confluence of the Owego creek with the north branch of the Susquehanna river. The Owego creek is crossed at this place by the New York and Erie railway, about two hundred and forty miles from New York. The Cayuga and Susquehanna railroad connects Owego with Ithaca. The town contains eight churches, three newspaper offices, a large number of stores, three banks, male and female academies, and numerous flour, plaster, cotton and woolen mills. Owego is extensively engaged in the lumber trade. Incorporated as a town in 1827; population, 5,000. (See views of Owego.)

STAPLETON HIGHTS,

A thriving town of Richmond county, New York, picturesquely situated among the hights, on the north-eastern side of Staten Island. It is seven miles south-west of New York, and five miles in the same direction from Brooklyn. It contains several churches, and some elegant private residences. It is, also, the seat of a Seamen's Retreat, an immense three story building, two hundred feet long, and fifty feet wide, erected at a cost of one hundred thousand dollars. (See view of Stapleton Hights.)

PORT JERVIS,

A thriving town of Orange county, New York, on the Hudson and Delaware canal and the Erie railroad, ninety-eight miles north-west of New York. It has five churches, two banks, and one engine house. Port Jervis is in a wild and picturesque region, surrounded by lofty elevations, the principal of which, Kittatinny mountain, changes the course of the Delaware from a south-westerly to a south-easterly direction. Population, about 4,000. (See views at Port Jervis.)

In 1860, New York had two thousand seven hundred and one miles of railroad, constructed at a cost of one hundred and thirty-one millions three hundred and twenty thousand five hundred and forty-two dollars. The Hudson and Erie canal, commenced in 1817, and completed in 1825, is three hundred and sixty-four miles long, and cost the state about seven millions of dollars. In regard to education, New York holds a prominent position among the United States. In 1860, the state contained seventeen colleges, attended by two thousand nine hundred and seventy students. The Normal School, at Albany, is attended by about two hundred and seventy-five students annually. The People's College, at Havana, Schuyler county, has property valued at one hundred thousand dollars, and is attended by forty-five students. At Ithaca, is the Cornell University, named in honor of Hon. E. Cornell, who donated five hundred thousand dollars to found the school, and the increase of a million acres of land for its support. (See views of Cornell University.)

In 1860, New York contained three millions eight hundred and eighty thousand seven hundred and thirty-five inhabitants, of whom three millions eight hundred and thirty-one thousand five hundred and ninety were white, forty-nine thousand and four colored, and one hundred and forty-one Indians. There are in the state five thousand and seventy-seven churches, eleven thousand six hundred and twenty-one public schools, one thousand five hundred and twenty private schools, two hundred and eight academies, seventeen colleges, and five hundred and fifty-nine newspaper publications. The governor of New York receives four thousand dollars per annum for his services. The senate consists of thirty-two, and the house of representatives of one hundred and twenty-eight, members. New York sends thirty one members to the national house of representatives, and is entitled to thirty-three electoral votes for president.

NEW JERSEY.

New Jersey, one of the middle states, and one of the thirteen original United States, lies between latitude 38° 55′ and 41° 21′ N., and longitude 73° 58′ and 75° 29′ W. It is bounded on the north by New York, on the south and south-east by the Delaware bay and river, on the east by New York, separated by the Hudson river, and the Atlantic ocean, and on the west by Pennsylvania and Delaware. Its greatest length is one hundred and sixty-seven miles; greatest breadth, ninety-six miles; area, eight thousand three hundred and twenty square miles, or five millions three hundred and twenty-four thousand eight hundred acres.

New Jersey, as a general thing, is low and sandy. The north-eastern portion of the state is traversed by a number of ridges, variously known as Blue, Schooley's, Romapo, and Second mountains. One of the grandest features of New Jersey scenery is the Palisades, a wall of trap-rock rising abruptly from the Hudson, to the hight of five hundred feet. One of the southern elevations of this ridge, is Bergen Hill, three miles west of New York, in Hudson county. (See views of Bergen Hill.) The Nevisink Hills, rising four hundred and fifty feet above an inlet of Raritan bay, are crowned with a light house, and commands an extensive and enchanting prospect.

The principal rivers, beside the Hudson and Delaware, are the Raritan, Hackensack and Passaic rivers. The Raritan, formed by the confluence of the north and south branches, in Somerset county, pours into the Raritan bay, after a course of thirty-three miles, about one-half of which distance is navigable for steamboats. The Hackensack, rising in Rockland county, New York, and emptying into Newark bay, New Jersey, is navigable for sloops for fifteen miles from its mouth. The Passaic river rises in Morris county, and, after a north-easterly course of one hundred miles, enters Newark bay, thirteen miles from Paterson. The scenery near the mouth of the river is highly picturesque. At Paterson, the river has a perpendicular pitch of fifty feet, and a total descent of seventy-two feet. During certain seasons of the year, the volume of water precipitated is small; but the falls have at all times a wild and romantic aspect. (See views of Passaic Falls.) In Warren county, there is a beautiful mountain lake, about two miles in circuit, and found at an elevation of one thousand four hundred feet.

The climate of New Jersey is mild, the soil north of the pine plains fertile, and the country healthy, with the exception of the malarious river bottoms. The northern part of the state is adapted to both tilling and pasturage. The staple productions are wheat, maize, oats, Irish and sweet potatoes, apples, peaches, plums, etc. The state has about twenty-four thousand farms, which produced in 1860, one million seven hundred and sixty-three thousand one hundred and twenty-eight bushels of wheat; nine millions seven hundred and twenty-three thousand three hundred and thirty-six bushels of corn, four millions five hundred and thirty-nine thousand one hundred and thirty-two bushels of oats, one hundred and forty-nine thousand four hundred and eighty-five pounds of tobacco, three hundred and forty-nine thousand two hundred and fifty pounds of wool, and five hundred and eight thousand seven hundred and twenty-six tons of hay.

Trenton is the capital. Other important cities are Newark, Jersey City, Paterson, Camden, Elizabeth, New Brunswick, and Hoboken.

TRENTON,

The capital of the state, and seat of justice of Mercer county, is on the eastern bank of the Delaware river, fifty-seven miles south-west of New York, and thirty miles north-east of Philadelphia. It is regularly laid off on somewhat uneven ground, and is intersected by, with few exceptions, straight streets, intersecting each other at right angles. Four railroads radiate from the city, and the Delaware and Raritan canal passes through the town.

Main street, the chief thoroughfare, contains the greater portion of the business buildings. State street crosses Main street at right angles, and contains the capitol, a handsome stone structure one hundred feet long and sixty feet wide, and many of the finest residences. Besides the capitol, the court house, a brick building, with a Grecian portico, penitentiary and state lunatic asylum are the principal buildings. Two bridges cross the Delaware at this place, one about a mile below and the other within the limits of the city. The latter is eleven hundred feet long. Trenton contains twenty churches, three banks, four paper mills, two rolling mills, and two wire factories. Population in 1860, 17,228.

NEWARK,

The largest city of New Jersey, and seat of justice of Essex county, is on the right bank of the Passaic river, twelve miles east by south of New York, on the New Jersey railroad. The site of the city is level, with the exception of an elevation extending entirely across the western suburbs of the city. Broad street, the principal thoroughfare, is two miles long, one hundred and thirty-two feet wide, and borders upon three fine public parks, shaded by beautiful elms.

The most important public buildings are the court house, a rich brown stone structure, in the Egyptian style, on the corner of Market and High streets, the custom house and post office, occupying an immense stone building, erected at a cost of one hundred and fifty thousand dollars, and the city hall. There are many elegant churches in the city, of which the Methodist, on Market street, the First Baptist, on Academy street, and the Catholic, on Washington, High, Warren, and Lafayette streets, are the most important. Newark contains seventy-five churches, five banks, forty public schools, nine newspaper publications, and five hundred and forty-seven manufacturing establishments, producing annually twenty-five millions of dollars. Population in 1860, 71,941.

JERSEY CITY,

Next to Newark, the largest city in New Jersey, is the seat of justice of Hudson county, on the western bank of the Hudson river, directly opposite New York. Five railroads, viz: Union, New Jersey, Morris and Essex, Easton, and Northern, radiate from the city, establishing an unrivaled line of communication with every section of the state. The Morris canal, for coal transport, extends from Jersey City to Easton, in Pennsylvania.

Jersey City is regularly laid off, with fine, broad streets, lighted with gas. There are about twenty churches in the city, one of the finest of which formerly stood in Wall street, New York, but was removed and built up stone by stone, on its present site. Large and powerful steamboats, lighted with gas, ply between New York and Jersey City, night and day. The city receives a supply of water from the Passaic river, seven miles distant, by means of water works, constructed at a cost of about six hundred thousand dollars. The distributing reservoir is on Bergen Hill, two miles from the city. The city has several seminaries, a high school, two newspaper offices, two banks, and a number of manufactories of machinery, locomotives, glass, crucibles, etc. Population in 1860, 29,226. (See views of Jersey City.)

PATERSON,

A city and seat of justice of Passaic county, New Jersey, is on the southern bank of the Passaic river, seventeen miles north-west of New York. It is on the line of the Union railroad, which connects it with New York city, and, also, with Goshen, on the Erie railway. The city is finely built, and is intersected by broad and well paved streets, generally direct, and lighted with gas. A short distance above Paterson, the Passaic river has a fall of seventy-two feet, affording a valuable hydraulic power, which has been greatly improved by the construction of a dam and several canals. The city contains fifteen churches, two newspaper offices, one bank, a number of large hotels, an academy, twenty cotton mills, a number of manufactories of locomotives, machinery, carriages, paper, etc., and an establishment manufacturing five thousand and five hundred pounds of silk monthly. Population in 1860, 19,506. (See views of Paterson.)

CAMDEN,

A city of New Jersey, and capitol of Camden county, is directly opposite Philadelphia, on the eastern bank of the Delaware river, thirty-two miles south-west of Trenton, and eighty-seven miles from New York. The city is finely laid off on an undulating plain, and contains a large number of elegant public buildings, and handsome private residences. It is connected with Philadelphia by steam ferries, and is the terminus of the Cape May, West Jersey, and Milville railroads. The city contains fifteen churches, three newspaper publications, a court house, an insurance office, two saw-mills, two iron foundries, and several ship yards. Population in 1865, 18,000.

ELIZABETH,

A city and seat of justice of Union county, New Jersey, is fifteen miles south-west of New York, at the junction of the

Central with the New Jersey railroad. The city was formerly known as Elizabethtown, and was the capital of the state. It is finely laid off, with broad and regular streets, on a plain considerably elevated above the sea. It contains twenty churches, two banks, an insurance office, three newspaper offices, a fine system of schools, and a large number of manufactories. Population in 1865, 13,500.

NEW BRUNSWICK,

A city and seat of justice of Middlesex county, New Jersey, is on the right bank of the Raritan river, thirty miles south-west of New York. It is on the line of the New Jersey railroad, which crosses the Raritan at this place, and is the eastern terminus of the Delaware and Raritan canal, a channel seventy-five feet wide and seven feet deep, extending to Bordentown. Rutger's college, a dark red free-stone structure, founded in 1770, is one of the finest buildings in the city. New Brunswick contains fifteen churches, several female academies, a theological seminary, five newspaper offices, and three banks. Population in 1865, 13,500.

HOBOKEN,

A city, and port of entry of Hudson county, is on the western bank of the Hudson river, one and one-half miles north of Jersey City, and opposite New York, with which it is connected by steam ferries. It has beautiful pleasure grounds, called "Elysian Fields," is a great summer resort, and is rapidly becoming an important town. It contains twelve churches, three newspaper publications, three banks, and twenty hotels. Two lines of European steamboats depart from this port. Population in 1865, 12,500. (See views of Hoboken.)

In 1860, New Jersey contained six hundred and seventy-two thousand and thirty five inhabitants, of whom six hundred and forty-six thousand six hundred and ninety-nine were white, twenty-five thousand three hundred and eighteen free colored, and eighteen slaves. The state contains one thousand one hundred and twenty-three churches, two hundred and fifty-one academies, one thousand four hundred and ninety-six public schools, about one hundred public libraries, containing four hundred and thirty-three thousand three hundred and twenty-one volumes; one hundred newspaper publications, twenty-one cotton and forty-one woollen factories, one hundred and nineteen iron foundries, with extensive manufactories of machinery, locomotives, carriages, glass, boots, etc. The governor of the state receives one thousand eight hundred dollars per annum for his services. The senate consists of twenty, and the house of representatives of sixty, members. New Jersey sends five members to the national house of representatives, and is entitled to seven electoral votes for president.

PENNSYLVANIA.

Pennsylvania, one of the thirteen original, and, next to New York, the most populous of the United States, lies between latitude 99° 43′ and 42° 15′ N., and longitude 74° 75′ and 80° 37′ W. It is bounded on the north by New York and Lake Erie; on the south by Delaware, Maryland and West Virginia; on the north-east by New York; on the east by New Jersey; and on the west by Ohio and West Virginia. It is three hundred and ten miles long, and one hundred and sixty miles wide, including an area of forty-six thousand square miles, or twenty-nine millions four hundred and forty thousand acres.

The Alleghany mountain range passes entirely across the state from north to south, forming the water-shed between the basin of the Ohio and the rivers which flow into the Atlantic ocean. The Blue mountains, the eastern ridge of the Alleghanies, extend first in a north-easterly direction, about one-third of the distance across the state, when they bend to the east-north-east, and enter New Jersey. The Delaware river here bursts through a deep and narrow gorge two miles long, and is walled in by almost perpendicular precipices, one thousand six hundred feet high, forming the Delaware Water Gap, one of the most remarkable curiosities in the state. (See views of Delaware Water Gap.) Chestnut ridge, the most western range of the Alleghanies, and Laurel ridge, reach no great hight, but are well defined mountain chains. The Broad mountains extend from the center of Carbon county, through Schuylkill into Dauphin county. Broad Top mountain, a peak of the Alleghanies, lies between Bedford and Huntington counties. This mountain contains rich beds of coal, from three to eight feet thick. On the summit of the mountain, is the Broad Top Mountain House, a delightful summer retreat in the heart of the coal region. (See views among the Alleghanies.)

The principal rivers, besides the Delaware, which forms the eastern boundary, are the Susquehanna and its branches, the Schuylkill and Lehigh, in the eastern part of the state, and Alleghany and Monongahela in the western part. The Susquehanna, formed by the confluence of the west with the north branch, one mile above Sunbury, has a course of one hundred and fifty miles, and empties into the northern extremity of Chesapeake bay. It contains a large number of picturesque islands, and is obstructed by rapids, which, at high water, render navigation difficult. The northern branch of the river originates in Otsego lake, in Otsego county, New York, and has a winding course of two hundred and fifty miles. The western branch originates in Cambria county, Pennsylvania, and has a course of two hundred miles. The Juniata river, formed by the confluence of the Little Juniata with the Frankstown branch, is one hundred and fifty miles long, and empties into the Susquehanna, twelve miles above Harrisburg. The Little Juniata rises in Blair county, and is thirty miles long. The scenery along the banks of the Juniata is in the highest degree grand and beautiful. The mountains, on either side of the river, frequently rise to the hight of one thousand five hundred feet. (See views on the Juniata.) The Schuylkill river, signifying "hidden creek," rises among the highlands in Schuyler county, and pours into the Delaware, five miles below Philadelphia, after a course of one hundred and twenty miles. The Lehigh river, originating in the lowlands of Luzerne and Pike counties, flows through a picturesque and beautiful region, and enters the Delaware at Easton, after a course of ninety miles. The Lackawaxen river, rising in Wayne county, passes through one of the wildest and most picturesque regions in the state. It drains the Wallenpaupack creek, and enters the Delaware in Pike county. The Wallenpaupack river, in a narrow, deep, and rocky channel, has a beautiful descent in falls and cascades, which deserves the attention of all lovers of the picturesque. (See views of Wallenpaupack falls.) The Alleghany river rises in Potter county, Pennsylvania, flows north through Cattaraugus county, New York, and bending south, again enters Pennsylvania, and unites with the Monongahela, at Pittsburgh, forming the Ohio. The Monongahela river is formed by the junction of the West Fork and Tygart's Valley rivers, in Marion county, West Virginia, and has a length from this point of one hundred and fifty miles.

The iron and coal mines of Pennsylvania far surpass those of any other state. The great anthracite and semi-anthracite deposits of coal are east of the Alleghanies; and west are the great beds of bituminous coal, which largely supply the Mississippi valley. In the latter districts are large deposits of petroleum. In the vicinity of Philadelphia are extensive quarries of fine white marble.

The climate of the state is mild, and the soil fertile. The staple productions are wheat, Indian corn, rye, oats, buckwheat, potatoes, hemp, flax, tobacco, hay, fruits, etc. In 1860, Pennsylvania produced thirteen millions forty-five thousand two hundred and thirty-one bushels of wheat, twenty-eight millions one hundred and ninety-six thousand eight hundred and twenty-one bushels of corn, twenty-seven millions three hundred and eighty-seven thousand one hundred and forty-seven bushels of oats, and three millions one hundred and eighty-one thousand five hundred and eighty-six pounds of tobacco. According to the manufacturing statistics of 1860, the amount of capital invested was one hundred and eighty-nine millions of dollars; value of raw material used, one hundred and forty-five millions and three hundred thousand dollars; value of the annual product, two hundred and eighty-five millions and five hundred thousand dollars.

Harrisburg, the sixth city in size in the state, is the capital, and Philadelphia is the largest city. Pittsburg, Alleghany city, Reading, and Lancaster city are the other most important towns.

HARRISBURG,

Capital of Pennsylvania, and also of Dauphin county, is pleasantly situated on the west bank of the Susquehanna river, one hundred and ten miles north of Washington. The capitol, occupying an elevation in the center of the city, and containing a valuable library, and the court-house, are the principal public buildings. The city has eighteen churches, six newspaper publications, ten public schools, a male and female seminary, four banks, and a county prison. Population, in 1865, about 20,000.

PHILADELPHIA,

The chief city of Pennsylvania, and, next to New York, the most populous in the United States, is on a peninsula formed by the confluence of the Schuylkill with the Delaware river, one hundred and thirty-six miles north-east of Washington, and eighty-seven miles south-west of New York. The ground on which the city is built, though generally level, is slightly elevated towards the north. The original plan of its founder, William Penn, though at the time followed to an extent, has, by succeeding generations, been wholly disregarded. The ten chief streets of the city extend from river to river, and are intersected at right angles by upwards of twenty-five others. The streets vary from fifty to one hundred and twenty-feet in width. The city is divided into four nearly equal parts, by Broad street, running north and south, and Market street, extending across the peninsula from east to west. At the intersection of the latter streets is a fine public park, divided by these thoroughfares into four sections. Each quarter of the city also contains a fine park.

The city is between five and six miles on the Delaware, two and one half miles on the Schuylkill, and covers an area of ten square miles. The narrowest portion of the peninsula is two miles wide, and it is here that the most compact and business portion of the city is found. Chestnut street, containing the custom house and United States mint, Third street and Market street are the chief business thoroughfares.

Among the public buildings, the state house, a plain brick edifice, in Independence square, on Chestnut street, demands universal attention. It was in the east wing of this building that congress convened and issued the declaration of independence, July 4th, 1776—a circumstance, which, connected as it is with the birth of our nation, has rendered it a national object of respect and interest. The east and west wings are connected by corridors, and the whole is surmounted by a dome, containing a town clock and an alarm bell. The custom house is a fine edifice of the Doric order, one hundred and sixty feet long, eighty-seven feet wide, and constructed at a cost of five hundred thousand dollars. The United States mint, on Chestnut street, is two hundred and twenty feet long, one hundred and twenty feet wide, and cost two hundred thousand dollars. The merchants' exchange is a rich marble edifice, one hundred and fourteen feet long, ninety-five feet wide, and containing, besides the great hall of the exchange, insurance and other offices. The Girard college buildings, constructed of white marble, surpass in beauty of architecture all other structures in the city. The entire cost of the buildings, including the grounds, was upwards of two millions of dollars, which sum was left the city by Stephen Girard, a Philadelphia merchant.

Philadelphia has a large number of excellent hotels. Of these, the Continental house, American house, and Washington house, on Chestnut street, Union house on Arch, and Merchants' house on Fourth street are the most important.

The Pennsylvania hospital, established in 1752, occupies a square at the intersection of Pine, Eighth, Spruce and Ninth streets. There are several buildings in this square belonging to the institution, one of which, the chief structure, is two hundred and eighty-two feet long, and all are constructed of brick. There are in the city fifteen military hospitals, with accommodations for upwards of fourteen thousand patients.

Among the principal libraries are the Philadelphia library, and American philosophical society, founded by Benjamin Franklin, the former containing eighty thousand, and the latter twenty thousand volumes.

Among the churches, the Catholic cathedral of St. Peter and St. Paul, greatly surpasses in architectural beauty all others in the city. This imposing edifice, constructed of red sandstone, is in Logan square, fronting on Eighteenth street. In front are four Corinthian columns, sixty feet high, with a tower at each angle of one hundred and ten degrees, the whole surmounted by a dome, the apex of which is two hundred and ten feet above the ground. The other important churches are Christ's church, St. Mark's church, a red sandstone structure, one hundred and fifty feet long, ninety feet wide, and crowned with a lofty tower and spire, Church of the Holy Trinity, Church of Calvary, and Baptist church.

Among the educational establishments of the city may be mentioned the Academy of the Episcopal church, Philadelphia academy, and Theological seminary, the latter two of which are Catholic institutions. There are also a girls' and a boys' high school, the former of which, on Sargeant street, is under the direction of a male principal and nine female assistants. The latter, established in 1837, is on Broad street, and has an average attendance of four hundred and seventy students. This building has a fine observatory, in which is a powerful telescope. Connected with the institution are fourteen professors, on salaries of one thousand two hundred dollars each.

Philadelphia is supplied with water by the Fairmount water works, located on the Schuylkill river, two miles north-east of the state house. By means of a dam across the river, eight wheels are turned, which work as many pumps. The water is received in four large reservoirs, on an eminence near the river, and from thence is conveyed through pipes to other reservoirs in different parts of the city.

The city has three hundred and sixty-five churches, fifty periodicals, forty weekly and twelve daily publications, sixty grammar schools, three hundred schools of lower grade, twenty-five banks, eight savings banks, five theatres, and a state penitentiary. It has manufactories of iron, machinery, cotton and woollen goods, boots, shoes, furniture, etc., amounting annually to one hundred and seventy-five millions of dollars. Population in 1860, 565,531. (See views of Philadelphia.)

PITTSBURG,

An important city of Pennsylvania, and seat of justice of Alleghany county, is at the confluence of the Alleghany and Monongahela rivers, which here unite to form the Ohio, five hundred and thirty-seven miles west of Philadelphia. Though there are considerable elevations along the rivers and in the western suburbs, the general character of the site of the city is level. When the town was laid off, the streets were made to follow the general direction of the rivers; consequently the cross-streets meet obliquely, a few blocks from the Monongahela. The numerous factories and foundries of the city, send forth columns of smoke, which fill the air for miles around, cover the buildings with soot, and give the city a dreary aspect. From this fact, Pittsburg has been appropriately styled the Birmingham of America. Directly across the Alleghany river, on the north, is Alleghany city, and on the opposite side of the Monongahela, is Birmingham, both of which cities might justly be regarded as extensions of Pittsburg.

Among the public buildings, the court house, on the summit of an elevation in the western part of the city, holds a conspicuous place. This building, constructed of stone, in the Doric order, is one hundred and sixty-five feet long, one hundred feet wide, and surmounted by a dome, which rises one hundred and forty-eight feet above the ground. The custom house, recently erected on the corner of Smithfield and Fifth streets, is a freestone structure of the Grecian order, constructed at a cost of one hundred and fifteen thousand dollars. Among the other important buildings may be mentioned the Monongahela house, one of the finest hotels in the United States, the Catholic cathedral, an imposing brick edifice, on the corner of Grant and Fifth streets, surmounted by a lofty spire, and the Episcopal church of St. Peter, on Grant street, directly opposite the court house.

Pittsburg is situated among the richest deposits of iron and bituminous coal in the United States. Sixty-five companies in the city produce yearly one million six hundred thousand tons of coal. There are in the city sixteen foundries, twenty-four iron and steel manufactories, several rolling mills, six cotton mills, and numerous manufactories of steam engines, boilers, nails, files, etc. Population in 1860, 49,220.

ALLEGHANY,

A city of Pennsylvania, is on the Alleghany river, directly opposite Pittsburg, with which it is closely connected in commercial and social interest. Three fine bridges, and a suspension aqueduct, extend across the river between the two cities.

Among the important buildings, may be mentioned the western penitentiary of Pennsylvania, a large stone building, constructed in the ancient Norman style, on Ohio street, the western Pennsylvania hospital, an imposing brick edifice in the eastern part of the city, and the house of industry, on Washington street.

Alleghany has fifteen churches, two theological seminaries, a fine system of public schools, three national banks, one hundred and twenty manufactories, and a large number of foundries.

READING,

An important city of Pennsylvania, and seat of justice of Berks county, is on the east bank of the Schuylkill river, fifty-two miles north-east of Philadelphia. The city is handsomely laid off on an undulating plain, and is intersected by wide and regular streets.

Prominent among the public buildings is the court-house, having a commanding situation, and adorned with a sandstone portico. Among the churches, the Episcopal church, a beautiful sandstone edifice, surmounted by a steeple two hundred feet high, and the Germans' Lutheran church, are the most important. Reading is on the Philadelphia, Reading, and Pottsville railroad, and is the terminus of the Lebanon Valley railroad.

The city has twenty-three churches, eight newspaper offices, several public libraries, an academy, four banks, two rolling mills, two flouring mills, a cotton mill, steam forges, and several foundries. It is also extensively engaged in the manufacture of machinery, steam engines, etc. Population in 1860, 23,162.

LANCASTER,

A finely built and important city of Pennsylvania, and seat of justice of Lancaster county, is seventy miles west of Philadelphia, on the Pennsylvania Central railroad. The city is regularly laid off, and is crossed by broad, and with few exceptions, direct streets. Wood and brick are the chief materials used in building.

The most important public buildings are the court house and county prison, both recently erected, the former in the Grecian style, and each costing in the vicinity of one hundred and twenty-five thousand dollars. The city contains a fine college, fifteen churches, ten newspaper publications, two public libraries, four banks, and manufactories of threshing machines, locomotives, carriages, rifles, axes, etc. Population in 1860, 17,603.

In 1860, Pennsylvania had two millions nine hundred and six thousand one hundred and fifteen inhabitants, of whom two millions eight hundred and forty-nine thousand two hundred and sixty-six were white, and fifty-six thousand eight hundred and forty-nine were colored. The state contains twenty-six colleges, twenty state academies, three hundred and thirty-five public schools, four thousand churches, about four hundred libraries, eight schools of medicine, and three hundred and ten periodical publications. The governor of Pennsylvania is elected for three years, and receives a salary of three thousand dollars per annum. The senate consists of thirty-three and the house of representatives of one hundred members. In 1862 there was in the state ninety-four banks, with an aggregate capital of twenty-five millions nine hundred and seventeen thousand six hundred and fifty dollars.

DELAWARE.

Delaware, one of the thirteen original states, the smallest of the middle, and, next to Rhode Island, the smallest of the United States, lies between latitude 38° 28′ and 39° 50′ north, and longitude 75° and 75° 45′ west. The eastern shore of the state is washed by the Atlantic ocean and the Delaware river and bay, the latter of which separates Delaware from New Jersey. Pennsylvania bounds the state on the north, and Maryland on the south and west. Length of the state, ninety-six miles; greatest breadth, thirty-seven miles; area, two thousand one hundred and twenty square miles, or one million three hundred and fifty-six thousand acres.

The surface of Delaware, as a general thing, is level, no elevations being found of sufficient altitude to be called mountains. The northern portion of the state is traversed by ranges of hills, and in the western part is a marshy elevation, partaking of the nature of a table land. The southern and central portions are low and level. The soil in this section is poor, consisting of a mixture of sand and clay. The most fertile districts occur in the north, and on the Delaware river and bay. The chief productions are Indian corn, wheat, rye, barley, buckwheat, hemp, flax, hops, honey, butter, etc.

Besides the Delaware, the most important rivers are Brandywine and Christiana, flowing into the Delaware river, Indian river, flowing into the Atlantic ocean, and Nanticoke and Choptank, flowing into the Chesapeake bay. The Delaware river rises in New York, on the western slope of the Catskills, and, after a course of three hundred miles, enters Delaware bay, an arm of the Atlantic. The river is navigable for large vessels as far as Philadelphia, and for steamboats to the head of tidewater, at Trenton.

Delaware has six hundred and fifteen manufacturing establishments, employing a capital of five millions three hundred sixty thousand dollars, and having an annual income of nine millions nine hundred and twenty thousand dollars. The commerce of Delaware is small, the trade of her cities being monopolized by the more important ones of Philadelphia and Baltimore. The chief exports are flour, grain, fruits, lumber, and sand.

Besides Dover, the capital, and Wilmington, the largest city, the places of any importance are Milford, Newcastle, and Smyrna.

DOVER,

The capital of the state, and also of Kent county, is on the Jones river and Delaware railroad, fifty miles north of Wilmington. It has a fine state house, four churches, and three large hotels. Population, 1,289.

WILMINGTON,

Chief city of Delaware, is in Newcastle county, on the Christiana creek, twenty-eight miles south-west of Philadelphia. It contains a custom house, twenty-three churches, a Catholic college, a fine library, four private and nine public schools, seven banks, six large machine shops, and a number of iron foundries, rolling and saw mills, and cotton factories. Population in 1860, 21,256.

MILFORD

Is a thriving town of Kent county, on the Mispillion creek, twenty-one miles south-east of Dover. It contains five churches, an academy, two banks, a newspaper office, a public library, and a ship yard. Population, 1,763.

NEWCASTLE

Is a city and seat of justice of Newcastle county, on the Delaware river, five miles south of Wilmington. It has eight churches, a court house, a public library, a bank, and manufactories of locomotives, machinery, etc. Population, 1,902.

SMYRNA

Is a thriving town of Kent county, thirty-six miles south of Wilmington, containing manufactories of carriages, a newspaper office and bank, five churches and three hotels. Population, 2,153.

In 1860, Delaware had one hundred and twelve thousand two hundred and sixteen inhabitants, of whom ninety thousand five hundred and eighty-nine were white, nineteen thousand eight hundred and twenty-nine free colored, and one thousand seven hundred and ninety-eight slaves. Delaware has two hundred and twenty churches, one college, two hundred and fifty-six public schools, forty academies, and one hundred and fourteen libraries, containing eighty-eight thousand four hundred and seventy volumes. The governor of Delaware is elected for four years, on a salary of one thousand three hundred and thirty-three dollars, and is not allowed to be re-elected. The senate consists of nine, and the house of representatives of twenty-one, members. Delaware sends one member to the national house of representatives, and is entitled to three electoral votes for president.

CHAPTER III.

THE SOUTHERN STATES.

MARYLAND.

Maryland is one of the thirteen original states, and the most northern of the southern states of which it is the smallest. It lies between latitude 38° and 39° 44′ N., and between longitude 75° 10′ and 79° 39′ W. It is bounded on the north by Pennsylvania, on the east by Delaware and the Atlantic ocean, and on the south and west by Virginia.

The outline of Maryland is very irregular. Its northern boundary has an extent of one hundred and ninety miles, but on the west side it contracts until its southern boundary is scarcely half that extent. The coast line of this state, including that of Chesapeake bay, is four hundred and eleven miles, without which it is only thirty-three miles.

The eastern portion of this state is level and the soil sandy. The mountainous portion is in the north-west part of the state, between the Potomac river and the Pennsylvania line. This section is crossed by several ridges of the Alleghanies. The coal, copper and iron mines of Maryland are productive.

The Chesapeake bay extends into the state about one hundred and twenty miles, varying in width from seven to ten miles. It divides the state into two parts, known as the eastern and western shore. A number of navigable rivers empty into this bay, the most important of which is the Potomac, being navigable for large vessels as far as Alexandria. The others are the Susquehanna, Potoxent, Patapsco, Elk, Chester, Chopotank, Nanticoke, and Pocomoke, all of which are navigable for small vessels. The falls of the Potomac are about fourteen miles above Georgetown; the perpendicular hight is not very great, being only about forty feet, but the beauty of the scene is hightened by the perpendicular cliffs on the Virginia side.

The staple productions are tobacco, wheat, and Indian corn. The forests are composed of a great variety of trees.

Maryland has a great amount of capital employed in various manufactures, producing forty-one millions seven hundred and thirty-five thousand one hundred and sixty dollars' worth of goods annually. It is the sixth state in the United States in commercial importance, being connected with Pennsylvania and southern New York by the Susquehanna river; with the west by Ohio and Baltimore railroad and the Ohio and Chesapeake canal, and the north-east by the Delaware and Ohio canal.

Maryland possesses great facilities for internal as well as foreign commerce.

The chief cities are Baltimore, Cumberland, Fredric City and Annapolis.

BALTIMORE,

The largest city of Maryland, has a population of two hundred and twelve thousand four hundred and eighteen. It is situated on the Patapsco river, about twelve miles from Chesapeake bay. The site of Baltimore is probably more picturesque than any other city in the union. It covers a number of eminences which furnish a pleasing variety for the tourist. From Washington monument, which is situated on a hill, a most beautiful panorama is spread out before the beholder. Baltimore has been called, from the number of its monuments, the "Monumental City." The most imposing of these is the Washington monument, which has a base fifty feet square and twenty feet high, supporting a column one hundred and seventy-six and a half feet in hight, crowned by a statue of Washington sixteen feet high. The summit of the monument is three hundred and twelve feet above the level of the harbor. It is constructed of white marble, and cost two hundred thousand dollars. Battle monument is also a beautiful structure of white marble; the base is square and finely ornamented; on it rests a facial column eighteen feet high, on the bands of which are inscribed the names of those who were killed while defending the city from the attack of the British in 1814. This column is surmounted by the Goddess of Liberty, seven and a half feet high. The Merchants' shot tower, the highest in the world, having an elevation of two hundred and forty-six feet, is also an object of interest to tourists. The Baltimore court house is a handsome structure two stories high, sixty-five feet wide and one hundred and forty-five feet long, constructed at a cost of one hundred and fifty thousand dollars. The United States court house is a handsome edifice built of granite. The Roman Catholic cathedral, a massive granite structure, is the most imposing church edifice in Baltimore. The total number of churches in the city is one hundred and sixty-one.

Among the literary and educational institutions, are the University of Maryland, Logola college, Baltimore college, and the Theological school. The athenæum has a library of nineteen thousand volumes. The Baltimore library has fifteen thousand volumes. The Maryland historical society has a collection of one thousand volumes, and in the gallery belonging to this society, are annually held exhibitions of painting and sculpture. There are about twenty-five newspaper publications, of which eight are dailies. The benevolent institutions of Baltimore, are the Maryland hospital for the insane, Mount Hope institution, the Church Home and Infirmary, five orphan asylums, and an alms-house. The state penitentiary, with the jail, occupies one square. There are eighty-two public schools, including the primaries, with an attendance of fifteen thousand six hundred and sixty-one scholars. Baltimore supports a great number of hotels, of which the city hotel, and Eutah house, are first-class.

Druid hill park encloses five hundred and forty-eight acres of land, situated just beyond the northern limits of the city. In Patterson's park are thirty-six acres, embracing the earthworks thrown up for the defense of the city during the war of 1812. Baltimore ranks among the first cities of the United States in commercial importance.

CUMBERLAND,

The county seat of Alleghany county, is situated on the Potomac river, and on the Ohio and Baltimore railroads, and about one hundred and eighty miles from Baltimore. It has a population of 8,478. It contains the county buildings, three banks, three printing offices, and a savings institution.

FREDRIC CITY,

Shire town of Fredric county, in wealth, population and commercial importance, takes the third rank in the state. It has a population of 8,142. It contains a handsome court-house, six tanneries, three banks, a college, an academy, two printing offices and eleven churches.

ANNAPOLIS,

The capital of Maryland, has a population of about 5,000. It is situated on the Severns river, about two miles from Chesapeake bay. In Annapolis are six churches, a bank, market-house, a fine state house, and two printing offices, from which are issued three newspapers.

The governor of Maryland holds his office four years, and has a salary of three thousand and six hundred dollars, with the use of a furnished house. The house of representatives consists of seventy-four members, and the senate of twenty-two. These, with the governor, are elected by the people.

DISTRICT OF COLUMBIA.

In 1790, Maryland and Virginia ceded one hundred square miles, situated on both sides of the Potomac river, to the United States. This tract was called the District of Columbia. It was designed for the site of the capital of the Republic, and, accordingly, a city was laid out and public buildings erected. The name of the city thus founded was Washington, and in 1800, the seat of government was removed thereto from Philadelphia. During the war of 1812, the British entered the city, burned the capitol, together with the library of congress, and the presidential mansion. These were rebuilt on the Maryland side of the Potomac, and the portion of the District on the Virginia side was retroceded to that state.

The District of Columbia is under the government of the United States congress, in which it has no representative, and is allowed no vote for the president. Georgetown and Washington are the only cities in the district. They are about two miles apart, and are separated by Rock creek.

GEORGETOWN

Is beautifully situated on a range of hills, the most elevated of which are called the Hights. (See views of Georgetown.) These eminences, which are occupied by handsome villas, command a view of Washington, the Potomac, Oak Hill cemetery, and an almost illimitable expanse of country. The Alexandria branch of the Ohio and Chesapeake canal is carried across the Potomac at Georgetown, by means of an enormous aqueduct one thousand four hundred and forty-six feet long and thirty-six feet above ordinary water level.

Georgetown is chiefly distinguished for its refined society and great literary advantages. The most important institution is the college, under the control of the Catholics, connected with which is a female academy, under management of the nuns, and a botanical garden. A United States hospital for soldiers is erected here. Georgetown being the only port in the District of Columbia, is important as a commercial town. It is situated at the head of navigation upon the Potomac, about one hundred and twenty-five miles from its mouth. Its trade in flour is supplied by fifty mills. It is one of the greatest markets in the United States for shad and herring, of which vast quantities are caught in the Potomac and brought here for barreling.

WASHINGTON,

The political metropolis of the United States, is located between the Potomac and a tributary call East Branch. The Potomac, at Washington, is about a mile in width, and of sufficient depth for the largest ships.

The principal edifices are the Capitol, White house, Treasury building, Patent office, Post office, and Smithsonian institute. The first of these, in point of interest and architectural merit, is

15

the Capitol, containing the supreme court room and halls of the national legislature. This building comprises the centre capitol and extensions. The corner stone of the centre building was laid by Washington in 1792. The extension was commenced by President Fillmore in 1851. The center capitol, built of freestone, painted white, is three hundred and fifty-two feet long by one hundred and twenty-one deep. The extensions, of pure white marble, are each two hundred and thirty-eight by one hundred and forty feet, connected by corridors forty-four feet long. The whole building is seven hundred and thirty-seven feet long, and covers three and a half acres of ground. (See views of the Capitol.) In the centre of the building is a rotunda ninety-six feet in diameter, surmounted by a dome of iron, on which rests Crawford's bronze statue of Liberty. The western front commands the finest view to be had in Washington, overlooking all the principal public buildings, and the central and western portions of the city. Groups of statuary by Persico and Greenough are on the eastern central portico. On the right of the entrance to the rotunda are placed the statues of War and Civilization; on the left of the entrance are the statues of Peace, and Columbus and the Indian girl. In the rotunda is a statue of Lincoln, and many historical paintings, among which are the baptism of Pocahontas, the landing of Columbus, the surrender of Cornwallis, General Washington resigning his commission at Annapolis, the surrender of Burgoyne, the embarkation of the Pilgrims, and others. In the dome of the capitol is an allegorical painting by Brumide. (See view of painting.) South of the rotunda is the old hall of representatives, now used for statuary, and as a passage way to the new hall. Above the south door is placed a statue of Liberty, supported by an eagle with spread wings. Over the north entrance is a statue regarded as one of the gems of the capitol. It is a figure representing History recording the events of the nation. The senate chamber is in the northern and the house of representatives in the southern extension of the capitol. They are both constructed of iron, ornamented alike, and differ only in size. The ceiling of the senators' retiring room is of Italian and the sides of gold veined

Tennessee marble. This room is more costly and beautifully ornamented than the others. (See views of retiring room.) The grounds around the capitol comprise about twenty-five acres, but they are soon to be increased to fifty acres. East of the capitol is a statue of Washington, by Greenough. (See view of statue.) In front of the capitol, between Maryland and Pennsylvania avenues, a botanical garden is being laid out, in which is a large collection of plants, secured by the South Sea and Japanese exploring expeditions.

The Presidential Mansion or White House, built of yellow free-stone, painted white, is about one and a half miles from the capitol, having been placed at this distance on Washington's suggestion, that the executive and legislative departments ought to be far enough apart to insure separate hours of business for each. It is two stories high, and has a front of one hundred and seventy feet by eighty-six deep. (See views of White House.) In the north lawn is a statue of Jefferson, and in Lafayette square, across Pennsylvania avenue, is an equestrian statue of Jackson, by Clark Mills, and in the circle near Georgetown is a statue of Washington by the same artist. (See views of statuary.)

The Treasury building, an immense edifice six hundred feet long and two hundred feet wide, is devoted to the state and treasury departments. (See views of Treasury building.) In this edifice are about five hundred rooms, in one of which is an immense printing and engraving establishment.

West of the president's house are the Navy and War departments and Pension office. They are large, plain brick buildings. The Postoffice, one of the finest structures in the city, is situated north of Pennsylvania avenue, about half way between the capitol and the president's house. It is built of white marble, two hundred and four feet long and one hundred and two feet wide, and contains upwards of two hundred rooms.

The Patent office occupies a whole square, and in structure, extent and elegance is not surpassed by any other building in the city except the capitol. (See views of Patent office.) Here may be found models of every invention or machine that has been patented.

A colossal monument to Washington has been commenced in the proposed new park, between the president's house and the capitol, to be erected by contributions of the people, the plan of which is an obelisk of white marble, at the base fifty-five feet square, diminishing to twenty-five feet square at the hight of five hundred feet. This stands on a pedestal seventeen feet high which is to be used as a receptacle for relics. A block of native wood or stone is furnished by each state, which is to be inserted at each landing of the inside staircase. East of the monument, and about half way between that and the capitol, situated on an eminence in the new park now being laid out, stands the Smithsonian institute. (See views of Smithsonian institute.) This imposing edifice, four hundred and fifty feet long and one hundred and forty feet deep, is built of red sandstone in the Norman style. James Smithson, an Englishman, left to the United States five hundred and fifteen thousand one hundred and ninety-six dollars, "to found at Washington an establishment for the increase and diffusion of knowledge among men." With a part of this fund and the accumulated interest the Smithsonian institute was founded. In this building are a museum for objects of natural history, and a gallery for painting and statuary. It has a library of forty thousand volumes, and one of the best supplied labratories in the United States. Works on ethnology and the antiquities have been published by this institution. The officers are the President, Vice President, Chief Justice of the United States, members of the cabinet, Commissioners of the Patent office, the Mayor of Washington, and a board of Regents, who elect a secretary, chancellor and executive committee.

One of the most creditable institutions of the United States is the National Observatory, lying in latitude 38° 53′ 39″ N., and longitude 77° 2′ 48″ W. from Greenwich. It is itself a meridian, and longitude is often reckoned from this city. The observatory occupies a commanding site on the Potomac, southwest of the white house. Astronomical observations are constantly made here, and chronometers for the use of the navy are tested. The largest telescope is a fourteen feet reflector, there are also a number of smaller ones.

The Arsenal is on Greenleaf point, at the junction of the east branch with the Potomac. The navy-yard, on the east branch, covering about twenty acres, enclosed by a wall, is about midway between the arsenal and capitol. This yard, one of the most extensive in the union, employs four hundred hands in the manufacture of anchors, boilers, steam engines, chain cables, in foundries, etc.

The government asylum for the insane of the District of Columbia, the army and the navy is situated on the opposite side of the east branch from the navy. About one mile east of the capitol is the congressional burying ground, where have been deposited some of the most eminent men of the nation.

VIRGINIA.

Virginia, one of the original states of the American confederacy, lies between latitude 36° 30′, and 40° 38′ N., and between longitude 75° 10′ and 83° 30′ W. It is bounded on the north by Ohio, Pennsylvania and Maryland; on the east by Maryland and the Atlantic ocean; on the south by North Carolina and Tennessee, and on the west by Kentucky and Ohio.

The state was settled in 1607, and being the first of the English colonies, was styled the "Ancient Dominion." The outline is irregular, the surface varied, and the state probably embraces a greater extent of mountainous territory than any other east of the Rocky mountains. White top, its highest elevation, is six thousand feet above the level of the sea. The principal productions are tobacco, wheat and corn. The inhabitants of Virginia were the first civilized people that were extensively engaged in raising tobacco.

Virginia possesses facilities, which, if properly improved, would render it one of the first manufacturing states in the union, but like the rest of the southern states, less attention is paid to the manufactures, than to agriculture.

The level and coast regions are hot, and subject to droughts during the summer. The mountainous part of the state has a salubrious temperature, with warm days and cool nights.

Virginia abounds in picturesque scenery. The most noted places are the Mineral Springs, Wyer's and Madison's caves, the Chimneys, the Natural bridge, Natural tunnel, Buffalo knob, and Hawk's nest. The Natural bridge spans a chasm ninety feet broad. The upper is two hundred and forty, and the under side two hundred feet above the water. The roads leading to the bridge, are, during wet weather, often impassable, and when best, the difficulties encountered in reaching the bridge are so great that they have been compared to purgatory. The bridge is in the form of an arch, through which, flows Creek river. Thirty feet from the bottom, and directly under the arch, are carved the letters G. W. These are the initials of George Washington, who, when a boy, scaled the rocks to this hight, and left his name indelibly traced on its surface. (See views of Natural bridge.) The Hawk's nest is a perpendicular cliff, one thousand feet above New river, on which it is situated. Through the Natural tunnel, passes a stream under an arch seventy feet in elevation, covered with a bed of earth twice that thickness.

RICHMOND,

The largest city and capital of the state, is situated on the James river. It has a population of 37,910. The city is built on several eminences, two of which are Richmond and Shokoe hills, separated by Shokoe creek. Main street is the principal business part of the city. The capitol is on Shokoe hill. Its size and elevated position render it the most conspicuous object in the city. The public square, in the center of which the capitol stands, embraces about eight acres. In it is a marble statue of Washington, around the center base of which are the statues of Patrick Henry, Thomas Jefferson, and Mason. The city hall, at an angle of Capitol square, is a handsome and costly building, constructed in the Doric style. The penitentiary has a front three hundred feet by one hundred and ten deep. It stands in the suburbs of the city, near the river. Richmond contains a court-house and jail, a new custom-house, two market-houses, a theater, a masonic hall, an orphan asylum, three banks, and about thirty churches. The public press issues seventeen papers and periodicals, several of which are dailies. Among the educational institutions, are Richmond college, St. Vincent's college, Sydney college, the Virginia historical and philosophical society, and the medical department of Hamden.

The city was founded in 1742, and became the capital of the state in 1780. During the rebellion it was the capital of the southern confederacy, and was taken by General Grant, of the union army, on the 2d of April, 1865, after a long siege. (See views of Richmond.)

NORFOLK,

Next to Richmond, the most populous city of Virginia, is situated on the north bank of Elizabeth river. It is one of the most important commercial and naval stations in the United States. The city hall, a structure eighty by sixty feet, has a granite front, and a cupola one hundred and ten feet high. Other conspicuous buildings, are the Norfolk military academy, the Mechanics' and Ashard halls. Norfolk has three banks, two reading rooms, nine seminaries, an orphan asylum, a hospital, fourteen churches, one of which has a steeple two hundred feet high, and several printing offices. The town was laid out in 1705, burned by the British in 1776, and incorporated as a city in 1845.

PETERSBURG,

A flourishing town of Virginia, is on the south bank of the Appomattox river. It has a population of eighteen thousand two hundred and sixty-six. The city is well built, and contains three banks, one woollen and several cotton factories, eight churches, and has three newspaper publications. It was taken by the union army in April, 1865.

ALEXANDRIA,

The county seat of Alexandria county, is pleasantly located on the west bank of the Potomac river. It has a court house, three banks, several excellent schools, two printing offices, and twelve churches. It is connected with Georgetown by means of a canal, and with Washington and Gordonsville by railroad.

MOUNT VERNON

Is about eight miles below Alexandria, on the Potomac. It is noted for being the residence and burial place of George Washington. (See views of Mount Vernon.)

WEST VIRGINIA.

West Virginia was admitted into the union as a state in 1862. It comprises about a third of the old state of Virginia. It lies between the Alleghany mountains and the Ohio and Big Sandy rivers. This state was separated from Virginia during the war of secession. Its climate, soil and productions resemble those of Kentucky and Ohio. Coal, iron, salt and petroleum exist in large quantities.

WHEELING,

The capital of West Virginia, is on the Ohio river, and on both sides of Wheeling creek. The site of the city is about six hundred and thirty feet above the level of the sea. In population, manufactures and trade, it is the chief city of the state.

Wheeling has a population of 22,500, and contains a handsome court house, custom house, four banks, three academies, nineteen churches, and publishes four or five newspapers. The river is here crossed by a beautiful suspension bridge, measuring in length one thousand and ten feet. The towers are sixty feet above the abutments, and one hundred and fifty-three feet above low water mark. The bridge is supported by four cable wires, each eight inches in diameter, and one thousand three hundred and eighty feet long. This bridge was constructed at a cost of two hundred and ten thousand dollars.

Inexhaustible beds of coal are found in the immediate vicinity of Wheeling, furnishing fuel at a small expense to its numerous manufactories.

The other principal places of West Virginia are Charlestown, Parkersburg, Point Pleasant, and Harper's Ferry.

CHARLESTOWN,

A handsome post village and county seat of Kanawha county, situated on the Kanawha river, is noted for its salt works. Its population numbers one thousand five hundred and twenty. Twice each year the district court of the United States is held at this place. The river at Charlestown is three hundred yards wide, and navigable for steamers at all seasons of the year.

PARKERSBURG,

The shire town of Wood county, is neatly built and pleasantly situated on the Ohio, at the mouth of the Little Kanawha. It has a population of six hundred, and contains a court house, four or five churches, a printing office, two national banks, and several steam mills. In the vicinity of Parkersburg, wells of coal oil abound.

POINT PLEASANT,

The seat of justice of Mason county, has a population of five hundred and nineteen, a court house, and several stores.

HARPER'S FERRY

Is at the junction of the Potomac and Shenandoah rivers, where the united waters break through the Blue Ridge. The scenery in this vicinity is beautiful and picturesque. Thomas Jefferson thought the "passage through the Blue Ridge one of the most stupendous scenes in nature, and well worth a voyage across the Atlantic to witness." The original name of this place was the Shenandoah Falls. (See views of Harper's Ferry.)

NORTH CAROLINA.

North Carolina, one of the thirteen original states, lies between latitude 33° 53′ and 36° 33′ N., and between longitude 75° 25′ and 84° 30′ W. It is bounded on the north by Virginia, on the east by the Atlantic ocean, on the south by the Atlantic ocean and South Carolina, and on the west by Tennessee. The east and south-east portions of the state are marshy, level and sandy, and abound in numerous shallow lakes, particularly between the Albemarle and Pamlico sounds. The level region extends about sixty miles from the coast. The center is hilly, and the western part mountainous. Through this part of the state pass several ridges of the Alleghany system, the highest peaks of which are, Clingman's peak, six thousand nine hundred and forty-one feet; Grandmother mountain, two thousand five hundred feet; Grandfather mountain, five thousand seven hundred and eighty-eight feet; Roan mountain, six thousand two hundred and seventy feet; and Mt. Mitchell, the most elevated peak east of the Rocky mountains, six thousand seven hundred and thirty-two feet above the level of the sea.

The principal minerals of North Carolina are gold, copper, iron, and coal. The state is traversed by a number of rivers, but the rapids and floating sand-bars of which prevent their being navigable for large vessels. The most important productions are cotton, rice, tobacco, wheat and corn. The chief exports are lumber and naval stores.

Attempts were made by Sir Walter Raleigh to settle North Carolina in 1585, but they were unsuccessful. The first permanent settlements were on the banks of the Roanoke and Chowara. These were attacked, in 1711, by the Tuscaroras, Creeks, and other Indians, who massacred one hundred and twelve settlers. The united forces of the Carolinas killed three hundred savages, and completely routed them.

North Carolina was the first to propose a separation from Great Britain, and took an active part in the revolution.

WILMINGTON,

The commercial metropolis and principal city of the state, is situated on the Cape Fear river. It has a population of nine thousand five hundred and fifty-two. Its business and population have greatly increased since the completion of the Wilmington and Raleigh railroad. The city has been recently connected with Manchester, in South Carolina. Communications with Charleston and Fayetteville, are kept up by means of steamboats. In 1819 a great portion of the city was consumed by fire. Wilmington was captured from the rebels in February, 1865, by the union army and navy. Many steam engines are employed in the manufactories, among which are saw, planing and rice mills, and distilleries. The city contains three banks, and publishes three newspapers.

FAYETTEVILLE,

The county seat of Cumberland county, is situated at the head of natural navigation, on the Cape Fear river. The town is symmetrically laid out, with streets one hundred feet wide. It has a population of four thousand seven hundred and ninety. The arsenal of construction at Fayetteville is a large establishment, embracing about fifty acres. Beside the county buildings, there are in this place three banks, and three printing offices. The city was captured by the federal troops in March, 1865.

BEAUFORT,

A port of entry, and shire town of Carteret county, has a population of one thousand six hundred and ten. It is situated on the Newport river, near its mouth; it is accessible by steamers, and has the finest harbor in the state, the entrance to which is defended by Fort Macon. Beaufort contains the county buildings, a number of seminaries, and one or two churches.

NEWBERN,

At the confluence of the Neuse and Trent, was formerly the capital of the state. The river at this point, is about a mile wide, and navigable for steamers for about eight months of the year. It is the capital of Craven county, and contains the county buildings, a number of churches, a theater, two banks, and several printing offices.

RALEIGH,

The capital of the state, occupying an elevated and healthy situation, has a population of four thousand seven hundred and eighty. The capitol, in the center of union square, which occupies the center of the city, is one of the most handsome state-houses in the union. It is one hundred and sixty-six feet long, ninety-six feet wide, and cost upwards of five hundred thousand dollars. It is a granite structure, surmounted by a dome, and surrounded by massive pillars of the same material as the building. In the city is an institution for the deaf and dumb, an insane asylum, a court house, two banks, several churches, a market house and two newspaper publications.

SOUTH CAROLINA.

South Carolina, one of the original states of the American confederacy, lies between latitude 32° and 35° 10′ N., and between longitude 78° 35′ and 83° 30′ W. It is bounded on the north by North Carolina, on the east by the Atlantic ocean, on the south by the Atlantic ocean and Georgia, and on the west by Georgia.

This state is next to Maryland, the smallest of the Southern states, but in proportion to its size one of the most populous and wealthy. It is often called the Palmetto state on account of the abundance of Palmetto trees growing within its borders.

The principal minerals are gold, iron and lead. The chief rivers are the Santee, formed by the confluence of the Wateree and Congaree, the Great Pedee and Little Pedee. Table mountain, one of the most interesting objects in the state, has a perpendicular elevation of eleven hundred feet above the surrounding country, and is a noted summer resort. At the foot of the mountain is a hotel. Cæsar's Head derives its name from its resembling the human head in shape. Glenn's and Limestone springs are watering places of considerable note. The climate and productions of South Carolina resemble those of southern Europe. There is more rice raised in this than any other state in the union. Large quantities of cotton are raised on the islands bordering on the coast of this state.

CHARLESTON,

The largest and principal city of South Carolina, has a population of forty thousand five hundred and twenty-two. The ground on which it is built lies between the Ashley and Cooper rivers. The city is symmetrically built, is about two miles in length and one and a half in breadth. The harbor of Charleston is defended by Forts Pinckney, Johnson, Moultrie and Sumter. The light house in this harbor is one hundred and twenty-five and a half feet high. The foundation of the city was laid in 1672, and was incorporated as a city in 1783.

Among the educational and literary institutions of the city are the state medical college, Charleston college, the literary and philosophical society, the apprentices' association, the mercantile library association, the city library, a high school, and several common schools. The city contains an orphan asylum, an almshouse, several first class hotels, thirty churches, a theatre, two banks, and several insurance offices.

Charleston is a great commercial city. The principal exports are cotton and rice. It exports more rice than any other city in the union, and the exportation of cotton is rivaled only by Mobile and New Orleans.

COLUMBIA,

The capital of South Carolina, is situated at the head of navigation on the Congaree river. It streets are one hundred feet wide and bordered with ornamental trees.

The South Carolina college is a brick structure three stories high and two hundred and fifteen feet long. The capitol has a front one hundred and seventy feet by sixty deep. The city contains, besides these, a court house, insane asylum, three banks, a market house, a number of churches, a theological school, several seminaries and printing offices.

GEORGETOWN,

A port of entry, is finely located on the west coast of Wingan bay. A short distance above the site of the town is the confluence of the Great Pedee, Black, and Waccamau rivers, the united waters of which render the position advantageous for trade. It has a population of one thousand seven hundred and twenty, and contains several churches and seminaries, a court house, a bank, and publishes two newspapers.

CAMDEN,

A flourishing town of south Carolina, situated at the head of navigation on the Wateree river, has a population of one thousand six hundred and twenty-one. It is surrounded by a fertile district, in which large quantities of cotton, corn and peaches are grown. In the town are an academy, library, bank, an arsenal and cotton factory.

GEORGIA.

Georgia, one of the thirteen original states, extends between latitude 30° 21′ 39″ and 35° N., and between longitude 81° and 85° 53′ 38″ W. It is bounded on the north by Tennessee and North Carolina, on the east by South Carolina and the Atlantic ocean, on the south by Florida, and on the west by Alabama. Every variety of surface is represented in this state; alluvial lands, swamps, undulating, rough, hilly and mountainous territory. The principal rivers are, Savannah, by which the state is separated from South Carolina; Chattahoochee, forming part of the boundary between Georgia and Alabama; and the Altamaha, formed by the confluence of the Oconee and Ocmulgee. Owing to the great diversity of soil and climate, the productions are of a great variety, embracing all those common to New England, Middle and Western states. The principal minerals are gold, silver, copper, iron, lead, marble and precious stones. Among the objects of interest to those who appreciate the beautiful and picturesque in nature, may be mentioned the falls of Tallulah, the stream in which they occur passing through cliffs from two to three hundred feet high, the Toccaso, Amicolah, Towaligo, Eastateah and Stochoa falls, Nicojack, Willson's and Nix's caves, Track Rock, and Pilot mountains.

SAVANNAH,

The largest and most important commercial city of Georgia, is situated on the south-west bank of the Savannah river. The city is laid out regularly, the streets wide, unpaved, and shaded with India trees. At every alternate corner there is a public square, usually in a circular or ellipse form. In these squares, also, are India trees growing. Broad and Bay streets have a carriage way on each side, and a grassy promenade in the middle.

The principal public buildings are Oglethorpe and St. Andrew's halls, the court house, jail, state arsenal, artillery armory, theatre, lyceum, city exchange, Chatham academy and custom house. Savannah has sixteen churches, a Hebrew synagogue, a historical society, several reading rooms, numerous private schools, a library of six thousand volumes, five banks, an orphan asylum, hospital, infirmary, a seamen's friend society, a Hibernian society, a free school, and publishes five daily newspapers. (See views of Savannah.)

AUGUSTA,

A flourishing city of Georgia and county seat of Richmond county, at the head of navigation on Savannah river, has a population of twelve thousand four hundred and ninety-three.

Among the important buildings are Richmond academy, a medical college, the city hall, a hospital, arsenal, six banks, five newspaper offices and fourteen churches. A bridge crossing the river at this point connects Augusta with Hamburg, South Carolina.

COLUMBUS,

A handsome city of Georgia and capital of Muscogee county, is on the east bank of the Chattahoochee river. The city is laid out in oblong blocks, in each of which there are eight square lots. The city extends a mile and a half along the river with a breadth of half a mile. It has a population of nine thousand six hundred and twenty one, a court house, an orphan asylum, several churches, excellent schools, and about one hundred and fifty stores.

MILLEDGEVILLE,

The capital of Georgia, situated on the Oconee river, has a population of two thousand four hundred and eighty. The city contains a fine gothic state house, a penitentiary, a state arsenal, a bank, an academy, five churches, and publishes five newspapers.

ATLANTA

Is about seven miles from the Chattahoochee river, on a line of railroad leading from Savannah to Chattanooga and Nashville, Tennessee. It was laid out in 1845, since which time it has increased in population and wealth until it is now one of the most important cities in northern Georgia, and has a population of nine thousand five hundred and fifty four. It was recaptured from the rebels in September, 1864, by General Sherman.

FLORIDA.

Florida, the most southern state in the union, extends between latitude 25° and 31° N., and between longitude 80° and 87° 44′ W. It is bounded on the north by Georgia and Alabama, on the east and south by the Atlantic ocean, and on the west by the Gulf of Mexico and Alabama.

The surface is generally level, no portion being more than three hundred feet above the level of the sea. The southern part, called the everglades, is covered with water. This tract is about one hundred and sixty miles long, by sixty broad. This state has a greater extent of seacoast than any other in the union. The principal rivers are the Appalachicola, Suwanee, and St. Johns. About twelve miles from Tallahassee, a beautiful lake is formed by a spring bursting from a vast depth. The lake is remarkably transparent, and the water nearly as cold as ice during the hottest weather. Some of these springs in which the state abounds, have sufficient force to turn a mill.

PENSACOLA,

The county seat of Escambia county, is situated on the Pensacola bay. The harbor of Pensacola is one of the safest in the Gulf of Mexico, and is strongly fortified. It has a population of two thousand eight hundred and seventy-six, and contains a market-house, custom-house, several churches, three newspaper offices, a United States naval station, and a marine hospital.

KEY WEST,

On Key West island, is the most populous city in the state. It was first settled in 1822. It now has a population of two thousand eight hundred and thirty-two. Its harbor is defended by Fort Taylor. It has no regular communication with the main land, except by steamers which enter its harbor once a week from Charleston and Savannah. About thirty thousand bushels of salt are made annually by solar evaporation.

ST. AUGUSTINE,

County seat of St. John's county, is situated in the eastern part of the state, on the Atlantic ocean. It is one of the largest places in the state and is the oldest city in the union. It was founded in 1565 by the Spaniards, and is built on a plain only a few feet above the level of the sea. The streets are narrow, most of the houses two stories, the upper of which projects over the street. The harbor is defended by Fort Marion, which is more than a hundred years old. It was erected by the Spaniards, and formerly called the Castle of St. Marcus.

The climate is mild, and the date-palm, the orange, olive and lemon thrive in this locality. In the town are about five hundred dwellings, one thousand nine hundred and fourteen inhabitants, a United States land office, court house, a newspaper office, three Protestant churches, and a Roman Catholic cathedral, the oldest in America, supposed to be three hundred years old. (See views of St. Augustine.)

ALABAMA.

Alabama extends between latitude 30° 10″ and 35° N., and between longitude 85° and 88° 30′ west. It is bounded on the north by Tennessee, on the east by Georgia, on the south by Florida and the Gulf of Mexico, and on the west by Mississippi.

The Alleghany mountains terminate in the northern part of this state. The centre is rough and hilly. The region along the coast is level. The principal minerals are coal, iron, lead, marble and limestone. The most important rivers are the Mobile, Alabama, Tombigbee and Tennessee, all of which are navigable for steamboats to some extent.

The climate and productions of Alabama closely resemble those of the tropical regions. It is one of the leading cotton

16

growing states. The other principal productions are corn, sweet potatoes, rice and lumber. The state formerly belonged to Georgia, and with it was included in the Mississippi territory. It was admitted into the union as a state in 1819.

MOBILE,

The largest and most populous city of Alabama, is situated on Mobile river, just above its entrance into the bay of the same name. Mobile is second only to New Orleans in the exportation of cotton. It exports, besides the productions of Alabama, a large portion of those of Mississippi. The streets of the city are wide and ornamented with shade trees. Mobile contains Spring Hill college, a marine hospital, two orphan asylums, a theatre and several newspaper offices, banks, churches and academies. A custom house is being constructed at a cost of three hundred thousand dollars. It has a population of twenty-nine thousand two hundred and fifty-eight.

MONTGOMERY,

A flourishing city and capital of Alabama, is situated on the Alabama river. It possesses greater facilities for communication with the surrounding country than any other city of the southern states. The waters of the Alabama never freeze, and are navigable for large steamboats all seasons of the year. The capital was removed from Tuscaloosa to this place in 1847. The city has a population of eight thousand eight hundred and forty-three, and contains beside the state buildings a bank and several newspaper offices.

TUSCALOOSA,

A flourishing town, situated on the Black Warrior river, was formerly the capital of Alabama. It is one of the principal towns of the state, and is noted for its active trade and literary institutions. It contains the state university, the buildings of which are pleasantly located about a half a mile from the river, and cost about one hundred and fifty thousand dollars, the state lunatic asylum, United States land office, a number of churches and newspaper offices, and several academies. It has a population of three thousand nine hundred and eighty-nine.

HUNSTVILLE,

A beautiful and thriving town, county seat of Madison county, Alabama, is on the Memphis and Charleston railroad. The court house, a handsome brick building, cost upwards of forty-five thousand dollars. The town has a population of three thousand six hundred and eighty-four, and contains a bank, United States land office, several churches, two female seminaries, one of which cost twenty thousand dollars, and publishes three newspapers.

MISSISSIPPI.

Mississippi, the ninth in order of the southern states, extends between latitude 30° 20′ and 35° N., and between longitude 88° 12′ and 91° 40′ W. It is bounded on the north by Tennessee, on the east by Alabama, on the south by the Gulf of Mexico and Louisiana, and on the west by Louisiana and Arkansas.

To this state belong a number of islands in the gulf, the principal of which are Ship, Deer and Horn islands. Though there are eighty-eight miles of sea coast, the state affords no good harbors. The eastern and central parts of the state are elevated table lands, descending toward the Mississippi river. The northern and southern portions are undulating and rolling. The principal rivers are the Mississippi, which forms the boundary between this state and Arkansas and a part of Louisiana, the Pearl, Black, Yazoo, and the Pascagoula. The chief productions are cotton, Indian corn, rice, sweet potatoes, sugar, peaches, figs and oranges.

Mississippi was admitted into the union as a state in 1817, from which it seceded in 1861, and joined the confederate states.

The principal cities are Natchez, Vicksburg, Jackson and Columbus.

NATCHEZ,

The largest and most important city of the state, is built on a bluff a hundred and fifty feet high which forms the bank of the river. The city derived its name from a noted tribe of Indians who peopled this part of the country. Natchez has thirteen thousand five hundred and fifty-three inhabitants, and elegant mansions, to some of which are attached orange groves. The city contains eight churches, a court house, jail, United States marine hospital, orphan asylum, masonic hall, two daily papers, numerous seminaries and flourishing public schools. It was settled by the French in 1716, and burned by the Indians in 1729.

JACKSON,

A thriving town and capital of Mississippi, is situated on the Pearl river. The town is built upon a plain, and symmetrically laid out. It has a population of three thousand one hundred and ninety-nine, and contains the state lunatic asylum, a United States land office, several churches, the executive mansion and a fine state house, constructed at a cost of more than half a million of dollars.

VICKSBURG,

The capital of Warren county, is located on the Mississippi river, and is of more commercial importance than any other city between Natchez and Memphis. There are four thousand five hundred and ninety-one inhabitants. It contains the county buildings, several academies and five churches. It was captured from the rebels by General Grant, after a long and obstinate defense, on the 4th of July, 1863.

COLUMBUS,

A flourishing post-town and county seat of Lowndes county, is on the Tombigbee river. It has a population of three thousand three hundred and eight. It contains the county buildings, a United States land office, newspaper office and several churches.

LOUISIANA.

Louisiana, one of the southern states, extends between latitude 29° and 33° N., and between longitude 88° 50′ and 94° 20′ W. It is bounded on the north by Arkansas, on the east by Mississippi, on the south by the Gulf of Mexico, and on the west by Texas. A large part of the state is below high water level, and is protected from inundations by dykes, called levees.

The staple productions are cotton and sugar cane, and of the latter Louisiana produces about nine-tenths of the whole amount raised in the union. Tobacco, rice, oranges, figs, peaches and bananas are also raised in large quantities.

The natural advantages for internal commerce which this state possesses are not rivaled by any other state or country on the globe. Steamers run from the Gulf of Mexico to the falls of St. Anthony on the Mississippi, to the foot of the Rocky mountains on the Missouri, and to the eastward on the Ohio, Cumberland, and Tennessee, carrying to her the production of fourteen states.

The principal rivers are the Mississippi, Red, and Washita. The Mississippi, the largest river of North America and the longest in the world, takes its rise in the northern part of Minnesota, in Itasca lake, flows in a south-easterly course and empties into the Gulf of Mexico. It is two thousand nine hundred and eighty-six miles in length. It is navigable for large steamers to the falls of St. Anthony, a distance of two thousand two hundred miles. This river separates Iowa, Missouri, Arkansas, and a part of Minnesota and Louisiana on the west from Illinois, Kentucky, Tennessee, and the greater part of Wisconsin and Mississippi on the east. The delta of the Mississippi has formed most of the lower part of Louisiana, and has advanced s everal leagues since the city of New Orleans has been built. The delta is a hundred and fifty miles wide, and contains an area of fourteen thousand square miles.

The chief cities are New Orleans, Baton Rouge, and Natchitoches.

NEW ORLEANS,

The great commercial metropolis of the south-west, is called the Crescent city from its location on a bend of the Mississippi. It exports more cotton than any other city in the world, and not only the productions of Louisiana, but a considerable part of those of the Mississippi valley. The population of the city numbers one hundred and sixty-eight thousand eight hundred and twenty-three. The public buildings of New Orleans are among the best and most extensive in the United States. The United

States custom house is exceeded in size by no building in the United States except the national capitol. The United States branch mint is a massive structure two hundred and eighty-two feet long and one hundred and eight feet wide and three stories high. The Municipal hall is an elegant structure in the Grecian style of architecture. Among other remarkable public buildings are the Odd Fellows' hall, Merchants' exchange, the Charity hospital, United States naval hospital, a Medical college, and numerous schools. The city also contains about forty churches and three Jewish synagogues.

On account of the marshy nature of the soil on which the city is built, there are no cellars under the houses, and no excavations for the interment of the dead can be made, and they are deposited in tombs or ovens above ground.

New Orleans was settled in 1717 by the French, and named in honor of the Duke of Orleans, regent of France during the minority of Louis XV.

BATON ROUGE,

The capital of Louisiana, is situated on the Mississippi, about one hundred and thirty miles above New Orleans. The site of the city is a bluff elevated about twenty-five feet above high water mark, and one of the healthiest towns in the southern portion of the Mississippi valley. Baton Rouge became the capital of the state in 1847, since which time the population and value of property has increased and business become more active. The population of the city numbers five thousand four hundred and twenty-eight.

TEXAS.

Texas, the largest state in the union, and the most south-western of the southern states, formerly belonged to Mexico. It extends between latitude 25° 50′ and 36° 30′ N., and between longitude 93° 30′ and 107° W. It is bounded on the north by Kansas and the Indian territory, on the east by Arkansas and Louisiana, on the south by the Gulf of Mexico and Mexico, and on the west by Mexico and New Mexico.

This state embraces every variety of surface, mountains, valleys, hills, plains, table lands and deserts. Only about one half of the state is settled. The western part is occupied by the Indians, and large herds of buffalo and wild horses roam over the unsettled regions. Texas abounds in minerals, and being so near the rich silver mines of Mexico and New Mexico may yet, possibly, yield rich supplies of this metal.

The staple productions are cotton, corn, sugar, tobacco and rice. Oranges, lemons, and other tropical fruits are grown with much success in this state. Camels were at one time introduced into this state for the purpose of traveling across the desert between Texas and the Pacific ocean.

The towns of Texas are not large. Austin is the capital and Galveston and Houston are the most important towns. San Antonio is the oldest in the state.

AUSTIN,

The capital of Texas and county seat of Travis county, is situated on the Colorado river. It has a population of three thousand four hundred and ninety-six, and contains besides the county and state buildings, several stores and printing offices. It became the capital in 1844.

GALVESTON,

The most populous and principal commercial town of Texas and capital of Galveston county, is pleasantly located on an island of the same name. It has the best harbor in the state, and one of the best on the Gulf of Mexico, carries on an active trade and contains a town hall, several large hotels, eight churches, a fine market house, and publishes several newspapers. It has a population of seven thousand three hundred and seven, and was first settled in 1837.

HOUSTON,

Shire town of Harris county, situated on Buffalo bayou, has a population of four thousand eight hundred and forty-five. It is the second town in commercial importance in the state, and the principal shipping port for an extensive and very fertile section of country. The city was at one time the capital of Texas. It contains a machine shop, an iron foundry, a hat factory and several newspaper offices.

SAN ANTONIO,

A flourishing post town of Bexar county, on the San Antonio river, has a population of eight thousand two hundred and thirty-five. It is a wealthy town, and contains many elegant residences, a United States arsenal, several churches and seminaries, and publishes two newspapers.

In this town is the Alamo fortress, renowned in the history of the state, where a band of Texans defended themselves for two weeks against a Mexican force of four thousand strong.

CHAPTER IV.

THE WESTERN STATES.

OHIO.

The first white settlement in Ohio was made April 7th, 1788, by a company from New England. In 1781 a territorial government was established over this region, called the territory north-west of the Ohio river, from which, in 1802, the present state of Ohio was separated.

The surface of the state, though not mountainous, is elevated in some places ten thousand feet above the level of the sea, and in other portions from six hundred to eight hundred feet. The northern part of the state is drained by Lake Erie, the southern by the Ohio river. The tributaries of the Ohio are much larger than those of Lake Erie. The Ohio river forms the entire southern boundary of the state, giving it access to the commerce of the great Mississippi valley. Its principal tributaries in Ohio are the Muskingum, Scioto, and Miami. These rivers vary in length from one hundred and ten to two hundred miles. The chief rivers of the northern slope are the Maumee, the Sandusky, Huron and Cuyahoga. Lake Erie forms the northern and northeastern boundary of the state for about one hundred and fifty miles. At the west end of the lake are the Maumee and Sandusky bays, besides several small islands belonging to the state.

Large stones, called boulders, are found on the plains of Ohio, and of several of the western states. These boulders are sometimes very large; they differ in character from the rocks of the surrounding country, and have evidently been brought from a distance. They appear to have been transported from their original resting place by the icebergs of an early sea, and dropped at random as the ice melted.

At Bryan, in Williams county, there is a natural fountain, supposed to proceed from a subterranean lake. The supply is never affected by droughts or rain, and small fish are sometimes thrown up. The celebrated white sulphur fountain is situated on the Scioto, eighteen miles above Columbus. It rises from the bed of the Scioto through solid rock. It was first discovered in 1820, while boring for salt water. The operators had pierced a hole about two and one half inches in diameter, through about ninety feet of solid rock, when the auger suddenly fell two feet, and there gushed up with great force a stream of strong white sulphur water. The water, which is pure, is supposed to be forced up by its own gas. It leaves on the ground, near the spring, a heavy white deposit.

"The source of Cold creek is a beautiful and curious flooding spring, rising from a level prairie at the village of Castalia. This spring is about two hundred feet in diameter, and sixty feet deep. The water is so pure that the smallest particle can be seen at the bottom, and when the sun is in the meridian, all the objects at the bottom, logs, stumps, etc., reflect the hues of the rainbow, forming a view of great beauty. The constituents of the water are lime, soda, magnesia, and iron, and it petrifies all objects, such as grass, stumps, bushes, moss, etc., with which it comes in contact. The stream courses about three miles through the prairie, and empties into Lake Erie. The water is very cold, but never freezes, and at its point of entrance into the lake, prevents the formation of ice. Upon it are the well known Castalia and Cold creek mills, the water wheels of which are imperishable from decay, in consequence of their being incrusted by petrifaction."

The climate in the southern part of the state is mild. The summers are warm and regular, but subject at times to severe drought. In the northern part of the state the winters are probably as severe as in the same latitude on the Atlantic coast.

In agricultural products Ohio stands among the first. The soil is fertile, especially on the river bottoms. Coal is abundant; it is found in twenty counties in the state.

COLUMBUS,

The capital of Ohio, is situated on the east bank of the Scioto river, ninety miles from its mouth. The surrounding country is rich and populous. The site of Columbus is level; the streets are wide and laid out with great neatness and regularity. It has many elegant public buildings, among which are a new state house, the Ohio lunatic asylum, the institution for the blind, the asylum for the deaf and dumb, and the Ohio penitentiary. The city was laid out in 1812, and incorporated in 1816. Its population in 1860 numbered eighteen thousand five hundred and fifty-four. The other important places are Cincinnati, Cleveland, Dayton, Toledo, Zanesville, Sandusky, Chillicothe, Hamilton, and Springfield.

CINCINNATI,

Called the Queen of the West, is the largest city in the state. It is situated on the right bank of the Ohio river, one hundred and twenty miles south-west of Columbus. It is situated near the eastern extremity of a valley, about three miles in diameter, surrounded by beautiful hills, some of which rise about four hundred feet above the river. A lovely view of the city and valley is obtained from the summit of these hills.

Cincinnati is remarkable for its rapid growth. It was first settled in 1788. It seems to have been originally laid out with great regularity. A large proportion of the entire valley is already built up, and the central and business portion is compactly and finely built with large warehouses, stores and handsome dwellings; but the outer portion is but partially built up, the streets being irregular and the houses scattered. The streets are wide, with sidewalks paved with brick and stone, and many of them lined with shade trees. The city contains one hundred and five churches, five colleges, three of which are medical, eighteen common schools, two intermediate, and three high schools. The charity institutions of the city are highly respectable. Under its control and support, are a house of refuge, an infirmary, a dispensary, and a lunatic asylum. Its population in 1864, was about one hundred and eighty-six thousand.

CLEVELAND

Is situated on the southern shore of Lake Erie, at the mouth of the Cuyahoga river, one hundred and thirty miles north-east of Columbus, and two hundred and fifty-five miles from Cincinnati. It is one of the most beautiful towns in the union. Nearly all of the city is situated on a gravelly plain, elevated about one hundred feet above the lake, of which it has a most commanding prospect. A public square of about ten acres occupies the center of the town. The court-house and one or two churches front on this square. In the center stands the statue of Commodore Perry, the hero of the battle of Lake Erie. It is the largest marble statue in the United States, and was erected by the citizens at a cost of eight thousand dollars.

The public schools of Cleveland rank among the first in the country. It has twenty primary schools, twenty secondary, twenty-three intermediate, nine grammar, and two high schools. The high schools are handsome edifices of stone and brick. The course of study prescribed fits the graduate to enter college without further preparation.

Cleveland was settled in 1796, and incorporated in 1836. In 1860 the population was forty-three thousand four hundred and seventeen. Since 1862, the population has rapidly increased, and in 1865, it was not less than sixty thousand.

DAYTON

Is situated on the east bank of the great Miami river, at the mouth of Mad river, sixty-seven miles west of Columbus, and fifty-two miles from Cincinnati. The town is laid out with streets one hundred feet wide, crossing each other at right angles. The public buildings are fine, and the city also contains many elegant private residences. The court-house, which cost the city one hundred and seventy thousand dollars, is one of the finest in the western states. The abundant water power which Dayton possesses, is one of the chief elements of its prosperity. It is extensively engaged in manufactures. In 1866 its population was about thirty thousand.

TOLEDO

Is situated at the western extremity of Lake Erie, on an elevated plain on the left bank of the Maumee river, about four miles from its mouth, one hundred and thirty-four miles northwest of Columbus, and one hundred and twelve miles west of Cleveland. At this point the river expands into a broad and beautiful harbor, affording accommodations for the largest vessels and steamers. The city stretches along the river for more than a mile, and has two points at which business centres, called the upper and lower landing. It was originally two distinct settlements. At these two points the stores, warehouses and dwellings are thickly crowded together, but between them it is rather thinly settled. It was incorporated as a city in 1836. The population in 1865 was between eighteen and twenty thousand.

ZANESVILLE

Is situated on the east bank, in a bend of the Muskingum river, about sixty-five miles above its mouth, and fifty-four miles east of Columbus. "The river seems once to have run nearly in a right line, from which, however, it has gradually diverged to the westward, forming a horse-shoe curve, and depositing, through successive centuries, an alluvium of gravel, sand, etc., of great depth, on which Zanesville now stands." In sweeping around this curve, through the space of about one and three-fourths miles, the river falls eight or ten feet, and, by the aid of a dam, a fall of between sixteen and seventeen feet is obtained, thus furnishing very extensive water-power. Steamboats ascend from the Ohio to this point, and several of them make regular passages between Zanesville and Cincinnati. The plan of the town is regular, the streets are wide and adorned by many fine buildings. The city contains fourteen churches, and a number of well organized public schools. It was laid out in 1799. The seat of state government was removed from Chillicothe to this place in 1810, and about two years later transferred to Columbus. In 1860, the population was nine thousand two hundred and twenty-nine.

SANDUSKY

Is situated on Sandusky bay, about one hundred and five miles from Columbus, and sixty from Cleveland. The bay is about twenty miles long and five or six miles wide, with an average depth of twelve feet, forming an excellent harbor, large enough to admit with safety vessels of all sizes, during the severest storms. The situation of the city is pleasant, rising gradually from the bay, and commanding a fine view of the harbor, thronged with steamboats and other vessels, taking in and discharging cargoes. The city is built upon an inexhaustible bed of the finest limestone, which is not only used for building purposes, but forms an important article of export. Sandusky contains many elegant churches, dwellings and warehouses. It was laid out in 1817, under the name of Portland. In 1865, it had about fourteen thousand inhabitants.

CHILLICOTHE

Is situated on the west bank of the Scioto, forty-five miles south of Columbus, and ninety-three miles from Cincinnati. The site of the city is remarkably beautiful, on a plain elevated about thirty feet above the river. The Scioto winds gracefully around the north of this plain, and Paint creek flows on the south. It is enclosed by verdant and cultivated hills, which attain an altitude of about five hundred feet, forming the background of a landscape which can scarcely be surpassed in the western states. The plan of the town is regular; the streets are wide, and adorned by many handsome buildings. It was founded in 1796. In 1860 the population was seven thousand six hundred and twenty-six.

HAMILTON

Is situated on both sides of the Miami, twenty-two miles north of Cincinnati, and ninety miles south-west of Columbus. It is neatly built, and has an elegant public square, on which stand the county buildings. It was incorporated in 1853. Previous to that time it included only the portion on the east side of the river, that on the west being called Rossville. The population is about seven thousand nine hundred and twenty-three.

SPRINGFIELD

Is situated at the confluence of Mad river with Lagonda creek, forty-three miles west of Columbus, and eighty-four miles north-east of Cincinnati. It is considered, by many, the most beautiful town in Ohio. It is surrounded by a handsome and fertile country, and is noted for the morality and intelligence of its inhabitants.

INDIANA.

Indiana was settled by the French in the early part of the eighteenth century. Like other French settlements its population did not increase very rapidly until the arrival of the Americans. The settlements remained without much accession to their numbers for some time after the close of the American revolution. In 1800, that portion of the United States which now comprises the states of Indiana and Illinois became a territorial government, and in 1816 Indiana became an independent member of the confederacy. In 1811 the American settlements were attacked by the Shawnee tribe, who committed great depredations. The Indians, it is said, were incited by the British, who furnished them with arms. General Harrison was sent against them, and routed them completely at Tippecanoe, but with the loss of two hundred of his own men.

Indiana has no mountains or great elevations, but portions south of the White river are somewhat hilly and rugged. Nearly all of the streams empty into the Ohio, showing a general inclination of the surface in that direction. Most of the rivers have rich alluvial bottoms of a few miles in width. The northern part of the state is heavily timbered. Bordering on Lake Michigan are some sand hills about two hundred feet in hight, behind which is a region covered with pine.

The climate of Indiana is somewhat milder than on the Atlantic coast, but subject to sudden changes. The soil is generally good, and much of it, especially on the river bottoms, very fertile. The country between the rivers is somewhat elevated, and the soil, though good, is not quite as fertile as on the river bottoms.

Indiana has no foreign commerce, but Lake Michigan, bordering on the north-western part of the state for about forty miles, opens to it the trade of the great lakes, while the Ohio, which forms the entire southern boundary of the state, gives it access to the commerce of the Ohio and Mississippi valleys.

Wyandotte cave, in Crawford county, is said to rival in extent and interest the celebrated Mammoth cave of Kentucky. In the year 1850, new chambers and galleries were discovered, abounding in stalactites and other calcareous concretions of great size and splendor. Previous to that time it had only been explored for about three miles. Epsom Salts cave is also quite celebrated. It is situated in the side of a hill four hundred feet high. The earth of the floor yields epsom salts, nitre, aluminous earth, and gypsum.

INDIANAPOLIS,

The largest city, and capital of the state, is situated on the west fork of White river, near the center of the state, one hundred and nine miles north-west of Cincinnati. When this place was selected for the capital of Indiana in 1820, the whole country for forty miles in every direction, was covered with a dense forest. In 1825, the seat of government was permanently established at this place. It is a regularly built and beautiful city, with a handsome state-house, court-house, jail, and state asylums for the blind, deaf and dumb, and insane. The lunatic hospital was established in 1848, and, in 1862 had two hundred and ninety-eight patients.

New Albany, Evansville, Fort Wayne, Lafayette, Terre Haute, Madison, Richmond, Laporte, Jeffersonville and Logansport, are also important places.

NEW ALBANY

Is situated on the right bank of the Ohio river, five miles below Louisville, and one hundred and thirty-six miles below Cincinnati. It is actively engaged in commerce. More steamboats are built at this place than any other town on the Ohio river. In the year 1864, twenty-six steamboats were launched.

The city is remarkable for its rapid growth. It was laid out in 1813. It now has eighteen churches, a collegiate institute, a Presbyterian theological seminary, four banks, and five large public school houses. Its population in 1865 numbered about eighteen thousand.

EVANSVILLE

Is situated on a high bank on the Ohio river, about two hundred miles below Louisville. The course of the river is here so winding that Evansville is not far from the center of the county. It is the principal shipping port for the grain and pork of south-western Indiana. The navigation of the Ohio is seldom obstructed either by drought or ice below this place.

Evansville contains about thirty churches, a fine court house, five banks, one theatre, and four public halls. Its population numbers about eleven thousand five hundred.

FORT WAYNE

Is situated at the confluence of the St. Joseph's and St. Mary's rivers, which form the Maumee, and on the Wabash and Erie canal, one hundred and twelve miles north-east of Indianapolis. It is a town of rapid growth, and one of the most important in the state. The surrounding region is highly productive, and a large portion of the land is under cultivation. The site of the town is that of the old Twightwee village of the Miami tribe. Fort Wayne was erected by order of General Wayne, in 1794, and continued to be a military post until 1819. Its present population is about twenty thousand.

LAFAYETTE

Is pleasantly situated on a gradually rising ground on the left bank of the Wabash river, sixty-six miles north-west of Indianapolis. Its situation affords a delightful view of the river and of the neighboring hills. It is a place of active trade, and one of the principal grain markets in the state. It contains a large and handsome court house which cost twenty thousand dollars, thirteen churches, some of which are large and handsome buildings, four banks, two of which are national, two academies and four public schools, one of which is a fine structure, having recently been completed at a cost of about twenty thousand dollars. Its population in 1860 numbered nine thousand three hundred and eighty-seven.

TERRE HAUTE

Is situated on the east bank of the Wabash river, seventy-three miles south-west of Indianapolis. The situation of the city is remarkably beautiful. The bank upon which the town is built is elevated about sixty feet above the river. The streets of the city are wide and bordered with numerous shade trees. The opposite banks of the river are connected by a fine bridge, over which the national road passes. Fort Harrison prairie, on the west border of which the town stands, is very fertile, and noted for its beautiful landscapes. The city contains a fine court house, a town hall, three banks, a large academy, and about twelve churches; also the State Normal school, which is one of the finest architectural structures in the state. Its population numbers about ten thousand six hundred.

MADISON

Is situated on the Ohio river, in a valley about three miles in length, which is enclosed on the north by steep and rugged hills about four hundred feet high. It is actively engaged in steamboat trade. The navigation of the river below this place is usually open all winter. The city is handsomely laid out and well built. It contains a fine court house, three public halls, thirteen churches, a United States hospital, four banks, and three large public schools. In 1865 its population was about fourteen thousand.

RICHMOND

Is pleasantly situated on the east fork of Whitewater river. More labor is employed in this place in the manufacture of cotton, wool, paper, flour, and iron than in any other city in the state. The Indiana yearly meeting of the society of Friends is held at this place. The surrounding country is the most populous and highly cultivated in the state. Its population in 1860 was about six thousand six hundred.

LAPORTE

Is situated on the border of a beautiful and highly cultivated prairie of the same name, twelve miles from Lake Michigan. It is a place of active trade. It contains the Indiana medical college, an academy and a bank. Its population in 1860 was about five thousand, but in consequence of its rapid growth, the census of 1870 will most likely nearly double that number.

JEFFERSONVILLE

Is situated on the Ohio river, nearly opposite Louisville. "The situation is elevated, and commands a delightful view of the city of Louisville, of the broad and winding river with its verdant islands, and a range of hills a few miles distant." It contains eight churches, one bank, three United States hospitals, and one of the state prisons of Indiana.

LOGANSPORT

Is situated on the Wabash river and canal, at the mouth of Eel river, seventy miles north-west of Indianapolis. The city is actively engaged in trade. It has valuable water power which is employed in manufactures to some extent. The city was laid out in 1827. It now contains eight churches, two academies, one bank, and a court house built of hewn stone, one of the finest in the state. The population numbers about five thousand.

ILLINOIS.

In 1673, Marquette, a French traveler, visited Illinois, and in the latter part of the seventeenth century, settlements were made by the French at Cahokia and Kaskaskia. These, however, like other French colonies, did not increase rapidly. In 1800, in connection with Indiana, it formed a part of a separate territory, called Indiana. In 1809, the present state was organized as the territory of Illinois, and in 1818 it was admitted into the union. Since that time its population has increased very rapidly. According to the census of 1860, it numbered one million seven hundred and eleven thousand seven hundred and fifty-three.

The state is generally level, having few hills, and no mountains. There are elevated bluffs on the Mississippi and Illinois rivers, also a small tract of hilly country in the southern part of the state. The lowest portion is about three hundred and forty feet, and the highest only eight hundred feet above the Gulf of Mexico. A large portion of the state consists of prairie land.

The scenery of Illinois presents few bold and striking features, yet it is not entirely without attractions. The prairies are not generally flat, but gracefully undulating, and covered with waving grass, and a profusion of lovely wild flowers. For quiet landscape beauty they are unsurpassed, and a person unaccustomed to prairie land, perhaps might find no object of natural scenery as interesting as these. Along the rivers are bluffs which, in rugged grandeur, almost rival mountain scenery. The most remarkable of these are on the Mississippi river, and are from one hundred to four hundred feet high. One of these, called Fountain Bluff, is of an oval shape, six miles in circuit, and three hundred feet high. The top of this bluff is full of sink-holes, or depressions in the surface of the ground. There are two eminences on the Illinois river, one of which is called Starved Rock, the other, Lover's Leap. Perhaps 'Thirsty Rock' would be a more appropriate name for the former. It received its name from a band of Illinois Indians having taken refuge here, who, being surrounded by the Pottawatomies, all died, not of starvation, but of thirst. It is a perpendicular mass of limestone, situated about eight miles below Ottawa, and one hundred and fifty feet above the river. Lover's Leap, consisting of a ledge of precipitous rocks, is situated some distance above Starved Rock. In Hardin county, on the Ohio river, there is a cave, the entrance to which is but a little above the bed of the river. This cave slopes gradually from its entrance for about one hundred and eighty feet, when a second entrance leads to another cave, the dimensions of which are not known. This cave was, in 1797, the abode of a band of robbers, who were the terror of Ohio boatmen. Since that time several bands of robbers have taken refuge in this cave.

A large portion of the great lead region is in the limits of Illinois. The coal-fields of Illinois are estimated to occupy an area of about forty-four thousand square miles. Bituminous coal is found in almost every county, and a bed of anthracite coal is reported to have been discovered in Jackson county. Copper, lime, zinc, marble, free-stone, gypsum, and quartz crystals are also found. The state contains several medicinal springs, one of which, in Jefferson county, is much resorted to.

Lake Michigan forms the north-eastern boundary of the state for about sixty miles, and adds greatly to its commercial importance. The Mississippi forms the entire western boundary, and the Ohio the southern, thus giving it access to the commerce of these great valleys. The Wabash forms its eastern boundary for about three hundred miles. The other principal rivers are the Illinois, Rock, Sangamon, and Kaskaskia. The Illinois is formed by the union of the Des Plaines and Kankakee rivers. It has a very sluggish current, and in times of freshets the waters of the Mississippi back up into it for about seventy miles. It is navigable at all times for about two hundred and eighty-six miles, and at high water, for some distance farther. Rock river is about three hundred and twenty miles in length. The current is obstructed by rapids in several places, but at a moderate expense it might be made navigable. Already the subject has been much agitated, and probably at no distant day, the improvement of the river will begin. It flows through an extensive plain noted for its fertility and beautiful scenery. The Sangamon is about two hundred miles in length. It is navigable for small steamboats at high water. The Kaskaskia, a fine, navigable stream, is about three hundred miles in length.

The climate of Illinois is somewhat milder than that of the Atlantic states in the same latitude. Its great length gives it considerable variation in climate. Its agricultural capabilities are unsurpassed by any state in the union. In some of the river bottoms the soil is twenty-five feet deep, and the upland prairies are nearly, if not quite, as fertile.

On the formation of the state constitution, one section in each township was appropriated to the support of common schools, and subsequently an additional income of three per cent. on the proceeds from the sale of the public lands within the state. In the year 1853, the school fund yielded an income of two hundred and ninety-nine thousand and forty-seven dollars.

Illinois has a state lunatic asylum at Jacksonville, a state penitentiary at Joliet, and a deaf and dumb asylum at Jacksonville.

SPRINGFIELD,

The capital, is situated three miles south of the Sangamon river. The streets are wide and straight. A new state house has been erected. Besides this, the town contains a court-house, four banks, a state arsenal, thirteen churches, and several academies. Springfield will ever be memorable as having been the residence of Abraham Lincoln, late president of the United States. (See view.)

The other important places are Chicago, Peoria, Quincy, Galena, Belleville, Alton, Rockford, Bloomington, Ottawa, Aurora, Lincoln, Rock Island and Galesburg.

CHICAGO,

The largest city, and the most important commercial center of the north-western states, is situated in the north-eastern part of the state, on Lake Michigan. The city is built on the lake shore, and along the banks of the Chicago river and its two branches, its limits extending westward for about five miles.

The city has, within the last thirty-five years, risen from a small military post or fur station, till now it is the great metropolis of the northwestern states, and the largest interior city of the United States. In 1833, the site of the city, together with the land which now forms the states of Illinois and Wisconsin, was purchased from the Indians. Walking in the imposing streets of the Chicago of to-day, it is difficult to realize that thirty-five years have not elapsed since the red men were dispossessed of the very site on which the city now stands.

The prairie on that part of the shore of Lake Michigan appears to the eye flat as the lake itself, and its average hight above the lake is not more than six feet. The entire business portion of the city has, during the last ten years, been raised from six to eight feet above its former level. This greatly facilitates drainage, besides rendering it possible to have dry cellars for store houses. The grading and filling up, and raising the buildings to the new grade, cost the city upwards of a million of dollars.

The river was originally but a small creek, that emptied into the lake; the inlet was twenty feet deep, but the mouth was obstructed by a sand-bar, and it only admitted vessels of thirty or forty tons. In 1833, the United States spent thirty thousand dollars in improving the harbor, and in 1834 a freshet swept away the bar at the mouth of the river, making it accessible to the largest ships that sail the lakes. At the present time, over nine hundred vessels, carrying in all, upwards of two hundred thousand tons, and employing about ten thousand sailors, ply between Chicago and the other lake ports. In the winter, after navigation is closed, four hundred vessels may be counted in the harbor, frozen up safely in the ice. Vessels can ascend the river a distance of five or six miles on the south branch, and from four to five on the north branch. Along the river and its branches, are immense warehouses, some of which are capable of storing one million five hundred thousand bushels of grain. Miles of timber yards extend along one of the forks, and the harbor is choked by arriving and departing vessels. (See views of Chicago river.) The people of Chicago have had a long and severe struggle with their river, and they have not yet made a complete conquest of it. The river and its two forks so divide the town, that it is impossible to go far in any direction without crossing one of them. In old times, the Indians carried people over in their canoes. In course of time, the canoes expanded into commodious row boats; next floating bridges were tried;

afterwards draw-bridges came into use, seventeen of which now span the river. These draw-bridges are rather in the way at present. Unfavorable winds sometimes detain vessels on the lake, until three hundred of them are waiting to enter. When the wind changes, the whole fleet comes streaming in, each towed by a puffing and snorting little tug-boat. Occasionally the bridges can be closed for a few moments, and then there is a tremendous rush to cross the river. These are exceptional cases, and some days the bridges are seldom opened; but as it is, they are a great inconvenience; however, this will soon be a thing of the past. Already one tunnel has been constructed (see view No. 40,) at a cost of two hundred thousand dollars, and in a short time these seventeen maddening draw-bridges will have been superseded by seventeen tunnels.

The streets of Chicago are regular, and nearly all of them eighty feet wide. The city is laid out in rectangular blocks. (See views from the dome of city hall.) The principal streets are now paved with Nicholson pavement, or wooden blocks, which are found to be more durable than stone pavement.

The business portion of the city was formerly built mostly of brick, but this is now almost entirely superseded by "Athens marble." An inexhaustible quarry of this stone was discovered by some workmen while digging a canal at Athens, a point about fourteen miles south-west of the city. It is soft, and of a light cream color. At first it was regarded as useless, but it was afterwards found to harden on exposure to the air, and it is now recognized as the very best and most elegant building material in the country. It possesses the virtue of being easily worked when first quarried, but is hard in the finished wall. The general use of this light colored stone gives to the principal streets of Chicago a cheerful, light and airy appearance. (See street views of Chicago.)

The principal public buildings are the city hall, built of stone brought from Lockport, New York, (see view,) and chamber of commerce, built of Athens stone. (See views.) This is an elegant, spacious apartment, decorated with fine fresco paintings by resident Italian artists. It is ninety-three feet in width, one hundred and eighty feet long and one hundred feet high. It cost the city about four hundred thousand dollars. Among the elegant church edifices are the First and Second Presbyterian, the latter of which is built of a dark oily stone, dug out of the prairie immediately west of the city; Trinity, St. James, Church of the Redeemer, Methodist, First Unitarian, Church of the Holy Name, Church of the Holy Family, Unity, and New England. (See views.)

Tremont and Sherman houses are among the first class hotels. (See views.) Among the other prominent buildings are Potter Palmer's building, Crosby's opera house and the custom house. (See views.) The city contains three large book stores, the shelves of which are crowded with the best literature. (See views.)

"Along the lake, south of the river, extend the beautiful avenues which change insensibly into those streets of cottages and gardens which have given to Chicago the name of the 'Garden City.'" (See avenue views.) "This is a pleasant umbrageous quarter where glimpses are caught of the blue lake that stretches away to the east for sixty miles."

There are seventeen public schools and a high school in Chicago, which are among the very best in the United States. The buildings are large, handsome and convenient. (See views.) The attendance at the high school ranges from seven hundred to two thousand. The university, under the auspices of the Baptist denomination, is situated just in the outskirts of the city, in Cottage Grove. (See views.)

The city is provided with water from the lake, but that near the shore is impure on account of the large amount of filth which runs out of the river. A tunnel has recently been constructed extending under the bed of the lake two miles from the shore, (See views,) so that the city is supplied with pure lake water. "The work is really something to be proud of, not for its magnitude, but for the simplicity, originality, and boldness of the idea." The tunnel is five feet in diameter, and cut thirty-five feet below the bed of the lake. A shaft is sunk on the shore eighty-seven feet deep, and an iron one nine feet in diameter in the lake at the extreme end of the tunnel. Around this shaft there is an immense crib built of heavy timber. (See views.)

Chicago is the great commercial metropolis of the north-west. It is the largest interior grain market in the world, the greatest lumber market in the United States, second only to New York as a beef and cattle market, and as a beef and pork packing point it stands first in the United States. It is the center of a railroad system which includes about five thousand miles of track. Its railroad depots are immense in extent and admirably constructed. (See views.) The great Union Central depot has under cover three quarters of a mile of track. Three trains can start from it at the same moment without the least danger of interference, and no passenger is obliged to cross a track in changing cars.

No city in the United States has increased in population so rapidly as Chicago. In 1830 there resided in Chicago four white families. In 1831 there were twelve. In 1837, when the first census was taken, the entire population numbered four thousand one hundred and seventy. In 1865 it was estimated at one hundred and seventy-five thousand.

PEORIA

Is situated on the west bank of the Illinois river, seventy miles north of Springfield. The river here expands into a broad and deep lake, which adds greatly to the scenery of the town. A draw-bridge connects the city with the opposite shore of the river. The town is situated on rising ground, while back of it extends one of the most beautiful rolling prairies in the state. Near the center of the city a public square has been reserved. The schools and churches are prosperous, and the society good. The population in 1860 was fourteen thousand and forty-five.

QUINCY

Is situated on the Mississippi river, one hundred and seventy-five miles above St. Louis. The country in the vicinity is a rich and rolling prairie, and one of the best cultivated in the state. The city is quite extensively engaged in commerce, by means of steamboats on the Mississippi river. It has a large public square, a good court-house, twenty-four churches, ten public halls, two national banks, an armory, and four United States hospitals. Its population in 1860 numbered sixteen thousand six hundred and seventy-two.

GALENA

Is situated on the Fevre river, six miles from its entrance to the Mississippi river, and four hundred and fifty miles above St. Louis. The Fevre river is navigable by steamboats, which make regular passages to St. Louis, St. Paul, and other ports on the Mississippi river. The river is more properly an arm of the Mississippi, setting up between lofty bluffs, and winding around their base with picturesque effect. The streets are built one above another, and communicate by means of steps. Galena owes its growth and importance mainly to the rich mines of lead with which it is surrounded in all directions. Its population in 1860 was eight thousand one hundred and ninety-six.

BELLEVILLE

Is situated fourteen miles south-east from St. Louis. It is actively engaged in trade and manufactures, and growing very rapidly. Its population in 1864 numbered ten thousand.

ALTON

Is situated on the Mississippi river, three miles above the mouth of the Missouri, and twenty-one miles above St. Louis. Alton is one of the oldest towns in the state. It is the seat of the diocese of the Roman Catholic church for Southern Illinois.

The state penitentiary was formerly located at this place, but has since been removed to Joliet.

ROCKFORD

Is beautifully situated on both sides of Rock river. It is a flourishing city, the center of an active business, and contains seventeen churches, seven public schools, a female seminary, and three newspaper offices. Its water power is one of the finest in the west, and its manufactures amount in value to about four millions of dollars per annum. Its growth since 1836 has been very rapid. Population at the present time, about twelve thousand. (See views of Rockford.)

BLOOMINGTON

Is situated on the Illinois Central railroad, one hundred and twenty-six miles south-west of Chicago. The State Normal University is situated two miles north of the city. It is an imposing building, said to have cost two hundred thousand dollars. It is attended by about five hundred students.

OTTAWA

Is situated on both sides of the Illinois river, just below the mouth of Fox river, eighty-four miles south-west of Chicago. The Fox river, at this point, has a fall of about twenty-nine feet, producing a city water-power which is said to be unsurpassed by any in the state. In 1865 the population numbered about ten thousand.

AURORA

Is a flourishing city situated on the Fox river, forty miles south-west of Chicago. Population in 1864, eight thousand seven hundred and fifty.

LINCOLN

Is a flourishing town, situated on Salt creek, twenty-eight miles north-east of Springfield. This place, the origin of which is quite recent, was named in honor of Abraham Lincoln. Its population is about five thousand seven hundred.

ROCK ISLAND

Is situated on the Mississippi river, two miles above the mouth of Rock river, and one hundred and eighty-two miles south-west of Chicago. The place derives its name from an island three miles in length, the southern extremity of which is nearly opposite the town. This island is partly covered with woods, and affords an agreeable retreat in the heat of the summer. It presents a perpendicular front of limestone twenty or thirty feet high. Rock Island is remarkable for its flourishing manufactures. A bridge across the river connects it with Davenport, Iowa. Its population in 1865 numbered about seven thousand five hundred.

GALESBURG

Is situated on the Chicago, Burlington and Quincy railroad, one hundred and sixty-five miles south-west of Chicago. It is situated in a rich farming district, and has an active business. Population in 1865, about seven thousand.

KENTUCKY.

This state formed a part of Virginia until 1792. It was first explored by Daniel Boone in 1769. The early settlers were much annoyed by the Indians, who made frequent incursions and attacks upon their villages. Their bloody contests with these savage foes gave rise to the name of Kentucky, which means "the dark and bloody ground."

The Cumberland mountains form the south-eastern boundary of the state. A range of hills runs nearly parallel with the Ohio river. West of the Cumberland river the surface is generally level; the rest of the state is undulating and hilly. Kentucky contains much that is picturesque in her natural scenery, and many wild and striking objects. The Mammoth cave is situated about one hundred miles south-west of Louisville, in Edmondson county, in the valley of Green river. The entrance to this cave is in a ravine, two hundred feet above Green river, and one hundred below the table land above. The cave abounds in interesting objects, such as streams, mounds, stalactites, stalagmites, etc. The stalactites and stalagmites are some of them very large; one of them, called the Temple, occupies an area of two acres, and is covered by a single dome of solid rock, one hundred and twenty feet high. Echo river, five miles from the entrance, is the deepest and widest of the rivers, being about ten feet deep and a quarter of a mile in width. The water is very transparent, the sand and pebbles on the bottom being as plainly visible as if seen in air. The surface of the river is nearly upon a level with that of Green river, and it is supposed that it empties into Green river as they usually rise and fall together. Near the shore of the river the roof of the cave descends within a few feet of the surface of the water, and appears like an arch sprung from one side of the cave to the other. About half way across the river the cavern expands into immense proportions. Here is the remarkable echo which gives its name to the river. Sounds are repeated millions of times, receding at each successive echo, until they die away in the most distant chambers with a strain of melody resembling that of a wind-harp.

A few miles farther on is Cleveland's Cabinet. This is an arch about twenty feet high, and twenty wide, incrusted with a thick coating of frost, through which protrude in all directions, buds, vine-tendrils, sun flowers, cactus leaves, etc., fashioned from a material the most delicate, and all of pearly whiteness. Thirteen miles from the entrance, is Serenna's bower, a small and deep grotto, guarded by an aperture difficult of entrance. The bottom, roof, and sides, of this bower are covered with stalactite formations. In the side, about three feet from the floor, is a basin of pure water, around the edge of which the most curiously shaped pillars form, as it were, a fence for its protection. Among the other remarkable objects of the cave, are the Devil's Arm Chair, the Elephant's Head, the Lover's Leap, the Gothic Chapel, the Cinder Pile, and the Bottomless Pit. (See views of Mammoth Cave.) There are a number of smaller caves in the state, which in almost any other place, would be considered remarkable. There are also a great many sink-holes or depressions in the surface of the ground. These are sometimes three hundred feet in circumference, and from sixty to seventy feet deep. They are shaped like an inverted cone. Frequently the sound of running water can be detected beneath them, and in one or two cases openings have been made revealing subterraneous streams. A number of streams of considerable size disappear for some distance, and afterwards rise again to the surface. In Breckenridge county, there is a stream called Sinking creek, which, a few miles from its source, sinks beneath the surface, and does not re-appear again for several miles. In Christian county, in the midst of romantic scenery, is a natural bridge, thirty feet high and sixty feet in span. There are numerous mounds or fortifications in the state, erected, it is supposed, by a race who occupied the country at some period antecedent to the Indians.

The climate of Kentucky is milder than the same latitude on the Atlantic coast, but subject to sudden changes. The soil is very fertile; there is but a small portion of the state which is not capable of cultivation.

The state is actively engaged in commerce. The Ohio forms its entire northern boundary, and the Mississippi its western, giving it access to the commerce of these great valleys. The other important rivers are the Cumberland, Tennessee, Licking, Kentucky, Salt, and Green rivers. The Cumberland rises in the south-eastern part of the state, in the Cumberland mountains. Its whole length is six hundred miles, three hundred and fifty of which passes through Kentucky. It is navigable for large steamboats as far as Nashville, Tennessee, about two hundred miles from its mouth, and small boats ascend about three hundred miles further. The Tennessee river crosses the western part of the state, and enters the Ohio river about forty-eight miles from its mouth. The navigation of the river is unobstructed as far as Florence, at the foot of Muscle Shoals. Here it is obstructed by rapids, but above the rapids it is navigable for some distance, making, in all, about five hundred miles of navigable water. Licking river rises in the Cumberland mountains, pursues a north-westerly direction, and empties into the Ohio, opposite Cincinnati. It is about two hundred miles in length, and navigable for small steamboats for about fifty miles from its mouth. Kentucky river is formed by the union of three small rivers. The length of the main stream is about two hundred miles. Steamboats ascend as far as Frankfort, and flatboats ascend about one hundred miles further. Salt river is formed from the union of two small rivers. It derives its name from the number of salt springs which abound near it. The main stream flows in a north-westerly direction, and empties into the Ohio twenty-two miles below Louisville. Green river rises in the east central part of the state. During its course it traverses the cavernous limestone formation and passes by Mammoth cave. It is about three hundred miles in length. The lower part of the river is navigable for steamboats at all seasons of the year, and during high water, small steamboats have ascended for about two hundred miles from its mouth.

FRANKFORT,

The capital of Kentucky, is beautifully situated on the right bank of Kentucky river, sixty miles from its mouth and fifty-three miles east of Louisville. The city stands on an elevated plain, commanding a delightful view of the picturesque scenery for which the Kentucky river is so remarkable. The town is regularly laid out and generally well built. It contains a handsome state house, built of Kentucky marble, quarried in the vicinity. The governor's house, a state penitentiary, a court house, six churches, one academy, and two banking houses. The population is about three thousand seven hundred. The other important places are Louisville, Covington, Newport and Lexington.

LOUISVILLE

Is situated on the Ohio river, one hundred and thirty miles below Cincinnati, and fifty-three miles west of Frankfort. The city stands upon a plain elevated about seventy feet above low water, and commanding a delightful view of the Ohio river and of the rapids immediately below. The city is well built and regularly laid out. Parallel to the river are eight handsome streets, about two miles in length, which are intersected at right angles by more than thirty different streets.

The principal public buildings are the city hall, court house, medical institute and the university. Besides these the city has a marine asylum, two orphan asylums, forty churches, two synagogues, a prison, four banks, and four large public school houses. In 1860 the population numbered sixty-eight thousand and thirty-three.

COVINGTON

Is situated on the Ohio river, opposite Cincinnati, and just below the mouth of Licking river. It may be considered as a suburb of Cincinnati, and is laid out according to the same plan. The city contains ten churches, three banks, a large city hall, two female academies and the western theological college, which is under the direction of the Baptists. In 1860 the population was sixteen thousand four hundred and seventy-one.

NEWPORT

Is situated on the Ohio river, opposite from Cincinnati, and just above the mouth of Licking river, which separates it from Covington. It owes its rapid growth to its proximity to Cincinnati and its beautiful situation. It contains twelve churches and one bank. Its population is about ten thousand.

LEXINGTON

Is situated twenty-five miles south-east of Frankfort, and ninety-four miles east of Louisville. It was formerly the capital of Kentucky. The situation is delightful, and its general appearance is surpassed by few inland towns. The city contains a university, a state lunatic asylum, a court house, two banks, a public library, several academies, a museum, an orphan asylum and twelve churches. A monument is contemplated, to be erected to the memory of Henry Clay, who resided at Ashland, a mile and a half from the city. Lexington was founded in 1776, while the news of the battle of that name was fresh in the minds of its founders. In 1860 its population was nine thousand five hundred and twenty-one.

TENNESSEE.

The country now constituting the state of Tennessee, was originally comprised within the state of North Carolina. It was ceded to the general government in 1784, but the grant was afterwards revoked. At that time hostilities had been commenced by the Indians; they were without a government of their own, and unprotected by the troops of North Carolina.

A large proportion of her people determined to form an independent state government, which would enable them to legally assemble a military force for defense. The new state was organized under the name of Frankland, in 1786. This gave rise to considerable trouble, and the state was finally ceded to the United States government, and formed a part of the Southwestern Territory until 1796, when it was admitted into the union.

The state is commonly divided into three sections, East, West and Middle Tennessee. East Tennessee includes that part east of the Cumberland mountains; Middle Tennessee that part between the Cumberland mountains and the Tennessee river; and West Tennessee, that portion west of the Tennessee river. East Tennessee is mountainous, Middle Tennessee is hilly, and West Tennessee is level or gently undulating. The Alleghany mountains form the entire eastern boundary of the state. The Cumberland mountains enter it from Kentucky and cross it in a south-westerly direction, into Alabama. There are a number of caves in these mountains, some of them several miles in extent. In one of these, four hundred feet below the surface, there was found a stream large enough to turn a mill. Another, on the top of one of the mountains, has a perpendicular descent, and its depth has never yet been ascertained. The climate of Tennessee is mild, the winters are not severe, and the summers are free from the intense heat of the Gulf States. The soil, especially in the valleys, is fertile. Some of the mountain land is not adapted to cultivation, but is favorable to grazing.

The Mississippi river forms the western boundary of the state. The other important rivers are the Cumberland, which flows for about one hundred and fifty miles through Tennessee; the Tennessee river, which crosses the state twice; the Clinch, about two hundred miles in length, and navigable for about half that distance, and the Holston, which is about two hundred miles in length, and navigable as far as Knoxville at all seasons of the year; besides these, there are several smaller streams, each more or less navigable for small boats during high water.

NASHVILLE,

The capital, is situated on the left bank of the Cumberland river, two hundred miles from its mouth, and two hundred and thirty miles north-east of Memphis. It is one of the wealthiest and most populous cities of Tennessee. The city is pleasantly situated, regularly laid out, and well built. It contains many elegant private buildings. The public buildings are also among the best in the United States. The capitol is estimated to have cost one million dollars. It is built of fine limestone, quarried in the vicinity, and very nearly resembles marble. It is one of the handsomest and most costly structures in America. A large lunatic asylum has recently been erected. Besides these, the city contains a state penitentiary, a university, several female seminaries, three banks and fourteen churches. A wire suspension bridge has recently been built across the Cumberland river, at a cost of one hundred thousand dollars. In 1860, the population was sixteen thousand nine hundred and eighty-eight. (See views of Nashville.)

The other important places are Memphis, Knoxville, Murfreesboro and Jackson.

MEMPHIS

Is beautifully situated on the Mississippi river, just below the mouth of Wolf river, and two hundred and nine miles south-west of Nashville. It is situated on a bluff about seventy feet high, and presents a very fine appearance from the river. It is rapidly increasing in population, and is full of life and commercial activity. It is the most populous and important city between St. Louis and New Orleans. The river is navigable for the largest ships from this point to its mouth. The city contains twenty-three public schools, eleven churches, one academy, four banks, and a telegraph office. In 1865 the population was about forty thousand.

KNOXVILLE

Is beautifully situated on the right bank of the Holston river, one hundred and eighty-five miles east of Nashville. The situation is elevated and commands a delightful view of the river, which is navigable at all seasons of the year from this point downwards. The city contains an asylum for the deaf and dumb, a university, five churches, three banks, and several academies. The city was laid out in 1794. In 1860 its population was about six thousand.

MURFREESBORO

Is situated in a beautiful plain, thirty miles south-east of Nashville. It contains a university, founded by the Baptists, a female institute, also under the direction of the Baptists, one bank, and five churches. It was formerly the capital of Tennessee. The population is about two thousand nine hundred.

JACKSON

Is situated on the Forked Deer river, one hundred and fifty miles south-west of Nashville. It is situated in the midst of a fertile region, and is actively engaged in trade. It contains a bank, two or three churches, and a flourishing college. Its population is about two thousand four hundred.

ARKANSAS.

Arkansas was settled by the French as early as 1685, and formed a part of the great tract purchased from France in 1803, under the name of Louisiana. It made little progress until after its formation into a territory of the United States in 1819. In 1836 it became a member of the American union.

Throughout its entire length it occupies the right bank of the Mississippi, which separates it from the states of Tennessee and Mississippi, and renders it accessible to the sea from many points. Its area is about fifty-two thousand one hundred and ninety-eight square miles, being about two hundred and forty miles in length from north to south, and two hundred and twenty-four in breadth from east to west.

The eastern part of Arkansas, for about one hundred miles back from the Mississippi, is covered with marshes, swamps and lagoons, occasionally interspersed with elevations, some of which are thirty miles or more in circuit, which, when the rivers overflow their banks, form temporary islands. In 1854, out of the equivalent thirty-three millions four hundred and six thousand seven hundred and twenty acres, only eight hundred and fifty-seven thousand one hundred and seventy-nine were cultivated, very little more than one-fourth of the whole, or one-seventh of the lands liable to taxation, as being allotted and occupied; but since the bill passed by congress giving to the southern and western states all the overflowed swamp lands within their respective limits, the state of Arkansas has constructed along its entire eastern boundary levees of great strength, by means of which extensive tracts that have hitherto been entirely worthless, have been converted into cultivable land of extraordinary fertility.

In climate and productions, Arkansas occupies, as it were, an intermediate position between the states of the west and those of the south. The state is divided into two unequal parts by the Ozark mountains, of which the northern has the climate and productions of the northern states, while the southern portion resembles that of the southern states. The northern region is well adapted to grazing. It produces, also, an abundance of excellent wheat, and, perhaps, the finest apples in the world. This section of the country is hilly, or rolling, and is interspersed with prairie, and abounds with fine springs of excellent water. The tops of the hills and mountains are often flat or rolling, and covered with a good soil and a heavy growth of timber. Indian corn, cotton, and live stock form the staple products of the state. On the bottom lands is generally found a heavy growth of cotton-wood, ash, cypress, and gum. The hickory and different kinds of oak flourish in the mountainous or hilly portions. From the central part of the state southward to the Red river, pine is found in great abundance. Beech is also found in considerable abundance on the St. Francis river. Besides these are found the black walnut, cherry, red cedar, dogwood, maple, poplar, sassafras and black locust. Immense quantities of these different kinds of timber are sent down the Mississippi to New Orleans.

Probably no state in the union is penetrated by so many navigable rivers as Arkansas. These rivers can only be ascended by vessels of any size, for about nine months in the year, owing to the long continued droughts which prevail in the hot season. The Arkansas is the principal river that passes wholly through the state. It enters the western border of the state from the Indian territory at Fort Smith, and sweeping almost directly through the middle of the state, after receiving a number of small tributaries, discharges its waters into the Mississippi. It is from three-eighths to half a mile wide through the last six hundred miles of its course, and navigable for about eight hundred miles from its mouth. The north-eastern part of the state is drained by the White river and the St. Francis with their affluents. They have their sources in the Missouri and their outlet in the Mississippi. The White river is navigable for about five hundred miles, the St. Francis for three hundred miles. Besides these there are the Red river, running through the south-western angle of the state, the Washita and its numerous affluents, having an aggregate of six hundred and thirty-five miles of navigable water, and the little Missouri. The state has no foreign commerce, though it has considerable boating trade with New Orleans, engaged in the export of its productions.

The mineral resources of the state are very extensive. The principal minerals are coal, iron, lead, zinc, manganese, gypsum, and salt. There is a celebrated quarry of oil stone near the Hot Springs, superior to any thing else of the kind known in the world. There are a great many varieties exhibiting all degrees of fineness. The quantity is said to be inexhaustible. There is in Pike county, on the Little Missouri river, a mountain of alabaster of the finest quality, and white as the driven snow. Gold is said to have been discovered in White county. Arkansas has more gypsum than all the other states put together, while it is equally well supplied with marble and salt.

The celebrated Hot Springs are situated in a county of the same name, about sixty miles south-west of Little Rock. More than one hundred of these springs issue, at different elevations, from a point or ridge of land forming a steep bank from one hundred and fifty to two hundred feet high, projecting over Hot Spring creek, an affluent of the Washita. This creek is warm enough to bathe in, even in the coldest weather. A considerable portion of the bank consists of calcareous deposits, formed from the water as it is exposed to the air. Near the top of the bank there is a fine cold spring, so near the warm springs, that a person can put one hand into cold, and the other into hot water at the same time. These springs are a great resort for invalids, their waters being considered particularly beneficial to persons suffering from rheumatism. Their temperature varies from one hundred and thirty-five to one hundred and sixty degrees.

LITTLE ROCK,

The capital of Arkansas, is situated on the right or southern bank of the Arkansas river, on a rocky promontory, or bluff, about fifty feet high, commanding a delightful and extensive view of the surrounding country. In ascending the river, there appears on the south bank, rising out of the water, a bald, igneous slate rock, which, at low water, is about twenty-five feet above the surface, but at high water is almost hidden from view. This gave to the place the name of Little Rock. Two miles above this point, there is another rocky bluff about two hundred feet high, which is called Big Rock. The town contains a state house, United States arsenal, state penitentiary, and six handsome churches. The population in 1860, was three thousand seven hundred and twenty-seven.

The other important places are Camden, Fort Smith, and Pine Bluff.

CAMDEN

Is situated on a high range of hills on the right bank of the Washita river, one hundred and ten miles south-west of Little Rock. Its growth has been very rapid. A few years ago, the land on which the city now stands was covered with a dense forest, and many of the trees are still standing in the streets. The city has great advantages for trade, being at the head of navigation for large steamers. It was settled in 1842, and in

1860 the population numbered two thousand two hundred and nineteen.

FORT SMITH

Is situated at the western boundary of the state, on the right bank of the Arkansas river, one hundred and sixty-three miles north-west of Little Rock. It is a military post of the United States, and is extensively engaged in trade with the Indians. Its population is about one thousand and five hundred.

PINE BLUFF

Is situated on the right bank of the Arkansas river, forty-eight miles south-east of Little Rock. It is situated in a rich cotton planting region, and ships twenty thousand bales of cotton annually. It has about one thousand three hundred inhabitants.

MISSOURI.

The early settlers of Missouri were French. The first settlement was made in the year 1719, near the site of the present capital. It was purchased by the United States as a part of the territory of Louisiana, in 1803. In 1812, when Louisiana was admitted into the union, the remainder of the territory was named Missouri. In 1821 the territory applied to congress for admission into the union. A bill was introduced admitting it as a state, but prohibiting slavery. This passed the house, but was arrested in the senate. After a stormy debate the question was settled by a compromise. A bill passed for the admission of Missouri without any restriction as to slavery, but prohibiting it throughout the United States north of latitude thirty-six degrees thirty minutes.

North of the Missouri river the surface is mostly level. South of this river it is varied, presenting mountains, marshes, and prairie lands. The climate is variable. The winters are cold and the summers very warm, but the air is dry and pure. The soil, especially on the river bottoms, is fertile. In the south-eastern part of the state there is considerable marsh land, which, with a proper system of drainage, would probably become the most fertile part of the state. The principal productions of the state are Indian corn, wheat, oats, tobacco, and wool.

The Mississippi river forms its eastern boundary, and the Missouri crosses it from west to east, thus giving it access to the commerce of the two largest rivers of the United States.

The Missouri river rises in the Rocky mountains. It is three thousand and ninety-six miles in length. Throughout the greater part of its course the current is very rapid, and the navigation is somewhat difficult. Steamboats, however, meet with but little difficulty in ascending for about two thousand five hundred and seventy-five miles from its mouth. It forms the north-western boundary of the state of Missouri for about two hundred miles, then crosses it in a south-easterly direction. On its southern shore there are a number of bluffs from one hundred to three hundred feet in hight. Its principal tributaries within the state are the Chariton, Grand, Osage, and Gasconade. The Chariton is navigable for about fifty miles from its mouth, the Grand for only a short distance, the Osage in high water for about two hundred, and the Gasconade for about sixty miles.

JEFFERSON CITY,

The capital of Missouri, is beautifully situated on the right bank of the Missouri river, one hundred and fifty-five miles west of St. Louis. The situation is elevated, and commands a fine view of the river and of the bluffs on the opposite shore. In 1865 the population was about three thousand five hundred.

The other important towns are St. Louis, St. Joseph, Hannibal, Kansas City, and Lexington.

ST. LOUIS,

The largest city, is situated on the right bank of the Mississippi, about twenty miles below the mouth of the Missouri. The thickly settled portion extends for about two and one half miles, but the whole extent is about seven miles along the river and three miles back. The natural commercial advantages of the city are very great. It is situated midway between the Atlantic and Pacific, in the center of the finest agricultural region in the world, on the largest river of the United States, and almost at the very point where the Missouri, Ohio, and Illinois rivers converge. The city is regularly laid out and well built. The streets are wide, and with few exceptions intercept each other at right angles. It contains many elegant public buildings. The new court house, built of Genevieve limestone, occupies an entire square. It cost the city about half a million of dollars. The United States arsenal is a large and handsome building, surrounded by handsomely ornamented grounds. Among the finest churches are St. George, the Catholic cathedral, and the Church of the Messiah. In the tower of the cathedral there is a chime of bells, the heaviest of which weighs two thousand six hundred pounds. The site of St. Louis was selected in 1764. In 1822 it was chartered as a city. In 1860 its population was one hundred and sixty thousand seven hundred and seventy-three.

ST. JOSEPH

Is situated on the left bank of the Missouri, four hundred and ninety-six miles, by water, from St. Louis. The town was laid out in 1843. The population in 1865 was about fifteen thousand.

HANNIBAL

Is situated on the Mississippi river, one hundred and fifty-three miles above St. Louis. It is a flourishing city, neatly laid out and well built. In 1865 the population was about eight thousand.

KANSAS CITY

Is situated on the right bank of the Missouri river, just below the mouth of the Kansas. It contains a court house, eleven churches and three banks. In 1864 the population was about five thousand four hundred.

LEXINGTON

Is situated on the right bank of the Missouri, one hundred and twenty miles west of Jefferson City. In 1860 the population was four thousand one hundred and twenty-two.

IOWA.

Iowa formed, originally, part of the Louisiana purchase; afterwards it became a part of Missouri, then of Wisconsin, and lastly of Iowa Territory. It was organized as a state, with governor and legislature, in 1846.

The surface of Iowa is undulating and beautiful, with alternate forests and prairies. There is nothing within its limits which approaches a mountain in elevation; but bold bluffs, with picturesque ravines, line the rivers. A plateau, which enters the northern part of the state from Minnesota, is the highest elevation. Table Mound, a conical elevation with a flat summit, three or four miles from Dubuque, is about five hundred feet high.

There are said to be some swamps in the north-western portion of the state. On Turkey river, in the northern part, there are numerous sinks, or circular depressions in the surface of the ground, some of them from ten to twenty feet across. On the same stream, within ten or fifteen miles of its mouth, are small mounds, from three to six feet high, and sometimes ten or twelve in a row. In Jackson county, there is a cave, several rods in extent, from which flows a stream large enough to turn a mill.

The state may be described as a rolling prairie, crossed by rivers whose banks are skirted with wood. The Mississippi and Missouri form its eastern and western boundary. The other important rivers are the Des Moines, Iowa, Red Cedar, and their branches. The Des Moines, the most important of these, has its sources in Minnesota, and, traversing the entire state of Iowa, forms, near its mouth, a small portion of the south-eastern boundary. It is thought that it can be made navigable for steamboats as far as Fort Des Moines, a distance of about two hundred miles, and the state government has recently undertaken the work. Small steamboats can ascend the Iowa river three months in the year, for about eighty miles from its mouth, as far as Iowa City. The Red Cedar is about three hundred miles in length, and passes almost entirely across the state, furnishing important water-power.

Iowa has not much direct foreign commerce, but trades extensively with the Atlantic and Gulf towns, and with the interior. The soil is exceedingly fertile and the climate healthful. The summers are warm, but the winters are quite severe. The rivers are frozen over from two to three months, on an average, each winter. Iowa, except along the rivers, is not well timbered. Between the belts of timber bordering on the streams, there are often prairies of from fifteen to twenty miles in extent, without as much as a shrub or tree to break the monotony of their surface.

DES MOINES,

The capital of the state, is situated at the junction of the Des Moines and Raccoon rivers, one hundred and seventy-five miles west of Davenport.

The other principal towns are Dubuque, Davenport, Keokuk, Burlington and Iowa City.

DUBUQUE

Is situated on the right bank of the Mississippi, about four hundred and fifty miles above St. Louis. Part of the city is built on a terrace, which extends along the bank of the river for several miles; the remainder is built upon a bluff, which rises about two hundred feet higher.

DAVENPORT

Is situated on the Mississippi, about three hundred and thirty miles above St. Louis. Next to Dubuque and Burlington it is the largest city of Iowa, and it is rapidly increasing in size. A handsome draw-bridge connects it with the city of Rock Island, on the opposite side of the river.

KEOKUK

Is situated on the Mississippi, two hundred and five miles above St. Louis. It stands on a basis of fine limestone, which affords an excellent material for building.

BURLINGTON

Is situated on the Mississippi river, about two hundred and fifty miles above St. Louis. It was at one time the capital of Iowa, and it continues to grow rapidly, notwithstanding the removal of the seat of government. At the present time its population is not equaled by any city in the state except Dubuque, which is about the same.

IOWA CITY

Was also at one time the capital of Iowa. It is situated on the Iowa river, about eighty miles from its mouth. The river at this point has excellent water-power, which is partially improved.

MICHIGAN.

The first settlements in Michigan were made by the French in the latter part of the seventeenth century, at Detroit and Mackinaw. In 1763, together with the other French possessions in North America, it passed into the hands of Great Britain. On the breaking out of the American revolution, it came into the hands of the United States. It was admitted into the union in 1837.

The state is divided by Lakes Michigan and Huron, into two irregular peninsulas. The northern peninsula is a wild and rough region of mountains and forests, and containing about two-fifths of the area of the state. The southern is a level, rich, fertile country of prairies and oak openings, and watered by numerous rivers. There is a striking contrast between the two peninsulas, the lower being level and fertile, while the upper is picturesque, rugged and sterile in soil. The climate is mild in the southern, and cold and bleak in the northern regions. The southern portion produces wheat, maize, butter, and cheese, in great abundance. The northern part is rich in minerals. Along the shores of Lake Superior are probably some of the richest copper mines in the world. A mass of copper weighing one hundred and fifty tons was uncovered in one of the mines in 1854. Silver is also found in considerable quantities in connection with the copper. In some instances the ore has yielded as high as fifty per cent. of silver. Iron also abounds along the shores of the same lake. (See views of the iron mines of Lake Superior.) Large quantities of this mineral are shipped from the town of Marquette, which owes its prosperity to the iron mines worked in the vicinity. Extensive ore docks are built along the shore of the bay. (See views of the bay of Marquette.)

Michigan is most favorably situated for internal trade, and trade with British America. It has a lake coast of over one thousand miles. The coast is indented by a number of bays, furnishing valuable harbors. The rivers are small and rapid in their course, obstructed by frequent waterfalls, which oppose navigation, but furnish valuable water power. The St. Joseph, Kalamazoo, Grand and Muskegon, are navigable for vessels of light draft from forty to fifty miles.

The towns of Michigan are remarkable for their rapid growth.

LANSING,

The capital, is situated on Grand river, one hundred and ten miles north-west of Detroit. When it was selected for the seat of government in 1847, it was surrounded by an almost unbroken wilderness. It now contains a large and handsome state house, twelve churches, two banks, a female college, an academy, and a reform school. In 1860, the population was three thousand and seventy-four. The other important places are Detroit, Grand Rapids, Adrian, Kalamazoo, Ann Arbor, Jackson and Monroe.

DETROIT,

The largest city, is situated on the west bank of Detroit river, eighteen miles from the head of Lake Erie. The city covers an area of about ten miles, and stretches along the bank of the river for about three miles. The city is regularly laid out, the streets are wide, well paved, and ornamented with forest trees. The city is supplied with pure lake water which is raised from the river by steam power. The position of Detroit on the great chain of lakes, gives it great commercial advantages. Several lines of large steamers are actively engaged in the copper and iron trade. In 1805, Detroit was entirely destroyed by fire. The city was then built up on an entirely different plan. It was the capital of the state from the admission of Michigan into the union in 1836, until 1850. The city contains a number of large and handsome public buildings, and many elegant private residences. In 1865, the population was about sixty thousand.

GRAND RAPIDS

Is situated on Grand river, forty miles from its mouth. The city takes its name from the rapids of the river at that place. It is beautifully situated on both banks of the river, in an elevated position, commanding a fine view of the river and surrounding country. It is actively engaged in commerce and manufactures. The city was laid out in 1833, and incorporated in 1850. It now contains twelve churches, two banks, and several seminaries. The population is about eight thousand one hundred.

ADRIAN

Is situated on a branch of the Raisin river, seventy miles south-west of Detroit. It is actively engaged in commerce, and is rapidly increasing in population. It has a number of large public buildings, and several places of worship. The population it about six thousand two hundred.

KALAMAZOO

Is situated on the left bank of Kalamazoo river, one hundred and forty miles west of Detroit. It is actively engaged in trade. The Michigan asylum for the insane is located here. It also contains a United States land office, nine churches, and three banks. In 1860 the population was six thousand and seventy.

ANN ARBOR

Is situated on the Huron river, thirty-eight miles west of Detroit. It contains a university, three colleges, eight churches, three banks, and a large union school. In 1864, the population was about eight thousand nine hundred.

JACKSON

Is situated on Grand river, seventy-six miles west of Detroit. It contains the county buildings, five churches, one seminary and the state penitentiary. In 1860 the population was four thousand nine hundred and seventy-nine.

MONROE

Is pleasantly situated on both sides of the Raisin river, two miles from its entrance into Lake Erie and forty miles south-west of Detroit. The place was settled in 1776, but has mostly been built since 1835. The population in 1860 was three thousand eight hundred and ninety-two.

WISCONSIN.

Wisconsin was settled in the latter part of the seventeenth century. For some time the population did not increase very rapidly, but within the last few years the rich soil, valuable minerals, and beautiful scenery of the state have attracted a large number of emigrants. It was admitted into the union in 1848.

The surface of Wisconsin is elevated, though it has no mountains. The climate is severe, the winters long, but almost entirely free from those sudden changes which occur in some of the states further south. The soil is fertile, and generally adapted to farming and grazing, especially in the southern part of the state. The mineral resources of the state are not yet fully developed. Considerable quantities of copper, iron and lead are found. The lead is frequently intermingled with copper, zinc, and silver.

The principal rivers of the state flow in a south-westerly direction, and empty into the Mississippi, which traverses the south-western border of the state for about two hundred miles. The other important rivers are the Wisconsin and the Chippewa. The Wisconsin rises in the northern part of the state, flows in a south-westerly direction, and empties into the Mississippi. It is about two hundred miles in length, and navigable for about one hundred and eighty miles of this distance. The Chippewa rises in the northern part of the state, flows in a south-westerly direction a distance of about two hundred miles, and discharges its waters into the Mississippi. The courses of the rivers are rapid, furnishing valuable water power, but unfavorable to navigation. They abound in rapids and falls. On the Wisconsin occur the St. Croix, Chippewa, and Big Bull falls. On the banks of this river are Pentenwell peak, and Pulpit rock. The former is an oval mass of rock, nine hundred feet long, three hundred feet wide, and elevated about two hundred feet above the surrounding country. The latter (see view,) is about one hundred feet in hight. One side has a perpendicular descent, and the other descends by a succession of terraces. About fifty miles below St. Anthony's falls the Mississippi river expands into a lake, some five miles in width and twenty-five miles in length. This is called Lake Pepin, which means "the Lake of Tears." This lake is noted for its beautiful scenery. On the east side is a bold rock over four hundred feet high called Maiden rock. (See view.)

This rock derived its name from an occurrence which took place about fifty years ago. An Indian girl, of the Wapasha tribe, became very much attached to a young hunter. Her parents, however, determined that she should marry a young warrior who had signalized himself in battle against the Chippewas. Rather than submit to this, she ascended this rock, and, with a loud voice commenced upbraiding her parents for their cruel conduct. They promised to relinquish all compulsory measures, but, regardless of their entreaties, she threw herself from the rock, and fell a lifeless corpse at their feet.

In the northern part of the state are a number of small lakes, remarkable for their beautiful scenery. Scattered throughout the state are mounds or earth works, which are evidently the work of a race who occupied the country previous to the people found by the Europeans on their arrival here. The cities of Wisconsin are growing rapidly, and new ones are constantly springing up.

MADISON,

The capital, is pleasantly situated in the center of a broad valley, on an isthmus between Lakes Mendota and Monona. The situation is remarkably beautiful, and it is much frequented by pleasure seekers as a summer resort. Since its origin the place has steadily and rapidly increased in population. When it was selected in 1836 for the seat of government, it contained but one house, and that was built of logs. It now contains a handsome capitol, a university, twelve churches, four banks and eighty stores. In 1865 the population was about ten thousand.

The other important places are Milwaukee, Racine, and Janesville.

MILWAUKEE,

The largest city, is situated on the western shore of Lake Michigan, at the mouth of Milwaukee river, seventy-five miles east of Madison. It is pleasantly situated on both sides of the river, and the general appearance of the place is very pleasing, on account of the large number of buildings made from the brick manufactured at that place. These bricks are of a light cream color. Large quantities of them are shipped to other parts of the United States. Milwaukee is remarkable for its rapid growth. The extensive water power of the Milwaukee river is an important element in the prosperity of the place. The town was settled in 1835, and incorporated as a city in 1846. It contains forty-three churches, eleven public schools, one female college, several academies, eight banks, three orphan asylums and two hospitals. In 1863 the population was about sixty-five thousand.

RACINE

Is beautifully situated on an elevated plain on the western shore of Lake Michigan, at the mouth of Root river, twenty-five miles south-east of Milwaukee. The city is regularly laid out, with wide streets, and contains a number of handsome public buildings and elegant private residences. Racine contains sixteen churches, one college, six public schools and two banks. It was settled in 1835, and incorporated in 1848. In 1865 the population was about ten thousand.

JANESVILLE

Is pleasantly situated on both sides of Rock river. It was settled in 1836, and incorporated in 1853. It contains a court house, nine churches, two banks, a high school, a female seminary, and the state institution for the blind. In 1860 the population was seven thousand seven hundred and three.

MINNESOTA.

Minnesota was first visited by white men in the year 1654. The first permanent settlement was made in 1811. The present state formed a part of the original Louisiana territory as purchased from France in 1803. It became a territory in 1847, and was admitted into the union in 1853.

The surface of the state is generally uniform. It contains no mountains, but is the most elevated tract of land between the Gulf of Mexico and Hudson's bay. There are a few elevations above the general average, called mounds ; but, with these exceptions, the surface is marked only by ravines running from the general level down to the beds of the streams. It is neither mountainous, hilly, or level, but a beautiful arrangement of upland and lowland plains. The climate is severe but remarkably uniform, sudden changes rarely occurring, so that there is far less suffering from cold than in the changeable weather of the winters further south.

The soil on the river bottoms is very fertile. In the northern part of the state the country is generally covered with drift, interspersed with marshes, too wet for cultivation. The climate is well adapted to the culture of wheat, barley, oats, and potatoes. Indian corn thrives as well as in northern New York or New England. Wild rice, strawberries, currants, plums, cranberries and grapes are found in great abundance.

Minnesota is one of the best watered states in the union. It abounds in beautiful lakes of almost every size. The largest of these lakes, with the exception of Lake Superior, are the Lake of the Woods, Rainy Lake, Red Lake, Lake Cass, Leech Lake, and Mille Lac, or Spirit Lake. Lake Pepin and White Bear lake (see views,) are noted for their beautiful scenery. The rivers of Minnesota abound in falls and rapids, which obstruct navigation, but afford valuable water power. St. Anthony Falls, on the Mississippi, have a perpendicular descent of sixteen and one half feet. These falls are celebrated, not so much for their hight, as for the wild and romantic scenery in the vicinity. (See views of the Falls of St. Anthony.) Near the Falls of St. Anthony is the beautiful cascade of Minnehaha. This is one of the small perfect works of nature, possessing all the greater charm, because it is not grand and overpowering, but simply beautiful. It has a perpendicular descent of about forty-five feet. As seen from beneath there is but a small portion of the sky visible, against which the fall seems projected, as though the waters were falling from some summer cloud. The precipice below the verge arches over, leaving a space wide enough for a foot path between it and the falls. (See views of Minnehaha.)

The principal rivers are the Mississippi, Minnesota, Red river of the North, St. Louis, and St. Croix. The scenery along the Mississippi is very beautiful. Near the confluence of the Mississippi and St. Peter's rivers there is an elevation two hundred and sixty-two feet in hight, called Pilot Knob, and another at Red Wing, three hundred feet in hight, called Barn Bluff. (See views.) Two or three miles above St. Paul there is an excavation in the white sand stone called Fountain cave. This opens by an arched passage into a chamber one hundred and fifty feet long and twenty wide, along the center of which runs a small stream. (See views of Fountain cave.) The scenery at St. Cloud and Fort Snelling is remarkably beautiful. (See views.) About thirty miles from the mouth of the St. Croix river there are some rapids which have a descent of about fifty feet in about three hundred yards. About half a mile below the rapids the river has forced its way through a perpendicular wall of trap rock, through which it rushes with great velocity. This pass is called the Dalles of the St. Croix. (See views.)

ST. PAUL,

The capital of the state, is situated on a bluff seventy or eighty feet high, on the left bank of the Mississippi river, eight miles below the Falls of St. Anthony. It is a place of active business, and is growing very rapidly. It was settled in 1840. The population in 1860 was ten thousand four hundred.

The other important places are St. Anthony, Minneapolis, Stillwater, Winona, and Hastings.

CALIFORNIA.

California was discovered in 1548, by Cabrillo, a Spanish navigator. In 1758, Sir Francis Drake visited its northern coast, and named the country New Albion. The original settlements in California were mission establishments, founded by Catholic priests for the conversion of the natives. The policy of these priests, who held absolute sway in California until 1833, was to discourage emigration. In the year 1840 the number of free whites and half breed inhabitants numbered less than six thousand. The emigration from the United States first commenced in 1838; this so increased from year to year that in 1846, Colonel Fremont had but little difficulty in calling to his aid some five hundred fighting men.

Geographically considered, the position of California is one of the best in the world, lying, as it does, on the Pacific, fronting Asia. It is about seven hundred and fifty miles long with an average breadth of about two hundred miles, giving an area of one hundred and fifty thousand square miles. Its great length, together with its diversity of surface, gives it a greater variation of climate and productions than any other state in the union.

The Colorado desert lies in the south-eastern part of the state, and is seventy miles wide by one hundred and forty long. It is a low, barren, dry, cheerless region. Part of it is seventy feet below the level of the sea, and, in times of very high water, the Colorado river frequently overflows its banks, and a large stream runs down into this basin and makes a lake. North of the Colorado desert lies the Mohave basin, which has no outlet. All its streams terminate in salt lakes, most of which dry up in summer. All these lakes are so strong with alkaline salts that no fish can live in the water, and one of them is so strong that it scalds the human cuticle. Most of the basin is four thousand feet above the level of the sea, but one portion, called Death valley, is three hundred and seventy-five feet below.

Sierra Nevada stretches along the coast, at the general distance of one hundred and fifty miles from it. This great mountain wall receives the warm winds, charged with vapor, which sweep across the Pacific ocean, precipitates their accumulated moisture in fertilizing rains and snows upon its western flank, and leaves cold and dry winds to pass on to the east. The region east of the mountains is comparatively barren and cold.

West of the Sierra Nevada is the inhabitable part of California. North and south, this region extends through about ten degrees of latitude, from Oregon to the peninsula of California. East and west it averages, in the middle part, one hundred and fifty, and in the northern part, two hundred miles, giving an area of about one hundred thousand square miles. Side ranges, parallel to the Sierra and the coast, make the structure of the rest of California, and break it into a surface of valleys and mountains—the valleys a few hundred, and the mountains two or three thousand feet above the sea.

The climate of California is mild. Snow never falls except in mountain regions. About one-third of all the land is susceptible of cultivation, and the soil is generally fertile, though not equal to the Mississippi valley. Where rain is abundant large crops are produced. Barley is cultivated to a greater extent than in any other state in the union. Fruit trees grow rapidly, and commence to bear when very young. The climate is peculiarly favorable for the cultivation of the grape. The vineyards of the state cover upwards of ten thousand acres. A single bunch of grapes has been known to weigh seventeen pounds. The vegetables are remarkable for their great size. At one of the agricultural fairs there was exhibited a cabbage weighing fifty-three pounds, a squash two hundred and sixty pounds, an onion forty-seven pounds, a turnip twenty-six pounds, a watermelon sixty-five pounds, a carrot ten pounds, and a beet one hundred and eighteen pounds, five feet long by one foot in diameter.

There are dense forests on the Sierra Nevada and on the coast north of the Golden Gate. The forests of the low land of the

Sacramento, the coast mountains south of thirty-seven degrees, the Colorado desert, and the Mohave basin are limited to some scattering groves of oak in the valleys and along the borders of the streams, and of red wood on the ridges and in the gorges of the hills, sometimes extending into the plains. The largest trees in the state are the *Sequoia Gigantea* or mammoth trees. These trees are found in the Sierra Nevada at an elevation of four thousand feet. Already twenty groves have been discovered in California. The Mariposa is the largest and finest, though the Calaveras, fifty miles to the northward, is better known. This grove contains ten trees thirty feet in diameter, eighty-two between fifteen and thirty, and a number of smaller ones. Nearly all of them are over two hundred and fifty feet high, and several of them three hundred. One of them was cut down by boring with augers and sawing the spaces between. The work employed five men for twenty-five days. When fully cut off the tree stubbornly continued to stand, only yielding at last to a mammoth wedge and a powerful battering-ram. Of the trees in the Mariposa grove, two hundred are more than twelve feet in diameter, fifty more than sixteen feet and six more than thirty feet. The largest, called the "Prostrate Monarch," is now lying upon the ground, leafless and branchless. It is believed to have fallen fully one hundred and fifty years ago. Part of the trunk has been consumed by fire, though enough of it remains to show that with the bark on it must have been at least forty feet in diameter. The largest of the trees are between three and four hundred feet high. The tops of many of the large trees have been broken off, leaving their average hight about two hundred and fifty feet. In one of the trees, there is a cavity about half the thickness of the trunk, which is large enough to admit fifteen persons on horseback, without crowding in the least. Through another, lying on the ground, a cavity has been burned, large enough to permit a man to ride through its entire length. The largest standing tree is the Grizzly Grant. If it was cut off smoothly, fifty horses could easily stand upon the stump. If the trunk were hollowed to a shell, it would hold more freight than a man-of-war or a first class ocean steamer two hundred and fifty feet long. (See views of mammoth trees in Mariposa and Calaveras groves.) The redwood pines which are scattered among these trees would elsewhere be considered kings of the forests, but among these hoary giants they dwarf into small shrubs. They are scattered over an area of about twelve hundred and eighty acres. Many of them are two hundred feet in hight.

The chief mineral is gold, and California is the chief gold producing country in the world. On the 19th of January, 1848, the gold mines of the Sierra Nevada were discovered by an American gentleman, James N. Marshall, and in about three months upwards of four thousand people were working them. Further explorations showed that these deposits of gold extended over a vast extent of country. The discovery of gold at once changed the character of California. Its people, before engaged in cultivating small patches of ground, and guarding their herds of cattle and horses, flocked to the mines. The laborers left their work, the tradesmen their shops, the soldiers deserted from the forts, and the sailors ran away from their ships. The mines astonished the world by the vast amount of their production. Information of the discovery spread rapidly, and in fifteen months after their discovery one hundred thousand people had started for the new El Dorado. Lower California was forgotten; the only California before the eyes of the world was the new land of gold, which thus usurped the name which once belonged exclusively to the peninsula.

The principal gold region of California is about five hundred miles long, and from forty to fifty miles broad, following the line of the Sierra Nevada. (See views of California mining.)

There are numerous streams which have their sources in the springs of the Sierra, and receive the waters from its melting snows and that which falls in rain during the wet season. These rivers in forming their channels, or breaking their way through the hills, have come in contact with the quartz containing the gold veins, and by constant attrition cut the gold into fine flakes and dust, and it is found among the sand and gravel of their beds at those places where the swiftness of the current reduces it, in the dry season, to the narrowest possible limits, and where a wide margin is consequently left on each side, over which the water rushes during the wet season with great force. (See views of Yuba river.)

Perhaps no state in the union is as remarkable for the combination of loveliness with sublimity, as California. Its natural scenery is unsurpassed by that of any other part of the world. The Geysers, in Lake county, a cluster of hot, steaming springs, and Lake Tahoe, or Bigler, near the summit of the Sierra Nevada, are fashionable watering places. The rivers have frequently cut for themselves beds, or canons, in the solid rock, narrow and deep, with the banks rising perpendicularly on either side. (See views of canons.) Lieutenant Ives' statements respecting the gorges upon the Colorado river are almost incredible, and are certainly without a parallel. At the head of navigation the deep and narrow current of the river flows between massive walls of rock, which rise sheer from the water for over a thousand feet, seeming almost to meet in the dizzy hight above. The sun rarely penetrates the depths of this "Black Canon," which is about twenty-five miles in length. Incomparably the grandest feature of California is the Yosemite valley. Unless the unexplored Himalayas hide some rival, there is no spot, the wide world over, of such varied beauty and measureless grandeur. The valley is from eight to ten miles long, and a little more than a mile wide, with steep, rocky sides, in some places four thousand feet high. Through this valley runs the Merced river. This river is about forty yards wide. Its waters are almost perfectly transparent. In the valley are five great cascades, the highest of which is the Yosemite. This is the loftiest waterfall in the world. It leaps one thousand six hundred feet at one fall, then it has four hundred and thirty-four feet of rapids and a second fall of six hundred feet, making in all a descent of two thousand six hundred and thirty-four feet. Next to the Yosemite is Bridal Veil fall, which is nine hundred and forty feet in hight. It is unbroken and much narrower than the Yosemite. Before reaching the end of its long descent it is completely transformed to spray. Its name is peculiarly fitting. It indeed looks like a veil of white lace, and, softened as it is by a delicate mist, notwithstanding its great hight, it strikes the beholder not so much with a feeling of awe, as with admiration of its own beauty. Nevada Fall is six hundred feet in hight. Its waters are always white as a snow drift. Its volume is much greater, still it is not lacking in the misty softness, which forms the principal beauty of Bridal Veil. South Fork Fall, six hundred feet high, is very difficult of access, and is seldom visited by travelers. Vernal Fall is on the middle or main fork of Vernal river. In spring each fall has twenty times as much water as in summer, and they are much more impressive and beautiful than later in the season. The view from the top of Vernal Fall is particularly impressive. In the distance, across the gorge, snow-streaked mountains loom up before the eye, while beneath is the valley, shut in by measureless inclosing walls, and fringed with groves of pines and spreading oaks.

The rock mountains are the principal feature of the Yosemite. Their dimensions are so vast as almost to exceed comprehension. South Dome is really a semi-dome. It is four thousand nine hundred and sixty-seven feet in hight. When we speak of a rock thirty feet in hight, it conveys some definite impression, but to tell of one four thousand feet high, only bewilders the mind. North Dome is three thousand seven hundred and twenty-nine feet in hight. Both these rocks are covered with vegetation. Hardy cedars, apparently growing out of the solid rock, have braved for a thousand years the war of elements. One large rock is named in honor of Thomas Starr King. The grandest of all the rocks is Tutoconuula. This rock is three thousand and twenty-nine feet in hight, with a smooth, seamless wall, entirely destitute of vegetation. Its surface is so smooth that it is impossible for a vine to fasten its tendrils upon its polished, weather-beaten wall. Mirror Lake is on the north fork of Merced river. The water is very transparent, reflecting the objects above so perfectly as almost to resemble an inverted dome of blue sky, dotted with mountains, rocks and trees. The United States authorities have taken measures to preserve the Yosemite valley and the Mariposa groves, as pleasure grounds for the people of the United States. They are set apart from the general public domain as a national park, and are under the care of a commissioner appointed by the governor of California, for their preservation and protection.

SACRAMENTO CITY

Is the capital of the state. It is situated on the left bank of Sacramento river, one hundred and twenty miles north-east of San Francisco. The river is navigable for steamers for some distance above the place, at all seasons of the year, giving it great commercial advantages. It was founded in 1849, and in 1865 the population was about eighteen thousand. (See views of Sacramento.)

SAN FRANCISCO,

The principal city, is situated on San Francisco bay, six miles south of the Golden Gate. It is regularly laid out, and contains many handsome buildings. There are within the city forty-six churches, twenty banks, a custom-house, a branch mint, a marine hospital, a number of public schools, a state normal school, and seventy-five private schools, besides a number of benevolent institutions. It is actively engaged in commerce, for which it has great natural advantages. The population is rapidly increasing; in 1865 it was about ninety thousand. (See views of San Francisco, harbor and bay.)

OREGON.

Oregon was first visited by the whites in 1775. From this time until 1804 the coast was occasionally visited by fur traders. In the year 1792, Captain Robert Gray, of the ship Columbia, of Boston, discovered and entered the Columbia river. In 1808 the Missouri fur company established a trading post on Lewis river, a branch of the Columbia, which was the first white settlement in the state. Emigration from the United States did not begin to any great extent until 1839. It was organized as a territory in 1848, and admitted into the union in 1859.

The state is divided into three natural sections; the lower or that portion next the ocean, the middle, or that part which lies between the Cascade range and the Blue mountains, and the upper, or that portion which lies between the Blue and Rocky mountains.

Oregon has a milder climate than that of the same latitude on the Atlantic coast. The climate of the coast region is mild throughout the year, neither experiencing the extreme cold of winter or the heat of summer. In the middle region the summers are drier and the winters colder than in the lower region, but free from sudden changes from heat to cold. The upper country is variable and colder than either of the others. The soil in the upper region is sterile and unfitted for agricultural operations. The central portion affords in many places excellent pasturage, though it is not in many places susceptible of cultivation, but that of the coast region is unsurpassed in fertility. Indian corn, wheat, barley, oats and turnips are the principal productions.

The principal river is the Columbia, which is the largest river on the Pacific slope of the continent. Its length, including that of its longest affluent, is about one thousand two hundred miles. It is navigable as far as the Cascades. Above this point the navigation is obstructed. The scenery along the river is remarkably beautiful. At the point where it breaks through the Cascade range, the channel narrows to one hundred and fifty yards. The river rushes through the narrow opening with great violence, and descends forty feet in two miles. At the dalles the channel again narrows for half a mile to one hundred yards, and descends fifty feet in two miles.

SALEM,

The capital of the state, is situated on the east bank of the Willamette river, fifty miles above Oregon City. The river is navigable to this point during high water for about nine months of the year. The city is growing rapidly. In 1865 the population was about two thousand five hundred. The other important towns are Portland, Oregon City, Salem, Albany, Corvallis, and Eugene City.

KANSAS.

This state was purchased from France in 1803, under what is called the Louisiana purchase. It was organized as a separate territory in 1854, and admitted into the union in 1861.

The surface of the state is gently undulating with no mountains or other high elevations. The climate is mild; the winters are very short. The days in summer are quite warm, but are always succeeded by cool and pleasant evenings. The soil is very fertile, equal to if not surpassing that of any other state in the union. The principal productions are corn, wheat, rye, oats, tobacco, buckwheat, potatoes, cotton and hemp. The principal rivers are the Missouri, which forms the north-eastern boundary of the state for some distance, the Kansas and Arkansas. The Kansas is formed by the union of the Republican and Smoky Hill Forks. The length of the main branch is about one hundred and twenty miles. The navigation is obstructed by sand-bars. The Arkansas flows through the south-eastern part of the state for some distance. The navigation is obstructed by rapids. The principal tributaries from the state, are the Walnut, Neosho, Verdigris, and Little Arkansas.

TOPEKA,

The capital, is pleasantly situated on the southern bank of the Kansas river, about fifty miles south-west of Leavenworth. It is regularly laid out, with wide streets, and is being rapidly and neatly built up. The population is about seven hundred and fifty.

The other important places are Leavenworth, Atchison and Lawrence.

LEAVENWORTH,

The largest city, is beautifully situated on the right bank of the Missouri, in the midst of a fine agricultural region. Steamboats navigate the river from this place to St. Louis. The city contains sixteen churches, seven banks, four academies, seven public schools, and one medical college. The population is rapidly increasing. In 1855, it numbered about one thousand, and in 1865, it was nearly eighteen thousand.

ATCHISON

Is situated on the right bank of the Missouri river, about twenty-five miles above Leavenworth. In 1865, the population was about three thousand five hundred.

LAWRENCE

Is situated on the right bank of the Kansas river. The city was founded in 1854. In 1863, the town was burned by the rebels under Quantrell, and about one hundred and fifty of the inhabitants killed. It has since been rapidly rebuilt. The population is now about one thousand six hundred.

NEBRASKA.

Nebraska originally formed a part of the Louisiana purchase. It became a separate territory in 1854. In 1861 its limits were greatly reduced by the formation of the territory of Dakota. It was admitted into the union in 1867.

The surface of the state, from the Missouri westward, is a rolling prairie, but little diversified in its aspect, except by the intersection of its streams. The soil for about one hundred miles west of the Missouri river resembles that of Iowa and Missouri. In the western part of the state is an extensive tract known as "bad lands." This consists of a rolling prairie, so largely intermixed with sand as to be almost unfit for ordinary agricultural purposes. The prairies, however, are covered with rich grass, which affords excellent pasturage. The principal productions of the state are corn, wheat, oats, hay, butter, and potatoes.

The climate is milder than that of the eastern states in the same latitude. The summers are very warm, but are generally relieved by cool winds from the prairies.

The principal rivers are the Missouri, Niobrara, and Nebraska. The Missouri forms its entire eastern boundary. The Niobrara crosses the north-western part of the state and empties into the

Missouri. The Nebraska is formed by the union of the North and South fork. Its length, including North fork is about one thousand two hundred miles.

OMAHA,

The capital, is pleasantly situated on the west bank of the Missouri, opposite Council Bluffs. The city contains a court house, ten churches, a female seminary and a number of other schools. The name of Omaha was derived from a tribe of Indians. It is a thriving town, and growing rapidly. In 1860 the population was about one thousand eight hundred, and in 1865 about four thousand five hundred. (See views of Omaha.) The other important places are Nebraska City and Brownsville.

The population of Nebraska City is about one thousand nine hundred. That of Brownsville, in 1860, was four hundred and twenty-five.

NEVADA.

Nevada was formerly comprised in the territory of Utah. It was organized as a territory in 1861, and admitted into the union in 1864.

The surface of Nevada consists of a succession of mountain ranges, with intervening valleys, and sandy plains. The soil is generally sterile, and a large portion of it is not capable of supporting a population. The climate is dry, and in many respects resembles that of Utah. It is rich is mineral resources. In Story county there are some silver mines said to be the richest in the world. Gold, silver, copper, lead, and iron, are also abundant.

It has no large streams. The only ones deserving of notice, are Humboldt, Walker, and Carson rivers. The lakes are small, and many of them have no outlet. Pyramid lake in the western part of the state, is inclosed by precipitous rocks which rise to a great hight. It derives its name from a rock shaped like a pyramid, about six hundred feet in hight.

CARSON CITY,

The capital, is situated at the eastern base of the Sierra Nevada, about four miles west of Carson river. In 1864, the silver mines at this place yielded upwards of one million dollars. In 1865, the population was about two thousand five hundred.

The other important places are Nevada City and Gold Hill. The population of Nevada City is about three thousand six hundred. That of Gold Hill in 1860, was six hundred and thirty-eight.

CHAPTER V.

TERRITORIES.

The territories of the United States are ten in number, viz: Washington, Idaho, Montana, Dakota, Wyoming, Utah, Colorado, Arizona, New Mexico, and Indian territory; the greater number of which are traversed by the Rocky mountain system, commencing in New Mexico, extending in a north-west direction across the North American continent, and terminating near the mouth of the Mackenzie river. The name Rocky mountains is, however, applied to only that part of the system within the United States. To this system belong the Sierra Madre, Wasutch, Bitter Root, Black Hills, and others. The great breadth of the base, and the gentle acclivity render the Rocky mountains more easily traversed than any others of the same altitude. The Union Pacific railroad crosses them at Bear mountain summit, eight thousand seven hundred and ninety feet above the level of the sea.

WASHINGTON

Is bounded on the north by British America, on the east by Idaho, on the south by Oregon, and on the west by the Pacific ocean. This territory was separated from Oregon by an act of Congress in 1853. A large portion of the surface is mountainous, and abounds in romantic scenery. Washington has a great coal trade, and gold has been found on the Columbia river, and on the east side of the Cascade mountains. The eastern and central portions are peopled by various Indian tribes. The white inhabitants live west of the Cascade range. Olympia, the capital, is on Shute's river, at its entrance into Puget sound. Steilacoom is one of the most important places.

IDAHO

Was organized in 1863. It is bounded on the north by British America and Montana, on the east by Montana and Wyoming, on the south by Utah and Nevada, and on the west by Oregon and Washington.

The surface is rugged and mountainous; the scenery picturesque and grand. In this territory is Fremont's peak, the highest of the Rocky mountains in the United States, having an altitude of thirteen thousand five hundred and ten feet.

Gold and silver, the chief minerals, are found in large quantities, and mining is actively engaged in.

Boise City, on the Boise or Big Wood river, is the capital.

MONTANA

Formed a part of Idaho until 1864, when it was organized as a territory. It is bounded on the north by British America, on the east by Dakota, on the south by Wyoming and Idaho, and on the west by Idaho.

The surface is rugged, mountainous, and in some places shows signs of volcanic action. Silver and iron exist in large quantities, and gold has been found to some extent.

The Missouri river has its source in Montana. In the northeastern part of this territory is Fort Union, on the proposed northern railroad route to the Pacific. Montana was organized as a territory in 1863.

The principal towns are Virginia City, the capital, Bannock City, Laburge City, Gallatin City, and Nevada.

DAKOTA,

The largest territory, was organized in 1861. It is bounded on the north by British America, on the east by Minnesota and Iowa, on the south by Nebraska, and on the west by Montana and Wyoming.

This territory presents every variety of surface, elevated table lands, rugged hills, plains, and sand hills. The Missouri river traverses nearly the entire length of this territory. On it are built several United States forts, among which are Forts Berthold, Clark, Sully, and others.

Yanktown is the capital, and Pembina the oldest city. (See views in Dakota.)

WYOMING,

The latest organized territory, is bounded on the north by Montana, on the east by Dakota and Nebraska, on the south by Colorado and Utah, and on the west by Utah, Idaho and Montana.

Through the central part of this territory passes a ridge of the Rocky mountains. In the south-eastern part occur the Black hills, the principal of which are Laramie peak and Mount Pisgah. South-west of this range of hills, and between them and the Rocky mountains, are the Laramie plains, on which are found huge red sandstone rocks. This territory formerly belonged to Dakota, from which it has recently been separated.

UTAH

Is bounded on the north by Idaho and Wyoming, on the east by Wyoming and Colorado, on the south by Arizona, and on the west by Nevada.

It was originally a part of California territory, ceded to the United States by Mexico in 1848. It became a separate territory in 1850. The general surface is mountainous, and the most barren and sterile region in the United States. Some of the villages are six thousand feet above the level of the sea. The climate in summer is hot and in winter mild, but subject to sudden changes. Great Salt Lake, in this territory, is the most remarkable body of water in the United States. This lake is in the northern part of the territory, about four thousand two hundred feet above the level of the sea, and so bitterly salt that no live animal can exist in it. It has no visible outlet, but four rivers empty into it, one of which is the river Jordan, connecting it with Utah Lake. The water of Salt Lake is so buoyant that one finds difficulty in wading in it, floats with ease, and would be in no danger of drowning, except by strangling. Three gallons of water produce one gallon of pure salt; and, during hot weather, the shores of the lake are covered with a thick incrustation of salt, caused by solar evaporation. The lake is one hundred and twenty miles long and forty miles broad. Utah Lake is about thirty miles from Great Salt Lake. It is a clear, fresh body of water, twenty miles wide and thirty-five miles long.

SALT LAKE CITY,

The capital of Utah, is about twenty miles from Great Salt Lake, and is situated near the Jordan river. The city was laid out by the Mormons in 1847, contains about twenty thousand inhabitants, and publishes three daily and one weekly papers. Camp Douglas, a garrisoned post of the United States army, restrains the despotic power of the Mormon church, affords shelter to all those who abandon that faith, and sends them to the states under military escort. Brigham Young, the president of the Mormon church, is popular among the "saints," and rules them with ease. His dwellings, the Lion House and the Bee-hive House, are in the heart of the city, surrounded by a wall eleven feet high, built of bowlders laid in mortar. In the city are four public squares, in one of which a magnificent temple is being erected. (See views of Salt Lake City.)

COLORADO,

Organized in 1861, is bounded on the north by Wyoming and Nebraska, on the east by Nebraska and Kansas, on the south by Indian Territory and New Mexico, and on the west by Utah.

The general surface is mountainous. Within this territory are some of the highest peaks of the Rocky mountains, the most noted of which are Long's Peak and Pike's Peak. The latter has an altitude of eleven thousand four hundred and ninety-seven feet. It was at this peak that gold was first discovered in Colorado.

The principal rivers are Arkansas, south fork of the Platte, Yampa, Bear, Bunkara and Gunnison. Big Thompson creek is in the northern part of the territory.

DENVER,

The capital, the most populous and principal commercial city of Colorado, is pleasantly located at the foot of the mountains, on the south fork of the Platte. Among the public buildings are the Colorado seminary, costing twenty thousand dollars; five churches, one of which cost twenty-four thousand dollars; a Catholic academy, and a United States branch mint, costing seventy-five thousand dollars.

ARIZONA

Is bounded on the north by Utah, on the east by New Mexico, on the south by Mexico, and on the west by California and Nevada.

It formerly belonged to New Mexico, and was made a separate territory in 1863. Its general surface is mountainous, and great portions are supposed to be of volcanic origin. This territory abounds in extensive treeless plains, or prairies.

Arizona is rich in gold and silver mines, which are found in almost every part of the territory. The capital is Prescott. The chief towns are Tucson and Tubac.

NEW MEXICO

Is bounded on the north by Colorado, on the east by Indian Territory and Texas, on the south by Texas and Mexico, and on the west by Arizona.

This territory is, for the most part, an elevated table-land, traversed by several mountain ranges. The greater portion of the inhabitants are Indians. It is probable that this territory abounds in precious metals, but the mines have not yet been worked very extensively, and the future may reveal vast treasures of gold, silver and other metals.

SANTA FE,

The capital, has a population of four thousand six hundred and thirty-eight. The other principal settlements are Albuquerque and Socorre.

INDIAN TERRITORY.

This territory is bounded on the north by Colorado and Kansas, on the east by Missouri and Arkansas, on the south by Texas, and on the west by Texas and New Mexico.

This territory was set apart by the United States as a permanent home for the Indians. The soil is fertile, productive, and well adapted to grazing. Some of the tribes which people this territory are advanced in civilization. Others are indolent, degraded, and are rapidly diminishing under the influence of intemperance.

Tahlequah, a Cherokee town, is the principal place of this territory.

The Union Pacific railroad is now completed, forming an easy mode of communication between the states and territories, and there is a prospect that they will now be more rapidly settled. The railroad passes through Nebraska, Wyoming, Utah, Nevada, touches Colorado, and terminates at Sacramento, California.

RUSSIAN AMERICA

Was purchased by the United States in 1867. Its area is nearly ten times as great as that of Pennsylvania. It is bounded on the north by the Arctic ocean, on the east by British America, on the south by the Pacific ocean, and on the west by Behring's sea, Behring's strait, and Arctic ocean.

The inhabitants are chiefly Esquimaux, living in huts partly under ground. They are a filthy and degraded race. There are, beside these, about six thousand Russians engaged in trapping and fishing.

South of the peninsula of Alaska the coast is mountainous, abounding in precipitous cliffs, descending abruptly to the sea.

North of this peninsula it is low and marshy. Along the coast are groups of volcanic islands, between which and the main land is a remarkable interior channel, safe for navigation at all times.

The climate is not as cold as it is in the same latitude on the eastern coasts of the American and Asiatic continents. Sitka, or New Archangel, the principal settlement, is on Baranoff island.

CHAPTER VI.

GEOGRAPHICAL HISTORY OF BRITISH AMERICA.

British America comprises Canada East, Canada West, New Brunswick, Nova Scotia, Cape Breton, Prince Edward's Island, Newfoundland, North-west Territory, and Hudson's Bay Territory.

The surface is generally level. The Alleghany mountain system extends into Canada, and terminates in low hills on the Gulf of St. Lawrence. A chain of hills called the Wotchish mountains, separates the basin of the St. Lawrence from that of Hudson's Bay. With these exceptions, it has few elevations of any considerable hight.

The climate is subject to great extremes. The summers are very warm, and the winters long and cold. The heat of summer, and the cold of winter is much greater than in the same latitude in Europe. In that portion bordering on the great lakes, the winters are not so cold and the heat of summer is less intense.

The Province of Canada is heavily timbered. In the south-eastern portion of this province, the soil is very fertile, and produces large crops of wheat and other grains; but near the mouth of the St. Lawrence, the climate is too severe and the soil too poor to admit cultivation.

The principal rivers are the St. Lawrence and Ottawa. The St. Lawrence, one of the largest rivers of North America, forms the outlet to the great lakes. It is about seven hundred and fifty miles in length, and navigable as far as Montreal for vessels of six hundred tons. Above this point, the navigation is obstructed by rapids. The Ottawa, with a volume of water almost equal to the St. Lawrence, enters this river about forty miles west of Montreal. It is about eight hundred miles in length. Its navigation is obstructed by rapids and cataracts. It abounds in beautiful scenery, and its banks are covered with valuable timber.

Canada shares with New York in the grand and beautiful scenery of Niagara Falls. The basin of the St. Lawrence is famous for the grandeur of its natural scenery. Besides Niagara, it contains the Falls of Montmorenci, seven miles from Quebec, with a perpendicular descent of two hundred and forty feet; the Falls of Chaudiere, ten miles from Quebec, rushing and foaming over a wild chasm one hundred and twenty-five feet in perpendicular descent; the Carrillon Falls of the Ottawa, a series of rapids twelve miles in length, and the romantic scenery of the Saguenay river. The banks of this river, varying in hight from five hundred to one thousand five hundred feet, are in many places perpendicular, while in other places they absolutely overhang the river. The water is very deep. Near its mouth a line of three thousand feet failed to reach the bottom. In other places, its depths varies from one hundred to one thousand feet.

The principal towns of British America are Montreal, Quebec, Toronto, Halifax, St. Johns, Hamilton, Ottawa, and Kingston.

MONTREAL

Was formerly the capital of Canada East. It is situated on the island of Montreal, in the St. Lawrence river, at the mouth of the Ottawa. The city occupies a tract of land about two miles wide, between the river and a beautiful elevation called Royal Mount. It possesses a fine harbor and is extensively engaged in commerce. It contains a number of elegant churches, the finest of which is the Roman Catholic Cathedral, one of the handsomest gothic buildings in North America, and capable of seating from ten to twelve thousand persons, a town hall, a French college, a university, a Roman Catholic theological school, and several classical and scientific academies. The city was founded in 1640. In 1861, the population was about ninety thousand. (See views of Montreal.)

QUEBEC

Is situated on the left bank of the St. Lawrence river one hundred and eighty miles above Montreal. The city is beautifully situated at the extremity of a narrow table land which forms the bank of the St. Lawrence for about eight miles. The city is actively engaged in commerce. Manufactures are not carried on to any great extent. It contains a large number of elegant public and private buildings. The population in 1861 was about fifty-one thousand. (See views of Quebec.)

TORONTO,

Formerly the capital of Canada West, is situated on a beautiful bay on the north-western shore of Lake Ontario, about three hundred and ninety miles south-west of Montreal. It is one of the most flourishing cities of British America. The harbor, formed by the bay, on which the town is situated, is beautiful and commodious. The city contains many elegant public buildings. The Government and Parliament houses are very plain and unpretending, and have long been in use, but they are soon to be superseded by new buildings. The city was founded in 1794. The population in 1861 was about forty-four thousand eight hundred.

HALIFAX,

The capital of Nova Scotia, is situated on a deep inlet of the sea on the southern shore of that peninsula. It is actively engaged in commerce with various parts of North America, West Indies and Europe. The population is about thirty thousand.

ST. JOHNS,

The capital of Newfoundland, and the most eastern seaport of North America, is situated on a peninsula which projects from the eastern coast of the island of Newfoundland. The shortest distance between any two seaports of Europe and America is from this point to Galway, Ireland, being one thousand six hundred and sixty-five miles. The town is situated on an elevation, and consists principally of one street about a mile in length. The population is about twenty-five thousand.

HAMILTON

Is situated at the head of Burlington bay, at the western extremity of Lake Ontario. In the rear of the city is a mountain rising to a considerable hight, and affording a delightful view of the city and surrounding country. The city was laid out in 1813. The population in 1861 was about nineteen thousand.

OTTAWA,

One of the most flourishing towns of Canada West, is situated on the right bank of the Ottawa river. It has recently been selected as the capital of Canada. The necessary public buildings were completed in 1867, and the seat of government removed to this place. The population in 1861 was about fourteen thousand six hundred.

KINGSTON

Is situated on the St. Lawrence river, at the foot of Lake Ontario, about two hundred miles south-west of Montreal. It is a flourishing city and growing rapidly. The population in 1861 was about thirteen thousand seven hundred.

CHAPTER VII.

GEOGRAPHICAL HISTORY OF MEXICO.

Mexico, of the grand divisions of North America the fourth in size, and second in population, lies between latitude 15° 58′ and 33° 5′ N., and longitude 86° 43′ and 117° 5′ W. This territory is bounded on the north-east and north by the United States—Texas, New Mexico, Arizona and California,—and on the east-south-east by Guatemala, a province of Central America. On the east the outline forms a semi-circle, which is washed by the Gulf of Mexico; and on the west, south and south-west is the Pacific Ocean. The general outline of the country is very irregular. The greatest length from north-west to south-east is one thousand nine hundred miles; greatest width on a parallel of latitude is nine hundred and sixty miles; area, six hundred and sixty-eight thousand square miles. The most important indentation in the coast line is the Gulf of California, about six hundred miles long and one hundred miles wide, and lying between the peninsula of California, and Sonora and Sinaloa.

The interior of Mexico consists of a vast table-land, rising from five thousand to nine thousand feet above the sea. The chief divisions of this great Mexican plateau are the Chihuahua and Anahuac table-lands, the former from four thousand to six thousand, and the latter from five thousand to nine thousand feet in hight. The table-land of Chihuahua is north of the twenty-fourth parallel, and is a bleak, barren and desolate region. Directly the reverse is the Anahuac plateau, a healthy, rich and fertile tract, where flourishes vegetation peculiar to the temperate zone. The Sierra Madre mountain chain, a continuation of the Rocky mountains, crosses the plateau from north to south. The loftiest summits of the mountains of Mexico occur in a chain which extends across the southern portion of the table-lands from east to west. Here are the Smoking Mountain, or volcano of Popocatapetl, seventeen thousand seven hundred and seventeen feet high; Iztaccihuatl, the White Lady, fifteen thousand seven hundred and five feet high; the peak of Orizaba, seventeen thousand three hundred and eighty feet high; Coffre de Perote, thirteen thousand four hundred feet high, and the volcano of Tuxtla, five thousand one hundred and eighteen feet high. About one hundred and seventy-five miles west of the White Lady, is the far-famed volcano of Jurullo, which rose, in September, 1789, from a level plain to the hight of four thousand two hundred and sixty-five feet.

The descents among the valleys of the Mexican plateau are so gradual, that carriages can travel over it without much difficulty. On the contrary, the approach from the sea is steep and precipitous, especially on the eastern side, where the summit can be reached only by two roads. Between the base of the table-land and the Gulf of Mexico, is a considerable interval of low and sandy land.

The rivers of Mexico are generally small, and are frequently obstructed by rapids. The largest of these is the Rio Grande del Norte, marking a portion of the boundary between Mexico and the United States. It has a course of one thousand eight hundred miles, and is navigable for small vessels to Matamoras, forty miles from the Gulf of Mexico, which it enters. The Rio de Tampico, formed by the confluence of the Tula and Panuco, enters the Gulf of Mexico after a course of four hundred miles. The other rivers worthy of note are Rio Grande de Santiago and Tecapan, entering the Pacific, the Sinaloa, entering the Gulf of California, and the Conchas, Sabinas and Salinas, affluents of the Rio Grande. The Rio Grande de Santiago, originating in Guanajuato, drains Lake Chapala, and, after a course of seven hundred miles, enters the Pacific near San Blas. Near Guadalaxara the river has sixty falls in the space of three miles.

Mexico, like all other countries within the tropics, containing high and low lands, exhibits a great variety of climate. The rainy season generally continues from May till October, and the dry from October till May. From the Gulf of Mexico to the summit of the table land will be found three climatic districts, viz.: the hot, swampy, and pestilential lowlands, the temperate regions, found between the hights of two and five thousand feet, and cold and desolate regions above. Vegetation varies with the climate, the lowlands yielding forests of oak, pine, mahogany, ebony, and palm, and the cooler regions wheat, barley, Indian corn, cotton, tobacco, sugar-cane, fruits and spices.

The wild animals of Mexico are numerous. The jungles of the lowlands are made the retreat of the cougar, or American lion, ocelot, jaguarundi, tiger-cat, and the more formidable jaguar, or American tiger. The American buffalo, known in Mexico as Cibolo, in mid-winter, sweep in immense herds over the lower districts from the plains of the north-west. The most ferocious of the species of grizzly bear inhabits the northern mountain districts. The tapir, wolf, American lynx, stag, deer, sloth, armadillo, and weasel, are also peculiar to Mexico. Various species of the monkey are found, and the cochineal insect is reared with great success. The forests swarm with countless varieties of the feathered family, as the parrot, humming-bird, and various species of wild game birds.

The mineral wealth of Mexico, particularly in gold and silver, is very great. The mines are, however, but imperfectly worked, and are not as productive as in former times. The chief deposits of gold occur north of the twenty-fourth parallel, on the west side of the Sierra Madre. Silver, variously mixed with sulphur, antimony and arsenic, is found in beds from twenty-five to one hundred and fifty feet thick in the state of Guanajuato. The annual product of gold and silver at the beginning of the present century, amounted to about fifteen millions of dollars, of which by far the greater portion was yielded by the silver. Mexico has also mines of iron, copper, lead, zinc, and other useful metals, which, however, have been but little worked.

The chief manufactures of Mexico are sugar, aloes, wine, earthenware, silk, paper, and glass. In the city of Mexico are fifty mills engaged in the manufacture of olive oil, and also manufactories of silk, producing forty thousand pounds annually.

The coast on the Gulf of Mexico is flat and sandy, and is therefore deficient in good harbors. On the contrary the Pacific shore is more bold, and abounds with excellent havens. Notwithstanding the unrivaled advantages which the country has for trade, being washed by the Atlantic on one hand and the Pacific on the other, and being rich in vegetable and mineral productions, the commerce of Mexico is extremely limited. Her commercial standing has been on the retrograde ever since her independence of Spain was recognized. The chief exports are gold, silver, cattle, hides, and cochineal.

The capital, and largest city of Mexico, is a city of the same name. The other most important cities are La Puebla, Guadalaxara, Guanajuato, Queretaro, Merida, Morelia, Zacatecas, Monterey, and Vera Cruz.

MEXICO,

The capital, is in the valley of Tenochititlan, on a table land seven thousand four hundred and thirty feet above the sea, and is environed on all sides by lofty mountain peaks. The city is on a plateau, covering an area of seventeen hundred square miles, and embracing in its extent five beautiful lakes. At the time of the conquest by Cortez, the city occupied three islands in Lake Tezcuco, and was approached by four large causeways, which met in the heart of the city. In the center of the city is a fine square of thirty or forty acres, known as Plaza Mayor, and contains besides the cathedral, the National Palace and town house. The chief streets converge towards this square, and are broad, well-paved, and lighted with gas.

The cathedral is an imposing building, occupying the site of the great *teocalli*, or temple of the Aztec god Mixitli. This structure, occupying an entire side of the Plaza Mayor, is five hundred feet long, four hundred and twenty feet wide, and has in front two towers, supported by immense pillars. The choir is of finely carved wood, and the high altar is adorned with gold and silver candle-sticks and crosses. On another side of the Plaza Mayor, is the palatial residence, formerly of the viceroys, and at the present time, of the president. The other buildings of interest are the university, directly opposite the National Palace, containing the National Museum, the Church of San Domingo, a beautiful structure surmounted with a dome and lofty spire, and the convents of St. Augustine and St. Francisco, elegant structures, adorned with a large number of domes and cupolas. In the Plaza Mayor, is the *kellenda*, a circular stone, on which are carved hieroglyphics, by which the Aztecs used to represent months of the year; and in the court-yard of the university is a colossal equestrian statue of Charles IV. The other objects worthy of notice, are the magnificent aqueducts, which supply the city with water; the Alameda, a fine public park of twelve acres, a great resort for the people on occasions of festivity, and the *Paseos*, two fine promenades, the one in the eastern, and the other in the western section of the city. Mexico has fifteen churches, fifty monasteries and convents, a large number of charitable institutions, a theatre, and a circus, a circular enclosure called the Plaza de Toros, capacious enough to accommodate three thousand five hundred persons, where are celebrated bull-fights and other public amusements.

Mexico is the great focus of the internal trade of the republic. The chief manufactures are carriages, leather, gold-lace, and cigars, which, in connection with gold and silver, are the chief articles of export. Population in 1860, two hundred and five thousand.

LA PUEBLA,

Called from the beauty of its location, the "city of angels," is a finely built city, and capital of the state of the same name, seventy-six miles south-east of Mexico. The streets are well paved. The city is built chiefly of stone, and has three colleges, and manufactories of glass, soap, earthenwares, etc. Population in 1860, seventy-one thousand.

GUADALAXARA,

An important city of Mexico, and capital of the state of Jalisco, is on the southern bank of the Rio Grande de Santiago, two hundred and seventy miles north-west of Mexico.

The most interesting building in the city is the cathedral, an imposing edifice in the Plaza Mayor. This building does not hold its former architectural rank, as both its towers were destroyed, and other injuries sustained, during the earthquake of 1818. The *Alameda*, or public walk, is a fine promenade, beautifully adorned with trees and flowers. The city has manufactories of iron, earthenware, leather and cloth. Population in 1860, sixty-three thousand.

GUANAJUATO,

A city of Mexico, and capital of a state of its own name, is in a narrow mountain defile, one hundred and sixty miles north-west of Mexico. The city is formed by a cluster of villages, and is extensively engaged in mining. It has seven fine churches, numerous chapels and convents, and a large public granary. Population, fifty thousand.

QUERETARO,

Capital of a state of the same name, is a manufacturing town, one hundred and ten miles north-west of Mexico. The city has a monastery, in the center of finely ornamented grounds, a large convent, and manufactories of cloth. It is supplied with water by an aqueduct ten miles long. Population, twenty-nine thousand eight hundred.

MERIDA

Is an important city in the north-western part of Yucatan, of which it is the capital. It is twenty-five miles from Sisal, its port, and has a considerable trade. The finest building is the cathedral, an imposing structure, in the central square. This square also contains the government house and Bishop's palace. The city has a university and thirteen churches. Population, forty thousand.

The inhabitants of Mexico, consisting of whites, Indians, negroes and mixed races, number eight millions two hundred and eighteen thousand.

HISTORY OF MEXICO.

Mexico was discovered by Francisco Hernandez Cordova, in 1517. At the time of the discovery, a large portion of the country was peopled by the Aztecs, a race of Indians farther advanced in civilization than the majority of American Indian tribes. The ruins of temples and cities still attest their skill in architecture. They cultivated the land, introduced Indian corn and cotton, built immense monuments and pyramids, and constructed bridges, aqueducts and roads. In 1518, Grijalva commanded a second expedition to Mexico, and on his return confirmed the glowing accounts of Cordova. The description of mines of gold and silver, and of treasures in cities, awakened the deepest cupidity of the Spaniards, and in 1518, Velasques, then governor of Cuba, dispatched Cortez, a Spanish adventurer, with an armed force, to Mexico, with instructions to conquer the people and possess himself of their wealth. Cortez landed at San Juan d'Ulloa, and marched, without opposition, to the city of Mexico. Two years of incessant and terrible war followed, till finally, by strategem, and the aid of the adjacent hostile tribes, the Spaniards succeeded in subduing the natives, overthrowing their empire, and adding the vast country of Montezuma to the Spanish American possessions. Mexico remained firm in her allegiance to Spain till the period immediately succeeding the French revolution, when the country began to assume a revolutionary aspect. This feeling was greatly intensified by the clergy, who favored the movement, and did much to disseminate the growing spirit of discontent. The first revolt was made in 1810, under the leadership of Hidalgo, a country priest. Hidalgo was defeated, and quiet was for a time restored. In 1820, however, the rebellious spirit broke forth anew, and, after a number of severe battles, the independence of the country was acknowledged, and Mexico was proclaimed a constitutional monarchy, with Don Augustin Iturbide as king, under the title of Augustin I. Ever since this period Mexico has been harassed by jealous and covetous nations from without, and torn by internal dissensions from within. Within the last forty years, there have been no less than seventy revolutions, or different governments, in Mexico. Iturbide was deposed, the constitutional government abolished, and a republican form of government established, in part resembling that of the United States. The first president, General Guadalupe Victoria, was elected in 1825. In 1835, Texas revolted, and became independent of Mexico, and ten years after, in 1845, became one of the United States. In 1845, difficulties arose between Mexico and the United States, concerning the boundary between the two countries, which occasioned a long and bloody war. (See United States.) After the close of the war, Mexico was under the direction first, of Santa Anna, and afterwards of Herrera. In 1852, the latter was deposed, and General Cevallos was, for a time, at the head of affairs. He, also, failed to satisfy the people, and was succeeded by a number of others, till 1859, when Benito Juarez was elected. His claims were contested by General Miramon, who was at the head of the priestly, or conservative party, and the country was plunged into a civil war.

Measures taken at this time by the Mexican authorities, adverse to the interests of several foreign nations, brought into the Mexican gulf a combined fleet of English, French, and Spanish, for the purpose of obtaining redress for the acts offensive to them. An armistice was agreed upon, a treaty negotiated, which was ratified by all the contending powers, except France, who, after the departure of the English and Spanish fleets, declared war against president Juarez. They obtained possession of Puebla, gained other advantages, and finally, in June, 1863, entered the capital. The feelings of the mass of the people, owing to the horrors of the civil war then raging, were in sympathy with the French; consequently the invaders were greeted with joyful demonstrations on their arrival at the city of Mexico. A provisional government was organized under the protection of the French troops, which met on the tenth of July, and voted almost unanimously to establish an imperial government, and to invite Archduke Maximilian, brother of the emperor of Austria, and son-in-law of King Leopold of Belgium, to accept the throne. This movement did not meet with the approval of the United States, and France could not deem it her duty to incur war with that power, in her efforts to rescue Mexico from barbarism. The French troops were withdrawn, and Maximilian was left to his own slender resources to establish the empire. In encountering the opposition of the moral and physical powers of the United States, and with Juarez concentrating his strengthened forces around him, his success became hopeless. He repulsed the latter in several hard fought battles, but was finally, by treachery and overwhelming numbers, defeated, taken prisoner, and, with his two chief generals, Miramon, (the former rival of Juarez) and Mejia, executed.

CHAPTER VIII.

GEOGRAPHICAL HISTORY OF CENTRAL AMERICA

Central America is the name applied to a narrow and irregular country between seven and eighteen degrees north latitude. It is bounded on the north-west, north, and north-east by Chiapas, Tabasco and Yucatan, provinces of Mexico, Bay of Honduras and Caribbean sea, and on the south-west by the Pacific ocean. At the Isthmus of Panama, its narrowest portion, it is only twenty miles from the Caribbean sea, on the east, to the Pacific ocean, on the west. Greatest length of the country eight hundred and seventy-five miles; greatest width, four hundred miles; area, two hundred thousand square miles.

In surface, Central America bears a general resemblance to Mexico. The table-lands decrease in hight as you advance south, where the surface is varied by a range of low hills, and at the Isthmus of Panama by a series of limestone elevations. Bordering on the south-western edge of the table-land is a line of volcanoes, which form in part the great volcanic chain on the Pacific coast of America. The culminating point of Central America is Volcan de Agua, having an altitude of fifteen thousand feet.

The chief river on the Pacific coast is the Lempa, rising in the north-western part of the country, forming the boundary between San Salvador and Honduras, and finally crossing the former state and entering an arm of the Pacific. On the Atlantic coast is the San Juan, draining Lake Nicaragua, Bluefield, Cape, and Patook rivers. The San Juan river has a course of one hundred miles, and forms a part of the overland route of one of the lines of California steamers. The chief lake, Nicaragua, found at an elevation of one hundred and twenty-five feet above the sea, is ninety miles long and thirty miles wide, is interspersed by a large number of islands, and, in some places, is two hundred and fifty feet deep. Lake Atitlan, in the north of

Central America, is twenty-five miles long by ten miles wide, is environed by lofty mountains, and is above eighteen hundred feet deep. The other important lakes are Managua, the waters of which flow into Lake Nicaragua, and Petens, in the northern part of Guatemala.

In climate and productions, Central America greatly resembles Mexico. The dry season lasts from October to May, and the rainy season from May to October. The thermometer rises as high as eighty-six degrees in March, but generally averages about seventy-eight degrees at mid-day. The low lands yield Indian corn, potatoes, sugar-cane, tobacco, and cocoa, while the more elevated regions are rich in the products of the temperate zone.

Central America comprises the five states of Guatemala, Honduras, San Salvador, Nicaragua, and Costa Rica. New Guatemala, the capital of the state of Guatemala, is the largest city. Other important towns are Comayagua, San Salvador, Leon, and San Jose.

NEW GUATEMALA

Is one hundred and six miles north-west of San Salvador, on a large and fertile plain, five thousand feet above the level of the sea. The great square contains the chief shops of the city, the cathedral, an archbishop's palace, a vice-regal palace, and government offices. The city is extensively engaged in manufactures, has sixty churches, five newspaper publications, a university, several other schools, a bull-ring, and a theatre. In the center of the city is a fine public fountain. Population sixty thousand.

LEON,

An important town of Central America, and capital of the state of Nicaragua, is built on the site of an old Indian town, on a rich and spacious plain between Lake Managua and the Pacific ocean. It contains the cathedral, an Episcopal palace, a number of churches, a college, and extensive manufactories of leather and cutlery. Population thirty-five thousand.

SAN JOSE,

A town of Central America, capital of Costa Rica, is fifteen miles west of Matina, and about equi-distant from the Caribbean sea and Pacific ocean. "It has grown up since the independence of this region was established, and has no buildings of note, but it has succeeded to the importance and commercial activity of Cartago, the former capital of the state." Population thirty thousand.

The population of Central America is estimated at about two millions one hundred and sixty-two thousand, and consists of whites and creoles, mestizoes, or the descendants of whites and Indians, and natives.

Central America was first discovered by Columbus in 1502, and in 1523 was visited by Pedro Alvarado, who was sent by Cortez to conquer the country. The country remained subject to Spain till 1823, when it threw off the yoke and became a federal republic.

CHAPTER IX.

GEOGRAPHICAL HISTORY OF THE WEST INDIES.

The West Indies form three divisions: the Greater Antilles, the Lesser Antilles, and the Bahamas. The Greater Antilles consist of Cuba, Hayti, Jamaica, and Porto Rico. The Lesser Antilles consist of a chain of islands which extend from Porto Rico to South America. The Bahamas are low islands of coral formation.

Most of these islands are in possession of European nations. Cuba and Porto Rico belong to Spain; Jamaica, the Bahamas, and most of the Lesser Antilles to Great Britain, and the remaining islands, with the exception of Hayti, which is independent, are owned by France, Denmark, Holland, Sweden, and Venezuela.

CUBA,

The largest and richest of the islands, is the most important colonial possession of Spain. The island was discovered by Columbus during his first voyage in 1492. He gave it the name of Juana, which was afterwards changed to Fernandina, and again to Santiago, but it is now called by its Indian name, Cuba. As early as 1511 a permanent settlement was made by the Spaniards, who, since that time, have retained possession of the island.

The city of Havana was taken possession of by the British in 1762, but was restored the following year. In 1851, Lopez, at the head of a band of United States adventurers, invaded Cuba. His men were all either slain or taken prisoners. Lopez, with six of his companions, was garroted, and fifty of the prisoners shot. The island is now undergoing a revolutionary movement. The Cubans are endeavoring to throw off the dominion of Spain and become an independent republic. The greater part of the island is now held by the Cubans, who will probably, ere long, succeed in establishing their independence.

The surface of the island is generally level. The only elevations of any importance are the Copper mountains, which extend from one extremity of the island to the other, reaching their culminating point at the eastern end at an altitude of about seven thousand feet. Reefs of rocky formation, and marshy tracts of country are found among the low lands of the coast. These reefs penetrate into the sea between two and three miles, rendering navigation difficult and dangerous. The coast is generally but little above the water level, and is subject to floods and inundations. There are some localities, however, where the sea is deep to the water's edge, and in these places are found some of the finest natural harbors in existence. The rivers are not large, and are navigable only for small boats.

The climate is tropical. Snow never falls, even on the highest mountains. Vegetation is very luxuriant. The principal productions are sugar, coffee, tobacco, cotton, cocoa, and indigo.

Havana was formerly the capital of the island, but since the breaking out of the revolution the Cuban congress has met at Guaimaro. This town is situated on a plain, and surrounded by a net work of seven small crooked rivers. The surrounding district is much of it covered with a dense wood, relieved only by the course of the various rivers. The wisdom of the Cubans in selecting Guaimaro as a capital, and fortifying it, is apparent. It would be a difficult battle field for the Spaniards. They would have fearful odds to encounter in plunging into a plain upon which grow dense woods, and through which half a dozen rivers wind and turn, so that none but a resident of the locality would know upon which side he was standing.

HAVANA,

The former capital, and the principal city of the island, is situated at the head of a beautiful bay on the north-western shore of the island. The harbor is entered by a channel one half mile long, and so narrow that only one ship can enter it at the same time. It is deep enough to receive vessels of the largest size. At the mouth of the channel are two strong castles, Punta on the west and Moro on the east. A light is fixed upon the latter, one hundred and forty-four feet high, which can be seen at a great distance.

Viewed from a distance, the city presents a picturesque and imposing appearance, but on a closer inspection it is found to possess but few attractions. The streets are narrow, ill-paved, and dirty, and are lined with massive stone buildings, with barred windows, which give the whole town a dreary and gloomy aspect. The city, however, is not entirely destitute of beauty, for, besides a number of handsome public buildings, it contains several parks and public squares, and a great many fountains. The Plaza de Armas is a beautiful enclosure, containing paved walks, fountains, and flowers, and is the site of the palaces of the governor, and the residences of the nobility.

Havana is a bishop's See, and has a handsome display of religious establishments. The bishop's garden is one of the most delightful retreats of the city. Shady walks, lined with flowers and plants and ornamental trees, among which the cocoanut and palm are conspicuous, are found in large numbers throughout the grounds.

The city contains a number of large churches, richly oramented with gold and silver lamps and images. A large cathedral contains the ashes of Columbus, which were brought from San Domingo in 1796. The population of the city, including its suburbs, is about one hundred and forty thousand. (See views of Havana.)

HAYTI,

The second in size of the West Indies, is a rich and beautiful island. The coast is irregular, being indented by numerous gulfs and bays, and presenting corresponding projections. The island was discovered by Columbus, during his first voyage. In 1773 the western part of the island was ceded to France. In

1821 a revolution broke out, and the inhabitants succeeded in establishing for themselves first an empire, then an independent republic.

The island is crossed by three mountain chains, between which are extensive plains and savannas. The vegetation, like all tropical countries, is very luxuriant. Majestic trees and the richest flowering plants clothe the mountains and adorn the valleys, forming some of the richest natural scenery on the globe. The usual tropical fruits and vegetables, such as oranges, pine apples, melons, grapes, plantains, bananas, yams, etc., are abundant.

There are several lakes in the south-western part of the island. The principal rivers rise in the central mountain chain. Their navigation is obstructed by sand-bars.

The population of the island is estimated at about nine hundred and forty-three thousand.

JAMAICA

Is a beautiful and fertile island. It has a coast line of about five hundred miles, and is indented by a number of excellent harbors. The general appearance of the island is very beautiful. It is traversed in all directions by lofty mountains, covered with stately forests and intersected by vales, exhibiting the most romantic scenery. The principal rivers are the Minho, Black, and Cobre.

The commerce of the island is not in a very flourishing condition. The productions and exports have fallen off considerably during the last two or three years.

The population of the island is estimated at about three hundred and seventy-eight thousand.

PORTO RICO,

The fourth in size of the West Indies, is about ninety miles in length, and thirty-six in width. The coast is indented by numerous bays and gulfs, deep enough for vessels of considerable burden, but, owing to the tremendous ground seas, only three of them are safe for vessels the year round. The climate is mild. The inhabitants are principally engaged in agricultural pursuits. The principal productions are sugar, molasses, coffee, cotton and tobacco.

The population numbers about five hundred thousand.

CHAPTER X.

GEOGRAPHICAL HISTORY OF SOUTH AMERICA.

South America is a great peninsula, stretching from the Isthmus of Panama, in latitude 12° 30′ N., to latitude 55° 59′ S., and terminating in the bold and rocky promontory of Cape Horn. From the latter point, passing north over the rocky wastes of Patagonia, the grassy plains and extensive forests of the La Plata and Amazon, and crossing the lofty mountains of the Parina system, Point Gallinas, the northern extremity of this division, is reached after a journey of over four thousand eight hundred miles. Its greatest breadth from east to west, is three thousand two hundred and thirty miles, and it contains over six hundred and fifty thousand square miles.

In South America there are three great mountain systems, viz.: Andean, the system of the Parina, and the Brazilian system. The Andean system extends, in a grand unbroken range, from the Isthmus of Panama, to the Straits of Magellan, a distance of four thousand five hundred miles. They run nearly parallel with the Pacific coast, and below 23° south latitude, consist of but a single chain. North of this point, several ranges run in parallel directions. The Andean mountains are inferior in hight only to the Himalaya range of Asia; and reach their culminating point with Sorata, twenty-four thousand eight hundred and twelve feet above the sea. The Parina range, also called the Highlands of Guiana, having a length of nine hundred miles, comprises several parallel ranges, and separates the basins of the Orinoco and Rionegro rivers. They extend over a tract of country about three hundred and fifty miles wide, and have an average elevation of four thousand feet, though many of the peaks rise to a much greater hight. The Duida has an altitude of eight thousand five hundred feet, and the Maravaca towers still higher, being ten thousand five hundred feet high. The Brazilian mountains extend along the south-eastern coast of Brazil, a distance of over two thousand miles. They have an average elevation of three thousand five hundred feet, and are found at a distance of from twenty to eighty miles from the shore. The culminating point of this range is mount Itamba, reaching an altitude of five thousand nine hundred and sixty feet. The Andes rise almost perpendicularly from the Pacific coast, but towards the interior the descent is more gradual.

Among the mountain peaks of South America, may be mentioned the Sahama, twenty-three thousand and fourteen, Aconcagua, twenty-three thousand, Tupungato, twenty-two thousand four hundred and fifty, Gualateiri, twenty-two thousand, and Chimborazo, twenty-one thousand and sixty-five feet high. Among the volcanoes, Cotopaxi, Pichincha and Tunguragua, in Equador, Aconcagua, in Chili, and Gualateiri and Arequipa, in Peru, are the most important. Cotopaxi is an active volcano on the eastern slope of the Andes, in latitude 41′ south, and longitude 78° 42′ west. It has an altitude of eighteen thousand eight hundred and eighty-seven feet above the level of the sea, and rises nine thousand eight hundred feet above the table-land of Quito. The upper four thousand feet forms a perfect cone, which, except in the immediate vicinity of the crater, is covered with snow throughout the year. The lava and stones, ejected from this volcano, cover an area around its base of sixty square miles. Flames have been known to issue from Cotopaxi three thousand feet above the crater; and the roaring caused by its eruptions can be heard at a distance of two hundred miles. During an eruption in 1743, the flames forced several new vents near the summit. The last great eruption occurred in 1803. (See views of Cotopaxi.)

The volcano of Pichincha is situated eleven miles north-west of Quito. The summit of the volcano, found at an altitude of fifteen thousand nine hundred and twenty-four feet, is covered with ice and snow throughout the year. The most remarkable feature of Pichincha is its crater, which is three miles in circumference and one and one-fourth miles deep. Prior to the

Spanish invasion, Pichincha was an active volcano, since which time it has been silent. (See views of Pichincha.) The Tunguragua volcano has a hight of sixteen thousand four hundred and twenty-four feet. Its greatest eruption occurred on the 23d of April, 1773, when an immense flood of lava was ejected from the volcano, which lies in hardened masses at its base. (See views of Tunguragua.)

Among the objects of interest in connection with the surface of South America, may be mentioned an immense rock, or bowlder, in the province of Antioquia, United States of Columbia, called El Penol. It covers six acres of ground, and rises four hundred and sixty-four feet above the level of the surrounding country. (See view.)

With the exception of the Brazilian mountains and table-land, and the Parina range, the section of country east of the Andes is one vast plain. The northern division of this plain is the *Llanos* of the Orinoco, a vast tract, almost as level as the ocean. During the rainy season this territory is covered with rich grass, but with the return of the dry season life and vegetation cease. The rich mould is crumbled into sand, and the surface becomes filled with large rents and cracks. The *Selvas*, or forest plains of the Amazon, extend from the mouth of that river to the region of the periodical inundation. The great moisture and heat of this region greatly promote the luxuriance of the vegetable kingdom. "Behold," says Guyot, "under the same parallel, where Africa presents only parched table-lands, those boundless virgin forests of the basin of the Amazon, those selvas, almost unbroken, over a length of over fifteen hundred miles, forming the most gigantic wilderness of this kind that exists on any continent. And what vigor, what luxuriance of vegetation! The palm trees, with their slender forms, boldly uplift their heads one hundred and fifty or two hundred feet above the ground, and domineer over all other trees of these wilds, by their hight, by their number, and by the majesty of their foliage. Climbing plants, woody-stemmed twining lianos, infinitely varied, surround them with their flexible branches, display their own flowers upon the foliage, and combine them in a solid mass of vegetation, impenetrable to man, which the axe alone can break through with success."

The *Pampas* of the La Plata, or plains of Buenos Ayres, are rich districts north of Patagonia, covered with a luxuriant growth of grass, which affords abundant pasturage for the herds of horses and cattle which exist in this region. A large tract of marsh country, a short distance north-west, abounds with lakes, and rich grassy meadows again appear above the head-waters of the Paraguay river. During the dry season, these plains, the same as the *Llanos*, become destitute of vegetation. The deserts of Patagonia extend from the Atlantic to the base of the Andes, and cover an area of one hundred thousand square miles. They occupy nearly all the territory south of the Rio Negro, and are frequently diversified by huge bowlders and rocky hights.

The chief rivers of South America are the Orinoco, Amazon, and La Plata. The Orinoco rises among the mountains in the southern part of Venezuela, flows first north and then east, and after a course of sixteen hundred miles, enters the Atlantic through several mouths. It drains an area of two hundred and seventy-two thousand square miles. There are rapids in the Orinoco, below its junction with the Guaviare, called the Altures, and thirty-six miles below they again appear, and are called Maypures. The mighty Amazon, rising among the Andes, receives the waters of the Rio Negro, Coqueta, Coary, Jurua, Purus, Madeira, Tapajos, Xingu, and Tocantius, and pours a volume of water into the ocean with such force that it remains unmixed with the waters of the sea for a distance of two hundred and fifty miles from the shore. It has a course of four thousand miles, and enters the ocean through several mouths, at which point it is, including the islands, two hundred and fifty miles wide. The La Plata river, formed by the confluence of the Salado with the Parana, enters the Atlantic with such force that its current is perceptible at a distance of one hundred and seventy-five miles from the shore. The river at Montevideo is fifty-three miles wide, and gradually expands, till at the mouth it has a width of one hundred and seventy miles.

The wild animals of South America are numerous, though not as ferocious as those of Asia and Africa. The jaguar, puma, ocelot, and tiger-cat are the most formidable. The ant-eater, sloth, armadillo, deer, antelope, ape, monkey, etc., are peculiar to the tropical regions of South America. Among the birds, the condor of the Andes, is conspicuous. There are also numbers of parrots, humming birds, toucans, macaws, and birds of prey, such as the eagle, vulture, falcons, etc.

South America has, for the most part, a tropical climate. In no section, however, of this country, do we find that intense heat, which its geographical position would lead us to expect. The prevalence of the trade-winds, the position of high mountains, and other physical causes, give the country a more uniform temperature, than it otherwise would enjoy. In passing south from the lowlands near the equator, or advancing up the mountain slopes, the heat of the torrid zone, is gradually succeeded by the more pleasing climate of the temperate zone. In Patagonia, the cold becomes severe; and snow falls almost daily, at the Strait of Magellan.

No other country can boast of a greater luxuriance, or variety of vegetation, than South America. On the slopes of the Andes and Cordilleras, is a vast amount of fertile land, which with proper attention would make a great agricultural district. In Ecuador, this region has three divisions, Ambato, Quito, and Cuenca, which includes the larger portion of the cultivated lands of the state. (See views in the valley of Ambato.)

In South America the forest trees are more various, and reach a greater size than those of the old world. The most important are the palm, cocoanut, balsam, passion-flower tree, and oak. Sugar-cane, wheat, barley, Indian corn, and potatoes are produced at elevations of from five thousand to ten thousand feet. Among the fruits produced may be mentioned mangabas, pomegranates, oranges, limes, cocoa-nuts, banannas, pine-apples, mangoes, mammoons, and jambas.

The countries embraced within the limits of South America are nine republics, viz: Venezuela, United States of Columbia,

Ecuador, Peru, Bolivia, Chili, Argentine Confederation, Urugray, and Paraguay; the empire of Brazil, the colonies of British, French, and Dutch Guana, and the unsettled district of Patagonia.

The chief towns of South America are Rio Janeiro and Bahia of Brazil, Buenos Ayres of the Argentine confederation, and Lima of Peru.

QUITO

Is a city situated among the Andes of Ecuador, on the Quito table-land, nine thousand five hundred and forty-three feet above the sea. The city contains a number of fine squares, one of which contains the town-hall, cathedral, palaces of the president and archbishop of the republic, and a fine bronze fountain. The university, orphan asylum, large hospital, work-house, and churches and convents comprise the other important buildings. Near the church of San Francisco is a fine public fountain, which supplies a large number of the people with water. (See views.)

The scenery which surrounds Quito is picturesque in the highest degree. " From the terrace of the government palace," says Humboldt, " there is one of the most enchanting prospects the human eye ever witnessed, or nature ever exhibited. Looking to the south, and glancing to the north, eleven mountains, covered with perpetual snow, present themselves, their bases apparently resting upon the verdant hills which surround the city." Quito was made a city in 1541, by Charles V. of Spain. Population seventy-six thousand. (See views of Quito.)

AMBATO

Is a town of Ecuador, one hundred miles south-east of Quito, on the northern slope of Chimborazo, eight thousand eight hundred and fifty-nine feet above the sea. It was destroyed by an eruption of Cotopaxi in 1698, but was rebuilt, and soon became more flourishing than before. It has some good buildings, and carries on an active trade in grain, sugar and cochineal, the products of the surrounding country. Population, fifteen thousand. (See views of Ambato.)

IBARA

Is an important town of Ecuador, fifty miles north-east of Quito, at the foot of the volcano of Imbabura. It is in a fertile region, well built, and has about fifteen thousand inhabitants. (See views at Ibara.)

MARAYCABO,

Is a city and port of entry of Venezuela, and capital of a province of its own name, on the western side of the entrance from Maraycabo Gulf into Maraycabo Lake. It has several monasteries and convents, and a large and handsome parish church. The harbor is obstructed by a bar, on which there is only eight feet of water at ebb tide. Population, eighteen thousand. (See views of Maraycabo.)

Within sight of Maraycabo is the town of Los Haticos, the streets of which are finely shaded with magnificent palms and cocoa-nut trees. (See views at Los Haticos.)

South America was discovered by Christopher Columbus, who landed at the mouth of the Orinoco river in 1498. All the country, except Brazil and Guana, was claimed by Spain, and remained subject to that power till the beginning of the present century, when the different provinces threw off the Spanish yoke, and established themselves as independent republics. Brazil was claimed by Portugal, and remained in her possession till 1822, when a peaceful separation was effected. Guana is divided between the British, French, and Dutch.

PART III.

FOREIGN OBJECTS

OF

INTEREST.

CHAPTER I.

BRITISH ISLES.

The British islands are west of Europe, and comprise England, Scotland, Ireland, Wales, and many adjacent islands.

England, the seat of government of Great Britain, is situated south of Scotland, and east of Wales. The surface is generally level or undulating, the climate moist and mild, and the soil fertile and productive.

LONDON,

The capital of the empire, and the largest city in the world, is situated on both sides of the Thames, in England. It had, according to the census of 1865, a population of three millions and fifteen thousand. It is the first city in commercial importance, and covers an area of one hundred and twenty-two square miles.

In the beginning of cold weather the city is sometimes enveloped in fogs so dense, that it is necessary, in the business part of the city, that the buildings should be lighted, and vehicles are unable to pass through the streets. The thick atmosphere and the cloud of smoke constantly hovering over the city, renders it difficult to view the whole metropolis from any one point. But from a number of positions views of portions of the great mass of buildings may be obtained, the magnificent dome of St. Paul's cathedral forming a conspicuous object in nearly every one. This church, in point of architecture, is the greatest ornament of the city. Its foundation was laid on Lodgate Hill in 1675. It is five hundred and ten feet long and two hundred and fifty wide, exclusive of the porticos. The building is surmounted by a massive and handsome dome, on the top of which is a lantern with a ball and cross, the hight of which is four hundred and four feet above the ground. The west front has a beautiful double portico of coupled columns and two clock towers, over which rises the cupola. This magnificent edifice is built of Portland stone, and was constructed at a cost of seven hundred and forty-seven thousand nine hundred and fifty-four pounds.

Westminster Abby, next to St. Paul's, the finest church edifice in London, was erected during the reign of Henry III. and Edward I. The beautiful chapel on the east end was built under the auspices of Henry VII., and is known as his chapel. This edifice is three hundred and sixty feet long and one hundred and ninety-five feet wide. In this building have been crowned all the kings and queens of England, from Edward, the Confessor, to Queen Victoria, and here a number of them have been interred.

London Tower occupies an area of twelve acres. It rises amidst an assemblage of ancient walls, battlements, and turrets. The central and most ancient part of the existing structure, known as the White tower, was erected in 1078, during the reign of William, the conqueror.

The House of Parliament is a vast and magnificent structure, containing the House of Lords, the House of Commons and various offices and apartments connected with parliamentary business. This massive edifice, covering about eight acres of ground, is situated between the river Thames and Westminster Abbey. The House of Lords is decorated with carved oak panelling, gilding, fresco paintings, and richly stained glass windows. This apartment is ninety-seven feet long, forty-five wide, and forty-five high. The House of Commons is somewhat smaller, and not so handsomely decorated.

St. James' palace was erected by Henry VIII. It is an irregular brick building, and has nothing striking in its appearance externally. In this palace royal levees are held. It has also drawing rooms, and is much resorted to during the fashionable season.

Buckingham palace, opposite St. James' park, was erected by George IV. The east front, in the Italian style, is higher than the rest of the building, and adds much to its beauty. The palace has a gallery one hundred and sixty feet long, in which are fine pictures. The Queen resides here during the greater part of the spring and summer months.

One of the greatest architectural ornaments of London is Whitehall, or the Banqueting house. Kensington palace, the birth-place of Queen Victoria, is a plain brick building situated in Kensington garden.

The Mansion house, constructed at a cost of seventy-one thousand pounds, is situated in the east end of the Boultry. It was built between the years 1739 and 1753, and is the residence of the Lord Mayor.

The British museum, on Russel street, is a large and imposing edifice, founded in 1753. It has an Ionic front, with sculptured ornaments, and contains Assyrian, Greek, Egyptian, and other antiquities, and also a large collection of sculptures, coins, minerals, books, manuscripts, stuffed animals, and a library of four hundred and sixty thousand volumes, to which the public have access three days of the week.

London university was founded in 1837 for the exclusive purpose of conferring degrees, the candidates for which are furnished by University college, and King's college. The course of education embraces history, science, medicine, jurisprudence, and the classical languages.

The great world's exhibition, originated by Prince Albert and held in a magnificent crystal palace, erected in Hyde Park, was first opened in 1851. This palace was nearly a half mile in length, the center forty-eight, and the sides twenty-four feet in hight. The whole structure which cost 347,937 pounds, has since been removed and re-erected at Sydenham, on a still more magnificent scale. (See views of London.)

The limits of London, as defined by a parliamentary act for parliamentary purposes, are within a circle, the center of which is the Post office, the radius being three miles. The actual area of this great metropolis greatly exceeds this, embracing the city of Westminster, the parliamentary boroughs of Tinsbury, Southwork, Lambeth, Marglebone, Tower Hamlets, and the towns of Greenwich, Dalwich, Clapham, Kensington, Hampstead and others.

GREENWICH,

Located on the right bank of the Thames, is about five miles south-east of London bridge. The older streets are narrow and irregular, but those recently laid out are wide, and numerous handsome houses have been built. The most interesting institution of Greenwich is the magnificent Naval hospital, a home for the superanuated seamen. It is one of the finest structures in England, and was erected in 1694 by the munificence of William and Mary. (See views of Hospital.)

On an eminence in Greenwich park, is the observatory, founded in 1674 by Charles II. From this meridian, longitude is reckoned in all British charts. The park was first enclosed by the Duke of Gloucester. It embraces about two hundred acres, a part of which is covered by a forest in which are numerous herds of deer, forming a great place of resort for the Londoners.

LIVERPOOL,

The second city in population, and the principal seaport of England, is about two hundred and ten miles from London. The city is about five miles in length, and nearly three in width. The principal public buildings are the town hall, exchange and revenue buildings, and St. George's hall. The latter, in which are the Assize Courts, is in the center of the city. This sumptuous building is five hundred feet in length, and is constructed in the Corinthian style. The most remarkable feature of Liverpool is the number and magnificence of its docks, covering an area of more than four hundred acres. (See views of Liverpool.)

CAMBRIDGE,

A parliamentary borough and seat of Cambridge university, is about fifty miles from London. The University of Cambridge, founded in the seventh century, now consists of thirteen colleges and four halls, viz.: St. Peter's, Caius, Corpus Christi, King's, Queen's, Jesus Christ's, St. John's, Magdalene, Trinity, Emmanuel, Sidney Sussex, Downing colleges, and Clare, Pembroke, Trinity, and Catharine halls. Some of these buildings are the most magnificent in the kingdom. A student of this university is called a Cantab. (See views of Cambridge.)

OXFORD,

County seat of Oxford county, is about fifty-five miles from London. On High street, the principal thoroughfare of the city, are the university colleges, nineteen in number, and the five halls connected with the university; also Magdalene, Queen's, and All Souls' colleges and University church. (See views of Oxford.)

DARTMOUTH,

A seaport town of Devon county, England, is most picturesquely built on a succession of terraces on the west side of the estuary of the Dart, the entrance to which is defended by a castle and strong batteries. (See views of Dartmouth.)

WARWICK,

A parliamentary borough, is situated on the right bank of the Avon. The principal object of interest in this town, is Warwick castle. The credit of founding this castle is bestowed on Ethelfleda, daughter of Alfred the Great. It is probably the most magnificent feudal fortress in England. (See views of Warwick castle.)

About two miles north of Warwick, is Guy's Cliff, containing the hermitage of Sir Guy, Earl of Warwick. During the reign of Henry VI, a chapel was here built by Beauchamp, Earl of Warwick, and contains a colossal statue of Sir Guy. (See views of Guy's Cliff.)

WINDSOR

Is a parish of Berks county. It is situated on the right bank of the Thames. The river is here crossed by an iron bridge, connecting Windsor with Eaton, the seat of Eaton college, founded by Henry VI., in 1446. (See views of Eaton college.)

The town is built principally upon one street, winding around the south and west sides of Windsor castle. It is well built, and contains some handsome private buildings. (See views of Windsor castle.)

Among the principal cathedrals of England, outside of London, are the Exeter, Wells, Petersborough, Durham, and Ely cathedrals. The Exeter cathedral, a noble edifice of great antiquity, is four hundred and eight feet long, and one hundred and thirty in hight. Its west facade is one of the most beautiful in the kingdom. Wells' cathedral dates from the time of Henry III. The interior is beautifully ornamented. The central tower of the building is one hundred and seventy-eight feet in hight. Petersborough cathedral was founded by Peada, in 635. The building is four hundred and seventy-one feet long. The front consists of three pointed arches, each eighty feet high, surmounted by spires and pinnacles. Durham cathedral was founded in 1093. Its greatest length and breadth are five hundred and seven feet, and two hundred feet respectively, and the hight of the central tower is two hundred and fourteen feet. Ely cathedral was built between the reigns of William Rufus and Edward III. It is a singular and magnificent edifice in the Norman, Saxon, and Gothic styles, and contains many interesting monuments. (See views of the different cathedrals.)

SCOTLAND.

This division of Great Britain is north of England, from which it is partly separated by the Chevoit hills. The Grampian mountains divide the surface of Scotland into the lowlands and highlands, the latter lying north and the former south of this range. The general surface, particularly in the northern part, is in striking contrast with that of England, possessing few of the valleys for which the latter is so remarkable. Many of the mountains belonging to the Grampian range, have a rounded form, terminating in fantastic peaks, among which are Ben Nevis, Ben Lomond, Ben Macdhue, and Ben Venue. A noted pass of this range is the Killiecrankie. The river Garro here flows for a distance of two miles, through a narrow, rocky and precipitous defile, along which a road has been cut. Another system, with their general level much lower, and their summits much more lofty than the Grampian range, lies to the north and west of lakes of Glenmore. The most elevated of these summits are Ben Wyvis, Ben Moore, Ben Clibbrick, Bendearge, and Morren. The lakes of Scotland are in the glens of the highlands, and are noted for their varied and picturesque scenery, and also for being much longer than wide. The most remarkable are Loch Lomond, Loch Ketrine, Lock Tummel, Lock Achray, Loch Rannoch, and Loch Tay. To Scotland, belong all the islands that line its coast. On the east side they are small and few in number, on the north are the groups of Orkneys and Shetlands, and on the west side is a series of groups called the Hebrides. Staffa, a much celebrated island belonging to the latter group, is composed of conglomerated trap. On this island are a number of caves resembling architectural designs. Of these, Fingal's Cave is the most remarkable. The entrance is formed by columnar ranges, supporting a magnificent and lofty arch. The entrance is thirty-three feet wide, and sixty feet high, and the length of the cave is two hundred and twenty-seven feet. The cave is composed of complicated ranges of gigantic columns. The floor is the sea, from which is reflected on the pendent roof, whitened with calcareous stalagmites, many colored lights. Of the other caves on the island, the most noteworthy is the Clam Shell Cave, deriving its name from the peculiar curve of the basaltic columns, giving it the appearance of pecten-shell. (See views.)

EDINBURGH,

The capital of Scotland, is situated on a picturesque cluster of hills, about one and a half miles from the Frith of Forth, in the county of Mid Lothian. Owing to the recent growth of the city, it is at present nearly connected with the town of Leith.

The Abbey of Holyrood was founded in the twelfth century, by David I., a pious Scottish king, who endowed the clergyman of this parish with power to found a burgh in a westerly direction up the slope, toward Edinburgh; and thus was built Canongate, a suburb now united to the city. A royal palace sprung up about this time, which became a favorite place of resort for Scottish kings and nobles. This edifice and the Holyrood palace were among the earliest buildings of Edinburgh. The Royal or Edinburgh Castle was undoubtedly the first erection in the city. Edinburgh being a fortified town, in 1436 the capital was removed to this place from Perth. After this event, while sur-surrounding cities sunk into obscurity, Edinburgh greatly increased in size and population. The city being walled, the houses were necessarily built high, consisting of a number of stories, each floor serving the purpose of a dwelling. The design of the buildings resembles those of Paris. One of the finest features of Edinburgh are the Public Gardens, which are laid out in the valley between the old town and the new. Of the public monuments in the city, the one erected in honor of Sir Walter Scott is the most remarkable. It was designed by George M. Kemp, is two hundred feet high, and is in the form of an elaborate gothic cross.

The chief educational establishments of the city are the High School, New Academy, University, and Medical Schools. Some of the buildings of interest in Edinburgh are the Castle, in which are shown the ancient regalia of Scotland; the extensive Library of the Faculty of Advocates; the Royal Institute, which contains the apartments of the Royal Society; the Museum of the Society of the Scottish Antiquaries; the general Register House, where the whole of the rights and pecuniary obligations connected with hereditable property are registered, and state documents preserved; the Parliament House, used by the Scottish parliament previous to the union with England; the University buildings; the National Gallery of Art; and the Palace and Abbey of Holyrood. (See views in Edinburgh.)

GLASGOW,

The principal commercial city of Scotland, situated on both sides of the Clyde, is, after London, one of the largest and most important cities of the British empire. By far the greater portion of the city is built on the northern bank of the river. Three handsome stone bridges span the river at this place, two of which are of solid granite, and are greatly admired for their light and graceful architecture. There are also two suspension bridges for the accommodation of foot passengers. The city has a somewhat smoky appearance, owing to its numerous workshops, factories, etc. It is about three miles in length and eight in circumference. The houses are built of freestone, and in much the same style as those of Edinburgh.

Glasgow has three parks, viz: Green, containing one hundred and forty acres, and occupying the level next to the Clyde; Queen's park, beautifully situated on rising ground; and Kelvingrove, embracing forty acres, sloping toward Kelvin river. The city of Glasgow originated with the cathedral and university, both of which are in the north-east part of the city. The site of the cathedral is an eminence on the bank of a ravine traversed by the Molendinar. This edifice was founded during the reign of David I. A lofty tower rises from the center two hundred and twenty-five feet in hight. The Necropolis, opposite the cathedral, is a handsome cemetery studded with monuments, and tastefully decorated with trees and shrubs. Several of the banks, many of the churches, and the royal exchange, in Green street, are excellent specimens of architecture. An obelisk, one hundred and forty-four feet high, is situated in the park, or green as it is generally called. This park embraces one hundred and forty acres, and is used by the inhabitants as a place of recreation. The botanic garden covers an area of forty acres, and every summer, during the fair holidays, it is thrown open, and visitors admitted. (See views in Glasgow.)

Glen Urquhart is a parish of Scotland. It contains the remains of an ancient castle and Druidic antiquities. Blair Athole is an extensive parish, in which are the mountains of Benygloe and Bendeare, the pass of Killiecrankie and Blair Athole castle, seat of the Duke of Athole. (See views of Glen Urquhart, Blair Athole, and Benygloe.)

BALMORAL CASTLE

Is in a picturesque dell in Bracmar, the south-western district of Aberdeenshire. This castle is the residence of Queen Victoria. It is located on an elevation sloping back from the river Dee, and commands a magnificent prospect on every side. Craigangowan rises in the background, and the castle, which is built of granite, when viewed at a distance, presents a strong and imposing appearance, looking as though it had been hewn out of one vast rock of that material. The old castle not being sufficiently commodious, Prince Albert erected a new one at his own expense in the Scottish balmoral style of architecture. The castle, which consists of two separate blocks of buildings, is united by wings, and surmounted by a massive tower thirty-five feet square, rising to the hight of eighty feet, and surmounted by a turret twenty feet high. Prince Albert has recently made great improvements upon the edifice and the property surrounding it. The estate, at present, includes Birkhall, the seat of Prince Albert, Knock castle ruins, Loch Muich, and dark Lochnagar, about seven miles south-west of Balmoral castle, and contains ten thousand acres in addition to thirty thousand acres of hill ground which has been converted into a deer forest.

Among other residences of the nobility are Inverary castle, west of the town of Inverary, the seat of the Duke of Argyle, Taymouth castle, the seat of the Marquis of Breadelbane, on the right bank of the Tay, in Perth county, Drummond, the seat of Lord Willoughby, and Abbotsford, the celebrated seat of Sir Walter Scott, in Roxburg county, on the Tweed. (See views of castles.

IRELAND,

The most western of the islands of Great Britain, is in the shape of a rhomboid. The surface is very irregular, no part of the island being more than fifty miles from the coast. The climate is moist and mild, and the atmosphere is seldom clear or free from fog. The mountainous regions are along the shore, and instead of being in continuous ranges, are in isolated masses. A considerable distance on the shore of Ireland is distinguished for its basaltic cliffs and caves, the most remarkable of which is the Giant's Causeway, which projects into the sea from the base of a stratified rock, about four hundred feet in hight, seven hundred in length, and three hundred and fifty in breadth. It is separated into three divisions by whinstone dykes. The name of this stupendous formation is derived from a popular legend, ascribing the work to some giants, who were endeavoring to construct a bridge across the sea to Scotland.

In the interior of the island are a vast number of lakes, some of which are so near together as to form a continued series. The lakes of Killarney are celebrated for their romantic scenery. Few countries of the same extent are traversed by as many rivers as Ireland. In some of them are waterfalls of great beauty, and the valleys through which they flow are noted for the magnificence of their scenery. (See views of natural scenery.)

DUBLIN,

The capital and largest city of Ireland, is situated on the Liffey, in the eastern part of the island. In the ancient part of the city occur Christ's Church and St. Patrick's Cathedral. This division of the town is not well built, and is irregular and filthy. In the east quarter is Sackville street, one of the finest thoroughfares in Europe. On this street are the Rotunda, Post-office, and the Nelson Pillar; also, Rutland, Mountjoy, and Marlborough squares. In the southern part of the city is the Dublin Castle, situated on an eminence, and containing an arsenal, an armory, the viceregal chapel, and various government offices. The principal church edifices are St. George Frindloter, twenty-nine Protestant and nine Roman Catholic parochial churches. (See views of Dublin.)

BELFAST,

A port and parliamentary borough of Ireland, is the principal commercial city, and the seat of the linen manufacture. The houses are of brick, and well built; the streets are spacious, well lighted, and macadamized. Among the educational institutions are Queen's College, an edifice of brick and stone; the Presbyterian College; the Royal Academical Institution, founded in 1810; the Belfast Academy, and other national and private schools. The chief public buildings are the custom-house, commercial buildings, hotels, offices, reading and music halls, and the new house of correction. (See views of Belfast.)

YOUGHAL

Is a seaport town of Munster county, situated on the west side of the Blackwater. The town was formerly enclosed by walls, the ruins of which still remain. It contains a court house, custom house, hospital, barracks, and also the former residence of Sir Walter Raleigh. The culture of the potato in Ireland was first introduced at this place by Sir Walter Raleigh.

WALES.

Wales, a part of the British empire, joins England on the west. The surface is rugged and mountainous, particularly in the northern part. Snowden, the culminating point of South Britain, rises to the hight of three thousand five hundred and seventy feet. Among the chief cities are Merthyr Tydvil, the largest town, noted for its iron works, Swansea, the principal seat of the copper trade, and much resorted to for sea-bathing, and Conway, the seat of the Conway castle, founded by Edward I. It is in a good state of preservation, and one of the greatest feudal fortresses in the kingdom. (See views of Wales.)

THE ISLE OF WIGHT

Is south of England, in the English channel. It has an area of one hundred and thirty-six square miles. The center is much more elevated than the margin, the highest elevation being eight hundred and thirty feet above the sea. Newport is the capital. The principal towns are Yarmouth, Ryde, Ventnor, and Cowes. Near the latter is the Osborn house, a favorite summer residence of Queen Victoria. (See views of the Osborn house.)

CHAPTER II.

FRANCE.

This is one of the most populous and influential empires on the globe. It is situated in the south-western part of Europe, and covers an area of about ninety-seven thousand square miles. It includes under its dominion, a large number of small islands and colonies in various parts of the world. The population, including that of its possessions, is forty-one millions sixty-three thousand three hundred and forty-nine.

The surface of the country is somewhat broken by mountain ranges, though it contains only a few lofty summits. The principal ranges are the Pyrenes, on the south, separating it from Spain, and the Alps, on the south-east, separating it from Italy. Both these ranges are celebrated for their beautiful scenery. At their base and along their sides, are beautiful villages, sometimes occupying an elevation of several thousand feet. Luz and St. Sauveur in the Pyrenes, are celebrated for their mineral springs. (See views.) Mount Blanc, the culminating point of the Alps, and the highest mountain of Europe, is situated in the province of Savoy, which was ceded to France in 1860. The mountain is about fifteen thousand eight hundred feet in hight. It is situated at the dividing line between France, Switzerland and Italy. The limit of the snow line is about eight thousand feet above the level of the sea. It forms the terminus of the Grurain Alps, one of the divisions of the western Alps. Thirty-four glaciers are found in this range, occupying an area of about ninety-five square miles. The largest of these is the Mer de Glace, or "sea of ice." The lower part of this glacier is called the Glacier des Bois. These glaciers extend north-east into Switzerland. It is thought that the whole extent covered by these fields of ice, in the different Alpine ranges, is not less than one thousand five hundred square miles, and averaging about one hundred feet in depth. The valley of the Chamouni, lying at the base of Mount Blanc, is remarkable for its beautiful scenery. The glaciers which descend into it are the grandest of the Alps. The valley contains three villages, Chamouni, lying at the foot of Mont Blanc, Argentine, and Ouches. (See views.)

The rivers of France are rapid in their course, and of but little value for navigable purposes.

PARIS,

The capital and principal city, is situated upon two islands formed by the river Seine, about one hundred and ten miles from its mouth. It is surrounded by a range of hills, the highest of which attains an elevation of about two hundred feet. Recently a line of fortifications has been built, enclosing the city and a large portion of the suburbs. The city proper is enclosed by an interior wall. Between this wall and the fortifications are what is called the outer Boulevards, making nearly the circuit of the town. The inner Boulevards, just within the interior wall, are a finely planted thoroughfare, bounded on either side by a double row of trees. These are a fashionable resort, and usually present a scene of gaiety and splendor.

The streets in the newer part of the town are regular, wide, and well paved, but in the older portions they are irregular, cutting each other at all kinds of angles, and in many places so narrow that carriages find difficulty in passing.

There are within the city several magnificent triumphal arches. The Arc de l'Etoile, surpasses anything of the kind ever erected, either in ancient or modern times. It is one hundred and sixty-two feet high by one hundred and forty-seven feet long and seventy feet broad. In the Place du Carrousel is another beautiful arch, designed after that of Septimius Severus, at Rome. This arch is forty-five feet high by sixty feet long and twenty feet broad. The top is crowned by a triumphal car drawn by four bronze horses.

The public buildings of Paris equal, if not surpass, those of any other city on the globe. Among the many elegant churches, that of Notre Dame is the most celebrated. It is situated on the site formerly occupied by a Pagan temple, and afterwards by a Christian basilica. The present building, which was erected between the twelfth and fifteenth century, ranks among the noblest specimens of Gothic architecture. It is built in the shape of a cruciform, with an octagonal east and west end, surmounted by two towers and a new central spire, remarkable for its delicate tracery.

Among the most celebrated palaces are the Tuileries, the Palais Royal, and the Louvre. The Tuileries, situated on the right bank of the Seine, have continued for centuries to be the chief Parisian residence of the sovereigns. The Palais Royal is situated not far from the Tuileries. It is surrounded by beautiful gardens, and much resorted to by the people of Paris. The Louvre, situated east of the Tuileries, has ceased to be a state residence, and is now occupied as the great national repository of works of art.

A large sandy plain, near the Quai d' Orsay, in which reviews and other military displays are held, is called the Champ de Mars. Not far from it is the Ecole Militaire, which was founded in 1752, and is now used as a military training school for infantry and cavalry.

The year 1867 witnessed, in Paris, a grand display of the products of different nations, called the Paris Exposition. The grounds, situated on the Champ de Mars, cover an area of thirty-seven acres. The building is oval in form, and consists of twelve circles around a common center, having an open central garden. This exhibition was visited by the principal monarchs of the world, and vast multitudes of people from all nations. (See views of Paris and Paris Exposition.)

LYONS,

The second city of France, is situated at the junction of two large rivers, the Saone, flowing from the north, and the Rhone, flowing from the east. The city extends to the opposite banks of both rivers, c ommunication being maintained by a large number of handsome and commodious bridges. The streets, in a large portion of the city, are narrow and irregular, and lined with ungainly buildings, crowded together in the smallest possible space. Some portions of the town, however, are well built with stately mansions, wide streets, and finely planted walks. The public buildings are more remarkable for their antiquity, than for the style of their architecture. Among the most interesting are the Cathedral, the Church of Notre Dame, the Church of St. Irenæus, the Palais de Justice, and the Abbey of Ainay.

As a manufacturing town it holds the first rank. Its silk manufactures are perhaps the most important in the world. It is admirably situated for commerce, and extensively engaged in trade. The population in 1862 was three hundred and eighteen thousand eight hundred and three. (See views of Lyons.)

VERSAILLES,

Situated ten miles south-west of Paris, is remarkable for the elegance and regularity of its construction. It is considered one of the handsomest towns in Europe. It contains a number of handsome public buildings, the most remarkable of which are the Palace of Versailles, the Church of St. Louis, the Prefecture, and the Chancery. The palace, built by Lous XIV., is now used as a historical museum. From 1672 to 1790 it was the residence of the kings of France. Connected with the palace are a chapel, a theatre, an orangery, large flower gardens, and a park, ornamented with numerous statues and fountains. The opening of the museum in 1837 did much to increase the prosperity of the city. In 1852 the population was thirty-five thousand three hundred and sixty-seven. (See views of Versailles.)

CHAPTER III.

SWITZERLAND.

Switzerland is a republic of central Europe, lying between latitude 45° 50′ and 47° 50′ N., and longitude 6° and 10° 25′ E. It is bounded on the north by Baden, on the south by Italy, Piedmont, and Savoy, on the north-east by Wurtemburg and Bavaria, on the east by Tyrol, and on the west by France. Greatest length of Switzerland from east to west, two hundred and sixteen miles, from north to south, one hundred and forty miles, area, fifteen thousand two hundred and sixty-one square miles.

The scenery of Switzerland is on the grandest scale. The inhabitants of level districts, accustomed only to the prairies or wooded plains which surround them, can form but a faint idea of the grandeur, the singularly beautiful natural scenery of the alpine regions of Switzerland. Nature has an infinite variety of aspects among the Alps. Beautiful lakes are embosomed among the mountains, the peaks of which tower far above the limits of perpetual snow; the naked rock is covered with hardened masses of glacier; immense glaciers glisten on the mountain sides; vast quantities of ice and snow are hurled into immeasurable abysses, and wild and picturesque valleys form the course of impetuous streams and mountain torrents.

Switzerland is the most mountainous country of Europe. The Jura mountains comprise several parallel ranges, which lie on the north-western side of the republic. The Alps, crossing the southern part of the country on the Italian frontier, cover over one half of the country.

One of the most striking physical features of Switzerland are glaciers, which are found here in greater numbers than in any other country. They exist in all latitudes, varying in hight according to the temperature of the country in which they are found, but those of the Alps have been more clearly and satisfactorily investigated than of any other region. They cover an area of fifteen hundred square miles, and are frequently from fifteen to twenty miles long, and three miles broad. "In elevated mountain valleys, glaciers are formed by the fall of snow, which is increased in amount by immense quantities precipitated from the adjacent mountain peaks. This mass is subject to alternate freezing and thawing, until, in the progress of centuries, the valley becomes filled with a body of ice constituting the glacial formation." Glaciers have a gradual downward motion, and are often found below the snow limit. The Lower Grindelwald is five hundred, and the Aar fifteen hundred feet below the snow line. They present the appearance of a frozen torrent, frequently traversed by deep rents called crevasses. The most important rivers of Switzerland owe their origin to glaciers. The Rhone issues from the Rhone glacier on the west side of Mount St. Gothard, between the mountains of Furka and Grimsel, and the Hinter Rhine from the Rheinwald glacier.

Switzerland is divided into twenty-two cantons or states.

BERN

Is one of the three leading states of the Swiss confederation, and celebrated above all others for the beauty and variety of its scenery. It has some of the loftiest peaks of the Alps, and contains the romantic valleys of the Lauterbrunnen, Grindelwald, Simmenthal, Gasternthal, and Kanderthal. In the Lauterbrunnen valley is the White Lutschine, celebrated for its picturesque beauty, and so confined, that, in winter, the sun does not appear till noon. In this valley, also, is the Staubbach fall, one of the highest and most beautiful in Europe. It occurs in a small stream of the same name, an affluent of the White Lutschine. The amount of water precipitated is small, and the whole, in its descent, is dashed noiselessly, by the mere resistance of the opposing air, into spray, and ere long into a fine mist-like rain. The hight of the fall is about eight hundred and sixty feet. "It is neither mist nor water," says Byron, "but a something between both; its immense hight gives it a wave or curve—a spreading here, or condensation there—wonderful and indescribable." Seen from the front, the Staubbach often presents the appearance of a white semi-transparent lace veil, flitting to and fro over the face of the rock, and contracting itself now and then into folds and undulations, as of drapery. (See views of the Staubbach.) From this fall, through the narrow valley of the Lutschine, is offered a distant vista gleam of the stainless Jungfrau, which towers far above the limits of perpetual snow, having an altitude of thirteen thousand seven hundred and twenty feet. The Jungfrau signifies the "Maiden," or the "Virgin mountain," and undoubtedly obtained its name from the purity and dazzling brightness of the snow and ice with which it is perpetually covered. This mountain is steep and precipitous, and it is but recently that travelers have succeeded in reaching its summit. (See views of the Jungfrau.)

Three miles north-east of the Jungfrau, is the Mouch, one of the loftiest of the Alpine peaks of Switzerland, having an altitude of thirteen thousand and forty-four feet. (See views of the Mouch.)

Two miles from Lake Thun the White Lutschine is joined by the Black Lutschine. The road up the valley of the latter stream leads to the valley of the Grindelwald and the Magic peak of the Wetterhorn. The valley of Grindelwald is surrounded on all sides by lofty and imposing mountain peaks, and is one of the most fertile and picturesque Alpine districts in Switzerland. It covers about fifty square miles, being about four miles wide and twelve miles long. Two immense glaciers branch off from the mass of snow and ice which clothe the Bernese Oberland, and furnish the principal inducement to tourists to visit the valley. (See views of the Grindelwald glaciers.)

On the right of the Grindelwald valley is the Wetterhorn, signifying "Peak of Tempest," one of the grandest and most picturesque mountains of Switzerland. It belongs to the group of the Bernese Oberland, and reaches an altitude, according to various authorities, of from twelve thousand two hundred to fourteen thousand one hundred and five feet. The summit is clothed with ice and snow, and is reached by a precipitous and irregular foot-path. (See views of the Wetterhorn.)

The Simmenthal valley is watered by the Simmen river, which has a course of thirty-five miles, and joins the Kander near where the latter empties into Lake Thun. In the Simmenthal valley the river flows through a deep, narrow, and romantic gorge, and has a number of beautiful falls and cascades. (See views of falls in the gorge of Simmen.) In this valley, also, is found the Peak of Amertenhorn, unsurpassed by few mountains of Switzerland in hight and grandeur. (See views.)

The Gastern, or Gasternthal valley, on the southern frontier of the state of Bern, is drained by a small stream called the Kander, which has a number of beautiful falls and cascades. This valley has scarcely a rival in savage grandeur, having for its background the great Tschingel glacier, which is between the peaks of the Schlithorn and Sackhorn, both of which attain an elevation of nine thousand feet. (See views in the Gasternthal valley.) A foot-path extends from this valley over the Hochweyden Alps and Lotschen glacier, to the valley of Lotschen, canton of Valais. The valley of Kanderthal is also drained by the Kander river, and contains the peaks of Doldenhorn, Eschinensee, Birrenstock and Fissistock. (See views.)

Bern contains the lakes of Neufchatel, Bienne, Thun, and Brienz, all of which are celebrated for the wildness and grandeur of their scenery.

The soil in the valleys of Bern is exceedingly rich, and the mountains are covered with majestic forests of pine. The canton has mines of iron, copper, lead, and marble.

BERN,

The capital, is finely built on a peninsula in the river Aar, which is here crossed by two substantial stone bridges. It has a large and imposing cathedral, an observatory, a museum of natural history, an arsenal, a public library, a mint, and manufactories of fire-arms, hats, paper, and leather. Population, twenty-nine thousand and sixteen.

INTERLAKEN

Is a village on the Aar, canton of Bern, consisting of a number of white-washed lodging-houses, and containing a subscription reading-room and library. It is a great summer resort. (See view.)

GRISONS,

Next to Bern the largest canton of Switzerland, is in the eastern part of that republic, and covers an area of two thousand nine hundred and seventy-five square miles. Population in 1860, ninety-one thousand one hundred and seventy-seven.

The canton is divided into three great valley-districts, the most important of which is the valley of the Rhine, occupying nearly the whole of the western portion of the canton. The valley or mountain pass of Albula extends across Mount Albula from the valley of Bergun to the Upper Engadine, and from the basin of the Rhine to that of the Inn. (See views in the valley of Albula.) The most remarkable feature, however, in connection with the surface of the Grisons, is the gorge of Viamala, a deep mountain defile, four miles long, between Chur and the Splugen. It is walled in by rocky precipices, sixteen hundred feet high, which nearly overarch the gorge, frequently approaching, at the top, within ten yards of each other, while far below, in the depths of the chasm, the Hinter Rhine darts like an arrow in its onward course. The walls run nearly parallel to each other, each indentation on one side corresponding to the projection on the other. The lower portion of this gorge was long deemed inaccessible, and had received the name of the Lost Gulf; but a difficult and precipitous road has recently been constructed about four hundred feet above the river, by means of blasting and cutting. The road is protected by a canopy of rocky projections and wooden roofing, from the rocks and stones which are hurled from the hights above. It winds from one side of the gorge to the other by means of three bridges, built about four hundred feet above the stream. Yet, so narrow is the chasm, that, during the flood of 1834, the river rose and washed away the upper bridge, and reached within a few feet of the others. (See views of the Viamala.)

There are two hundred and forty glaciers in the Grisons, one of which, Rheinwald, forms the source of the Hinter Rhine. In the valleys of the Grisons are a number of villages, more noted for their beautiful situations and grandeur of the scenery which surrounds them, than for size and wealth. Among these may be mentioned Schiersch, Grusch, Malix, Rhazuns, and Alvaschein. The village of Fideris is in the Landquart valley, twelve miles north-east of Chur. Klosters is on the Landquart, four miles north-east of Fideris. (See views.)

GLARUS

Is a canton of Switzerland, between St. Gall, the Grisons, Schwytz, and Uri, containing an area of two hundred and eighty square miles. The chief river, Linth, having a course of twenty-five miles, and its affluents, enter Lake Wallenstatt. It flows through a picturesque country, and on its banks is Glarus, the capital of the canton, in the rear of which rises Glarnisch, a steep and precipitous mountain, the peak of which is eight thousand nine hundred and twenty-five feet above the level of the sea. (See views.) The culminating point of this canton, and also of East Switzerland, is Mount Dodi, having an altitude of eleven thousand eight hundred and eighty-seven feet. The chief town is

GLARUS,

The capital, on the Linth, at the foot of Mount Glarnisch, containing a hospital, free school, public library and reading-room, and manufactories of muslins, cottons, woolen cloths, etc. Population of the city, four thousand and eighty-two. (See views.)

Population of the canton, thirty-three thousand three hundred and sixty-three.

VALAIS

Is a canton in the south-eastern part of Switzerland, bounded on the north by Vand and Bern, and on the south by Italy.

Area, about two thousand and sixteen square miles; population in 1860, ninety thousand seven hundred and ninety-two. It forms a single long and deep valley, between the Bernese and Pennine Alps, two of the loftiest mountain chains of Europe, and is drained by the Rhone, which originates in the glacier of Gallenstock, (see view) and enters Lake Geneva. This valley has been described as an immense trough, seventy miles in length, one and one-half miles in depth, and two miles wide at the bottom. The higher elevations are covered with the greatest of Swiss glaciers, and the whole canton is exposed to impetuous torrents and destructive avalanches. In the north are the Goimsel and Gemmi, and in the south the Great St. Bernard and Simplon passes.

Two important peaks of this canton are Mont Rosa, having an altitude of fifteen thousand two hundred and eight feet, and Mount Cervin, having an altitude of fourteen thousand seven hundred and seventy-one feet. The former is inferior in hight only to Mount Blanc, of the Pennine Alps, from which it is fifty miles distant. (See view of Mont Rosa.)

The cultivated portion of Valais comprises a strip of land from one-half to three-fourths of a mile wide, on each side of the Rhone. Considerable quantities of corn are here produced. A railroad ascends this valley as far as Sion. The chief towns are Sion, the capital, Martigny, and Vispach.

The other cantons of Switzerland, not yet described, are Aargau, Appenzell, Basel, Freyburg, Geneva, Lucerne, Neufchatel, St. Gall, Schaffhausen, Swytz, Soleure, Ticino, Thurgau, Unterwalden, Uri, Vaud, Zug, and Zurich. The best cultivated are Basel, Aargau, Thurgan, Vaud, and Geneva. The chief productions are spelt, wheat, rye, barley, Turkish corn, oats, and tobacco.

The chief cities are Geneva, Bern, Basel, Lausanne, Zurich, St. Gall, Lucerne, Freyburg, Neufchatel, Schaffhausen, Soleure, Lugano, Aarau, Glarus, and Appenzell.

GENEVA,

The most populous city of Switzerland, and capital of a canton of its own name, occupies the slope of two hills, at the western end of Lake Geneva, where that body discharges the Blue Rhone. The city is built on both sides of the river, which is crossed by several bridges. The lower portion of the city is the chief district of trade, and is irregularly and poorly built. The upper portion, however, the seat of the aristocracy, contains a large number of elegant hotels and private residences and villas.

The most important public buildings are the cathedral, town house, casino, penitentiary, and Musee Rath, a tasty building named after its founder. The cathedral is a Gothic edifice, flanked by three massive towers, and occupying a commanding situation on the highest ground in the city. Among the educational establishments may be mentioned the Calvin college and academy. Geneva has a museum of natural history, a botanic garden, and is extensively engaged in the manufacture of watches and jewelry. It is surrounded on three sides by walls, and is entered by three gates. Population twenty-nine thousand one hundred and eight. (See views of Geneva.)

ST. GALL,

A city and capital of a canton of the same name, is eighteen miles south-east of Constance, in a mountain valley, two thousand one hundred and fifty feet above sea-level. The environs of the city are beautiful, and contain many fine walks and promenades. It contains a cathedral, monastery, town house, post office, three churches, a public square, a number of fountains, and manufactories of linen, cotton, fine muslins, etc. Population in 1860, fourteen thousand five hundred and thirty-two. (See views of St. Gall.)

APPENZELL,

An important city of Switzerland, and capital of Inner Rhodes, in the canton of Appenzell, is six miles south of St. Gall. It has a number of churches, a council house, an arsenal, baths, and manufactories of linen. Population two thousand nine hundred and ten, chiefly Roman Catholics. (See view of Appenzell.)

CHAPTER IV.

AUSTRIA, PRUSSIA, GERMANY, AND RUSSIA.

AUSTRIA.

Austria, next to Russia, is the largest province of Europe. The inhabitants are of different races, speaking as many different languages. The general surface is mountainous, abounding in beautiful and romantic scenery. The plains are not extensive, occupying less than one-fifth of the surface. The principal valleys are found in Tyrol, Solsburg, Styria, and Illyria. The loftiest mountains are in Tyrol, Styria, and Illyria.

VIENNA,

The capital and largest city of Austria, is situated on a branch of the Danube, about two miles from the main stream. It consists of the city proper and upwards of thirty suburbs. The most important of the church edifices, are the Cathedral of St. Stephen, a massive gothic structure three hundred and fifty feet long, by two hundred and thirty-five deep, ninety feet high, and built of hewn limestone ; and the court parish church, founded by Frederick the Fair, in 1330. It contains a beautiful monument to the Archduchess, Christina, and in the chapel the hearts of the imperial family are preserved. Among the palaces and government edifices are the imperial palace, the palaces of Archduke Charles, Belvedere, one built by Prince Eugene, and those of Count Schonborn, Prince Auersperg, etc. The chief government buildings are the national bank, mint, town house, and the Imperial and Civil arsenals, in both of which are collections of ancient armor. The monuments of the city are not numerous. The finest are an equestrian and colossal statue of Joseph II., one of the late Emperor Francis I., the monument and statue to the Virgin, and the marble statue of Theseus. (See views in Vienna.)

LINZ,

A city of upper Austria, is fortified by a circle of thirty-two forts, nine on the north side of the Danube, and twenty-three on the south side. The city is well built, and has three suburbs, larger than the city proper. The river is here crossed by a wooden bridge two hundred and eighty yards in length. The city contains several fine churches, a bank, theater, custom house, and an old castle. (See views of Linz.)

TYROL,

A division of Austria, occupies the south-western portion of that province. It is for the most part a mountainous region, being crossed by three ranges of the Alps, the center range dividing it into two parts. The summits of many of these mountains are covered with perpetual snow, and glaciers to the number of eighty, covering an area of one hundred and seventy square miles, descend into the valleys. The scenery of Tyrol is second only to Switzerland. The principal rivers are the Danube, Po, and Rhine. These rivers are fed by numerous streams and torrents from the glaciers and regions of perpetual snow. Brenaver, one of the culminating points of the mountains of Tyrol, has an elevation of six thousand seven hundred and eighty-eight feet above the sea. The road between Insprick and Brexen crosses this mountain at an elevation of four thousand six hundred and fifty feet. (See views among the mountains of Tyrol.)

SALTZBURG,

A city of Tyrol, has a picturesque site at the base of two precipitous hights. The scenery around this city is scarcely surpassed by the finest and most romantic parts of Switzerland. The greater part of the town is built on the left bank of the Salza. In this part of the city is a lofty hight, crowned by a magnificent ancient castle. The principal squares are Resideng and the Damplatz. Between these is an Italian Cathedral, adjoining to which is the Archbishop's palace. In the same vicinity is the collegiate church of St. Peter, and a cemetery distinguished for its remarkable ancient tombs. The castle has been sometime used for barracks. In one of the towers is preserved a part of the torturing apparatus employed on the protestants, who were here cruelly persecuted, and some of whom suffered martyrdom. (See views of Saltzburg.)

BORMIO,

A town of Tyrol, Austria, is about twenty-nine miles from the Adda, on which occur the ancient and celebrated salt baths called Bagni di Bormio. (See views of Baths.)

PRUSSIA.

The kingdom of Prussia ranks as a leading power of Europe. By its late victories over Austria, it has added to its territory, Hanover, Holstein, Hesse-Cassel, Nassau, and several other divisions. The surface is generally level, the mountains occurring only in the south and south-western parts of the country. The soil is fertile and productive. Prussia lies in the basins of the North and Baltic seas, and is drained by large rivers, the most celebrated of which is the Rhine. Along this river the scenery is mountainous and picturesque. The inhabitants are mostly Germans, and are well educated and intelligent people. All children are obliged by law to attend school until they are fourteen years old.

BERLIN,

The capital, is, next to Vienna, the largest city of Central Europe, and is remarkable for the regularity of its streets, the size and beauty of its buildings, and for its institutions of science and art. It is finely located on both sides of the Spree, is about ten miles in circumference, and comprises the city proper, Cologne, Lewsenstadt, Friedrichstadt, Friedrichswerder, Neustadt, Friedrich Wilhelmstadt, and the suburbs of Stralhau, Spandau and Konigstadt, Oranienburg and Potsdam. Forty bridges cross the Spree and its branches at this place. The city is enclosed by a wall sixteen feet high. One of the gates through which the city is entered, is one of the most splendid in Europe.

Among the numerous public buildings are the royal palace and castle, the palaces of the princes, the museum, arsenal, opera house, and university. (See views in Berlin.)

COLOGNE,

A city of Prussia, situated on the Rhine, is one of the most populous in the kingdom. It is connected with Deutz, on the opposite side of the river, by a handsome double bridge. The cathedral is the greatest object of interest in the town, and is the best specimen of Gothic monuments in Europe. It was begun in 1248, is five hundred and eleven feet in length, and two hundred and thirty-one in breadth. The roof is supported by one hundred columns, the center four of which are thirty feet in circumference. The cost of the completion of this structure is estimated at seven hundred and fifty thousand pounds. This part of the work was commenced in 1842. The city contains eight chapels, a synagogue and twenty-seven churches. (See views in Cologne.)

COBLENTZ,

A fortified city of Prussia, is situated on the Rhine, about fifty miles from Cologne. The Rhine is here crossed by a bridge of boats. The city is well and regularly built, and contains a noble palace and several fine churches, the residences of several families of the nobility, valuable collections of coins, minerals and antiquities, and a town library. (See views in Coblentz.)

BACHARACH,

A walled town, is on the left bank of the Rhine, about twenty-three miles from Coblentz. (See views.)

ANDERNACH

Is a town of Prussia, on the Rhine, about ten miles from Coblentz. It has become distinguished for the production of millstones and cement. (See views.)

GERMANY.

Germany comprises Bavaria, Saxony, Baden, Wurtemberg, a number of smaller states, three free cities, and a part of Prussia and Austria. The inhabitants are an industrious and intelligent people. The free cities are Hamburg, Bremen, and Lubeck. Many of the smaller towns are noted for remarkable historical events, and others for their magnificent palaces, churches and universities.

HAMBURG,

A commercial city of Germany, is situated on the river Elbe. Within the city is a lake called the Inner Alster. This is a favorite place of resort for the inhabitants, and during some seasons of the year the lake is covered with pleasure boats. The canal and branches of the Alster river pass through the city. In many places the buildings come to the waters edge, and communications between the buildings are carried on by means of boats. (See views of Hamburg.)

LIMBURG,

An ancient town of Germany, on the Lahn, has a hospital, a Roman Catholic seminary, and a palace. (See views.)

WEILBURG,

On the Lahn, contains a castle and manufactories of paper. The river is crossed by an iron bridge. (See views.)

NEUBURG

Contains a theatre, museum, barracks, a church, a castle, remains of ancient fortifications, and a royal institute. The river Danube is here crossed by two bridges. (See views.)

CANNSTATT

Is in a beautiful and fertile valley of Wurtemburg. Near the town are a number of mineral springs. It contains the royal seats of Bellevue and Rosenstein. (See views.)

NENHAUS

Contains a handsome palace of Count Czernin, and a Jesuit college. (See views.)

BADEN BADEN,

A celebrated watering place, and summer resort for visitors from all parts of Europe, is in Germany, in the valley of Schwarzwald. Over the principal spring, a pump-house has been erected, from which water is conveyed by numerous pipes to different hotels for the accommodation of visitors. (See views.)

RUSSIA.

Russia is the largest empire in the world, embracing European Russia, Siberia and Trans-caucasian Russia. Russian America also belonged to this empire until 1867, when it was purchased by the United States government. The surface is for the most part, very level, the only mountainous section being north of the Caucasus mountains. The government is an absolute monarchy. The people are divided into four classes—the nobles, clergy, merchants, and the recently emancipated serfs.

ST. PETERSBURG,

The capital, is situated on the river Neva, near its mouth. It is the largest and most populous city of the empire, and in the splendor of its public buildings, is surpassed by few cities. The most distinguished of the ecclesiastical edifices is the cathedral of our Lady of Kezan. It is in the form of a Greek cross, and cost upwards of twenty millions of dollars. The Winter palace, probably the most magnificent in the world, is seven hundred feet square, and during the residence of the emperor within it, is inhabited by six thousand people. The city was founded by Peter the Great, in 1703. The little cottage in which he lived, is in the city in a remarkable state of preservation.

MOSCOW,

Formerly the capital, and at present a famous city of Russia, is about four hundred miles from St. Petersburg. The site of the city is on undulating ground. On the highest eminence, near the center of the city, stands the Kremlin, which is of a triangular shape, surrounded by a wall sixty feet high, and nearly a mile in circuit. Among the buildings of the Kremlin is the famous Ivan Veliki, rising without ornament to the hight of two hundred and nine feet, surmounted by a gilded dome, on which is a cross. This tower consists of a number of stories, in each of which is suspended a massive bell, one of which weighs sixty-four tons. Another bell, weighing about one hundred and ninety tons, is on a pedestal of granite in the bottom of the tower. The tower in which it was first suspended was burnt, and the bell in falling was broken. Its hight is upwards of twenty-one feet, its circumference twenty-two and a half feet, and its least thickness three inches. (See views in Moscow.)

CHAPTER V.

ITALY AND PAPAL STATES.

ITALY,

Formerly the center of the Roman Empire, comprises a number of islands in the Mediterranean sea, and a large peninsula, between the latter body and the Adriatic sea. It lies between latitude 47° and including Sicily, 36° 41′ 30″ north, and longitude 6° 35′ and 18° 35′ east. Its greatest length from north to south, is six hundred miles; from east to west, three hundred miles; area, one hundred and seventeen thousand nine hundred and fourteen square miles.

The Alps separate Italy from France, Switzerland, and Austria, and send ramifications over the northern part of the country. The Apennine mountain range winds through the entire length of the peninsula from north to south. The valleys between the mountains are extremely fertile, and well adapted to cultivation. The Apennines contribute beauty and grandeur to central Italy, which in the southern districts assumes a wilder aspect. In the vicinity of Mount Vesuvius and the city of Naples, the scenery approaches almost a savage grandeur. This volcanic peak rises out of a fertile and luxuriant plain, three thousand nine hundred and forty-eight feet above the sea. The crater is fifteen hundred feet in diameter, and five hundred feet deep. Around the base of Vesuvius are immense fields of hardened lava and scoriæ, which have been ejected from the volcano. Its first recorded eruption occurred in A. D. 63, and in 79 the cities of Herculaneum, Pompeii, and Stabiæ, were buried in lava and ashes, which were emitted from this volcano. The site of Herculaneum was discovered in 1713, but though extensively excavated, only a small portion of the ancient theater is visible. Pompeii, not having been buried in lava, but ashes, is much more easily excavated than Herculaneum, and a large number of statues, urns, etc., here found, have been deposited in the museum at Naples. After being buried nearly eighteen hundred years, these cities are gradually being removed of their covering, and are found to be in a remarkable state of preservation. (See views of Herculaneum, Pompeii, and Vesuvius.)

Sicily is crossed by a mountain chain from east to west, known first as Neptunian, and afterwards as Madonian mountains. This chain so greatly resembles the Appenines, and the physical character of the Strait of Messina is such as to give strength to the assertion that Sicily formerly constituted a part of the mainland, from which it has been separated by some terrible convulsion of nature. The prevalence of earthquakes, and the frequency of volcanic eruptions, are facts that further support this theory. Etna, Stromboli, and Lipari, are still subject to terrible eruptions. The former is an isolated peak, forming a perfect cone, which has a circumference at its base of eighty-seven miles, and is one of the greatest curiosities of the world. It has an altitude of ten thousand eight hundred and seventy-four feet. It is nearly encircled, except on the east, where it is bordered by the sea, by the Alcantara and Giaretta rivers. There are about sixty recorded eruptions of Etna, the most remarkable of which are those of the years 1669, 1792, 1811, 1819, and 1832. Numerous new vents were formed near the summit in 1832, from which issued sheets of flame, and immense quantities of ashes and cinders. In 1669, one of these burning streams of molten matter overtopped the ramparts of Catania, sixty feet in hight, and fell in a fiery cascade into the city, a part of which it destroyed. It however, ultimately cooled, and the solid lava may still be seen curling over the top of the rampart, like a cascade in the act of falling. (See view.) In the northern part of Italy are the great plains of Lombardy, which are drained by the river Po.

The rivers of Italy, owing chiefly to the narrowness of the country, are generally small, sometimes obstructed with rapids, and navigable only for small boats. The Po is much the largest, and rises in Mount Piso. Among the others may be mentioned

Adige, Brenta, Piave, Tagliamento, Aterno, Saugro, Metauro, Ofanto, Arno, and Tiber. The chief lakes are Como, Garda, Maggiore, Lugano, Iseo, and a part of Geneva. The Como lake might properly be regarded as an expansion of the Adda river, which enters it at the foot of the Rhetian Alps, and flows from it at Lecco. It is environed on the south by mountains from one thousand to thirteen hundred feet in hight, and is separated into its two branches of Como and Lecco by a peninsular projection known as Bellagio. It is thirty-five miles long, and three miles wide, and is surrounded by the richest of Italian scenery. The water abounds with fish, and the lake is exposed to sudden storms, which greatly impede water communication. On the shore are a number of villas, among which may be mentioned Villa Lenno, on the supposed site of Pliny's villa, and Villa d' Este, once the residence of Caroline, Queen of England. (See views of Como.)

The climate of Italy is varied. In the north flourishes vegetation peculiar to the temperate zone, while in the south it reaches the richness and luxuriance of that in tropical countries. The singular clearness of the atmosphere sets off the landscape beauties of Italy with brilliant effect, giving a brightness of color, and distinctness of outline rarely known in other countries. The lakes in the basin of the river Po, and the lagoons and marshes of Venice are frequently frozen in winter, but the climate of Calabria, Sicily, and the adjacent islands, is such as to promote the vegetation of the tropical zone. Silk is extensively manufactured in the northern provinces, and sugar-cane flourishes in Sicily. Corn is produced in large quantities, as is also cotton, hemp, flax, oil, rice, olives, wine, and fruits.

Florence is the capital of Italy, and Naples, Milan, Turin, Venice, Geneva, Leghorn, and Verona are the most important towns.

FLORENCE

Is an important city and capital of Italy, in the division of Tuscany, chiefly on the northern bank of the Arno river. The river is here spanned by four bridges, the finest of which, Ponte del la Santa Trinita, remarkable for its light and graceful architecture, is constructed of marble, has three arches, and is adorned with statues. The general appearance of Florence is neat and prepossessing. The streets, though narrow, are clean, and are lined with public and private edifices of every description and style. There are a great many noble and elegant palaces, among which the Pitti palace, the former residence of Luca Pitti, and now of the grand duke, holds a conspicuous place. (See view.) The most important building of Florence is the Cathedral of Santa Maria del Flore, an imposing structure, surmounted by a dome, the largest in the world. The walls are of brick, and are incrusted with marble. Among the other buildings may be mentioned the church of Santa Croce, containing the ashes of Michael Angelo, Galileo, and other celebrated men, the church of St. John, now used as a city baptistery, the Biblioteca Marucelliana, Magliabecchian, and Laurentian libraries, the latter of which occupies a long and lofty gallery, with windows of stained glass. Florence is surrounded by a wall, four and one-fourth miles in circuit, and is entered by seven gates. Population in 1862, one hundred and fourteen thousand three hundred and sixty-three.

NAPLES,

Formerly the capital of the state of Naples, and at present capital of Napoli, is the most populous city of Italy. It is near the north-eastern extremity of the Bay of Naples, at the base of Mount Vesuvius, one hundred and eighteen miles south-east of Rome. Opposite Vesuvius, on the east, rises the peak of Pausilippo, and in the background recede the ramifications of the Apennines. The city itself has scarcely a rival in beauty of location and grandeur of surrounding scenery. The streets are paved with blocks of hardened lava, and, with but few exceptions, are straight and clean. The most important building is a fine Gothic cathedral, occupying the site of a Temple of Apollo, and containing relics of St. Januarius. The royal palace is an immense building, three stories high, each of which is composed of a different order of architecture. Its original design has not been carried out, but it is richly furnished, and adorned with paintings, statues, etc. (See views.) The other buildings worthy of note are the Palace of Capo di Monte, the Palazzo Degli Studij Publici, a building of the seventeenth century, the churchs Dei Santi Apostoli, St. Martin, St. Philip de Neri, Del Parto, and San Severo, and royal library. The chief manufactures are silk, lace, gloves, carriages, soap, violins and other musical instruments, hats, woollen, linen, etc. Population, four hundred and eighteen thousand nine hundred and sixty-eight.

TURIN,

One of the most important cities of Italy, and capital of Piedmont, is on a rich plain among the Alps, on the right bank of the river Po, at the mouth of the Dora Susina, eighty miles south-west of Milan. The most important building is the cathedral, the interior of which is richly ornamented with frescoes and paintings, and containing the remarkable chapel of Santo Sudario. Among the other ecclesiastical buildings may be mentioned the churches of San Filippo Neri, Santa Christina, Corpus Christi, Sant 'Andrea, and San Rocco. Turin has a university, an Episcopal seminary, a royal military academy, and two colleges. Population in 1862, one hundred and eighty thousand five hundred and twenty.

MILAN,

Third city in size in Italy, is on a fertile plain, between the basins of the Ticino and Adda, eighty miles north-east of Turin, and one hundred and seventy-five miles west of Venice. The city is encircled by a wall, and is entered through eleven gates. The buildings are generally of brick, and frequently have elegant exteriors.

The chief object of interest, however, of Milan, is the cathedral, a massive structure, which ranks in size and beauty of architecture among the finest buildings of the world. It is in a square in the heart of the city, called Piazza del Duomo, and is four hundred and ninety feet long, two hundred and ninety-eight feet wide, and three hundred and fifty-five feet high to the apex of the dome, above which rises an obelisk spire. Around the roof and sides of the building are four thousand six hundred niches, of which four thousand are occupied by statues. The interior is as gorgeous as the exterior, almost overcoming the beholder, who gazes in rapt wonder at the splendor and magnificence of the countless objects which surround him. The floor is formed of marble of various colors, the arches of the naves are supported by fifty immense pillars, the walls are adorned with the work of the most renowned painters, and the windows with groups of figures of a size probably unequaled in the world. (See views of Milan cathedral.) Other important buildings are the churches of Sant' Ambrogio, Sant' Eustorgio, and Santa Maria della Passione. Milan has a royal academy of arts and sciences, a normal school, a military and geographical institute, and a military, orphan, and several foundling asylums. Population in 1862, one hundred and ninety-six thousand three hundred and eighty.

VENICE,

A city of Italy, and semi-capital of the Lombardo-Venetian kingdom, is situated in the lagoons of Venice, a swampy district resembling a vast lake, which is separated from the Adriatic by a narrow strip of land, and connected with the main land by a bridge of two hundred and twenty-two arches, and two miles long. Venice was formerly the greatest commercial city in the world. Its site is formed by eighty small islands, separated by one hundred and fifty canals, and united by three hundred and sixty bridges. The most important buildings are the Palazzo di San Marco, and the church of San Marco. The latter may justly be regarded as one of the grandest and most interesting buildings in Christendom. It is of the Byzantine style, partly of Gothic and partly of the Italian order, and is constructed in the form of a Greek cross. It is flanked by five domes, the central one being ninety feet high, and the others each eighty feet. The main front has five hundred columns of black, white, and veined marble, and terminates in pointed arches supporting crosses, pinacles, and spires. "Over the portal of this magnificent temple were replaced, in 1815, the four celebrated bronze horses which were found at Corinth, and successively adorned Athens, Rome, Constantinople, Venice, and Paris." Among the other buildings may be mentioned the churches of Santa Maria Gloriosa dei Frari, La Madonna dell 'Orto, San Francisco, Santa Maria della Salute, and San Giovannie Paolo.

Venice has a lyceum, marine college, normal high school, and an academy and school of the fine arts. Population one hundred and eighteen thousand one hundred and seventy-two.

VERONA

Is a city of Italy, government of Venice, on the Adige, twenty miles east of Venice. The city was founded by the Romans in the fourth century before the Christian era, and has still relics of Roman architecture. The most important of these antiquities is the celebrated ampitheatre, the most perfect of its kind, and the only one in which public exhibitions are still held. (See view.) The principal buildings are the churches of St. Zeno, St. Anastasia, and St. George. The city has a botanic garden, a philharmonic academy, two valuable libraries, and manufactures of cottons and woollens, and an extensive trade in silk and rural produce. Population fifty-nine thousand one hundred and sixty-nine.

POZZUOLI,

Is an important town of Naples, seven miles south-west of the city of Naples. Population eight thousand four hundred. Its environs were formerly crowded with villas of wealthy Romans, and contain the ruins of an amphitheatre. (See view.)

CAPUA

Is a fortified city of Italy, twenty miles north of Naples. It was built by the Lombards in 855, out of the ruins of ancient Capua, the remains of which, about two miles east, include a gate, and the ruins of a large amphitheatre. The only important building in the town is the cathedral. Population eight thousand one hundred. (See view.)

PAPAL STATES.

The territory belonging to the Papal States formerly occupied Central Italy, stretching from the Mediterranean to the Adriatic, and from Naples to the river Po. It has recently been greatly reduced by the incursions of Italy, and, at present, comprises only the states of Roma et Comarca, Velletri, Viterbo, Civita Vecchia, and Frosinone.

The country, though generally rugged and hilly, has few mountains. The Pontine Marshes is the name of a swampy tract of land, twenty-five miles long, which lie along the Mediterranean sea, between Cisterna and Terracina. During the time of the Romans, these marshes were intersected by a number of canals, which rendered a considerable portion of them dry; but they have recently been neglected, and allowed to return to their former condition. The Appian Way, formed by the Romans, is the present road from Rome to Naples.

The chief river, the Tiber, originating in the Tuscan Apennines, has a course of one hundred and eighty-five miles, and enters the Mediterranean through two mouths, seventeen miles below Rome. In the spring, the river, generally sluggish, is rapid, and brings down with it a yellowish mud, which caused it to be called "Yellow Tiber." It is three hundred feet wide at Rome.

The Papal States enjoy one of the finest climates in the world. The intense heat of summer is greatly mitigated by refreshing sea-breezes, which originate in the Mediterranean. The soil is rich, and is generally well cultivated.

ANCIENT ROME.

This city was the capital of ancient Italy, and was built on the left bank of the Tiber. It was founded by Romulus, and laid out in the form of a square. The city became rapidly extended under the direction of the early Roman Kings, who founded buildings still famous in history, and embellished the city with works of utility and art. In the reign of Servius Tullius, the city had covered the famous seven hills—Palatine, Capitoline, Quirinal, Cælian, Aventine, Viminal, and Esquilline. The city being laid in ashes by the Gauls in 390, B. C., was hastily rebuilt, with little regard to regularity or beauty. After the wars with Carthage, numerous buildings of great architectural pretentions were planned and executed, while the narrow and filthy streets were left unmolested. In the reign of Nero the city was burned a second time, to gratify, it is said by various authorities, the curiosity of the reigning prince. Be that as it may, it is certain that when Rome revived from her ashes, she presented an entirely different aspect than before. The city was entirely remodeled, the hight of the houses being restricted, and the streets widened and straightened. In the reign of Vespasian, the city was thirteen miles in circumference, and had a population of over two millions. The wall built by Romulus enclosed merely the Palatine, and was pierced by three gates. That of Servius Tullius was not continuous, but consisted of fortifications drawn across the intervening valleys, and was pierced by thirty-seven gates. The walls of Aurelian, with the exception of the portions beyond the Tiber, are the same as those that surround the modern city.

The principal public place in the city was the Forum, an oblong open space, where were held the assemblies of the people. It was surrounded with arched porticos, within which were spacious halls, where courts of justice might sit on private affairs. The Campus Martius, or Field of Mars, was a large plain without the city, where was practiced the use of arms, athletic exercises, and sports. It was adorned with statues of famous men, and triumphal arches, columns and porticos, and other magnificent structures. One of the most interesting buildings of Ancient Rome is the Flavian Amphitheatre, or Colliseum, commenced by Vespasian, and completed by his son Titus. It is probably the largest structure of its kind, and is fortunately, also, the best preserved. It is of an elliptical form, is six hundred and twenty feet long, five hundred and thirteen feet broad, and was capacious enough to seat eighty-seven thousand persons.

Five thousand beasts were slain in the arena, on the occasion of the dedication, and the games and sports of the amphitheatre lasted one hundred days. " The exterior is about one hundred and sixty feet in hight, and consists of three rows of columns, doric, ionic and corinthian, and, above all, a row of corinthian pilasters." (See views of Amphitheatre.)

The celebrated Via Sacra was the chief street of the city, remains of which can still be seen in the Forum of Modern Rome. According to various authorities, the city contained four hundred temples, of which the Feretrian Jupiter was the oldest, having been founded by Romulus, and restored by Augustus. There was, also, a number of elegant palaces, the most noted of which was the Palatium, formerly the residence of the orator Hortensus, and afterward the seat of the imperial family. Two palaces, exceeding the latter in beauty, were built by Nero, one of which covered the whole of Palatine Hill and a portion of Esquilline, and was burned down during the great fire.

MODERN ROME

Occupies a sandy plain on both sides of the Tiber, and is divided by that stream into two unequal parts. The wall enclosing the city is twelve miles in circuit, and is pierced by sixteen gates. About one-half of the section enclosed is occupied by pleasure grounds, gardens, and vineyards, which lie south of the capitol. The most densely populated, as well as the business part, is on the site of the ancient Field of Mars. A street about one mile long, called the Corso, extends from Piazza del Popolo, the northern entrance, through the heart of the city, to the Plazza di Venezia, at the foot of the capitol. The houses on the Corso are regular and substantial, and consist of elegant churches and palaces, the Ghigi, Borghese and Ruspoli being found among the latter.

By far the finest building of Rome, and the most stupendous ever constructed, is the Cathedral, or Church of St. Peters, which is on the right bank of the Tiber, between the Vatican and Janiculum. The building is erected in the form of a Greek cross, and is approached through a richly ornamented piazza.

On either side of the latter, the buildings are hid from view by a magnificent colonnade, forming two semi-circular porticos of two hundred and eighty-four columns. On the entablement of the columns are one hundred and ninety-two statues of saints, each eleven feet high. The dome, rising four hundred and fifty-eight feet above the ground, is supported by four immense piers, and may justly be regarded as the most astonishing and perfect work of architecture ever submitted to the gaze of an admiring world. Within the cathedral everything is gorgeous beyond description. The walls are six hundred and seven feet long, and four hundred and fifty-eight feet wide. The Baldacchino, a splendid bronze canopy, under the dome, and immediately over the high altar, is one hundred and twenty feet above the floor. The interior of the dome is adorned with magnificent mosaic paintings. This truly wonderful building was produced by the genius of Bramante, Raphael, and Michael Angelo, and cost, with all of its embellishments, from sixty to eighty millions of dollars. (See views of St. Peter's.)

Among other ecclesiastical structures of Rome, may be mentioned the Santa Crose, richer in relics of ancient days, than in architecture. It is supposed to possess a portion of the cross of our Savior, and has mixed with its foundation earth brought from Jerusalem. St. John Lateran, regarded as mother church of the "Eternal City," occupies an isolated spot near the south wall, and is the place where the popes were formerly crowned. Among the other churches may be numbered Santa Maria Maggiore, Santa Agnese, St. Agostino, St. Antonio Abate, San Bonosa, and Santa Maria sopra Minerva.

Among the many palaces of Rome the Vatican, occupying a hill of the same name, in point of architecture and matter of history, is the most deserving of attention. It is regarded by various writers, as having been founded in the reign of Constantine, and is at present the seat of the Romish Popes. They first took possession of it in 1377, and from that period continued to embellish it till the time of the Pontificate of Alexander VI. It was by him renovated on a grander scale, and finished in nearly its present style. It covers a large square, and consists of an irregular pile of buildings, the entire mass being one thousand one hundred and fifty-one feet long, and seven hundred and sixty-seven feet wide. This great building has twenty courts, and four thousand four hundred and twenty-two apartments. (See views of the Vatican.)

The other palaces deserving notice are the Piazza del Campidoglio, on the summit of the capitol, in the piazza of which is a bronze equestrian statue of Marcus Aurelius Antonius; the Capitoline museum; and the Conservatori.

Among the educational establishments of Rome, the university is the most important. The school was founded by Leo X.; has forty-two professors, and is attended by one thousand students. There is also a Roman college, under the direction of the Jesuits, and twenty other colleges, three of which are English, Irish, and Scotch institutions.

Rome has numerous hospitals and charitable institutions, and is well supplied with theatres, museums, and enclosures for horse races and other public amusements. The manufactures are of little importance, consisting of woollen, silk fabrics, hats, gloves, etc. Population in 1863, two hundred and one thousand one hundred and sixty-one, including foreigners and strangers.

CHAPTER VI.

CHINA AND JAPAN.

China is a vast empire of Asia, stretching from 18° 20′ to 54° north latitude, and from 72° to 134° west longitude. Its greatest length from north to south is one thousand four hundred and seventy-four miles; from east to west, one thousand three hundred and fifty-five miles; area, four million seven hundred thousand square miles.

The outline of the country is very irregular. On the north of China is Asiatic Russia, from which it is nearly separated by the Altai mountain range and the Amoor river; on the south and south-west is Hindoostan,—separated by the Himalaya mountains—Birmah, and Tonquin; on the south-east and east are the China, Yellow, and Japan Seas; and on the west is Turkestan.

China is one of the most mountainous regions on the globe. All of the great mountain chains of Asia either intersect or bound the country. Owing to the rigid exclusion of foreigners, and the natural and artificial barriers which guard the frontier, the interior of China has been but imperfectly explored. The Himalaya mountains, the loftiest range in the world, lie in the south-western part of the empire, on the northern frontier of Hindoostan, and attain their greatest elevation with Mount Everest, the culminating point of the globe, at an altitude of twenty-nine thousand one hundred feet. The Himalaya mountains are continued to the sea by the Nanling range, which forms the water-shed between the Yang tse Kiang and Hong Kiang rivers. The Kuen Lun and Peling mountains constitute a grand chain extending through the central part of southern China. North of this chain branches off an irregular range called the Khin Gau mountains, which terminate in Siberia, at the northern extremity of the Channel of Tartary. The Altai mountains, after forming a portion of the boundary line between Russia and China, branch off in a north-easterly direction through the former empire, and extend to the north-eastern extremity of Siberia.

The Great Wall of China, perhaps the greatest monument of human industry and skill in existence, forms a barrier between Mongolia and China for about fifteen hundred miles. It was begun in 214 B. C., and completed in 204 B. C., and employed in its construction several millions of men at one time. Its design was to protect the country from the incursions of the Tartars from the north. It is twenty feet high, and is carried in a single instance over a mountain having an altitude of one mile. It is about twenty feet thick, and throughout its whole extent supports towers at regular intervals from each other, which were occupied by the archers and soldiers. "It has been estimated that the materials employed in this immense fortification would be sufficient for constructing a wall six feet high and two feet thick, twice around the world."

South of the Altai are the Thian Shan mountains, between which and the Kuen Lun range is the Great Desert of Gobi. It covers an area of about five hundred thousand square miles, and is covered with shingly gravel and fields of drifting sand. In the central part it is two thousand four hundred feet high; and at the great wall it has a hight of five thousand eight hundred feet; average height four thousand feet. The table land of Thibet, having an average elevation of eleven thousand feet, lies between the Kuen Lun and Himalaya ranges, and is traversed in every direction by the ramifications of these mountains.

The chief rivers of China are the Yang tse Kiang and Hoang Ho. The former rises on the southern slope of the Kuen Lun mountains, and has a course of about two thousand seven hundred miles; the latter, rising among the Peling mountains, has a course of two thousand miles, and both enter the Yellow Sea.

The Chinese belong to the Mongolian, or yellow race. They are generally low in stature, have black hair, thick lips, flat nose, expanded at the nostrils, and are generally of a dark complexion. The smallness of the hands and feet of the males, reaches almost a deformity with the females. The good qualities of a portion of the population, who are not debased by foreign intercourse, are counterbalanced by the immorality and vice of the majority of the people, who practice lying, deceit, treachery, and nameless abominations. Population of the empire, four hundred and seventy-seven millions.

The chief cities are Pekin, Canton, Soo-chow, Hang-Chow, Fuh-Chow, Amoy, and Shanghai.

CANTON,

The great emporium city of China, is on the left bank of the Canton river, seventy miles from the sea. It is very irregularly built, the streets being narrow and crooked, and averaging about eight feet in width. Canton has upwards of one hundred and twenty temples, fourteen high schools, and thirty colleges. Manufacturing is also extensively carried on. The poorer portions of the people live in mud huts, which line the canal, and one apartment is often crowded with from fifteen to twenty persons. The wealthy class reside in elegant and richly furnished houses. No wheeled carriages are used in the streets of Canton. The nobles and officers are borne by their attendants in sedan chairs, often taking up the whole of the walk, to the great annoyance of the foot passengers. The city is surrounded by a wall about seven miles in circuit, and is entered through twelve gates. Population, one million. (See views of Canton.)

MACAO

Is a city on the island of Macao, at the entrance of the Canton river, having a population of forty thousand. The harbor forms a semi-circle, around which is built the town, consisting chiefly of an intermingling of European and Chinese residences. The harbor is defended by six forts. The principal buildings are a number of Chinese temples, the church of St. Joseph and college of St. Joseph, a royal grammar school, and a female orphan asylum. (See views of Macao.)

THE EMPIRE OF JAPAN.

The several islands which comprise this empire are east of Asia, and have an area of one hundred and sixty thousand square miles. The surface is uneven and broken, rising in places to mountains of considerable elevation. The highest peak is about twelve thousand feet high. It was formerly a burning volcano, but now is a snow-capped mountain.

YEDDO,

The seat of the military emperor, and capital of the empire, has a population of two millions. It is surrounded by a trench, and contains a fortified castle, large temples and numerous public buildings.

MIAKO,

The ecclesiastical capital, is situated on a plain surrounded by mountains. It contains a strong citadel, a number of temples, in one of which is suspended the largest bell in the world. It is eighteen feet high, and weighs about one thousand tons. The population of the city is about five hundred thousand.

SIMONOSEKI

Is a small town and harbor of Japan, on the strait of Kioo Sioo, on Niphon Island. The site of the town is a plain partially surrounded by mountains. (See views of Somonoseki.)

NAGASAKI,

A foreign settlement, principal seaport, and commercial city of Japan, stands on a hill-side, and is regularly built. The harbor is about one mile in width and seven in length. Before the treaty which was recently concluded between the Japanese and the United States, this was the only port open to foreign commerce. The chief edifices in the town are the palaces of the nobility, the arsenal, theatres, and numerous temples, which are enclosed in gardens, forming a place of public resort for the people.

CHAPTER VII.

HISTORICAL AND DESCRIPTIVE SKETCH

OF

PALESTINE AND ADJACENT COUNTRIES.

The name *Palestine* or *Palestina* was at first applied to a small tract of country on the south-eastern shore of the Mediterranean sea. It received this name from the Philistines who settled it. The whole country inhabited by the Jews, God's chosen people, soon became known by this name, and, at the present time, it is called Palestine almost exclusively. This country, in ancient times, was also designated by a variety of other names, among which are the following: *Canaan*, so called from the fourth son of Ham, because it was first settled by descendants from his eleven sons; *Holy Land*, because it was inhabited by the Jews, who were the chosen people of God, and because it was the scene of the deeds, sufferings, and final triumph of the Savior; *Land of God*, because, under the Mosaic dispensation, God was considered as the Supreme Ruler of the land; *Land of Promise*, because God promised to Abraham that it should be peopled and owned by his posterity; *Land of Israel*, because the Israelites, descendants of Jacob or Israel, inhabited it; and *Land of Judah* or *Judea*, because the tribe of Judah was the largest of the Israelitish tribes.

Palestine is bounded on the "north by Syria, east by Syria and Arabia Deserta, south by Arabia Petraea, and west by the Mediterranean sea." When first occupied by the twelve tribes of Israel, the country was divided between them by lot. One-half of the tribe of Manasseh, and the tribes of Gad and Reuben, settled on the east of the river Jordan; the remaining nine tribes and the half tribe of Manasseh settled between Jordan and the Mediterranean sea. In the time of Christ, the country was divided into provinces. *Judea* occupied the southern part of Palestine east of the Jordan, and included the tribes of Judah, Simeon, Benjamin, and Dan; the name of *Samaria* was applied to the central part of the country, including the tribe of Ephraim and the half tribe of Manasseh; the province north of Samaria, including the tribes of Issachar, Zebulon, Asher, and Naphtali, was called *Galilee;* and the province of *Perea* was west of the Jordan. The country is about one hundred and eighty miles in length, and in width ranges from forty to ninety miles, being widest at the south.

In the time of Christ, Palestine belonged to the Roman empire. It was taken from them in the seventh century by the Mohammedans, who held it until 1099. From that time until 1291, the Crusaders were in possession of the country; from 1291 until 1517, the Egyptians; and since that time the Turkish government has held it.

The land is fertile and productive. Fig, pomegranate, olive, sycamore, palm, and oleander trees abound. The land is now the same as it was in the time of the prophets and apostles, but almost barren on account of neglect. The natural physical condition of the country is the same. "The hills still stand round about Jerusalem as they stood in the days of David and of Solomon. The dew falls in Hermon; the cedars grow in Lebanon, and Kishon, 'that ancient river,' (Judges, v:21,) still draws its stream from Tabor as in the times of old." "The Sea of Galilee still presents the same natural accompaniments; the fig tree springs up by the wayside (See views of Fig trees); the sycamore spreads its branches, and the vines and olives still climb the sides of the mountains. The desolation which covered the cities of the plain is not less striking at the present hour than when Moses, with an inspired pen, recorded the judgment of God. The swellings of the Jordan are not less regular in their rise than when the Hebrews first approached its banks; and he who goes down from Jerusalem to Jericho, still incurs the greatest hazard of falling among thieves. There is, in fact, in the scenery and manners of this ancient land a perpetuity that accords well with the everlasting import of its historical records, and which enables us to identify, with the utmost readiness, the local imagery of every great transaction."

MOUNTAINS.

Palestine is a very mountainous country. Its principal mountains are Lebanon, Hermon, Tabor, Carmel, Little Hermon, Gilboa, Ebal and Gerizin, Mountains of Ephraim, Mountains of Judah and Mountains of Jerusalem.

LEBANON.

The mountains of Lebanon are north of Palestine, in Syria. They consist of two principal ranges running parallel with the coast. The range nearer the sea is called Lebanon, the other Anti-Lebanon. They are divided by an extensive valley called Coele-Syria, or "the valley of Lebanon." The tops of the mountains are perpetually covered with snow, and, either on account of this, or from the fact that the limestone of which they are composed is white, they have received the name of *Lebanon*, which, in Hebrew, means the "White Mountains." As the snow is not in very large quantities, however, it is probably the white limestone which has given the name to the mountain. (See view No. 94.) These mountains are famous in sacred history for their lofty cedars. (See views of Cedars of Lebanon.) The celebrated temple of Solomon on Mount Moriah in Jerusalem was built chiefly of cedar of Lebanon. There are not at present many cedars found in Lebanon except in a space about three quarters of a mile in circumference at the base of one mountain.

HERMON.

This mountain forms the southern extremity of the anti-Lebanon range. It is also called *Sion*, *Shenir*, *Sirion*, and *Baal-hermon*. It is about ten thousand feet above the level of the sea. The "tower of Lebanon, which looketh toward Damascus," mentioned in Canticles vii:4, is supposed by some commentators to refer to Hermon, as it is the most lofty and imposing peak of the range. (See views of Mount Hermon.)

TABOR.

Mount Tabor is situated in the north-eastern extremity of the plain of Esdrælon, about six miles south-east of Nazareth, and fifty north-east of Jerusalem. In shape, it resembles a cone. It is about one thousand feet high, and may be ascended by an ancient path to the summit. The mountain is formed of limestone, and its sides are very nearly covered with trees and bushes. By some, this mountain is supposed to be the one upon which the Savior was transfigured; but this supposition has been proven groundless by very good evidence.

CARMEL.

This mountain, the highest peak of a range of the same name, is much renowned in Jewish history. The range of mountains extends from the plain of Esdrælon to the coast of the Mediterranean, south of the bay of Acre, a distance of five or six miles. The mountain, in shape resembling a flattened cone, is from fifteen hundred to two thousand feet above the level of the Mediterranean sea. (See view of Mount Carmel, No. 90.) Its soil in the time of the prophets was exceedingly fertile and productive, from which fact it derived its name *Carmel*, which signifies "a fruitful field," or "The Garden of God." It has now, in accordance with the prediction of the prophet (Amos i:2), lost a great deal of its former productiveness. This mountain is famous in Biblical history as being the place where Elijah in the presence of the king and people of Israel, confounded the four hundred and fifty prophets of Baal, and proved that the Lord was God. (1 Kings, xviii:17–41.) During the eighteenth century, Mount Carmel was the resort of many christian devotees, and an order of monks called Carmelites, established a convent there. This convent was destroyed in 1799, after the retreat of the French army, by the Arabs, who used it during the siege of Acre, as a hospital for their sick and wounded soldiers. (See view of the convent, No. 23.)

LITTLE HERMON

Is a short range of mountains in the southern part of Galilee, in the tribe of Issachar, about eight miles south of Mount Tabor, and five miles north of Gilboa.

GILBOA.

Mount Gilboa is situated in the south-eastern part of Galilee, in the tribe of Issachar. This mountain is famous as the scene of the battle between the armies of Saul and the Philistines, where occurred the death of Jonathan, and the suicide of Saul, as recorded in the last chapter of 1 Samuel. The lamentation of David after this event (2 Samuel, i:19–27) is one of his most touching productions.

MOUNTS EBAL AND GERIZIM

Are in Samaria, in the tribe of Ephraim, one on the north-east, and the other on the south-east of the city of Shechem. From these mountains the blessings and curses of the law were declared to the Israelites. (Deuteronomy xxvii, 11–26 ; Joshua viii:30–35.) In accordance with the command of Moses (Deuteronomy xxvii:4–6,) the children of Israel built an altar upon Mount Ebal, "the mountain of curses," after their entrance into the promised land. The Samaritans believed that this altar should have been built on Gerizim, and they afterwards erected a temple on this mountain, where they worshipped. It was to this mountain that the woman of Samaria referred in her conversation with the Savior, recorded in the beginning of the fourth chapter of John.

MOUNTAINS OF EPHRAIM.

This is the general name applied to the mountains in the tribe of Ephraim in the southern part of Samaria; and those in Judea, including the tribes of Judah, Simeon, Benjamin, and Dan, are called the *Mountains of Judah.*

MOUNTAINS OF JERUSALEM.

The mountains of Jerusalem are Bezetha on the north, Bezetha, Moriah and Ophel on the east, Zion on the south, and Zion and Acra on the west. Without the city are Mount Olivet on the east, Mount of Corruption on the south-east, and the Hill of Evil Counsel on the south.

SEAS.

DEAD SEA.

The seas of Palistine are the *Dead Sea*, *Sea of Galilee*, and *Waters of Merom*. The Dead sea is situated in the southern part of Palestine, between Judah on the west, and Reuben and the kingdom of the Moabites on the east. In the Bible it is called the *Salt sea*, (Genesis xiv:3, numbers xxxiv:3–12; Deuteronomy iii:17; Joshua iii:16, xii:3, xv:2–5, xviii:19); *Sea of the Plain* (Deuteronomy iii:17, iv:49; Joshua iii:16, xii:3, II Kings, xiv:25); *the Sea* (Ezekiel xlvii:8); *East sea* (Ezekiel xlvii: 18, Joel ii:20); in the Talmud it is called the *Sea of Sodom*. Josephus calls it the *Asphaltic Lake;* the Greeks call it *Asphaltites*, and the Arabs *Sea of Lot*. The name *Dead Sea* was not used until about the second century after Christ. This sea is the receptacle of the rivers Jordan, Kidron and Arnon, besides several smaller streams. It is about forty miles long and from four to ten wide. Its depth ranges from thirteen to thirteen hundred feet. The water of the Dead Sea is extremely nauseating and sluggish. A gallon of this water weighs over twelve pounds, or over two pounds more than pure water. Some have advanced the theory that this sea did not exist until the destruction of Sodom and Gomorah, and that they were at that time submerged. This supposition is based solely upon Genesis xiv:3, which makes the vale of Siddim identical with the Salt sea. As the waters of the Jordan were always discharged in the same place, believers in this theory suppose that there before existed a subterranean lake which received the waters of which the Dead Sea is now the receptacle. Others contradict this theory on the ground that Genesis xiv:3 is the only passage in the whole Bible which at all gives countenance to this belief; that the cities of Sodom and Gomorrah, lying, as they did, in the "Plain of the Jordan," must have been north, or at least on the northern extremity of the sea; and, which is a still stronger proof of the fallacy of this belief, that it is in direct opposition to the description of the manner of the destruction of these cities as given in Genesis xix:24.

SEA OF GALILEE.

The Sea of Galilee is situated between Zebulon and Naphtali on the west, and the half tribe of Manasseh on the east. It is called in the Bible, *Sea of Chinereth* (numbers xxxiv:11, Deuteronomy iii:17, Joshua xiii:27); *Chineroth* (Joshua xi:2, xii:3); *Sea of Galilee* (Matthew iv:18, xv:29, Mark i:16, vii:31, John vi:1); *Lake of Gennesaret* (Luke v:1); *Sea of Tiberias* (John vi:1, xxi:1). The sea is about fifteen miles long, and from six to eight wide. There are in this lake several kinds of fish; and it is famous from the fact that the first four of Christ's disciples, Peter, Andrew, James and John, were fishermen on this lake, (Matthew iv:18–22, Mark i:16–20, Luke v:1–11), and that it was the scene of several interesting incidents in the life of our Savior. The river Jordan passes through this lake on its course to the Dead sea. (See view of Sea of Galilee, No. 24.)

WATERS OF MEROM.

This is a small, triangular shaped lake in the northern part of Palestine, in the territory of the tribe of Naphtali. Josephus calls it *Lake Samochonitis*, and it is now called *Huleh*. It is celebrated as being the scene of a battle during the conquest of Palestine between the Israelites under Joshua, and Jabin, king of Hazor, Jobab, king of Madon, and divers other kings. (Joshua, xi:1–9.)

RIVERS.

JORDAN.

This river, the most important and celebrated of the rivers of the Bible, has two sources. One of these is a fountain south-west of Mount Hermon, near a place called Hasbeiya, whence the river, between that place and the waters of Merom, is called the Hasbany. The principal source of the Jordan, however, is among the mountains of Naphtali, near Caesarea Philippi. (See view of the source of the Jordan, No. 93.) These two branches unite in the waters of Merom. The river then flows in a southerly direction, passing in a direct current by itself through the

Sea of Galilee, and discharges its waters into the Dead sea. It is a remarkably tortuous stream. From its most remote source to its mouth it will not measure more than one hundred and fifteen to one hundred and twenty miles in a straight line, but the river is in reality more than twice that length. The current of the river is very rapid. Its average breadth is about ninety feet, but at its mouth it is said to be over five hundred and thirty feet wide. The Jordan was the scene of many interesting transactions, both in the times of the prophets and in the time of Christ, the most important of which were the overflowing of its banks at the time of the dividing of the waters of the Dead sea, in order that the Israelites might pass over (Joshua, iii:14–17); the waters divided by Elijah and Elisha (II. Kings ii:8–14); Naaman, the Syrian captain, cured of the leprosy (II. Kings, v:1–14); and the baptism of Christ (Matthew, iii:13–17; Mark, i:9–11; Luke, iii:21–22; John, i:32–34).

OTHER RIVERS.

Abana and *Pharpar*, rivers of Damascus, a city of Syria, rise among the mountains of Anti-Lebanon, and flow, Pharpar through the city of Damascus, and Abana in the immediate vicinity. They are lost among the marshes to the east of Damascus. These rivers are mentioned but once in the Bible (II. Kings, v:12). Abana is also called Amana, and some have supposed the expression in Solomon's Song, iv:8, to refer to this river. *Belus* is a small river which rises among the mountains in the territory of the tribe of Asher, and empties into the Bay of Acre, a short distance below the city.

Besor, meaning "cold," is the name of a brook passed over by David when he was in pursuit of the Amalekites (I. Samuel, xxx:9–10–21). It rises among the mountains of Judah in the tribe of Simeon, and flows through the land of the Philistines, emptying into the Mediterranean at the little town of Anthedon, about five miles south-west of Gaza.

"That ancient river, the river *Kishon*," rises in the territory of the tribe of Issachar, and flows through the beautiful plain of Esdrælon, entering the Bay of Acre near the base of Mount

Carmel. Its other names are *the river before Jokneam* (Joshua, xix:11), and the *waters of Megiddo* (Judges, v:19). This river is famous as the scene of the overthrow and defeat of the hosts of Jabin, king of Canaan, under Sisera, by Deborah and Barak (Judges, iv:1–16), and the destruction of the four hundred and fifty prophets of Baal (I. Kings, xviii:40).

The river *Kanah* is in Samaria, and flows into the Mediterranean sea. In the division of Palestine into tribes, this river formed the boundary between Ephraim and Manasseh (Joshua, xvi:8, and xvii:9).

The river *Leontes* rises among the mountains of Anti-Lebanon, a few miles above the town of Baalbek, and flows through the valley of Lebanon or Coele-Syria, emptying into the Mediterranean sea a short distance above Tyre.

The rivers *Hieromax* and *Jabbok* are branches of the Jordan on the east; the former flowing from Bashan through the half tribe of Manasseh and the northern portion of Gad, and discharging its waters into the Jordan at a point about eight miles south of the Sea of Galilee, and the latter flowing from the country of the Ammonites, across the central part of Gad, and entering the Jordan about four miles north-west of the town of Succoth.

Arnon and *Zered* are rivers emptying into the Dead sea on the east. The river Arnon formed the boundary between the country of the Moabites and Reuben (Deuteronomy, iii:8–12–16, iv:48; Joshua, xii:1–2, xiii:9–16; Judges, xi:13–18–26), and Zered (Deuteronomy, ii:13–14), called also Zared (Numbers, xxi:12) and "the brook of the wilderness" (Isaiah, xv:7) was the boundary between Moab and Edom.

The brook *Kedron* runs through the valley of Jehoshaphat which separates Jerusalem from the Mount of Olives, and empties into the Dead sea. The name *Kedron* does not appear in the Bible. It is called *Kidron* (II. Samuel, xv:23; II. Kings, xxiii:6), and *Cedron* (John, xviii:1). The brook *Cherith* flows through Jerico eastward, and empties into the Jordan. It was near this brook that Elijah was fed by the ravens when he was hiding from the presence of King Ahab (I. Kings, xvii:2–6).

CITIES.

JERUSALEM,

The capital, and principal city of Palestine, is situated in the south-western part of the land of the tribe of Benjamin, in Judea. (See views of Jerusalem.) This city, the most sacred of all cities, received, in the Bible, a variety of names, viz: *Salem* (Genesis, xiv:18; Psalm, lxxvi:2; Hebrews, vii:1–2); *The Jebusite* (Joshua, xv:8); *Jebusi* (Joshua, xviii:28); *Jebus* (Judges, xix:10–11); *City of the Jebusites* (Judges, xix:11); *Stronghold of Zion* (II. Samuel, v:7); *City of David* (II. Samuel, v:7–9, vi:10–12–16; I. Kings, ii:10, viii:1); *Zion* (I. Kings, viii:1; Psalm, xlviii:12, lxxxvii:2–5; Isaiah, xxxiii:20, lx:14); *City of God* (Psalm, xlvi:4, xlviii:1–8, lxxxvii:3); *City of the Lord* (Psalm, xlviii:8; Isaiah, lx:14); *City of the Great King* (Psalm, xlviii:2; Matthew, v:35). Herodotus called it *Kadytus*, and Homer gave it the name of *Solyma*. The modern Arabian name is *El-Khuds*, signifying "the holy."

Jerusalem is situated in latitude 31° 46′ 35″ N., and longitude 35° 18′ 30″ E. from Greenwich, thirty miles from the Mediterranean, thirty-five southeast of Joppa, six north of Bethlehem, eighteen north of Hebron, twenty from the Jordan, fifteen south-west of Jericho, and thirty-six south of Samaria. It is built upon several hills, Bezetha on the north, Moriah and Ophel on the east, Zion on the south, and Zion and Acra on the west. In the time of Christ, the wall extended between Acra and Bezetha on the north, Calvary being just outside the city, between these hills. After the death of Christ, king Agrippa built a wall, which was the same as the former on the east, west and south, but on the north it included Calvary and Bezetha in the city. The modern wall is wider at the north than that built by Agrippa. It extends, on the north, across Bezetha, cutting off its northern part, and on the south, across Mount Zion, leaving the southern portion of this mountain outside of the wall.

In the wall are four principal gates, which are always open from morning until sunset. They are as follows: On the east side of the city, near the pool of Bethesda, is *St. Stephen's gate*, which is also called the *Sheep gate*, and the *Gate of the Virgin*

Mary; on the south side is *Zion gate,* called likewise the *Gate of David;* between Mounts Bezetha and Calvary, on the west side, is the *Damascus gate;* and near the bend on the west side is the *Joppa gate* (see view No. 86). This gate is also called the *Pilgrim's gate, Gate of Bethlehem,* and *Bab el Khaleel,* meaning "the gate of the beloved," *i. e.,* Abraham. Two smaller gates, which are opened occasionally, are, one a little west of Mount Moriah, on the south side, which Maundrell calls the *Dung gate,* and the other, going out from Bezetha, on the west side, to which the same writer gives the name of *Herod's gate.* Another gate, which Maundrell calls the *Golden gate,* is on the east side of Mount Moriah. It was used as a gate at the time the Christians were in possession of the city, but it is now completely walled up. (See view No. 18.) There are several other gates mentioned in the scriptures, among which are the following: *Gate Sur* (II Kings, xi:6); *Gate of* or *behind the Guard* (II Kings, xi:6,19); *Horse gate* (II Kings, xi:16, II Chronicles, xxiii:15, Nehemiah, iii:28, Jeremiah, xxxi:40); *Corner gate* (II Kings, xiv:13, II Chronicles, xxv:23, xxvi:9, Nehemiah, iii:35, Jeremiah, xxxi:38, Zechariah, xiv:10); *Gate of Ephraim* (II Kings, xiv:13, II Chronicles, xxv:23, Nehemiah, viii:16, xii:39); *Gate of Joshua* (II Kings, xxiii:8); *Gate between the two walls* (II Kings, xxv:4, Jeremiah, xxxix,4): *Gate of foundation* (II Chronicles, xxxiii:5); *High gate* (II Kings, xv:35, II Chronicles, xxiii:20, xxvii:3); *Valley gate* (II Chronicles, xxvi:9, Nehemiah, ii:13, iii:13); *Gate Shallecheth* (I Chronicles, xxvi:16); *Fish gate* (II Chronicles, xxxiii:14, Nehemiah, iii:3, xii:39, Zephaniah, i:10); *Fountain gate* (Nehemiah, ii:14, iii:15, xii:37); *Old gate* (Nehemiah, iii:6, xii:39); *Water gate* (Nehemiah, iii:26, viii:1–3–16, xii:37); *East gate* (Nehemiah, iii:29, Jeremiah, xix:2); *Gate Miphkad* (Nehemiah, iii:31) *Prison gate* (Nehemiah, xii:39); *Gate of Benjamin* (Jeremiah xx:2, xxxvii:13, Zechariah, xiv:10); *First gate* (Zechariah, xiv:10). Josephus mentions *Essenes' gate* and the *gate Gennath.*

There are one Catholic and twelve Greek convents on Mount Calvary. The Greeks have another near Zion gate. The

Armenians have two in the city, three on Mount Zion, and one outside of Zion gate, where the house of Caiaphas, in which our Savior was tried and denied by Peter, is supposed to have stood. There are also a Syrian convent and an English church (see view No. 16) on Mount Zion, a Coptic convent on Calvary, a Dervise convent on Mount Moriah, and a Latin convent on Acra. (See view No. 13.) The Jews have a number of synagogues, the principal of which is the church of the Holy Sepulchre, on Calvary. (See view No. 12.) "This is an edifice distinguished for its size and massiveness. It forms altogether a block one hundred and sixty feet long, and one hundred wide; and includes what are called the chapel of the crucifixion, the church of the sepulchre, seven small chapels, a monastery and cloisters. The traditions with which the various apartments are associated are scarcely worthy to be preserved, and yet the votaries of superstition have contrived to group and connect them in such a manner as to excite strong and probably salutary emotions in the mind of the reflecting visitor." On Mount Moriah, in the eastern part of the city, on the site of Solomon's temple (I Kings, vi), stands the mosque of Omar. This mosque is walled in on all sides, and none but Mussulmen are permitted to enter its sacred precincts on pain of death. It is a very large building, and there are strong proofs that it is built on the same foundation on which the temple of Solomon stood. (See views of the mosque of Omar.) On the south of Mount Moriah the Mohammedans have another large and beautiful mosque, which they call the mosque of Aksa. (See views of the mosque of Aksa.)

On the east side of the city, in the street leading up from the gate of St. Stephen, commences the *Via Dolorosa*, or "grievous way." This is the path in which tradition says our Savior walked from the house of Pontius Pilate, the governor, to the place of crucifixion. (See view No. 14.) Without the city are several places of interest. The valley of Gihon is memorable as the place of the anointing of Solomon as king (I Kings, i: 33–38–45); and the fountain of Gihon is mentioned as having its course turned by king Hezekiah (II Chronicles, xxxii:38).

(See view No. 85.) The valley of Hinnom, which is a continuation of Gihon, is immediately below Jerusalem, and joins Jehoshaphat south-east of the city. In this valley, at one time, the most abominable idolatries were practiced (II Chronicles xxxiii: 6). It is also called Topheth (II Kings, xxiii:10), from *toph*, (a drum), because that instrument was often used to drown the cries of victims. The valley of Hinnom is situated at the foot of Mount Zion, along the western branch of the brook Kedron (see view No. 82). On the slope of a lofty mountain opposite to Mount Ophel, at the foot of which runs the brook Kedron, is situated the village of Siloam, to the south-west of Jerusalem. (See view No. 10.) South-east of Jerusalem, at the foot of Mount Zion, is the pool of Siloam, memorable as the pool in which the blind man washed and received sight (John, ix:7). (See view No. 11.) The garden of Gethsemane, where our Savior agonized before his crucifixion, is east of Jerusalem, on the western slope of Mount Olivet (see view No. 9). Mount Olivet, celebrated as the mountain from which Christ made his public entry into Jerusalem, and also from which He ascended into heaven, is west of Jerusalem. (See views Nos. 9 and 81.) South of Jerusalem, across the western branch of the brook Kedron, is *Aceldama* or "the field of blood," which was bought with the money paid to Judas Iscariot for betraying his Master (Matthew, xxvii:7). (See view No. 83.)

BAALBEK.

This is an ancient city of Syria, the origin of which is not known. It is situated in the valley of Lebanon, on the river Leontes, a short distance below its source. It is supposed to have been built by the Phoenicians at a very ancient date, and afterwards greatly enlarged and beautified by the Romans. The ruins of this ancient city are supposed to exceed in extent even those of Rome. (See views Nos. 35 to 45 inclusive.) This is probably the same as Baalgad, mentioned in Joshua, xi:17.

DAMASCUS.

This city, the oldest in the world, and capital of Syria, is situated on the Pharpar river, in a plain covered with olive, chestnut, and fig trees, apricots and vines. No Christian is permitted to enter within the walls of the city. It is at the present time under the government of the Mohammedans. A mosque in that city, which is a very old building, is supposed to be the longest structure in the world which is used as a place of worship. (See view No. 30.) This place is memorable as the residence of Naaman, the leper, and captain of the hosts of Syria, whom Elisha healed of leprosy, (II. Kings, v.,) and for the conversion of the Apostle Paul, (Acts, ix:1–18). (See views of Damascus.)

RUKHLEH

Is an ancient city north of Mount Hermon, at the foot of the Anti-Lebanon range. The town is now in ruins. (See view No. 29.)

TYRE AND SIDON

Are ancient cities of Phoenicia, on the coast of the Mediterranean, the former about one hundred and ten, and the latter about one hundred and thirty miles north-west of Jerusalem. The Hebrew name of Tyre was *Tsor* or *Tsur*. The modern name is *Sur*. Sidon was also called Zidon several times in scripture, and was the subject of several remarkable prophecies. (Isaiah, xxiii:4–18; Jeremiah, xxv:17–38; Ezekiel, xxviii:21–24.) It is now called "Saida." In the division of Canaan by lot to the twelve tribes, Tyre and Sidon were in the territory assigned to the tribe of Asher (Joshua, xix:28–29), but the Israelites never succeeded in wholly expelling the native inhabitants, who were to them a source of great annoyance. These cities are now in Phoenicia. They are supposed to have been built over a thousand years before the Christian era. The ancient inhabitants lived in a style of great luxuriance, which caused the prophet to utter maledictions against the cities (Isaiah, xxiii). Their crimes were, however, in some degree palliated on account of their non-enlightenment when Christ "upbraided the cities wherein most of his mighty works were done, because they repented not." (Matthew, xi:21–22; Luke, x:13–14.) These cities were formerly very beautiful, but they are now in ruins. (See views of Tyre.)

CAPERNAUM

Was situated on the western coast of the Sea of Galilee. In this city Christ performed some of his most wonderful works, and delivered some of his most pointed discourses. Notwithstanding Capernaum was so highly favored by the Savior's instructions and presence, it was a wicked and ungrateful city, and was the subject of some of the Lord's most fearful denunciations. The prediction of its downfall, contained in Matthew xi:23–24, and Luke x:15, was long ago fulfilled, and now even the site it occupied is uncertain, although it was once the metropolis of all Galilee, and a city of great renown. Dr. Robinson believes it to be the same as "Kaln Minyeh" on the north-western shore of the Sea of Galilee; but Dr. Thomson thinks it is "Tell Hum," three miles above "Kaln Minyeh," on the same shore, and nearly ninety miles from Jerusalem. (See view No. 26.)

BETHSAIDA.

The town of Bethsaida was situated on the western shore of the river Jordan, and near the Sea of Galilee. There is at the present day scarcely any trace of the town, it being entirely destroyed. It is celebrated in sacred history as being the birth-place of Philip, Andrew, and Peter, who were among the first followers of Christ, and who were all subsequently chosen Apostles, (John i:44.) (See view No. 24.)

CHORAZIN.

This town, which is somewhere in Galilee, was once a city of some note, and was included in the curse (Matthew xi:21–22, Luke x:13–14) because it would not repent. Its exact location is not now known, but it is supposed to be identical with "Khorazy," two miles above "Tell Hum," and ninety-two from Jerusalem.

CÆSREA PHILIPPI.

This town was situated in the north-eastern part of Galilee, near Mount Hermon, about one hundred and ten miles from Jerusalem. The town is now in ruins. (See view No. 92.) Near this place is the principal source of the river Jordan. "Philip, the tetrarch, son of Herod, contributed largely to its prosperity, and gave it the name of Cæsarea, in honor of Tiberius Cæsar." It is called Cæsarea of Philip, or Cæsarea Philippi, to distinguish it from

CÆSAREA OF PALESTINE.

This town is in Samaria, on the coast of the Mediterranean sea, about sixty miles north-west of Jerusalem. It was built by Herod the great, about twenty years before Christ. It was called Cæsarea in honor of Augustus Cæsar. This place was at one time the principal city of Palestine, and it was here that Paul made his celebrated defense before King Agrippa (Acts xxiii:33, xxvi:30.) In Cæsarea was the residence of Cornelius, the centurion (Acts x:1,) and also of Philip the evangelist (Acts xxi:8.)

NAZARETH.

This town is situated from fifty to seventy miles north of Jerusalem, and six miles north-west of Mount Tabor. It is described by a modern traveler as "situated upon the declivity of a hill, the vale of which spreads out before it resembling a circular basin, encompassed by mountains." The streets are narrow and steep; the average estimate of the population is about three thousand; and the houses, of which there are about two hundred and fifty, are all flat-roofed. About five hundred of the inhabitants are Turks, and the remainder are nominal Christians. This town is celebrated in scripture as being the place where the parents of Jesus dwelt after their return from their flight into Egypt. (Matthew, ii:23.) (See view No. 89.)

SAMARIA.

The province of Samaria received its name from the city of the same name. This city is situated about forty miles north of Jerusalem, and six miles north-west of the ancient city of Shechem. It was built about the year 925 B. C., by Omri, king of Israel, as the capital of the kingdom of Israel, and named in honor of Shemer, from whom the land on which it was built was purchased (I. Kings, xvi:24). The Hebrew name of the city was *Shomeron*. The position of the city was extremely beautiful, and it was strongly fortified. It withstood an unsuccessful siege by Benhadad, king of Syria, who was assisted by thirty-two other kings (I. Kings, xx:1–21) ; but was finally taken by Shalmaneser, king of Assyria, during the reign of Hosea (II. Kings, xvii:1–6), after a siege of three years. The Romans called the city *Sebaste.* It is now but a small village, and is called by the Arabs *Sebustiyeh,* a corruption of Sebaste. " Some architectural remains it has, partly of Christian construction or adaptation, as the ruined church of St. John the Baptist " (see view No. 88), and " partly, perhaps, traces of Idumaean magnificence. St. Jerome, whose acquaintance with Palestine imparts a sort of probability to the tradition which prevailed so strongly in later days, asserts that Sebaste, which he invariably identifies with Samaria, was the place in which St. John the Baptist was imprisoned and suffered death. He also makes it the burial place of the prophets Elisha and Obadiah."

SHECHEM

Was one of the most ancient cities of Palestine. It was also called *Sichem* (Genesis xii:6), *Sychar* (John iv:5), and *Sychem* (Acts vii:16). The Romans called it *Neapolis* or *Nablous,* and it is still known by the latter name. Mount Ebal is north and Gerizim south of the city. In the modern town two long streets run parallel with the valley. The view of the city from the surrounding hights is said to be exceedingly beautiful, situated as it is in a delightful and fertile valley. There are in the town six Mohammedan mosques, a church of the Greek Christians, and a Samaritan synagogue, in which service is held every Saturday, which is the Samaritan sabbath. It has a population of eight or ten thousand, all Mohammedans, with the exception of twelve or fifteen Jews, from fifty to one hundred Greek Christians, and about forty Samaritans. (See view No. 87.)

SHILOH

Was a city of Samaria in the land of the tribe of Ephraim, about twenty-two miles north of Jerusalem, and twelve miles south-east of Shechem. Its modern name is *Seilun.* It is celebrated in Scripture as being the residence of Eli, where Samuel was taken by his mother (I. Samuel, i:24–25), and where he began to prophesy (iii:20–21). It was also the residence of the prophet Ahijah (I. Kings, xiv:2). The ruinous condition of Shiloh was proverbial in the times of the prophets (Jeremiah, vii:14, xxvi:6–9). It is now wholly in ruins. (See view No. 22.)

JOPPA

Was and is yet the principal seaport of Palestine, though its harbor is a poor one, ships being obliged to anchor about a mile from the city. It is called *Japho* in Joshua xix:46, and is now known as *Jaffa* or *Yaffa.* It is situated in the tribe of Dan, about thirty-five miles north-west of Jerusalem, and about the same distance south-west of Shechem. Joppa was the residence of Dorcas, a woman "full of good works" (Acts, ix:36), and, also, of Simon, the tanner, with whom Peter lodged, and where he had his celebrated vision (Acts x:6–9–16).

JERICHO

Is one of the oldest cities of Palestine. It is situated in the tribe of Benjamin, about sixteen miles north-east of Jerusalem. Its modern name is *Riha.* There are a great many palm trees in the vicinity; and in Deuteronomy, xxxiv:3, it is called the *city of palm trees.* When the Israelites crossed into Palestine, they went immediately to Jericho. The city was compassed seven days; the walls fell on the seventh at the shouting of the people, and by the command of God the city was completely destroyed and all the inhabitants slain, except Rahab and her family, and the very ground on which the city stood was cursed (Joshua, vi). It was at the fountain of Jericho, near this place, that Elisha effected a miraculous change in the unwholesome waters (II. Kings, ii:19–22). (See view No. 7.) Jericho was also the residence of Zaccheus, the publican. (Luke xix: 1–10.)

BETHANY

Was a village on the south-eastern side of the Mount of Olives, two miles from Jerusalem. It was the scene of many interesting events in the life of Christ, among which are the cursing of the fig tree (Matthew, xxi:18–22, Mark, xi:12–14–20–23); the anointing of His feet (Matthew, xxvi:6-13, Mark, xiv:3-9, Luke, vii:36-50, John, xii:3-8); and the raising of Lazarus (John, xi: 1-44). The village is now in ruins. (See view No. 79.)

BETHLEHEM.

This village, celebrated in sacred history as the birth-place of David (Luke, ii:4-11), and of Christ (Matthew, ii:1, Luke, ii:4-6, John, vii:42), is about six miles south-west of Jerusalem. It was so small a place that it was generally omitted in the lists of the cities of Judah. Travelers speak of it as being reduced to a miserable state, from the ravages of war. When Mr. Whiting, an American missionary, was there, in 1834, "it had just suffered severely from some tyrannical measures of the government; and he passed over the ruins of houses and fields that had just then been demolished, and parks of olive and fig trees which had been cut down by order of the pasha, to punish their proprietors for an alleged rebellion and flight." (See view No. 78.)

HEBRON.

This town is situated about twenty miles south of Jerusalem. It was, also, called *Kirjath-Arba* (Genesis, xxiii:2, Joshua, xiv:15, Judges, i:10); *City of Arba* (Joshua, xv:13); *Mamre* (Genesis, xxiii:16, xxv:9, xlix:30, i:13). The Arabs now call it "*El-Khaleel*, which signifies 'the friend,' or 'the beloved,' from the remarkable title given to Abraham, namely, 'the friend of God.'" Here Abraham lived (Genesis, xiii:18), and here was his family burial-place, the cave of Machpelah (Genesis, xxiii:19-20, xxv: 9-10, xlix:29-32, i:13). After the conquest of Canaan, Hebron was in the territory assigned to Caleb (Joshua, xiv:13-14), and it was afterwards one of the cities of refuge (Joshua, xx:7, xxi: 13). The cave of Machpelah is now covered by a mosque, which is the most prominent object in the town. (See view No. 77.) It is supposed by some that Hebron was the residence of Zacharias and Elizabeth, at the time of the birth of John the Baptist. "About a mile from the town, up the valley, is one of the largest oak trees in Palestine. This, say some, is the very tree beneath which Abraham pitched his tent, and it still bears the name of the patriarch."

SINAI.

Sinai, the scene of the Israelite wanderings in the desert, is situated between the Gulfs of Suez and Akabuh. The surface is generally mountainous and rocky. Nearly in the centre of this peninsula is a wedge of granite, rising upwards of eight thousand feet in hight. Mount Horeb forms the north end of the ridge. Mount Sinai, one of the peaks, is generally identified with Jebel-Moosa, or "Mount of Moses," the supposed site of the burning bush, though many conjecture that Mount Horeb was the original Sinai, celebrated in holy writ. The culminating point of this cluster of mountains is Mount St. Catharine.

Wady Mukatteb, or the Written Valley, is celebrated for the inscriptions which line the rocks. These are thought to be the work of christian hands, probably of some passing pilgrims. On the north-east side is the fortified convent of Sinai, now tenanted by about twenty Greek monks. (See views of Sinai.)

GREECE.

In ancient times this country was in advance of all others in freedom, literature, art, philosophy, and of civilization generally. Its early history is involved in obscurity. The only approach to it is through the marvelous legends of gods and heroes, but how much truth may underlie these stories it is difficult to say. In the fifteenth century it was conquered by the Turks, but in 1821 the inhabitants revolted, and the country is now independent. It is situated in the southern part of Europe, and covers an area about half the size of Scotland.

The surface of Greece is generally mountainous, more so than any other country of Europe, except Switzerland and parts of Scotland. The province of Arcadia almost rivals Switzerland in the rugged grandeur of its mountain scenery. The mountains are more remarkable for the abruptness of their rise than for their great elevation, though some of the peaks rise to a great hight. Olympus is nine thousand seven hundred feet in hight, and is covered with perpetual snow.

The rivers of Greece are small, and none of them navigable; but it has an extensive coast-line, with numerous bays extending far up in the land, affording important commercial advantages.

ATHENS,

The capital of Attica, and the chief city of Greece, is situated about three miles from the coast, in the central plain of Attica, surrounded by hills on all sides except towards the sea. The plain is broken by a number of hills, of moderate hight, several of which, with their intervening valleys, are partially occupied by the city, while the highest, rising abruptly for about one hundred and fifty feet, forms the Acropolis, or citadel, on which most of the noblest monuments are placed. This is an isolated rocky hight, with a flat summit of about one thousand feet long from east to west, by five hundred feet broad from north to south.

Immediately west of the Acropolis is a second hill, of irregular form, called the Areopagus, or Mars' Hill. (See view No. 99.) According to tradition, it is called Mars' Hill on account of this god being brought to trial before the assembled gods by Neptune, for the murder of his son. It was the place of meeting of the Council of Areopagus, the most ancient and venerable of all the Athenian courts, enjoying a high reputation not only in Athens, but throughout all Greece. To the Christian it possesses a peculiar interest as the spot from which St. Paul delivered his eloquent address to the people of Athens.

The city of Athens is crowded in every direction with temples, alters, and other sacred buildings. The Acropolis is covered with temples of gods and heroes. The Propylaca, standing at the top of a flight of marble steps, seventy feet broad, serves as an entrance to the works within. It is constructed entirely of Pentelic marble, and forms one of the master pieces of Athenian art. (See view No. 48.)

In the highest part of the Acropolis, and near the center, stands the Parthenon, adorned by the most exquisite sculptures, and forming the most perfect production of Grecian architecture. (See view No. 102.) North of the Parthenon and close to the northern wall of the Acropolis stands a magnificent building called the Erechtheum. (See view No. 100.) In front of the sacred area which Athens dedicated to her tutelary divinity, stands a temple called the Wingless Victory. On the marble balustrade, which encircles the edifice, are pictured a troop of personified Victories. (See view No. 51.) Pausanias informs us that the Athenians gave no wings to victory because they would prevent her flying away from them. In many of these buildings female figures called Caryatides are used in the place of columns. (See view No. 49.) Occupying the slope at the south-eastern extremity of the Acropolis is the theatre of Bacchus. This is excavated out of solid rock, with rows of seats extending one above the other. (See views Nos. 53, 54 and 55).

EGYPT.

The early history of Egypt is involved in obscurity. History throws but little light on the building of its ancient cities, and the construction of the magnificent monuments which still continue to be the wonder and admiration of the world. At the present time, it is principally under the French government. It is situated in the north-eastern part of Africa, embracing the northern division of the Nile, and extending from the Mediterranean to the cataract of the Syene.

Scattered throughout Egypt are a number of remarkable works of art, among which are the Pyramids, Lake Mæris, an immense artificial reservoir, the Great Sphinx at Gizeh, a colossal form hewn out of the solid rock, one hundred and seventy-two feet long, by fifty-six feet high; the Labyrinth, an enormous structure of marble, built underground, and the Catacombs, subterraneous galleries of great extent, appropriated to the reception of the dead.

The Pyramids are one of the wonders, both of the ancient and modern world. They are solid mounds raised over the chambers containing the remains of the kings who flourished from the fourth to the twelfth dynasty. One of the first acts of an Egyptian monarch, was to prepare his tomb. For this purpose a rectangular chamber was first excavated in the solid rock. Over this chamber, a cubical mass of masonry of square blocks was then placed, leaving the orifice of the shaft open. Additions to this mass continued to be made during the life of the monarch. At his death the outer surface was smoothed off, and the entrance carefully filled up to prevent ingress to the sepulchral chamber. In the construction of the largest of these pyramids, one hundred thousand men are said to have been employed for upwards of thirty years, (See views of the Pyramids.)

The only river of Egypt is the Nile. It is about half a mile in width, and receives no tributaries for the last one thousand five hundred miles of its course. It yearly overflows its banks, furnishing, in a country where rain seldom or never falls, valuable irrigation to the soil. The scenery along the river in upper Egypt is wild and romantic, but in the lower part of its course, it is monotonous and uninteresting. Herodotus describes it as having seven mouths, but at the present day only two of them continue to flow in an uninterrupted course to the sea. West of the Nile, is the fertile valley of Fagoon. From this valley a road leads west to the oasis of El Dukhel. Other roads from Girgesh, Esneh and Ezion Geber, offer communication with the fertile spots which characterize the regions west of this river. The usual manner of traveling is by means of camels and dromedaries. (See view No. 5.)

CAIRO,

The capital, is situated on the right bank of the Nile, about five miles above the commencement of its delta. Its streets are narrow, dark, irregular, and unpaved. It covers an area of about three square miles, and is surrounded by a low wall. The most remarkable buildings are the minarets and mosques. It has two elegant and high minarets. Under the rule of the Mameluke kings, the celebrated mosque, on account of its great size and the thickness of its walls, was frequently seized and made use of as a fortress.

Among the objects of interest, situated in the environs of the city, are the tombs of the Caliphs. These are magnificent and imposing buildings, forming beautiful specimens of Arabian architecture. (See view No. 96.) On the south, outside the walls, are the celebrated tombs of the Mamelukes. (See view No. 60.) The public gardens, which consist of groves of orange, citron, palms, and vines, are considered very beautiful. The population of the city is estimated at about two hundred and fifty thousand. (See view of Cairo.)

CATALOGUE OF VIEWS.

MISCELLANEOUS.

NO. VIEW.		NO. PAGE.
224	The Tomb of Washington (Mount Vernon),	232
1414	Mount Vernon, the Residence of George Washington,	232
667	1339 669 668 The Genesee Falls, at Rochester,	176
702	Loch Lomond. The Ferry (Scotch),	349
1775	1776 Saloon of the Steamer St. John, on the Hudson,	175
1875	1283, 1873, 1874 Fort La Fayette, New York Harbor,	184
1410	1411 1412 1413 Harvard College, Cambridge, Mass.,	159
4115	Upper Saloon of the North River Steamer Dean Richmond,	175
4571	Group of Officers on board the Italian Man-of-War, N. Y. Harbor,	188
4579	Wall Street Ferry, New York Harbor,	188
4584	Castle Garden, New York,	185
4596	Funeral of President Lincoln, N. Y. City, 7th Regiment passing in view,	93
5268	Residence of President Brigham Young and Daniel H. Wells, Salt Lake City, Utah Territory,	308
5269	Section of Roof of the New Tabernacle, Salt Lake City,	308
5432	View on Stapleton Hights, Staten Island,	202
5438	5437 Interior view of Fort Lafayette, showing the spot where Kennedy was executed,	184
5899	5900 Saloon of the Steamer "Drew," Central Park,	185
5974	5902 The Sound Steamer "Bristol," on the Hudson,	175
5973	5974 Cohoes Falls, N. Y.,	176
6708	6709 The Cornell University at Ithica, N. Y.,	203
5978	5977 Looking across the Hudson, Jersey City in the distance,	206
5979	Looking across the Hudson, Hoboken in the distance,	206
6087	Upper Saloon of the Steamer Providence, (on the Hudson,)	175
6609	6610 Natural Bridge, in Virginia,	230
6617	Monument and Attendant Statue of Victory, Lowell, Mass.,	158
6289	Washington Monument, Union Square, N. Y.,	188
450	444 440 432 429 Fourth of July in and about New York,	184
816	Georgetown, from Camp Cameron. A view of exquisite beauty,	225
944	View of Harper's Ferry, showing the ruin wrought by war,	72
1263	1264 Flag Ship of the Russian fleet in New York Harbor,	188
2166	2167 Harper's Ferry and the Shenandoah Valley from Maryland Heights,	81
2018	2020 Views at Chambersburg,	90

VIEWS IN AND ABOUT SARATOGA SPRINGS.

NO. VIEW.		NO. PAGE.
3996	View from the front of the United States Hotel, looking down Broadway,	201
4051	Front of the Union Hotel, looking down Broadway,	201
4057	Group of Actors on the Stage of Leland's Opera House,	201
4058	Entrance to Congress Hall,	201
4067	4066 Congress Spring,	201

NO. VIEW.		NO. PAGE.
4075	4074 Columbia Spring,	201
4078	Reservoir in Congress Spring Park,	201
4079	Entrance to the Washington Spring,	201
4081	4080 Washington Spring,	201
4084	4083 Saratoga Spring,	201
4088	4087 Empire Spring,	201
4092	4091 High Rock Spring,	201
4100	Congress Street and Park,	201

INSTANTANEOUS VIEWS, NEW YORK.

308	Broadway, from the balcony of St. Germain's, looking north, showing the Worth Monument and the spires of the Collegiate Church and the Tabernacle,	188
904	905, Omnibuses starting from South Ferry, N. Y.,	188
900	Bird's eye view of New York City, from Shot Tower,	184
3696	The junction of Chatham and Center streets, from Printing House Square,	184
2950	2952, 2956, the Funeral of President Lincoln, New York, April 25th, 1865,	93
5078	5079, 5080, Broadway, from the corner of Broome street, looking up,	184
5337	Looking north from the corner of Fulton street, showing Broadway and City Hall Park,	184
5093	Broadway—Burst of Sunshine after a Shower,	184
5095	Broadway on a Rainy Day,	184
2121	Looking up the East River from the Roosevelt St. Ferry,	184

MAJESTY AND BEAUTY OF NIAGARA.

639	The American Fall, from the Canada side, near the Museum,	177
644	The American Fall, from the Museum grounds, Canada side,	177
868	The Scenery of the Niagara,	177
1943	The Suspension Bridge, from Canada side,	179
1949	The Suspension Bridge, from the Monteagle House,	179
1951	The Rapids, looking towards the Three Sisters,	177
1952	Horse Shoe Fall, from the Canada side,	177
1967	1968, View from Lewiston Mountain, looking towards Lake Ontario,	180
1969	View looking down the river from Terrapin Tower,	177
1973	Gate and Carriage Way, Suspension Bridge,	179
1974	Table Rock, Canada side,	179
1976	Sectional view of Suspension Bridge,	179
1985	The Clifton House, from the Museum grounds, Canada side,	179
1982	1987, The American Fall, from the Museum grounds,	177
2977	The Falls from Point View, American side,	177
2980	Terrapin Tower and Horse Shoe Fall, from Goat Island,	177
3007	Bridge to Goat Island,	179
3729	The Suspension Bridge, Niagara Falls,	179
3732	Table Rock and Clifton House,	179
3736	Table Rock and Horse Shoe Fall,	179
5392	From Point View, American side,	177
5798	The Horse Shoe Fall, from the Custom House,	177
5801	Horse Shoe Fall,	177
6010	The Falls from Victoria Island,	177
6043	Cataract House, from Goat Island Bridge,	179

BEAUTIES OF THE HUDSON.

GLENS OF THE CATSKILLS.

NO. VIEW.		NO. PAGE.
4207	4208 View from the top of Haines' Fall. South Mountain in the distance,	173
4213	4214 View from the top of the Kauterskill Fall looking down the Glen,	173
4215	The Bastion Fall, Kauterskill Glen, near the Laurel House,	173
5757	4217 The Kauterskill Fall, near the Laurel House,	173

VIEWS IN WASHINGTON CITY, AND DISTRICT OF COLUMBIA.

226	The United States Treasury Building at Washington,	227
226	Interior view. Retiring room of the United States Senate,	126
1309	South front of the White House,	127
1315	The Navy and War Department,	127
1316	The Post Office,	227
1323	The Smithsonian Institute,	228
1325	Smithsonian Institute Grounds—Capitol in the distance,	228
1326	Lafayette Square ; Jackson's Statue in the distance,	227
1333	Washington Monument,	228
1991	Clark Mills' Equestrian Statue of Washington,	227
2732	The President's House, Washington,	227
2733	President's Summer House, Washington,	227
2743	Picturesque view of Georgetown, the Potomac, and the Chesapeake Canal, from rear of the observatory,	225
2747	View of the Potomac and the Washington Monument,	228
2981	Pennsylvania Avenue, looking north from Metropolitan Hotel	227
2982	Statue of Civilization, by Greenough,	226
2986	White House ; front view,	226
2987	The Treasury Buildings ; east front,	227
6453	6452, The Post Office from S. E. and S. W.,	227
6455	The War Department,	227
6456	The Navy Department,	227
6457	East Capitol Square,	227
6459	Walk in the East Capitol Square,	227
6461	6462, Marble Statue of Washington (by Greenough) in East Capitol Square,	227
6464	West Capitol Grounds or Park,	227
465	View in the United States Botanical Garden, west side of the Capitol,	227
6466	The Capitol from the Botanical Gardens,	227
6467	The United States Capitol from Maryland avenue, (distant view),	227
6470	The Capitol from East Capitol Square ; Marble Statue of Washington in the foreground,	227
6471	6472, The Capitol from East Capitol Square,	225
6473	6474, 6475, East front of the Capitol from north-east,	225
6479	East front of the Capitol from south-east,	225
6484	Western entrance to the U. S. Capitol,	226
6485	6486, Eastern portico of the Capitol,	226
6490	6491, Statue of Columbus and Indian Girl, (by Persico),	226
6492	6493, 6494, Statue of Civilization, (by Greenough),	226
6595	9496, Statue of A. Lincoln, in the Rotunda of the Capitol,	226
6497	6498, Statue of Ceres, or Peace, (by Persico),	226
6499	Statue of Mars, or War, (by Persico),	226
6500	Brumidi's Allegorical Painting in the dome of the Capitol,	226
6501	West or Middle Room, Congressional Library of the Capitol,	226

NO. VIEW.		NO. PAGE.
6502	North Room, Congressional Library of the Capitol,	226
6503	Bronze Statue of Jackson, in Lafayette Square, (by Clark Mills),	227
6504	Statue of Jefferson, in the lawn, Executive Mansion grounds,	227
6506	6607, 6508, South Front of White House, fountain in foreground,	227
6509	The Executive Mansion, south front,	227
6511	The President's House, south front,	227
6513	The President's House, north front,	227
6516	President's House, from eastern carriage entrance,	227
6519	6520, The White House, from Treasury buildings,	227
6524	6526, The U. S. Treasury, from the south-west,	227
6530	U. S. Patent Office, east front,	227
6631	U. S. Patent Office, south front,	227
6533	Model Room, U. S. Patent Office,	227
6534	Blue Corridor, U. S. Patent Office,	226

PUBLIC BUILDINGS IN NEW YORK CITY AND BROOKLYN.

1284	Plymouth Church, Brooklyn, Rev. Henry Ward Beecher,	189
1285	Christ Church, Brooklyn, E. D., Rev. Mr. Patridge,	189
912	N. Y. Academy of Music, cor. 14th street and Irving Place,	187
1656	Church of the Puritans, Rev. Dr. Cheever,	189
1587	Fifth Avenue Hotel, New York,	187
1588	Church of the Holy Trinity, Brooklyn, Rev. Dr. Littlejohn,	189
2245	Fifth avenue and 37th street, looking north,	185
3699	City Hall, from Broadway,	185
3704	Rutger's Institute, corner of 5th avenue and 42d street,	186
3950	View of City Hall from Broadway,	185
4624	Hoffman House, Broadway and 24th street,	187
4402	Cooper Institute,	187
4615	Free Academy, East 23d street and Lexington avenue,	186
4793	New York University from Washington Parade Ground,	186
4997	The St. Nicholas Hotel from corner of Broome street,	
5082	U. S. Treasury, corner of Wall and Nassau streets,	186
5084	Trinity Church,	187
5090	Entrance to City Hospital, view from Broadway,	186
5089	City Hospital, view from south side,	186
5092	City Hospital, view from north side,	186
5308	Mercantile Library Association Building, (Clinton Hall,) Astor Place,	187
5310	Fifth Avenue Hotel,	187
5172	The Broadway Bridge, including St. Paul's Church and the Astor House,	188
5808	Broadway and City Hall Square from Fulton street,	185
6294	National Academy of Design,	186
6598	6599 City Hall,	185
6601	Looking down Wall street from Trinity spire,	185
6602	Looking across the Hudson, from Trinity spire,	184
6603	Up Broadway, from Trinity spire,	184
6828	A. T. Stewart's Retail Store,	187

BROOKLYN NAVY YARD.

6717	Looking down from the entrance,	189
6721	Shot and Shell Pyramids,	189

NO. VIEW.		NO. PAGE.
6722	Pyramids of Shot,	189
6723	Shell Pyramids,	189
6725	The Torpedo Boat, Midge,	189
	WEST POINT VIEWS.	
4279	View of West Point from the Cemetery,	199
4283	Arsenal and portion of Sea View Battery, W. P. M. A.,	199
4285	Sea View Battery,	199
5769	North-east corner of Cadet Barracks, looking north-west over plains,	199
5775	Plain of West Point from area of Cadet Barracks, looking north,	199
	West Point from R. R. Tunnel at Garrisons,	199
	VIEWS ON THE SOUTHERN TIER OF THE ERIE RAILROAD.	
670	At Elmira—View on the Chemung, looking up the river,	200
671	Owego, and Valley of the Susquehanna,	201
760	Owego, from Evergreen Cemetery, looking south,	201
701	Bird's-eye view of Owego from the north, Susquehanna river in the distance,	201
657	View at Lackawaxen, looking down the Delaware river,	210
754	View of Port Jervis, from the east,	202
753	View near Port Jervis,	202
755	764, View from the Deep Cut, near Port Jervis,	202
744	Down the Neversink, near Port Jervis,	202
5602	Owego, view from Evergreen Cemetery,	201
	WHITE MOUNTAIN VIEWS, N. H.	
4403	Summit of Mount Lafayette from the top of Canon Mountain,	145
4409	4410, Profile or Canon Mountain,	145
4412	Silver Forest on Canon Mountain,	145
4413	Summit of Canon Mountain,	145
4427	Echo Lake from the Boat House, showing the summit of Mount Lafayette,	145
4430	4429, Echo Lake from the outlet, showing the Notch,	145
4447	South-east side of Canon Mountain,	145
4449	The Franconia Notch, from the Profile House,	145
4453	4787, 4454, East side of Canon Mountain,	145
	HILLS AND DALES OF NEW ENGLAND.	
454	In the Gold Miner's Glen, Plymouth, Vt.	150
577	The Passumpsic at St. Johnsbury, Vt. The village in the distance	152
596	Looking north from Ox Bow Cliff, Waterford, Vt.,	152
599	View across the Passumpsic at St. Johnsbury, Vt.,	152
772	The Crossings; View of Village of St. Johnsbury Center, Vt.,	152
761	Village of St. Johnsbury Centre, Vt.,	152
122	221, Prof. Wise inflating his Balloon, Ganymede at St. Johnsbury, Vt.,	152
	VALLEY OF THE RAMAPO, ERIE RAILWAY.	
6244	Hotel and Turner's Station, Erie Railroad,	176
6249	The old Albany Post Road, below Turner's Station, looking east,	176

NO. VIEW.		NO. PAGE.
6250	Valley of the Ramapo, below Turner's Station, looking up the clove towards Newburg,	176
6256	The Valley at Greenwood, Erie Railroad,	176
6259	At Greenwood,	176
6263	Bridge over the Ramapo, at Greenwood,	176
6265	The everlasting Hills,	176
6266	The Valley below Greenwood Station,	176
6270	Erie Railroad at Southfield in the Ramapo valley,	176
6276	The Dam and Terrace House at the Village of Ramapo,	176
6278	At the Village of Ramapo,	176
6279	View of Southfield from the Church,	176
6280	The Dam at Ramapo,	176
6281	The Windings of the Ramapo,	176
6283	Quiet on the Ramapo,	176
6251	Valley of the Ramapo between Turner's and Greenwood Station,	176
6260	Greenwood Furnace in the Ramapo valley,	176
6275	Terrace House, Torn Mountain in the distance,	176

GREENWOOD CEMETERY VIEWS.

NO. VIEW.		NO. PAGE.
948	Tomb of W. W. Grosbeck, Dale avenue, Crescent Water foreground,	192
1487	The Fountain, on Fountain Hill,	190
1592	Monument of Henry Ruggles,	192
2185	2186 2187 Monument of Miss Charlotte Canda, Battle ave.,	191
2189	New Entrance to Greenwood Cemetery,	190
5290	2191 The Sea Captain's Monument, on Vista Hill,	192
2192	Monument of De Witt Clinton,	190
2197	Crescent Lake,	190
5271	View on Willow avenue. New Gateway in the distance,	190
5278	Crescent Water, Dale avenue,	190
5279	Sylvan Water,	190
5280	Niblo's Tomb, Dale avenue,	192
5282	Monuments on Ocean Hill,	190
6842	From Vine Dell looking towards Ocean Hill,	190

PASSAIC FALLS, PATTERSON, NEW JERSEY.

NO. VIEW.		NO. PAGE.
2132	2131 2130 Bird's-eye view of Patterson,	204
2138	2140 2136 2134 Passaic Falls, (different views,)	204

CENTRAL PARK VIEWS.

NO. VIEW.		NO. PAGE.
1065	From the Bell Tower, looking south. The Terrace and Mall in the distance,	185
1066	From Bell Tower, looking south-east,	185
1068	From the Summer House, north-west of 6th ave. entrance,	185
1075	The Mall, looking north,	185
1078	Grounds east of the Mall, now temporarily occupied by the animals for the Zoological collection,	185
1079	From the Casino, looking north-east,	185
1081	The Valley. Harlem Plains in the distance,	185
1096	Transverse Road No. 2, south of Old Reservoir,	185
1102	The Cave,	185
1108	A Music Day on the Park,	185
1113	1111 Swans on the Lake,	185

NO. VIEW.		NO. PAGE.
1121	The Lake, with the Bow Bridge in the distance,	185
1124	Bronze Group of Eagles and Alpine Goats, west of the Mall,	185
1137	The Music Pavilion,	185
1138	From Walk near Artist' Gate, 6th avenue and 59th street entrance, looking east. Old Arsenal in the distance,	185
1162	Lake and Bow Bridge,	185
1887	1888 Rustic Bridge near West Drive,	185
3712	3705 Instantaneous View of the Lake from the Terrace,	185
3716	3714 Rustic Bridge, near the 8th avenue,	185
3725	3726 3727 The Music Stand,	185
4503	5350 The Terrace,	185
4804	4798 Skating Scene in Central Park,	185
4406	4407 View in the Ramble,	185
5911	5912 The Camel and his Rider,	185
5914	The Fountain on the Mall,	185
5917	The Fountain. The Esplanade of the Terrace, the Lake and Ramble in the distance,	185 185
6204	Ornamental Water west of the Conservatory,	185
6208	The Casino and Statue of "Auld Lang Syne,"	185
6233	6217 6231 The Fountain on the Mall,	185

CALIFORNIA VIEWS.

1	The Yo-Semite Valley,	297
3	2 The Yo-Semite Fall, 2500 feet high,	297
4	The Bridal Veil, 937 feet high, near view,	297
5	Fall on the South Fork, 600 feet high,	298
6	Nevada Fall, with South Dome and Valley,	298
9	8 Nevada Fall, 600 feet in hight,	298
13	The Big Tree in Mariposa Grove,	298
14	Vernal Fall, 600 feet in hight,	298
21	19 17 Scene in a Canon,	297
23	The South Dome, 4967 feet high,	298
26	Tu-to-con-u-u-ta, 3039 feet high,	298
28	The North Dome, 3729 feet high,	298
22	The Domes,	298
29	The South Dome from the South Fork,	298
35	View on the Merced River,	298
33	From the top of Vernal Fall, looking west,	298
39	Group of Big Trees in Mariposa Grove,	295
45	52 Panoramic View of San Francisco taken from the corner of Sacramento and Taylor streets,	299
40	Group of Big Trees in Mariposa Grove,	295
42	78 The Heads; entrance to the Bay of San Francisco. Golden Gate in the distance,	299
60	South Park, San Francisco,	299
67	View of Sacramento,	299

VIEWS IN CUBA.

15	164, Cocoanut trees in the Bishop's garden, Havana,	330
18	The large Cactus, in the Bishop's garden, Havana,	330
19	The avenue of Royal Palms, in the Bishop's garden, Havana,	330
20	An Instantaneous View. The Harbor of Havana,	329
22	An Instantaneous View. The steamer DeSoto leaving the harbor of Havana,	329

NO. VIEW.		NO. PAGE.
6622	Little Falls, Lover's Rock, looking north-west,	200
6634	6641, Locks and Dry Dock, Erie Canal,	200
6636	6637, Falls and Bridge on the Mohawk river,	176
6638	6639, Profile Rocks, east and west sides,	200
6642	Little Falls, looking west,	200
6643	Little Falls, looking east,	200

VIEWS IN MONTREAL AND QUEBEC.

21227	Victoria Square, Montreal,	313
20980	Beaver Hall, from Victoria Square, Montreal,	313
16710	View looking west across the city, from tower of French Church, Montreal,	313
16762	Court House, Montreal,	313
21275	Great St. James Street, Montreal,	313
20851	Notre Dame Street, looking east, Montreal,	313
16828	Wharves at Montreal, with steamers and bridge in distance,	313
17326	Marine Hospital, Quebec,	314

MAMMOTH CAVE VIEWS, KENTUCKY.

5	Mouth of the Cave,	269
17	Deserted Chamber, Guide entering, equipped for the long route,	269
18	Gorin's Dome. This is sixty feet wide and two hundred feet high, the sides beautifully fluted is if by the hands of skillful artists,	269
19	Bridge of Sighs, over the far-famed "Bottomless Pit,"	269
23	Wild Hall, surpassing in wierd gloom Dore's conception of the inferno,	269
24	Snowball Arcade. A regular arched way, the ceiling of which is covered with white gypsum, resembling snow,	269
25	Grand Crossing, showing two avenues, one passing over the other,	269

SCOTCH AND CONTINENTAL VIEWS.

984	Power's Court, Waterfall, County of Wicklow, (Ireland,)	353
1009	General View of Paris, taken from the Pantheon, (France,)	356
1393	Church of Notre Dame, (France,)	357
1402	Champ de Mars, Ecole Militaire, (France,)	357
1579	St. George's Hall, Liverpool, (England,)	346
1629	Panorama of Lyons, (France,)	357
1631	General View of the Mer de Glace, Savoy, (France,)	355
1649	Osborn House, (Isle of Wight,)	354
1739	Giant's Causeway, (Ireland,)	353
1797	Panoramic view of the Cathedral of Cologne, (Prussia,)	370
1805	Church of St. Peter and Obelisk at Rome,	383
1834	New Houses of Parliament, London, (England,)	344
1902	Ice Glaciers, (Switzerland,)	359
1903	" " "	359
1904	" " "	359
2006	Ice Glaciers (Switzerland),	359
2010	Ice Glaciers, Switzerland,	259
3959	Fingal's Cave, Staffa, (Scotland),	349
3961	The mouth of the Clam Shell Cave, Staffa,	349
3963	Windsor Castle. The Garden Terrace, (England),	347

SWISS AND AUSTRIAN VIEWS.

PARIS AND PARIS EXPOSITION.

NO. VIEW.		NO. PAGE.
6095	The French Park. Paris Exposition,	357
6118	Gallery of Machinery. French Section,	357
6122	Crystal. French Section,	357
6147	Gallery of Machinery. English Section,	357
6152	Crystal. Austrian Section,	357
6157	Gallery of Machinery. Portuguese Section,	357
6161	Gallery of Workmanship. Russian Section,	357
6168	The Egyptian Park. Paris Exposition,	357
6181	Gallery of Workmanship. Italian Section,	357
6186	Saloon of Awards. Paris Exposition,	357
6199	Panoramic view of the Building. Paris Exposition,	357

VIEWS IN CALIFORNIA.

429	Black Point and Golden Gate, from Telegraph Hill, San Francisco,	299
430	The Presidio and Golden Gate, from Russian Hill, San Francisco,	299
690	Swift's Station, Carson and Lake Bigler Road, eastern summit of the Sierra Nevada Mountains,	294
798	Hydraulic Mining, Timbucto Diggings, Yuba county,	296
803	Hydraulic Mining, the Pipe and Tank,	296
875	The Sentinels; hight 315 feet; Mammoth Grove, Calaveras County,	295
878	Section of the original Big Tree; diameter 30 feet; Calaveras County,	295
882	Big Tree Hercules, from a point 250 feet from the base, Calaveras County,	295
887	Big Tree, Abraham Lincoln; hight, 281 feet, circumference, 44 feet,	295
907	Abraham Lincoln, near view, 281 feet high, 44 feet in circumference, Calaveras County Big Tree Grove,	295
1107	The Three Brothers, 4,000 feet high, Yosemite Valley, Mariposa County,	297
1109	The Three Brothers, reflected in the Merced river, Yosemite Valley, Mariposa County,	298
1111	The Yosemite Fall, 2,634 feet high, Yosemite Valley, Mariposa County,	297
1113	View down the Yosemite Valley, Cathedral Rocks in the distance, Mariposa County,	297
1114	The North Dome, 3,725 feet high, Royal Arch, and Washington Tower, Yosemite Valley, Mariposa County,	298
1118	Mirror Lake and Reflections, Yosemite Valley, Mariposa Co.,	298
1119	The Vernal Fall, 350 feet high, " " " "	298
1124	The South Dome, from the little " " " "	298
1225	Mount Starr King, 5,600 f. high, " " " "	298
1020	Placer Mining. The Flume and Boulders, Columbia, Toulumne County,	296
1023	Placer Mines. The Boulder Range, Knapp's Ranch, Columbia, Toulumne County,	296

VIEWS ABOUT LAKE SUPERIOR AND VICINITY.

266	Bay of Marquette, Lake Superior,	286
265	Ore Docks, Bay of Marquette, Lake Superior,	286
270	The Superior Iron Mine, Main Working,	286

NO. VIEW.		NO. PAGE.
3171	3173, Panoramic view of Richmond, Va., from Libby Hill, looking west; in the distance, Pontoon Bridge and Belle Island, the place where so many union prisoners were confined,	230
3253	Panoramic view of Richmond, Va., from Gamble Hill, looking east. Lynchburg Canal and ruins of City Armory in the foreground; in the distance, Church Hill,	230
3372	3373, Pontoon Bridge on the James river, Richmond, Va.; in the middle ground are large Woolen Factories,	230
3540	Gen. Sherman's Headquarters, Savannah, Georgia,	90
3547	Gen. Sherman's Wagon Train, near Savannah, Georgia,	90
3647	3648, 3649, The place where Maj. Gen. J. B. McPherson was killed, Atlanta, Ga.,	89
3661	3662, Pulpit Rock, Lookout Mountain, the place where Jeff. Davis addressed the Confederate Armies, Tenn.,	87
3663	Fortifications and Bombproofs, Atlanta, Ga.,	89
3666	View in the City of Atlanta, Ga.,	240
3410	Quarter Deck and Starboard Battery of U. S. Ship Pawnee, the Fighting Ship of U. S. Navy, taken at Charleston Harbor, S. C.,	237
3168	Washington Monument in the Capitol Grounds, Richmond, Va. The statues around the center base, are those of Patrick Henry, Thomas Jefferson, and Mason,	230

ALPINE CLUB.

67	Mont Rosa, taken from the Gorner Gratt, Switzerland,	365
77	Panorama of Interlaken, with Jungfrau in the distance,	363
89	The Wetterhorn in the Valley of Grindelwald, Switzerland,	361
90	View of the Wetterhorn, Grindelwald, Switzerland,	361
103	Staubbach Fall, Valley of Lauterbrunnen, Switzerland,	360
172	Panorama of Glarus and Glarnish Mountain, Switzerland,	364
210	Mount Blanc, and panorama of Chamounix, France,	355
215	View on the Mer de Glace, Chamouuix, Savoy, France,	355
216	Grand Pyramids on the Mer de Glace, Savoy, France,	355
221	The summit of Mount Blanc, and view of Servoz, France,	355
228	The Mer de Glace, Chamounix, Savoy, France,	355
274	The Jungfrau, taken in the Wengern Alps, Switzerland,	361
275	Hotel of the Jungfrau, Wengern Alps, Switzerland,	361
276	The Monch, view in the Wengern Alps, Switzerland,	361
277	The Monch, and the Eiger, Wengern Alps, Switzerland,	361
278	The Jungfrau, view on the Route of Murren, Switzerland,	361
299	General view of the Superior Glacier of Grindelwald, Switz.,	361
302	Interior of an Ice Cavern, Glacier of Grindelwald, Switz.,	361

ENGLISH AND SCOTCH VIEWS.

	St. Paul's, South-west, England,	343
	The Tower of London, England,	344
10	Loch Katrine, the path by the Loch, Scotland,	349
13	Balmoral Castle, from the south-east, Scotland,	352
14	Balmoral Castle, from the river, Scotland,	352
16	Clamshell Cave, Staffa, Scotland,	349
17	Fingal's Cave, Staffa, Scotland,	349
19	The Thames. Eton College, England,	347
43	Glasgow Bridge, Scotland,	351

NO. VIEW.		NO. PAGE.
45	Glasgow. View on the Clyde, Scotland,	350
59	Loch Archray and Ben Venue, Scotland,	349
70	Guy's Cliff, from Mill Meadow, England,	347
103	Abbotsford, from the river, Scotland,	352
111	Edinburgh Castle, from Princess street, Scotland,	350
114	Sir Walter Scott's Monument, Edinburgh, Scotland,	350
131	Ely Cathedral; view from the Park, England,	348
132	Balmoral Castle, from the south-west, Scotland,	352
134	Balmoral Castle, from the north-west, Scotland,	352
145	Fingal's Cave, Staffa, Scotland,	349
201	The city of Oxford, from the top of Magdalen Tower, Eng.,	347
440	Balmoral Castle, from the south-east, Scotland,	352
443	Windsor Castle—the Garden Terrace, England,	347
445	Windsor Castle—the North Terrace, England,	347
471	In the Pass of Killiecrankie, looking towards Ben-y-gloe, Scotland,	351
478	Blair Athole, from Tulloch Hill, Scotland,	351
480	Bridge of Tilt, looking towards Ben-y-gloe, Scotland,	351
485	Taymouth Castle, from the Fort, Scotland,	352
490	Peterborough Cathedral, from the south-east, England,	348
496	Drummond Castle, from the Garden, Scotland,	348
497	Drummond Castle, from the Garden, Scotland,	348
508	Loch Zummel—the Queen's View, Scotland,	348
530	Abbotsford—the Garden Front, Scotland,	352
668	View from above Tarbot, Loch Lomond, Scotland,	349
730	Ben Nevis, from above Banavie, Scotland,	348
763	The Necropolis, Glasgow, Scotland,	351
769	The Queen's View—Pass of Killiecrankie, Scotland,	351
773	Faskally House, Pass of Killiecrankie, Scotland,	351
812	Glasgow—in the West End Park, Scotland,	351
829	Luss—Loch Lomond, Scotland,	349
837	Ben Lomond, from Luss,	348
842	Ben Lomond, from near Tarbot, Scotland,	348
869	Ellen's Isle, Loch Katrine, Scotland,	349
872	Loch Katrine, from the Goblin's Cave, Scotland,	349
1931	Dartmouth, from Hill above Warfleet, England,	347
19	St. John's College, Cambridge, new buildings, from the south-east, England,	346

PRUSSIA AND GERMANY.

NO. VIEW.		NO. PAGE.
46	View of Bacharach and Durhin, Prussia,	370
77	Abside of the Cathedral of Limburg on the Lahn, Germany,	370
80	View of the Bridge and the Chateau of Welburg, on the Lahn, Germany,	371
325	Baden Baden. View on the Oosbach, Germany,	372

ITALY AND PAPAL STATES.

NO. VIEW.		NO. PAGE.
754	Interior of the Amphitheatre at Pozzuoli, Italy,	380
825	Excavations of Herculaneum in 1828. Mosaic Branch, Italy,	374
1094	Entrance to the Cathedral of Milan, Italy,	378
1531	General view of Naples, Italy,	377
1546	Observatory of Vesuvius, near Naples, Italy,	374
1578	Garden of the Vatican, and Cupola of St. Peter's, Italy,	384

VIEWS OF PALESTINE AND ADJACENT COUNTRIES.

NO. VIEW.		NO. PAGE.
1	Sinai. Wady Mukatteb. The Written Valley. A good specimen of the mysterious "Sinaitic" Writing,	409
2	6, Sinai. Wady Feiran. Paran. Wild Palms and Arab Figure,	409
3	Sinai. The Plain of the Assemblage from the Convent,	404
4	Sinai. Convent of Sinai. The Abbott and Monks,	409
5	15, Travelers on Dromedaries, near Ezion Geber,	412
6	Hebron. A Group of Natives,	409
7	The Fountain of Jericho. Ain Sultan healed by Elisha,	407
8	22, Jerusalem from Mount Zion, with Mosque of Omar, etc., showing much of the modern City,	399
9	Jerusalem. The Garden of Gethsemane and Mount of Olives,	402
10	25, Jerusalem. The Village of Siloam, and Valley of the Kedron,	402
11	Jerusalem. The Pool of Siloam,	402
12	" Facade of Church of the Holy Sepulchre,	401
13	" Latin Monks,	402
14	27, " Via Dolorosa,	401
16	" The English Church,	401
17	32, " The Mosque of Aksa,	401
18	32, " The Golden Gate,	400
19	33, " The Mosque of Omar; the Site of Solomon's Temple,	401
20	33, Jerusalem. View of the Court of the Mosque of Omar; specimen of Saracenic Architecture,	401
22	Shiloh (Seilun,)	407
23	43, Mount Carmel. The Convent.	393
24	Site of Bethsaida. Sea of Galilee,	396
25	Sea of Galilee. Bethsaida. The Castor Oil Plant,	396
26	Site of Capernaum. Tell Hum. Ruins of Synagogue, Cornice, Capitals, etc.,	404
29	Rukhleh. Huge Medallion Face, supposed to be of Baal,	403
30	Damascus, with Ancient Great Mosque,	403
31	Damascus. A view from a House Top,	402
35	Baalbek. The Great Columns,	402
36	Baalbek. View of the Great Columns and Temple of Jupiter,	402
37	Baalbek. Ornamental Door and Niche on the south side of the Great Court,	402
38	Baalbek. General view of the Temple of Jupiter,	402
39	" " " "	402
40	" " " " Fallen mass of Ceiling of the Perystyle,	402
41	69, Baalbek. Temple of Jupiter. The Great Portal with Slipped Key Stone, measuring 42 by 21 feet,	402
42	70, Baalbek. Temple of Jupiter. Capitals, etc.,	402
43	" " " " Columns, Capitals, etc.,	402
44	71, " " " " " " "	402
45	72, " The Circular Temple,	402
46	75, Cedars of Lebanon. Near View, Old and Young Trees,	392
47	" " The largest of the Cedars,	392
48	Athens. The Propylæ,	410
49	84 " The Caryatides,	411

NO. VIEW.		NO. PAGE.
50	Athens. Sculptured Heads, etc., in the Acropolis,	410
51	" Sculptures of the Wingless Victory,	410
53	91, " Theatre of Bacchus,	411
54	" " " " State Chair,	411
55	" " " " " "	411
56	Egypt. The Great Pyramid and Excavated Temple,	411
57	" The Second Pyramid and Sphinx,	411
58	" Step Pyramid of Sakhara,	411
59	" Pyramid of Dashoor,	411
60	" Cairo. Tombs of the Mamelukes, showing the Citadel,	412
63	109, Egypt, Cairo. Mosque of Mohammed Ali,	412
64	110, " " " " "	412
65	" " " of Sultan Kassan. The Fountain,	412
66	112, Egypt, Old Cairo. Mosque of Sultan Amer,	412
67	Egypt, Old Cairo. Ruined Mosque in the Desert,	412
68	" " " Street view from Mosque of Sultan Hassan,	412
69	Egypt, Cairo. Street view, from road to Citadel,	412
72	1, Sinai. The Valley of the Cave,	409
73	" The Wilderness of Paran,	409
74	" Wild Palms,	391
75	8, " Mount Horeb,	409
76	10, " The supposed Site of the Burning Bush,	409
77	Hebron, with Mosque covering the Cave of Machpelah,	408
78	17, Bethlehem, from the Church of the Nativity,	408
79	Bethany,	407
80	22, Jerusalem, from the Mount of Olives,	402
81	28, " from the Walls, looking east,	402
82	" The Valley of Hinnom,	402
83	" Aceldama,	402
84	" The Mosque of Omar,	401
85	34, " The Fountain of Gihon,	401
86	35, " The Joppa Gate,	400
87	Shechem. Nablous, between Ebal and Gerizim,	406
88	39, Samaria. Ruins of the Church of St. John,	406
89	40, Nazareth, from the west,	405
90	Mount Carmel,	393
92	Cæsarea Philippi, Roman Ruins,	404
93	Cæsarea Philippi, principal source of the Jordan,	396
96	106, Egypt, Cairo, Tombs of the Caliphs,	412
97	Egypt, Cairo, Bedouin and Dromedary,	412
98	Egypt, Cairo, Arab Tombs,	411
99	77, Athens and Mars' Hill,	410
100	Athens, and the Erectheum,	410
102	81, Athens, the Parthenon,	410
23	Jerusalem, Pool of Hezekiah,	401
33	" View from near Mount Zion, Mosque of Omar,	399
97	Egypt. The Great Pyramid and Sphinx,	411
102	Egypt. Cario. From the Citadel, with Mosque of Sultan Hassan,	412
94	Athens. The Modern City from the Acropilis,	410
105	Egypt. Cairo. Tombs of the Mamelukes,	412
61	Baalbek. A general view of the Temples, and the range of the Lebanon,	402

NO. VIEW.		NO. PAGE.
	SCENERY AT ITHACA AND VICINITY, N. Y.	
6923	Ithaca Fall, 160 feet high and 150 feet broad, from the north bank, Fall creek,	180
6924	Ithaca Fall, 160 feet high and 150 feet broad, Fall creek,	180
	SCENERY AT PORTAGE AND VICINITY, N. Y.	
6988	View from High Bank, Middle. Horse Shoe Falls and Bridge in the distance,	176
6990	High Bank, (380 feet,) Genesee river, below Middle Falls,	176
6991	View of High Bank, (380 feet,) Genesee river, below Middle Falls,	176
6992	Middle Falls, Genesee river. Bridge in the distance,	176
6994	The Genesee Falls, 96 feet high, Rochester, N. Y.,	176
6995	" " " " " " "	176
6996	" " " " " " "	176
6999	The Lower Genesee Falls, below Rochester,	176
7000	" " " " " "	176
	VIEWS IN BALTIMORE AND VICINITY, MD.	
7027	Catholic Cathedral,	223
7032	Delaware Row, Franklin Square,	222
7042	Bay View Asylum,	223
7044	Baltimore from Federal Hill, looking north-east,	222
7045	" " " " " north,	222
7046	Baltimore Harbor from Federal Hill, looking south-east,	222
7048	Battle Monument,	222
7049	" "	222
7050	Washington Monument,	222
7051	" "	222
7054	The Grand Promenade, Druid Hill Park,	223
7055	Mansion House, south view, Druid Hill Park,	223
7056	Mansion House and Fountain, Druid Hill Park,	223
7058	Woodbury, from Prospect Hill, Druid Hill Park,	223
7059	The Music Stand, Druid Hill Park,	223
7063	Looking towards the Lake, Druid Hill Park,	223

LIST OF HEADINGS.

www.ingramcontent.com/pod-product-compliance
Lightning Source LLC
LaVergne TN
LVHW021138110826
845150LV00005B/1058

* 9 7 8 1 4 2 5 5 4 8 7 5 9 *